Flyfisher's Guide to™ the

NEW ENGLAND COAST

Fishing Titles Available from Wilderness Adventures Press, Inc.™

Flyfishers Guide to™

Flyfisher's Guide to Alaska

Flyfisher's Guide to Arizona

Flyfisher's Guide to Chesapeake Bay

Flyfisher's Guide to Colorado

Flyfisher's Guide to the Florida Keys

Flyfisher's Guide to Freshwater Florida

Flyfisher's Guide to Idaho

Flyfisher's Guide to Montana

Flyfisher's Guide to Michigan

Flyfisher's Guide to Minnesota

Flyfisher's Guide to Missouri & Arkansas

Flyfisher's Guide to Nevada

Flyfisher's Guide to the New England Coast

Flyfisher's Guide to New Mexico

Flyfisher's Guide to New York

Flyfisher's Guide to the Northeast Coast

Flyfisher's Guide to Northern California

Flyfisher's Guide to Northern New England

Flyfisher's Guide to Oregon

Flyfisher's Guide to Pennsylvania

Flyfisher's Guide to Saltwater Florida

Flyfisher's Guide to Texas

Flyfisher's Guide to the Texas Gulf Coast

Flyfisher's Guide to Utah

Flyfisher's Guide to Virginia

Flyfisher's Guide to Washington

Flyfisher's Guide to Wisconsin & Iowa

Flyfisher's Guide to Wyoming

Flyfisher's Guide to Yellowstone National Park

On the Fly Guide to™

On the Fly Guide to the Northwest

On the Fly Guide to the Northern Rockies

Anglers Guide to™

Complete Anglers Guide to Oregon

Saltwater Angler's Guide to the Southeast

Saltwater Angler's Guide to Southern California

Best Fishing Waters™

California's Best Fishing Waters

Colorado's Best Fishing Waters

Idaho's Best Fishing Waters

Montana's Best Fishing Waters

Oregon's Best Fishing Waters

Washington's Best Fishing Waters

Field Guide to™

Field Guide to Fishing Knots

Fly Tying

Go-To Flies™

Flyfishing Adventures™

Montana

Flyfisher's Guide to[TM] the

NEW ENGLAND COAST

Tom Keer

Flyfisher's Guide to[TM] Series

Wilderness
Adventures
Press, Inc.[TM]

Belgrade, Montana

Flyfisher's Guide to˜ Series

Published by Wilderness Adventures Press, Inc.˜
45 Buckskin Road
Belgrade, MT 59714
866-400-2012
Website: www.wildadvpress.com
email: books@wildadvpress.com

First Edition 2011

Printed in South Korea through Four Colour Print Group, Louisville, Kentucky.

ISBN 978 -1-932098-75-4 (8-09206-98754-8)

Table of Contents

Acknowledgements

In 35 years of flyfishing and nearly 20 years of direct involvement in the fishing business, there are far too many folks to thank. And to do it properly, I should write a chapter thanking everyone who has helped me along the way. From fishermen I've met, to fly shop owners in Rhode Island, Massachusetts, New Hampshire and Maine and to charter captains and wade guides, the list is long. To you all I owe a debt of gratitude for thoughts, for observations, for theories and conjecture, and, above all, for camaraderie.

There are editors and art directors from some of the magazines for which I have written. Some were strictly flyfishing oriented while others were outdoors or lifestyle publications. There have been numerous changes in the ownership of the magazines, as well as the editorial staffs. So, thanks to: Joe Healy, John Randolph, Steve Walburn, Dave Dibenedetto, Ross Purnell, Phil Monahan, Brian McClintock, Jim Butler, Crispin Battles, Mary Grauerholz, and Deb Martin. Thank you all for working with me. A special thanks to those of you who worked with me on the cutting-edge pieces. Those are the ones that were the most fun to write, and they were useful to fishermen.

Thanks go to Hayden Price for my first flyfishing lesson and to John Bosnyak and John Lunny for early fly-tying lessons and fishing trips.

Thanks to Phil Shook for suggesting I write a companion book to his fine 512-page whopper (the Flyfisher's Guide to the Northeast Coast: Connecticut, New York, New Jersey) and to Chuck Johnson, Josh Bergan and Mandy Connelley for creating a great product.

To Peter Jenkins at the Saltwater Edge for friendship and input into Rhode Island and to Mac McKeever from L.L. Bean for his understanding of the Maine coastal fishery. And to Barry and Cathy Beck for the fun photo shoots we've had, and for their friendship.

To Tim Shields for help with Rhode Island and Massachusetts, Capt. Rusty Barry for the South Shore, Capt. Tom King and Capt. Mike Bartlett for Boston, Ted Storm for Nantucket and Dave Griskovich and Al Wanamakere for New Hampshire and Maine.

A debt of gratitude goes to Kenny Abrames for his thoughts and insight into the saltwater environment. The enormous amount of time that we spent fishing, observing and talking are among my most cherished times. Of equal importance to me is the time I was priviledged to spend with Sgt. Major Tim Didas, USMC, Cabe Loring, and Jeff Doyle. The countless hours we spent on the water, in the uplands and duck blinds, and in the turkey woods are some of my favorite memories. I look forward to more.

Most of all I am indebted to my family. A special thanks to my wife Angela for her constant willingness to complete many of my responsibilities so that I could concentrate on this book, and who was more kind and loving than I deserve. My step-children Morgan and Isaac have earned an unending amount of fishing, boating, and hunting trips in future years. Your patience and understanding of why I spent most hot, summer days writing instead of on the water was mature beyond your years. We'll catch 'em up next year, I promise.

The texture around Cape Neddick's rocky shoreline offers structure and current. You can see the current seam in the background.

Introduction

For centuries, people have believed that the ocean is a mysterious place. Part of that belief was rooted in seafaring history. Under the water were alleged sea dragons and serpents that destroyed ships, giant squid that engulfed boats, and seductive mermaids luring ship captains to run aground. Jules Verne and 20,000 Leagues Under the Sea and Captain Nemo. Whales like Moby Dick furthered the lore. Top-water mysteries included pirates like Blackbeard looting ships, and mooncussers, the groups of privateers who carried lanterns along the dunes in the darkness of the new moon, thereby suggesting a lighthouse that moved, disoriented captains and caused them to run their ships aground. The top-water looters raced down to the bars and claimed their prizes. Add the deepest part of the ocean, the Mariana Trench in the Pacific Ocean off the Japanese coast, and you've got a complete package. At 35,810 feet deep (6.7 miles), who knows what lurks below the water line.

The ocean is a mysterious place indeed, but it is also somewhat predictable. Its predictability gives us anglers the opportunity to create a game plan so we can catch more fish. We fishermen are like 5th graders discussing a quarterback's stats or a pitcher's earned run average to determine the best places to fish. That's heady stuff for a kid. For us? All we are trying to do is to increase our odds at catching fish, and big ones at that.

During rough seas, we reflect on what lurks below. While fishing at night we wonder what those bumps against our waders really are. We breathe a sign of relief when we can take a step after that bump knowing our leg is intact, particularly if fishing a place with the name like Dogfish Bar. But in this thoroughly modern world, we have demystified some of those issues. We have tide charts that explain how much water is moving. The tide charts feature nuances for hundreds of different areas along the coastline. They tell us that low tide along the ocean is at 3:00am and a few miles away in the adjacent estuary where we will fish three hours later. They also tell us about the lunar phase and if the spring tides will be higher than normal or lower than normal. The approximate 2-foot difference to a wade fisherman can mean that he can walk farther out on a bar and target the honey hole. Or know when the next full moon is so he can target a cinder worm hatch in a favorite bay or cove.

Nautical charts show us the terrain of what is below the water surface. If you're a traveling angler and bounce from state to state, the Maptech NOAA Chartkit series offers an encyclopedic collection of charts. In the past, anglers bought individual charts that wound up costing a pretty penny. The Chartkit is a fraction of the cost of the sum of the total charts, and includes additional information such as boat ramps, parking restrictions, and food and lodging options. Nautical charts are as important to an angler as his tackle, and if you toss a version in your truck at the beginning of the season, you'll have an easy reference guide for the year. For internet junkies, the charts are online as well.

Nothing, of course, beats scouting and fishing. Driving to a beach or cove or estuary during a full-moon low tide will give you the actual information that you need. You will be able to see the combined result of the tide chart and the nautical chart, and the information you learn will be invaluable. You'll see many things that you did not see when the water was up, like oyster beds, undercut banks, channels, and recesses in the ocean floor where the bait and the fish will hold. You can see how the wind and the tide interact, where to enter, where to exit, and just how far you can go. You can plan your sortie accordingly and increase your catch in the process.

Anglers will find a great variety of coastline, and a tremendous amount of opportunities. They will find beachfronts, river estuaries, saltponds, coves, reefs, flats, inshore islands, rips and rocky drop-offs. Some areas are quiet and peaceful, others are urban and energetic. Some are perfectly suited for wade fishing, other areas are best reached by kayak, and still others by boat. The best part of a fishing trip to Rhode Island, Massachusetts, New Hampshire or Maine is the seemingly endless list of options.

RHODE ISLAND

The Ocean State comes by its name honestly. Sometimes the smallest state in the union gets picked on, but while its diminutive size can be construed as a negative, I think of it as a positive: with over 400 miles of coastline jam-packed into a state, it does not take much time to get from an estuary to a saltpond to a reef to a beach or to the rocks. As the tides ebb and flow, an angler's location can be changed quickly and easily with success at every stop. Rhode Island and its coastline is accessible and fisherman friendly.

One of my favorite areas in Rhode Island is South County. With long, expansive beaches and saltponds, an angler can have a heyday, particularly in September. You'll find bass, bluefish, false albacore, bonito, and shad. You'll also find squeateague, too, which is Narragansett Indian for weakfish. Watch Hill Reef in May and June is squid time, and it is no small reason that striped bass are known as squid hounds.

Head east to Point Judith and see for yourself. Sure you'll see the ferry departing for Block Island, but you'll also see an enormous fishing fleet. There are charter boats, private boats, head boats, draggers, trawlers, all types of boats. Fishing is ingrained in the Rhode Island culture and as a result, Rhode Islanders are some of the best fishermen on the East Coast.

There is a tremendous amount of history as well. Fishing off the rocks in Newport harkens back to the Great Gatsby era – while catching striped bass, bluefish, or false albacore along Ocean Avenue you'll bear witness to the cottages. By no means is that description accurate, for these cottages are really mansions. The Rockefellers, Vanderbilts, and the Astors, among others, threw gala events, the kind that may have inspired F. Scott Fitzgerald to pen his novel. The fishing in front of their homes is excellent, and you'll touch angling history as you pass the old, rusty fish stands. Over a century ago, anglers would hang their gear and lanterns on the stands and lean against them while they caught striped bass with lobster tails for bait. Of course they would hang on to the stands when the seas were rough or when a rogue wave hit, thereby preventing being washed into the sea. When you hook up to a big fish in the rocks, lean on him hard so he doesn't break you off on a sharp rock edge. Watch for red flags with a white slash, for it's a "diver down" flag. It goes without saying that you should avoid hooking scuba divers.

Narragansett Bay covers 147 miles of Rhode Island's coastline. With Jamestown at the southern end and Providence at the northern end, the bay is New England's largest estuary. Some consider it a large, natural harbor, but with thirty islands spread throughout it may very well be an archipelago. The rivers, bays, and rocks are perfect examples of the diversity an angler can find in a short drive in Rhode Island.

In late 2009, Rhode Island vetoed a saltwater fishing license. That said, stay tuned for more details.

Be sure to handle bluefish carefully as shown with this Sachuest Point bluefish.

MASSACHUSETTS

The Bay State got its name from the first settlers. While en route to try another settlement in Virgina, the Mayflower was blown on a westward course and arrived inside the hook that is Provincetown. The sea weary travelers first disembarked and then explored, finding a cache of corn that provided them with sustenance to make it through the first winter. Back in the boat, they tried to get on course, but in 1620 there was no Cape Cod Canal and they ran aground in Plymouth. Massachusetts is Pilgrim country, and a visit to the state includes an up close view of history.

There are 192 miles of coastline in Massachusetts, and the terrain varies considerably. In southwestern Massachusetts along Buzzards Bay, there are numerous rivers, coves, and harbors. New Bedford was immortalized as Captain Ahab set forth after the white whale, and Lizzie Borden and her 40 whacks made Fall River famous. And the Pilgrims, not being well versed in the American wild turkey, thought the birds roosting in trees were buzzards. There were a lot of these birds near the bay, hence the name Buzzards Bay. With the proximity to the Gulf Stream, anglers find stripers, bluefish, bonito, false albacore, skipjack, shad and, if it's a warm year, mahi mahi.

Anglers are concerned about a lot of issues – herring being one of them. Herring stocks are so depleted that live-bait fishermen can't net herring for use. And the problem with the status of herring isn't just land-based anglers. There is an even greater concern that the herring are being overfished, either deliberately or as a bycatch in federal waters, which extends for more than 3 miles off shore.

The expansiveness of the Rhode Island and Massachusetts beaches makes for great fishing. Long casts are not needed as the fish are typically in the wash, and picking fishing times around the wind can make for an epic day. Photo by Barry & Cathy Beck.

Some folks are working hard on the herring. Joe Costa is the executive director of the Buzzards Bay Coalition, an environmental group that works to improve habitat as well as fish stocks. Costa said his group has spent a lot of money on anadromous runs in the Buzzards Bay area. Said Costa, "The confounding factor is what is happening in the off-shore fishery. Commercial fishing has so altered the off-shore stocks it has been difficult for us to restore stocks even though we are working on runs. Herring are an important resource, and this problem has to be addressed."

Perhaps that is why there is the Herring Alliance. The Herring Alliance is an organization that focuses more on Atlantic herring in the open ocean. Its main mission is to protect forage fish, basically from Cape Cod Bay to the Gulf of Maine. The alliance's Nancy Civetta said her organization, which is made up of other conservation organizations as well, wants to protect the herring for future harvest and because of its importance to the general health of the ecosystem. The organization has run a campaign to stop large fishing boats from netting herring and other baitfish in the Gulf of Maine. This kind of advocacy is invaluable for improving fishing conditions. Between the Coalition and the Alliance, Bay State anglers should see some positive movement.

Eastward ho to Cape Cod and the islands. In its original form, the Cape was connected to the mainland. When the Cape Cod Canal was completed in 1935, it connected Buzzards and Cape Cod Bays. One of the region's best fisheries, Cape Cod instantly became an island. No matter, it has been said that if the striped bass were to become extinct, the last one will be found on Cape Cod. With a diverse structure from the rocky Elizabeth Islands to the saltponds and estuaries on the south side, to the flats and beaches from Chatham to Provincetown, there is more water to fish on Cape Cod than an angler could cover in a lifetime. Then there is the bay side. You'll find flats, tidelines, rivers, coves, pockets. Some of it is wadeable, some is best fished from a kayak, and some by boat. You'll find bass and blues and tuna in all of the Cape Cod waters, and from Chatham west you can add bonito, false albacore, and Spanish mackerel.

If you want, you can take a ferry or plane to the Vineyard or Nantucket. Martha's Vineyard is close, only half a dozen miles from the Cape, while Nantucket is a bit father, just over a dozen miles away. Both islands are well known for celebrities and politicians, but at their heart is fishing. Whether you're catching albies next to the Edgartown Lighthouse on the Vineyard or bluefish off of Nantucket's Eel Point, you'll probably want to make one of the islands your home. Many folks do.

The robust South Shore is the Massachusetts' unsung hero. The South Shore's beaches, the Plymouth/Duxbury flats, Marshfield's North and South Rivers, and Cohassett's rocks are year-round striper and bluefish haunts. With their proximity to Boston, it is easy to get in a morning of fishing and still be at work on time. The farther north you go, the more urban the fishery. The water shuttle transports businessmen from Hingham to Boston, and planes fly overhead en route to Logan International Airport. Still, "Striper Mike" Cragin beached a tuna from Hummarock, and that's not an everyday occurrence (Cragin is a fanatical fisherman and is usually one of the first anglers to catch spring stripers and one of the last to wave them goodbye – visit www.

stripermike.com for more information). Boston Harbor, that once-polluted cesspool, is and has been clean. The Polar Bear Club isn't the only group that jumps in the water – it is so clean that triathlons are regularly held in the drink. There are wade spots and boat spots, and you can take a ferry out to one of the Harbor Islands for the day. On some of them you can even camp out on. Think about it: for the cost of a campsite and a ferry ride you can have your own private fishing grounds. And you won't have to pay taxes on it, either.

There is something interesting about planes flying in while you're catching bass, blues, and mackerel. It gets loud sometimes, but with Paul Revere's house in the background, a Delta jet ready to land and catching a fish? That's a powerful statement about the cleanliness of the water. Catch a Red Sox or Patriots game, enjoy dinner at a wide variety of restaurants that range from pizza to a celebrity chef's restaurant, and then go fishing. Can't beat that.

Boston's North Shore is a combination of rocky shoreline and barrier beaches and river estuary systems. From the island of Nahant to Rockport, you'll find rocks, ledges and inshore islands galore. The fishing season starts a bit later due to the cold water, but it's one place that the stripers head to in the summer heat. Marblehead is known for sailing, but it also has a number of inshore islands that run the gamut all the way to Manchester-by-the-Sea. And be sure to tip your hat when you pass the Gloucester Fisherman (a bronze statue of a fisherman at the wheel of his ship looking out over the sea, in memoriam to the fishermen who have been lost throughout the years).

From Annisquam to Salisbury is a labyrinth of beaches, rivers, and estuaries. On calm days, you'll see kayakers fishing in the Parker, Ipswich, and Essex Rivers, and on skiffs looking for bass on the flats at the mouth of the Ipswich River. The Scarlet Letter was filmed on Hog Island, and you can catch bass throughout the river system. Plum Island – all 11 miles of its barrier beach – connects the Merrimack River at the north with Plum Island Sound at the south. The gradually sloping shelf makes for softer swells. It comes by its name honestly – there are lots of plums nearby.

The Merrimack River is a giant. Treacherous at its mouth, it runs 110-miles inland to its New Hampshire headwaters. The well-known Joppa Flats run along Water Street, and the famous flyfishing author Col. Joe Bates' daughter Pam owns the house on stilts. Fishing is excellent in May and June when the alewives and menhaden move up into the river to spawn, and in the summer when the blues roll into town. With numerous side channels to explore, you can't go wrong.

There has been a tremendous amount of conservation movement in the Bay State that has changed the way we fish. Stripers Forever, a Maine-based advocacy group, has enlisted the help of State Rep. Matthew Patrick, a Barnstable democrat, to end commercial fishing for striped bass in Massachusetts. If you're interested in tracking the bill's movement, it is House Bill 796. Patrick's position is that since fewer than 30 people fish commercially for striped bass in this $24 million fishery and that they are not full-time striped-bass fishermen, it makes sense to permanently close a fishery that supports so few jobs. Instead, by improving fish stocks, the recreational fishery that increases will create far more jobs in the travel and tourism sector. Stripers

Forever maintains that commercial fishing targets the striped bass brood stock and that commercial fishing contributes to the species decline. House Bill 796 is similar to an identical law in Maine, and if the bill passes, striped bass recreational anglers would also be affected. Their daily limit would drop from two fish to one fish per day. The bill was still being debated as of press time.

On another note, anglers will need to register for fishing in the saltwater. In time, and as early as 2011, this registration could turn into a fee-based saltwater fishing license. The National Marine Fisheries Service created its Saltwater Angler Registry mandated by the Magnuson-Stevens Act Reauthorization of 2006 that requires all saltwater fishermen fishing in federal and tidal waters to have registered by January 1, 2010 with NMSF. Registration by mail or online should include the angler's name, date of birth, address, telephone number and the regions where they intend to fish. A certificate – essentially an annual license – will be issued. As of this writing, the registration is free, but will probably cost $15 to $25 starting in 2011. Check with your local fly or bait shop or visit the NOAA website (www.nmfs.noaa.gov). In the search box, type in Massachusetts Saltwater Fishing License and click on the frequently asked questions section. Curious parties can also visit www.countmyfish.noaa.gov/mrip for more information.

First Encounter Beach in Eastham is an excellent early-season fishing spot.

NEW HAMPSHIRE

You won't find much of the Granite State's namesake on the coast, for the quarries that gave the state its nickname are much further inland. You won't find much of a coastline, either. The 13-mile stretch is the shortest coastline of any state that connects with the saltwater. Tell New Hampshire anglers that and you're likely to get a different story.

Its beaches serve as corridors for migrating striped bass and bluefish. Every spring you'll find the fish moving along the beachfronts. In the summer you'll find bluefish blitzing at first and last light, and a good number of striped bass at night. The Piscataqua River gets a lot of attention, and rightfully so. It's a big river with strong currents, lots of baitfish, and plenty of holding water. The Piscataqua connects with Great Bay where you'll find plenty of inshore islands, river systems, herring and alewife runs, and bass and blues to beat the band.

Boat anglers oftentimes sail to the legendary Isle of Shoals. The Shoals is a chain of nine islands that is shared by both New Hampshire and Maine. Located 10

Thirteen inches is all that's left of this striped bass. In the salt, gamefish oftentime become bait. This fish was chopped off of Old Orchard Beach in Maine.

miles from Portsmouth Harbor and 6 miles off the coast from Rye, the islands have interesting names: Appledor, Star, Seavey, Malaga, Smuttynose, Cedar, Lunging, Duck, and White. These privately-owned islands boast some excellent concentrations of bass during the warm months. And as every traditional island should have, ghost stories and legends abound. One legend supports a visit to the island chain by none other than Captain John Smith (of Pocahontas fame). White Island had a lighthouse keeper whose daughter wrote poetry. The girl's name was Celia Thaxter, and the poetry wasn't that attention grabbing; the fact that she was visited by the famous pirate Blackbeard, however, is more notable. Private boats are not permitted to come ashore, but the fishing around the rocks and ledges can be excellent. Visits to the Oceanic Hotel can be arranged, and conferences are routinely held on Star Island.

MAINE

When flyfishermen think of heading to Maine to catch some fish, they typically think of the old-line sporting camps. The venerable Maine outfitter, L.L. Bean, has pictures of anglers with stringers of brook trout, also known as squaretails, and lake trout, also known by their Indian name of togue. These fish, among the native crustacean the lobster, were the catch of the day for several generations. The sweetwater (freshwater) fishing traditions continue to this day, but Down East vacationland has become increasingly popular for its coastal striped bass, bluefish, and tuna fishing.

Because of its northern proximity and water temperatures, Maine's season gets started later and ends earlier than the other states. The sections along coastal Route 1 vary dramatically. Just over the New Hampshire border you'll find river systems, coves, harbors, points, and the beaches of southern Maine. Cape Neddick Lighthouse, also known as the Nubble because it sits on Nubble Island, rests about 200 yards off of Cape Neddick Point. Two President Bushes have fished the rocks around Saco Bay's Kennebunkport in past summers. Beaches, rocks, and reefs lead the way farther north to the burgeoning seaport of Portland. With its recently renovated seaport district, the town has a feel of a younger brother to Boston, complete with inshore islands, rocks, and ledges. Finding a great meal, live entertainment, and an active social scene after fishing isn't difficult.

Many Mainers consider southern Maine to be a part of northern Massachusetts, and when you get to Down East you'll see why. There is the laconic way of speaking that blends perfectly with the lobster boats and buoys. With Casco Bay, Merrymeeting Bay, Sheepscot Bay, and Penobscot Bay, there are plenty of inshore islands, rocks, ledges, beaches, coves, points, and harbors. Quaint seaside towns, all complete with picture-perfect harbors, are filled with some of the most passionate striper fishermen along the eastern seaboard. Stripers Forever, a conservation-minded group, continues to lobby for strict regulations to protected the heavily fished species.

Because the Gulf Stream runs far to the east, you won't find pelagic species like bonito or false albacore. Every year, Boston (or Atlantic) mackerel are mistaken for albies, but that's ok. When they're around, so are the bass and blues.

Tips on Using this Book

One question that anglers frequently ask is: Where are the fish? A follow-up question is: What fly or plug should they use? The third and final question completes the cycle: When should they go?

To use this book properly you should think of the places listed as a starting point to learn of some spots that consistently hold fish for a good portion of the season. Some fish may be replaced by other species due to water temperatures or changing baitfish patterns, but they are as good and as likely as any. The only mistake that you can make by using this book is if you plant your feet in the sand and do not move. Unlike sweetwater fishing, the ocean is a dynamic environment. The areas that may hold fish at the top of the tide may be exposed sand at low. With 9- to 13-foot tides, you'll need to move accordingly so you can stay with the fish during those cycles.

A serviceable way to move is obvious and random. When you get to a spot listed in this book, you'll be likely to move up or down a beach, higher or lower in an estuary, or to another side of a breakwall or inshore island. Random movement combined with fan casting, variable retrieve speeds, or fly or plug and depth changes is prospecting. Prospecting is a serviceable approach to catching fish, and once you begin catching fish you can continue to repeat your success. If the tide is low, go to the farthest point you can. When the water begins to move you can see how the water interfaces with the structure. Look for bait. If it is present in good amounts then the fish are likely to find it. The bait will move along the current line until the water gives it passage either onto a structure like a flat or into a structure like an estuary. Note the depth at which the bait holds. Is it at the surface? Is it 2 feet deep, 4 feet deep? Now you'll know where to swim your fly or plug. Keep a winning gameplan; change a losing game plan.

A better method saves both time and effort, and it incorporates some basic fish behavior. First, by nature and design, all fish must swim into the current. They may swim with the current for short bursts, such as getting off a flat as the tide is dropping. After that short period of time, the fish must return to a position where they are facing the current. The reason that fish move into the current is so that water will pass over their gills for oxygen. But they also move into the current to feed; afterall, the bait moves into the current, too. So when you arrive at a location in this book, particularly one that is new to you, look for the current. If you can't tell the direction of the current, toss a piece of driftwood into the drink and watch it for a while. Or, if there are surfers in the area, ask them (they need the current in order to pop onto their boards).

Next, study the wind. Notice where it is coming from and where it intersects with the current. Where the wind and the current intersect is a perfect place to start your search. Every angler knows there is a tremendous amount of energy where the wind and the waves connect. Your job is to find out if the fish are high up on that line, in the middle, far down below, just on the inside, or over on the outside. If the wind is stronger than the current, the fish may move into the wind. If the current is stronger than the tide then the fish may move into the current.

Once you start catching fish, note not the location as much as the process. If you've combined your knowledge of the tide (tide chart) with the terrain (nautical chart) with your current and wind reconnaissance, you may be far from a place detailed in this book. Good for you, you'll be using the book properly.

What fly or plug should you use to catch the fish you have found? There are lots of choices and no shortage of new ones on the way. Fly tiers and plug makers are a creative bunch.

There are a few important points to consider. First, there is the attraction versus imitation school of thought. Then there is that of matching the bait by aligning your fly with the natural's size, silhouette, and color.

Attractors, those brightly colored, oftentimes noise-making artificials, will work well at times. If there are small fish or aggressively feeding fish you will have no shortage of responsive fish that wind up in your boat. Attractors – like poppers and suface flies – are great for prospecting. Seeing a fish blow up on them is a total thrill. If you want, you can match your offering to the size of the bait in the water. Or, you can simply tie on the biggest, brightest fly in your kit and let 'er rip. Pinks, purples, oranges, or yellows are all good options. Mix and match, the colors are right when you get a fish to hit.

Be careful of using attractors to solve a rational problem. Just because the water is murky and cloudy, possibly roiled up by a storm or a dropping tide doesn't mean that you need to fish an attractor pattern. Just because you can see it more clearly doesn't mean that the fish will respond. Saltwater fish are predators and can see naturals in cloudy or murky water. Not many of them starve because they can't see bait in a tea-colored surf. Experiment with naturals and attractors. You may find that for every fish you catch on a chartreuse fly in dirty water you catch 10 with an imitator.

If you're going to imitate the bait, there is a three-step process with a kicker. The first step is to match your offering by the old standard of size, silhouette, and color. The fly does not need to consist of half a rooster neck and three quarters of a bucktail. Just outline the shape of the bait with your materials, match the length and color scheme and go fishing. It's a very important method that Kenney Abrames covers in his fly-tying book, *A Perfect Fish*. It's how you can cast a 14-inch fly with a 6-weight.

The second step is to match the movement of your fly and plug with how the bait moves in the current. Squid, cinder worms, eels, and sand eels undulate in the water while menhaden, herring, and mackerel are stiffer. The current affects how the baitfish moves, too, and it is the reason a plug fisherman uses a broken-back in soft current and a stickbait in a hard current. A jointed plug in heavy current looks like a hula dancer at the ballet.

The third step is to match your imitation with how the bait looks in the water. Matching the water color is the kicker and it is a critical element. It is why we anglers fish black and bronze imitations on rainy nights and it is why yellow and chartreuse work well on a sunny flat. The water color is what is key, and it is important because the bait swims in the water. Whatever color the water, so too shall be your fly.

My friend Kenney Abrames has spent a lifetime observing and photographing baitfish underwater. Understanding the baitfish and how they move and what they do is the underpinning of fly selection. His website (www.stripermoon.com) and his book *Striper Moon* are invaluable references, and will fast-track even veteran anglers towards additional success. If you can find his fly-tying book, you will gain valuable insight into solving the imitation equation. And if you don't know what a baitfish looks like in the water, check out his site, too.

A final few tips for using this book with regard to the rigging. There are many fine books that cover the subject of knots and leaders in great detail, but consider dropper rigs when fishing in the salt. Most freshwater anglers will use droppers in the sweetwater (freshwater), but very few do in the salt. Gamefish are efficient feeders, and sometimes they can be fussy. If you've ever had a 30-plus-pound bass or 15-pound bluefish trail your fly up to the boat but never eat it, you know what I mean. When fish do that they like what you're throwing. They just don't love it.

To get around that equation, try fishing a dropper rig. Simply put, a dropper rig is the surest way to understand what baitfish the predator has keyed in on. You may see silversides at your feet, but 100 feet away, which is where your fly lands, there may be squid that moved in to feed on the silversides. Rigging a dropper with multiple flies offers uncanny insight into your fishing process. Some predators may hit the attractor, others a sand eel imitation, still others a shrimp. There are so many different types of bait that are present in the water at all times, that the fish have a choice. During a bluefish blitz one fall, there were nine different baits washed up on the beach: silversides, sand eels, squid, tinker mackerel, adult butterfish, peanut bunker, blueback herring, shrimp and, get this, snapper blues. That day, the adult bluefish were not selective and they'd hit anything. But on other days when they are selective, think of fishing a dropper rig. With so many different baitfish in the water, you'll improve your odds. And if you're a plug fisherman, add a fly dropper. After all, Tony Stetzko caught his 73-pound bass on a dropper. You win either way, so let the fish decide.

Tides can sometimes be confusing. They change every six hours or so, and an area can go from water that is 10 feet deep to a dry, exposed sand bar. The sand bar at low tide is useless for fishing but perfect for digging littlenecks. So, you'll need to know when the best time to fish your spot will be.

TIDES

Slack low tide is when the tide has run out, and is neither coming in nor going out. Slack high tide is when the tide is at its fullest and is neither rising nor falling. Higher water marks are generally from the third hour of the coming tide, past slack high tide, and through the third hour of the falling tide. Lower water marks are generally from the third hour of the falling tide through slack low tide and through the third hour of the rising tide. Full and new moons move more water while quarter moons move less water.

For specific up-to-date information on tides along the New England coast, visit www.saltwatertides.com.

The two currents of a bull-nose bar at Marconi Beach offer great currents and structure.

Popular Gamefish of the Northeast Coast

STRIPED BASS

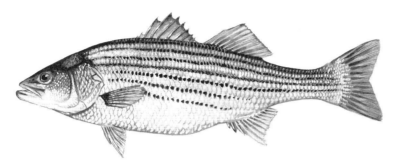

Striped bass (*Morone saxatilis*, modern Latin name; *Roccus lineatus saxatilis*, old Latin name). Common names and nicknames: striper, rockfish, rock, linesiders, Old Pajamas, Brown Dog, Squid Hound. Striped bass feed on small baitfish by inhaling the water column and purging the water through their gills. They engulf large baitfish heads first, so the dorsal fins of the frightened baitfish don't stick in their throat. They'll feed on herring, menhaden, silversides, sand eels, shrimp, crabs, lobster, you name it. Striped bass have a white, flaky flesh, perfect for a summer meal. Four important bodies of water with breeding stocks of striped bass are: Chesapeake Bay, Massachusetts Bay/Cape Cod, the Hudson River, and the Delaware River. Everyone loves the striped bass, and it's the state fish of Maryland, Rhode Island, South Carolina, and the state saltwater (marine) fish of New York. The largest striped bass ever caught by angling was a 78.5-pound fish taken in Atlantic City, New Jersey, on September 21, 1982. Here's how some other fish compare. Note that Vican's 2008 fish was very close to beating the world record. The spot where that fish was caught is in this book.

NEW ENGLAND NOTABLE CATCHES

State	Angler	Location	Size	Date
RI	P. Vican	Block Island	76 lbs 14 oz	July 2008
MA	Charles Church	Quick's Hole	73 lbs	1913
MA	Charles Cinto	Sow and Pig's Reef	73 lbs	1967
MA	Tony Stetzko	Nauset Beach	73 lbs	1981
NH	Robert Lindholm	Great Bay	60 lbs	June 1980
ME	Douglas Dodge	Sheepscot River	67 lbs	Sept. 1978

BLUEFISH

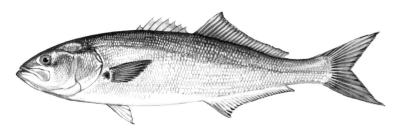

Bluefish (*Pomatomus saltatrix*). Common names and nicknames: blues, blue dogs. Baby bluefish are known as snappers, 3- to 5-pounders are called cocktail blues, double-digit-pound bluefish are known as choppers. The bluefish is a moderately proportioned fish, with a broad, forked tail – their tail being a dead give away when they're mixed in with striped bass in shallow water. Bluefish fresh from their migration are known as racers, mostly because of their long length, big heads and shoulders, and emaciated bodies. Bluefish have vision equally keen out of the water as they have in the water. Bluefish are voracious, predatory fish and are the only fish known to kill for the sake of killing. Their razor sharp teeth chop the tail off of their prey and then they circle around and eat the head and body. Extreme caution should be used when landing bluefish. They have dark, oily flesh and strong flavor. Cocktail blues that are bled and iced are preferable.

NEW ENGLAND NOTABLE CATCHES

State	Angler	Location	Size	Date
RI	D. Deziel	Unknown	26 lbs	Aug. 1981
MA	Louis Gordon	Graves Light	27 lbs 4 oz	Sept. 1982
NH	Henry Krook	Great Bay	21 lbs	Aug. 1975
ME	Denis Moran	Boothbay Harbor	19 lbs 12 oz	Aug. 1994

WEAKFISH

Weakfish (*Cynoscion regalis*). Common names and nicknames: weakies, squeateague, tide runners, grey trout. Weakfish are known to inhabit beachfronts and saltponds, feeding on small baitfish and most commonly on shrimp. The head and back of this fish are dark brown in color with a hint of green. Their flanks have a faint silvery tint with dusky specks, and their stomach is white. The origin of its name is based on the weakness of the mouth muscles, which often cause a hook to tear free, allowing the fish to escape the angler. New England populations are low, and they're not found in New Hampshire or in Maine. The weakfish is the state fish of Delaware.

NEW ENGLAND NOTABLE CATCHES

State	Angler	Location	Size	Date
RI	R. Moeller	Greenwich Bay	16 lbs 8 oz	May 2007
MA	George Mahoney	Buzzards Bay	18 lbs 12 oz	Aug. 1984

FALSE ALBACORE

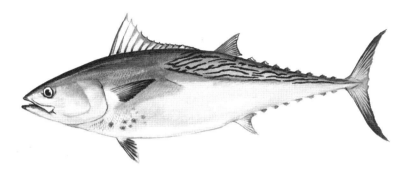

False albacore (*Euthynnus alletteratus*). Common names and nicknames: little tunny, albies, appleknockers (as they leave in the fall when the apples fall from the trees), hardtails. False albacore are school fish and are very muscular, hydro-dynamically designed fish. They're often linked to bonito and skipjacks. They have keen vision and favor edges, sharp drop-offs, and rips. False albacore make for poor table fare. Like the squeateague, they're not found in New Hampshire or Maine.

NEW ENGLAND NOTABLE CATCHES:

State	Angler	Location	Size	Date
RI	E. Cole	Matunuck	12 lbs 5 oz.	Sept. 1990
MA	Donald Mac Gillvray	Edgartown	19 lbs 5 oz.	Sept. 1990

ATLANTIC BONITO

Atlantic bonito (*Sarda sarda*). Common names and nicknames: Green bonito, bonito, bones. Like the false albacore, bonito have keen vision and favor edges, sharp drop-offs, and rips. The first bonito of the season are historically caught at 30- to 35-foot depths on umbrella rigs with colorful surgical tubing, trolled on wire. Atlantic bonito eat mackerel, menhaden, alewives, silversides, sand lance, and other fishes, as well as squid. They are strong swimmers. Normally they travel in fairly large schools and are common offshore in the vicinity of New York City where they are known as 'skipjack' because of their habit of jumping from the water. That said, the

name 'skipjack' more commonly refers to the skipjack tuna. The spawning season is June and specimens 12 to 15 centimeters (5 to 6 inches) long are taken in September off Long Island. Atlantic bonito are delicious. Bonito aren't found east or north of Chatham, Massachusetts.

NEW ENGLAND NOTABLE CATCHES:

State	Angler	Location	Size	Date
RI	R. Gliottone	Westerly	13 lbs	Oct. 1995
MA	Eddie Gomez	NB Dike	13 lbs 8 oz.	Sept. 2002

SKIPJACK TUNA

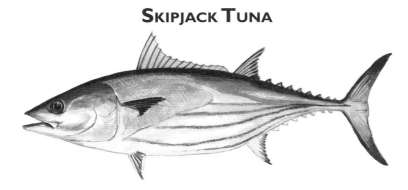

Skipjack tuna (*Katsuwonus pelamis*). Common names and nicknames: skippies, mushmouth, skipjack. Skipjack tuna feed in a simlar pattern as albies and bonito. They are not regular fish in the southern New England inshore regions. Skipjack are frequently seen in offshore waters, but some years they never appear inshore. They are a streamlined, fast-swimming pelagic fish, and are also common in tropical waters throughout the world. They can inhabit surface water in large shoals of up to 50,000 fish. These fish are good eating.

NEW ENGLAND NOTABLE CATCHES

Fishing for Skipjack has become popular among fly rodders as pods of those fish have moved inshore in recent years, but no record catches have been recorded.

SPANISH MACKEREL

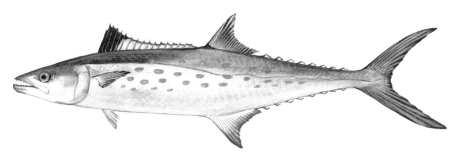

Spanish mackerel (*Scomberomorous maculates*). Common names and nicknames: Spanish macks. Spanish mackerel frequent the southern New England waters. The fish exhibits a green back; with silvery sides and rows of roundish, orange spots. They are toothy, and feed on small baitfish on hard edges, much like false albacore, bonito, and skipjack. As tropical water temperatures rise, the Atlantic group migrates along the coast from Miami, Florida, beginning in late February through July reaching as far as southern Cape Cod, then returning in fall. They are exceptionally good table fare.

NEW ENGLAND NOTABLE CATCHES

Fishing for Spanish mackerel has become popular among fly rodders, but no record catches have been recorded.

BLUEFIN TUNA

Bluefin tuna (*Thunnus thynnus*). Common names and nicknames: football tuna, school bluefin. Small tuna have been all the rage in the past decade. They have a cigar shape and incredible muscular strength that runs down to a pair of tendons connected to a sickle-shaped tail. Unlike other fish, the tuna's body stays rigid while the tail flicks back and forth, thereby increasing the efficiency of each stroke. Tuna have an unusual temperature regulation, which keeps them perfectly warm and perfectly cool, as the water temperatures dictate. As a result of a regulated temperature, they can fight for extend periods of time. School bluefin tuna feed into the wind along edges that are formed by drop-offs in the ocean floor. Permits for catching school tuna are required, and can be obtained from the individual states' Department of Marine Fisheries website.

NEW ENGLAND NOTABLE CATCHES

Fishing for school tuna is a recent phenomenon, and therefore only records are maintained for giants.

New England Coastal Bait

ALEWIVES

Alewives have large eyes and a single shoulder spot. Their lower jaws extend beyond the top jaw. Alewives begin to arrive in Rhode Island and Massachusetts on the first full moon in March, and continue to arrive in waves. They typically arrive in New Hampshire and Maine in April and May. These anadromous fish move into the bays and estuary systems that have freshwater origins and that typically end in a pond. They feed on plankton and have a grayish green/violet back with a silvery belly. Later in the fall, fry drop out of the river systems and small bucktails with blended black, blue, and purple hair work best. Adult patterns should be between 7 and 15 inches long, juvenile patterns between 1 and 3 inches long. Effective fly patterns are Deceivers and Clousers in blended blue, grey and black, Cowen's Magnum Herring, Abrames' Razzle Dazzle, Armand's Herring Fly, Semper Fli, Blue and White Angus, Blados' Crease Fly, Catherwood's Hair-Head Herring, Sedotti's Slammer, Abrames RLS Supervisor, RLS False Dawn, and RLS Striper Moon.

ATLANTIC MENHADEN (POGY, BUNKER)

Menhaden are members of the herring family, and have a bluish-green or bluish-brown back with silver sides. They also have a dark shoulder spot. They have a big, boney head and a large mouth. Like herring, their lower jaw extends beyond the top jaw. Menhaden move into the southern New England areas in early May. They move around quite a bit, and will stay inshore throughout the summer, typically at or near the surface and near large estuaries. The juveniles return in large numbers in the fall and are known as peanut bunker. The adults get up to 18 inches long, and the juveniles grow to 2 to 5 inches. Adult: Peanut Bunker: Menhaden Bucktail, Semper Fli, Brown and White Angus, Brock's Bulky Deceiver, Blados' Crease Fly, Catherwood's Pogy, Kintz Major Bunker, Sedotti's Slammer, Abrames RLS Razzle Dazzle, Abrames, RLS Crazy Menhaden, Puglisi's Peanut Bunker.

AMERICAN SAND LANCE (SAND EEL)

The American sand lance is long and thin, with a bluish green to olive brown dorsal side and a silvery-steel blue side and white belly. The lower jaw extends beyond the upper jaw and it's found in the sandy shorelines, and rarely over mud, rocks, or deep water. The sand lance is up to 7 inches long, and arrive in late May through early June in southern New England, and in mid-June through early July in northern New England. Good patterns are Abrames' Ray's Fly Flatwing in brown, Mikkleson's Epoxy Baitfish, Gartside Soft Hackle Streamer, Windram's Sparkling Bucktail, Gartsides Marabou Fishhead Sand Eel, Mikkleson's Lavender Sand Eel, Veverka's Marabou Sand Eel, Windram's Sand Eel Special, Abrames' Little Sueshe, Abrames' RLS Stormy Sea, and the RLS Bullraker.

ATLANTIC SILVERSIDE (SILVERSIDES)

Atlantic silversides are long and thin like the sand lance, but they have a pale green dorsal side and a silver lateral stripe. Their snout is shorter than their eye, and they live in salt and brackish waters, typically over a sand bottom. They may be up to 5 inches in length and arrive in May. Patterns include Surf Candy, Herb Chase Striper Fly, Abrames' Ray's Fly Flatwing, Ray's Fly, Mikkleson's Epoxy Baitfish, Gartside Soft Hackle Streamer, Windram's Sparkling Bucktail, Abrames RLS Stinger, and the RLS Sure Thing.

BLUEBACK HERRING

Blueback herring begin to arrive in Rhode Island and Massachusetts on the first full moon in March. Like alewives, they continue to arrive throughout the spring and arrive in waves. They move into river estuary systems for spawning, and are easily differentiated from alewives by the distinct blue hues on their dorsal sides. They'll arrive in New Hampshire and Maine two months later in May. Adult patterns should be between 7-11 inches long, juvenile patterns between 1-3 inches long. Effective patterns include Deceivers in blue over white, Clousers in blue over white, Armand's Herring Fly, Blue and White Angus, Brock's Bulky Deceiver, Blados' Crease Fly, Sedotti's Slammer, Abrames RLS Herr Blue, RLS 9-3, RLS False Dawn, Puglisi's Blueback Herring.

BAY ANCHOVY

While herring have lower jaws that extend beyond the top jaw, the opposite is true of their relative, the anchovy, which have an overhanging snout. They are abundant in inshore waters, mostly in shallow bays and estuaries. They are up to 4 inches long. Patterns include Surf Candy, Abrames' Electric Anchovy, Mikkleson's Epoxy Baitfish, Thunder Bunny, Windram's Sparkling Bucktail, Kintz Anchovy Fly, and Abrames' RLS Easterly.

BUTTERFISH

Butterfish resemble jacks, and have a very compressed and thin width but a very wide profile. They are silver with irregular dark spots and have similar dorsal and anal fins. They can be as large as a foot. Patterns include Monty's Pretender, or Enrico Puglasi's EP flies.

CLAM WORM

Clam worms are found in a wide variety of environments and can hatch for most of the year. Some inhabit muddy areas and hatch around the spring full moons while others hatch in the ocean in the summer. Most anglers will target them in saltponds around the spring full moons.

Patterns include Ken's Clam Worm Fly, Windram's Worm Fly, Caolo's Witch Doctor.

CRABS, BLUE AND GREEN

Most of the action with a crab pattern is on the flats, so patterns like a Merkin, Skok's Blind Crab, Caolo's Diablo Crab work best.

EEL

Patterns include Abrames' Eel Punt and Tabory's Snake Fly.

ISOPODS

Isopods (the Latinate for "same foot") are small crustaceans with seven legs on each side and inhabit shallow waters. There are many different subspecies, and an angler who has been unsuccessful at catching actively feeding striped bass may be the victim of isopods in the water. Like a crab or lobster, the isopod will shed its skin, but they don't swim. As a result, they are easy prey for a gamefish. Beach fleas are isopods, as are sow bugs in your backyard. When they're in big concentrations in the ocean, they'll drive bass crazy. Saltwater scud patterns.....deadly.

LOBSTER

As strange as it sounds, lobsters comprise a part of a striper's diet. Around late May through early July, the lobsters molt, shedding their hard exoskeleton and growing into a new shell. During this time their shell has not calcified, and they are soft. When this happens, you'll find the lobsters in the rocks trying to root out the bugs from their crevices. Fish that are caught in the midst of such feeding behavior typically have reddish patches around their jaws and their bellies where they rub against the rocks. Remember, too, that during the late 1800s through the early 1900s, lobster tails were used as striper bait. Nat Moody's Lobsta is the best pattern.

MACKEREL (TINKER MACKEREL)

Atlantic mackerel are the baitfish, but their cousins, the Atlantic bonito, false albacore, and Spanish mackerel are gamefish. The firm fish have a large head and bluish-green with black worm-like markings on their backs. They favor the open seas and moving current, though they are sometimes found in bays and harbors. Mackerel can get to be 22 inches long. Patterns include Blanton's Sar-Mul-Mac, Brock's Bulky Deceiver, Catherwood's Mackerel, Lewis' Tinker Mackerel, Mikkleson's Acrylic Tinker Mackerel, Gail's Tinker Mackerel, Abrames' RLS Tinker's Green, RLS Skinny Mack, RLS Rosey Mack.

MULLET

Striped mullet run as far north as Cape Cod, so they are more important in the southern New England states than in either New Hampshire or Maine. They have a rounded head that is flat between the eyes and have an olive/blue-green back and silvery belly. They favor coastal waters and estuaries and can be up to 18 inches long. Patterns include Catherwood's Finger Mullet, Abrames' September Night Fly, Tabory's Slab Side, Blanton's Sar-Mul-Mac, Popovics' Siliclone, or Enrico Puglisi's Rattle Finger Mullet.

SHRIMP

Shrimp are an important part of a striped bass' diet. The most common shrimp are grass shrimp, and they live in tidal areas such as river systems, coves, marshes, and bays. Some may be large and others are small, but they first appear in May in southern New England and later in June in northern New England. The translucency of the shrimp means you should carry a variety of colored fly patterns. You can cover all bases with a selection of Abrames' General Practitioner in honey, bronze, ginger, black, olive, and pink.

SQUID

Long fin squid and boreal squid are the two common squid that we find on the East Coast. Like shrimp, they change their colors very easily. Squid use their tentacles to grasp their prey, and they are found in any area that has baitfish and elvers. Reefs, saltponds, mouths of rivers, and harbors are the more common spots. They move backwards and when frightened emit a black ink. Some popular patterns are Abrames RLS Moonstone Squid, and RLS Amber Squidazzle, and RLS Razzledazzle, Blados Crease Squid, Kintz Big Reef Squid, Chris Windram's Chris' Squid, Caolo's Magic Squid.

Fishing Techniques

ESTUARIES AND SALTPONDS

Estuaries and saltponds are some of the sweetest saltwater fishing spots. They are seldom far from the crashing surf, strong tidal rips, or surging rocks and are protected by land and trees which minimize the impact from the wind. Freshwater anglers love estuaries and saltponds as they are reminded of their home waters.

Estuaries are river systems that divide into smaller branches, each of which ultimately ends. Some, like the Merrimack, have freshwater origins and can be traced to their headwaters, both of which are in New Hampshire. The headwaters of the Connecticut River, for example, are in Pittsburgh, New Hampshire, a short poke from the Canadian border. The river runs south through the states of Vermont, Massachusetts, and Connecticut until it reaches the coast in Old Saybrook. Rivers with sweetwater (freshwater) flows are expansive at the mouth and gradually shrink, the higher up anglers travel. Saltwater estuaries, like Cape Cod's Sandwich or Scorton Creek, are smaller in size and in scope. They do not run upriver for miles and miles and are far more intimate fisheries.

My fascination with estuaries is how each river subdivides into smaller offshoots. River branches divert the flow past spits of land and form labyrinths. Some estuaries are quite complex whereas others are simple. That said, their structures are all unique.

Saltponds are just as their name implies: a pond of saltwater. At some point, these ponds must connect with the sea. Like estuaries, each saltpond's size and features are different. Some are small while others, like Block Island's Great Salt Pond or Martha's Vineyard's Menemsha Pond, would take several hours to walk around. Freshwater may enter the ponds at different points but there usually is not a high concentration of sweetwater (freshwater).

Occasionally you may see combinations of estuaries and saltponds as you see in Cape Cod's Bass River. At the southern reach lies the open ocean, at the northern reach is a saltpond, and connecting the two is an estuary. Small wonder it's named the Bass River.

The interaction of the currents and the structures is what makes both estuaries and saltponds interesting fisheries. You'll find bars and bays, islands and fingers, mussel beds and grass beds, and cuts and channels; simply put, there is enough diversity in a given area to hold any angler's interest.

Because of the various types of bait in these areas, estuaries and saltponds fish well throughout the entire northeast saltwater season. In the early season (April and May), we find silversides and river herring, also known as alewives. The silversides move from the deeper continental shelf water into the shallows in March to spawn. Alewives migrate into the estuaries and the saltponds in late March through May to access the freshwater reaches so that they, like the silversides, can spawn.

Around the mid-season (June, July, August), sand eels and menhaden reach the saltponds and estuaries. Sand eels love the bottom terrains, for they offer perfect spots for food and lodging. Menhaden in these areas are usually big adults. Ask any kid hanging out under a summer dock light and he'll tell you he's jigging for squid.

The late season (fall) brings juvenile menhaden that stage on the quarter moons in preparation for their migration. You'll also find glass minnows (herring fry) and, in some southern New England areas, mullet.

As if this is not enough bait, you can add other species such as clam and cinder worms, shrimp, krill, and small flounder. Striped bass will eat them like any opportunistic fish will, but these baits tend to be secondary or tertiary food groups.

Bait in estuaries and saltponds is fairly consistent, but there are some nuances. For instance, saltponds with no freshwater inflows won't support alewives that need freshwater to spawn. Others, like Rhode Island's Ninigrit Pond, have rich mud, ideal for strong worm hatches. Part of the fun of fishing these waters is spending the time to identify the baitfish patterns; matching the bait is one of the keys to successful fishing. At any time of the season you will find bait and, therefore, fish.

BEACHES

There are three types of beaches: sand, rock, and combination. The sand beaches are found in close proximity to a river system. The river's current is what transports the beach to its resting spot. Whatever the terrain upriver is what you'll find on the beach. So, if it's a sandy/marshy area you'll have a sandy beach, if it's a rocky environment upriver you'll find large boulders that ultimately break down into smaller rock gardens over time. Around those areas you'll also find cobble – those nearly perfectly symmetrical-sized rocks that are about the size of an orange or a grapefruit. The larger the river, the larger the beach. Consider the Merrimack River and its adjoining Plum Island. Then, consider the Essex River and Crane's Beach. There are some exceptions that can be explained, but that's pretty much the way beaches get formed.

When fishing beaches you'll need to determine the bar structures. There are several different bars on the beaches that you need to identify during the day so you'll know how to fish them at night. A bull-nosed bar is rounded and attaches to shore. Offshore bars are separated from the beach by deeper water. While you may be able to wade out to the offshore bar at low tide, you may get wet if you stay out too long when the tide comes in. Onshore bars jut out into the ocean and connect to the beach and are prime spots for night fishing. Points are just that, spits of sand that stick out into the ocean. Bowls or holes are basins that have deeper water and lots of current. Remember, too, all bars are unique so scouting during the day saves hassles at night.

Wellfleet's Blackfish Creek has ample structure that early-season striped bass like.

There are a couple of pointers for fishing some of these areas. First, use ranges wherever you can. A range is where you take a longitudinal point and match it with a latitudinal point to mark your spot. If you have two convenient points, such as the right end of a cottage porch and a lobster bouy you're all set. You can use water towers, bouys, breakwalls, channel markers, rock piles, or tree lines to mark your spot. If there are no ranges you can make one. If you're on a wide open beach and want to mark an ocean hole you can take a piece of driftwood and tie an orange ribbon on it (like the kind used for marking trees you want to cut down) and stake it in an inconspicuous area for later use.

Onshore bars are a bit different. The appeal is that you can walk way out to some primo fishing spots, but finding your way back in can be a chore. I'll stake out the point of contact where the bar meets shore with a chemical glow stick. After I wade far out and want to come back in, the light helps me find my way off the bar when the tide comes in. After you do it a bunch of times the patterns become familiar and you'll develop a feel for the beach.

COVES

There is a great variety of sizes to coves. Some are small and rounded and cut into rocks and inshore islands while others are long and large, feathered by marsh grass and soft sand. Rocky coves tend to fish better when baitfish gather on the quarter moons, particularly during the fall run. If they have a section of beach sand, kelp, and eel grass, then they may fish well all season long. Coves featuring a sandy or muddy terrain are usually chock-a-block with a variety of baitfish, from silversides, sand eels, shrimp and crabs, to worms. As water temperatures warm, they tend to fish well at night, and there are few sounds as spectacular as a striped bass popping small bait at night. Some of the areas can be muddy, and if your boots keep pulling off your feet, wrap a zip tie around your ankles and cinch relatively tight.

INSHORE ISLANDS, ROCKS, AND LEDGES

Structure in the form of rocks and ledges are what differentiate Rhode Island, Massachusetts, New Hampshire, and Maine from other eastern saltwater fisheries. The rocks arrived by default, a gift of the glaciers. In these spots, there were no estuaries to sweep sand along the way and form luscious beachfronts, areas suitable certainly for fishing, swimming, sun bathing, and picnicking. But not far around the horn from these beaches are the cold, hard facts – rocks and ledges. As nor'easters, storms, heavy seas, etc. wash away land, they leave rocks and ledges.

There are jagged promontories and cliffs like you'd find in Newport and Jamestown, Cohasset and Scituate, Marblehead and Manchester, Gloucester and Rockport, Cape Neddick and Boothbay Harbor, and Camden and Rockland. These are areas that get pummeled by winter nor'easters and soothed by summer's sou'westers. They are areas inhabited by rugged fishermen where, if allowed, true magic can happen. Shore anglers wear cleats to get around the rocks. More often than not they look like Dall sheep in Colorado and sound like New Orleans tap dancers trying to make a buck. They take a few casts and move, take a few casts and move, and clamber in, around, and over the rocks until they find the slot that holds fish. Hook points are easily dulled and must be sharpened frequently. Tippets get frayed and must be checked routinely and changed often. Fly patterns are big and natural.

In between wavelengths, when the ocean is quieter, they may see fish follow a fly and take it when it gets close to the end of their retrieve. Sometimes they see a big bass appear out of nowhere in hot pursuit of a meal. But most of the time, it's prospecting for fish, blind-casting, and keeping their wits about them for the telltale strike. Only steely-nerved boat handlers need apply to fish the rocks. You've got to get in tight to the structure to make a cast and keep the boat ready to get out of harm's way quickly. A sudden ground swell, an increase in wind speed, or a rogue wave can toss a boat on to the rocks or temporarily pin it until the next wave fills it to the gunnels. Running around in the rocks is like navigating a minefield. Hidden ledges that will tear off a lower unit appear at the last moment and force a skipper to be constantly vigilant. It's a tough game out here among the rafts of sea ducks and the small packs of harbor seals diving for snacks. But as you pick pocket your way through the crevices, rifling casts just far enough so that they hit the white wash but not so far as a hang up on the rocks, there is the potential for fish, and big fish at that. Along some of the particularly dangerous rocks are lighthouses or buildings. I think of Marblehead Light, Minot's Light, and Graves.

FLATS

Sand, rock, and cobble that is exposed at low tide or nearly exposed at low tide is a flat. Some are very wide and long, others are short and narrow, and others are variations. The point is that flats in New York are different from those in Rhode Island and still they are different from those in Massachusetts. Every year flats change due to the current and erosion, and they change dramatically in the winter when the nor'easters hit. If you watch your flats over time, you may see patterns develop. It is peculiar, but there is a series of flats not far from my home that takes on almost the same shape every five years or so. As the flats change, so will the dynamics of the fishery. It makes good sense to survey your flats at the beginning of every season to see how they have changed.

Depending on the height of the tides in your area, flats are either fully exposed at low tide or mostly exposed. The bottoms of the flats vary by the region as well as by proximity to the mainland. Some flats are all sand, others have patches of eel-grass beds, and others have a cobble bottom – the cobble being washed into the ocean from natural erosion on the mainland. Water clarity varies as well. Flats in Long Island Sound tend to be a bit murkier than the flats that are closer to the open ocean. They are murkier due to the lower current exchange and due to their distance from the open ocean. Small flats in estuaries get that way, too. Flats are sensitive, and a stiff wind or an overnight storm can cloud even the clearest of water. A day or two of calm weather following a storm clears up most all flats.

Most flats end at some point, and where they end they drop off into deeper water. Some flats have a series of bars, and others have cuts and troughs, known in Massachusetts as guzzles. These cuts and troughs drain the water from the flat as the tide drops and fill the flat as the tide floods. The cuts and troughs are likely areas for the fish to move about to get up onto the flat.

Whether you have cuts and troughs, sand bars, high spots or low spots, you ultimately wind up with an edge. Most predators favor edges, for they are the areas where the deeper water offers protection as well as stronger, more erratic currents. They are great feeding areas; as the baitfish drop-off the flat, the striped bass lie in wait of their room service and they follow the baitfish up onto the flat when the water allows. Hard edges (sharp angles and stronger current) make the fish more aggressive than soft edges. The fish need to move quickly in order to get a meal in harder edges or else it washes by them.

Fish move predictably on flats. They are predators and predators follow edges, which formed by structure or current. A structural edge may be a bar, a depth variation or drop-off, an eel-grass bed, a channel, or a high-spot. A current edge is the way the water moves off of structure. Depending on the height of the tides and the phase of the moon, the water may move fast or slow. Here, too, wind will affect the current speed. Wind moving with the tide will smooth the surface and speed up the water flow. Wind moving against the tide will create a chop and slow the current.

Channels are a good place to wade fish for saltwater fish, and if the channel is in a place called the Bass River on Cape Cod, you're probably in a good place.

Bait swim into the current and predators follow them. (Fish swim with the current if they're spooked or are bailing off a flat because the tide is dropping; if they swim for too long with the current they will drown.) First, you'll need to know in which direction the current is moving; meaning, is it going left-to-right, right-to-left, or some variation in between.

The fish will move along an edge and into a current. They'll find a particular depth that they like and stay with it as the tide rises. The bait will gather at a particular point and the fish will follow. They find a depth in which they're comfortable, meaning that they have enough water over them to feel safe and can feed opportunistically. When there is enough water for them to move they will stay at that depth and move. They'll move until the edge runs out and then they'll look for another edge of similar proportions.

Start at a low depth and motor around for a bit. Look for fish, not just singles, but groups. You may start to see patterns of baitfish and then fish. Keep looking until you see situations that make sense. I learned to pattern fish from my friend Kenney Abrames. Sometimes when we fish, we'll spend hours just looking for fish. You'll come away with some very interesting observations.

You'll note that all the fish are holding on the southwest corner of a point bar. You'll see that they are moving into the current and with the wind. If you watch the depth, you'll find that they hang at a specific depth, say 2.3 feet, and when the tide rises the fish move up, staying at that 2.3-foot mark. You'll see that they work up a series of edges until the tide is so high that they change direction and move off the flat. Fish patterning is hunting and once you get started it opens up a predictable way of catching fish on a flat.

WETSUITING

As a shorebound angler looking to access more tasty water, I stumbled on it by accident. I simply combined two of my favorite sports: flyfishing and scuba diving.

Before I owned my Maritime Skiff, I wade fished the rocks. I met ample success, but never could shake off the possibility of accessing the rocks and ledges that were a few hundred yards from shore. If I got on a pod of school bass, I was convinced there was a pod of 25-pound fish just out of reach. If I caught a good fish, I suspected that there were better fish to be had. After wetsuiting for a few years I learned that this method of fishing developed around Montauk and had been popularized by both spin and flyfishers in the 1960s. Wetsuiting is so much fun that there are numerous days in the season when I leave the boat on the trailer and don my farmer john.

To be sure, the act of wetsuiting is actually swimming to a rock ledge, inshore island, or reef and climbing out on the structure to fish from there.

First off, you should be a decent swimmer, and comfortable in potentially rough water. You'll need the farmer john section of a diver's wetsuit. Wetsuits are made from open-cell neoprene and will soak up water. That's good because you'll stay cool when you're fishing. After the initial shock of the cold water has worn off and your body temperature has warmed the layer of water, the wet suit acts as an insulator. As we all know from waders, neoprene makes swimmers positively buoyant. The farmer john style covers the legs, torso, and shoulders and leaves the arms free for casting. Add a pair of hard-soled neoprene booties and either one or two scuba fins and you're set to go.

Divers approaching boat ladders always remove one fin so that they have a free foot to stick into the ladder's rungs. By wearing one fin they still have the ability to propel themselves through a current. Unless I'm swimming a few hundred yards from shore, I'll always use only one fin. My entrances and, more importantly, my exits are quick. In my first attempts at wetsuiting, I simply stuck some tippet spools, shock material, a hook hone, a scissor/forceps, and handful of big flies under my hat. It worked well until a wave showed me I was foolish. Now I tow behind a small wet/dry bag. I've attached a 1-pound H anchor and 10 feet of nylon line borrowed for the season from a mallard duck decoy. In the event that I drop the line the anchor slows the drift of the bag. The anchor also secures my bag in the rocks when I'm fishing so a stiff wind doesn't blow it into the water. In the bag I carry a stripping basket into which I'll toss a few boxes of flies, tippet and shock material, a scissor/forceps, a waterproof camera, a pair of sunglasses, a bottle of water, wading chains, a flashlight, and a compass – you never know when a fog could roll in.

The only difficult part about entering and exiting the water is the surge. As all shore divers know, watch the wavelengths. One out of every few waves will usually be the biggest. Scout out your terrain for an open slot, wait for the biggest wave to crash, and enter the water at the beginning part of the drop of the lowest wave. Take a giant stride so that you enter away from the rocks and with a few quick thrusts with your fin, you're out of the break zone. To exit, find the leeward side of your island or ledge. The waves don't crash as hard as on the windward side, and if you're wearing only one fin, it's easy to climb out and on to the rocks.

NIGHT FISHING

Night fishing is tactile. If you're used to fishing during the day then your vision is probably very keen but your tactile senses may be undeveloped. On some nights, particularly on high-pressure nights or around full moons, you might not even need a light to re-rig. But on low pressure nights, especially on a dark, new moon, you won't be able to see much. Here are a couple of pointers that will make the difference.

START FISHING BEFORE SUNSET

You'll be able to see your terrain, feel the current flow, and get comfortable as the light gently fades. Your eyes will adjust and it won't be as much of a jolt as if you show up on the beach at midnight.

RELY ON FEEL

Casting and fishing will be based on feel. Most night fishermen will drop their casting arms towards the side to keep the fly line and the fly a slight distance from their head. The stroke remains the same, but by dropping your arm you'll prevent hook ups. Stop your backcasts a bit higher than you normally would; your sense of distance will be changed and chances are you'll tick the water or the beach on your backcast. Swim your fly. You'll have to feel your line to know where it and your fly are. Floating or sink-tip lines work best for line control and after you make your cast, feel where the rod is bending and where the line is drifting and you'll know exactly what is happening. If you need to get deeper, you can always add a pinch of split shot or some extra weight to a tippet. Since you won't be able to see a fish inhale your fly, consider every bump a strike, just as you would when nymph fishing for trout.

When the sun rises above the horizon, Grave's Lighthouse seems to appear out of nowhere. During the spring and fall runs, it's common to find enormous schools of bass on the surface.

LISTEN

When the wind isn't too stiff or if you're downwind, you can hear a long way off. On quiet nights you'll oftentimes here fish slurping silversides or sand eels or slapping herring.

SMELL

I remember night fishing with Kenney Abrames and he suddenly yelled, "STOP! LET'S FISH!" We got out walked the beach and within a few minutes were catching fish. When I asked him how he knew there were fish there he said he smelled them. How did he smell them? Remember what a fish smells like. After you catch one, hold your hand to your nose. As you wander around at night you will be able to key in on the scent just as you distinguish a grilled steak at a barbecue.

POINTS ON FULL MOONS, COVES ON QUARTER MOONS

In the fall, most bait stages on the quarter moons and migrates on the big moons. Points are great ambush spots on the full or new moons, and areas with slower current are better on the quarter moons.

FISH DROPPER RIGS

Your odds for hook up during the day or night improve if you're fishing a few different flies. A large bait pattern on the point with a small bait pattern farther up the leader and a clam worm pattern higher up gets you matching more of the diverse bait in the water. Since it is dark and you can't see as well, it makes sense to cover the bases with multiple patterns.

FLY COLOR

Most fly rodders will use black flies at night due to the low-light conditions. But baitfish don't always respond to black-tie events. True, they will pick up the color that corresponds with their environment or light but daytime patterns with brown or olive blends many times work just as well.

SHUFFLE WHEN WADING

It's tough to see where you're walking, but you don't need to if you shuffle your feet. You'll feel if the bottom starts to get soft or if the water gets deeper before you leap.

KEEP UNNATURAL LIGHT TO A MINIMUM

Turn away from the water you're fishing before you click on your light. Bright lights are unnatural to striped bass. And while it's fun to take pictures at night, flash bulbs at night tell other anglers you're hooking up.

Landing fish

With luck you're hooking nothing but big fish, but that's not always the case. Small fish are easy to lip and release. But scout out an area for the times when you get a big fish. If you're on a beach it's easy to watch the wave patterns and surf the fish onto shore. Out on a bar it helps to have a friend help out. If you don't have a friend, back up to some high ground and beach your bass on your own.

Summer and Fall Water Temps

Striped bass feed most aggressively in cooler water temperatures (mid-50s to low 60s). In the summer and in the early fall, the water will cool down after the sun sets and it's coolest just before the sun rises.

Fish with a pal

It's easier to drink coffee and stay awake with a pal. You also err on the side of caution when you have a partner watching your back.

Kayak Fishing

Some fishing spots fit somewhere in between a wade spot and a boat spot. Those areas may be an estuary with a muddy bottom, a long, shallow flat, or a quiet saltwater estuary, where fish spook easily. Hard-chine kayaks are the perfect answer. They are affordable, easy to paddle, easy to maintain, and can get you to where the fish are.

There are two types of ocean kayaks: open sit-a-tops and open cockpit boats. The sit-a-top enables anglers close access to the water and great balance. The extra balance can be helpful in accommodating the athletic fly cast. During warmer months they work well. The down side to sit-a-top boats has to do with the northeast water temperatures. Stripers typically arrive in late April and stay through November or December. The water temperatures are still very cold. For most-of-the-year fishing, an open cockpit boat solves that problem.

I've used a lot of different boats and, as of right now, my favorite is the Wilderness Systems Pamilco in a tandem version. There is a lot of room, it's 14 feet long (and that extra length helps me balance in stiffer winds and seas), and I can fit all sorts of stuff in the large cockpit. There are foot braces in the front to help me stabilize while casting or leaning over to grab a fish. I like the tandem because sometimes I'll paddle my wife or a friend into casting range, and sitting in the back seat helps me to do that easily. They're so well-made that all I do is rinse off the boat with a little freshwater after each trip.

Some accessories are helpful for your boat. You'll want to have a compass and a whistle on board. An easy way to handle those is to attach them to one of the bungee cords that store gear. The compass is critical for navigating when a fog rolls in, and the whistle helps you to get your friend's attention. The loud tone cuts through the ever-present wind. A spray skirt is helpful during rainy weather. Fly rodders like to strip their line onto the spray skirt, and it serves as a stripping basket. An anchor helps in most situations. You can buy a small Danforth-style anchor and line, or you can make your own out of a gallon jug and some anchor line. I'll fill mine with sand and rocks when I get to my location and empty it before my portage back to the truck (saves weight). The best part of the make-it-yourself anchor is that you can tie it off and make a drift anchor by cutting the water depth in half, and tying a half-hitch on your seat. You'll slow your drift and be able to better work the area you're fishing. You'll also want a paddle tether. You'll attach the tether to the paddle when you're not stroking so that you don't watch your paddle fall overboard and drift away. There are a number of kayak racks and personal floatation devices available to suit every paddling angler's tastes and preferences.

Over-sand Driving

Check the Local Rules First

Vehicles that drive on the beaches must follow a number of rules specific to the state and the governing body's regulations. After you target a beach you want to run, conduct research with the individual governing bodies to ensure compliance. You'll find some rules cover common sense (no riding on fenders, tailgates, roofs or in any other position outside the rig) or practical (no towing dune skiers, paragliders, or water skiers).

Some Tips for Driving on the Beach:

Deflate your tires to about 12 pounds per square inch before hitting the beach. You'll get a smoother ride with a broader surface and keep from bottoming out. When you come off the beach, look for an air station for re-inflation. Air pumps are typically located within 150 feet of exit points. They may be covered with shrubs, and out of site. If there is none, drive slowly to the nearest gas station.

Run your rig in four-wheel-drive high gear. The following gear is usually required by the governing body, and if it's not, you still should pack it before deflating your tires: shovel, jack, towrope or tow strap, full-sized spare tire, two jack support boards, and an air gauge. I pack a hand winch and a crow bar as well.

Stay on established paths to prevent damage to the dunes and vegetation. Loose, dry, or wet intertidal sand can be especially dangerous. If you're unsure of the path, get out and walk it first. Drive under 15 miles per hour. If you're going faster you'll probably bounce a lot and you may miss subtle signs of warning. I saw one truck with a steel sign post run through its radiator. It blew down in a storm and acted like a spear to the unsuspecting speeder. Limits around shorebird nesting habitats (usually plovers) are under 5 mph.

If you get stuck, let out a little more air from your tires to increase the surface area. If you wind up spinning your tires and your frame digs into the sand, then jack up each wheel and fill in holes under each tire. Then, back up and roll forward.

Vehicles coming off the beach have the right of way. As you're driving out to your fishin' hole, watch for turnouts. Pull in to them so the rig coming off the beach can keep rolling. When running at night, pack a few flashlights so you can scan the sides and watch for drop-offs, soft spots, vegetation, or holes.

Make sure your gas, oil, and coolant levels are topped off. If you're going to run the beaches on a regular basis or if you add a camper to the top of a pickup then you might want to add an over-sized radiator to keep your engine temperature low.

Rinse the undercarriage when you get off the beach to reduce rusted frames.

RIGGING TECHNIQUES

For the most part, northeast saltwater gamefish aren't leader shy. The conditions, such as bright light, the wrong fly, or running out of room on a retrieve usually result in a low hook-up ratio, and many anglers will blame their terminal gear. If you feel more comfortable going to light tippets, so be it, but many plug fishermen are catching as many or bigger fish with 40- to 60-pound leaders.

Shorter leaders tend to be the norm, usually between 4 and 9 feet long. Many anglers will use a simple 3-foot section of leader material, others will use two sections of 2 or 3 feet of heavy and 2 or 3 feet of light (as in 40- and 20-pound test), while others will mimic a trout leader with a graduation (as in 3 feet of 40-pound, 3 feet of 30-pound, and 3 feet of 20-pound). When fishing with sinking lines, a shorter leader makes sense to keep the fly at the same depth as the line. With any leader, the use of droppers makes absolute sense. You'll figure out the type of bait that the fish are interested in and it will help you put more fish on the beach.

For a simple leader, you can use one knot to do it all: the double surgeon's knot. Tie a double surgeon's loop in the butt to connect with your fly line, use a double surgeon's knot for graduations and a double surgeon's loop to attach your fly. Other ways would include a bimini or a spider hitch in the butt section to attach to your leaders for shock absorption. A five-turn surgeon's knot at each graduation is the way to create a dropper.

For bass in the rocks or bluefish you'll need some type of tippet protection. Wire biteguards are best for bluefish and monofilament sections are preferred for leader-shy bluefish and bass in the rocks. An Albright knot from your leader to the bite guard works best. A haywire twist gets the nod for attaching a fly on to wire and a Homer Rhode or Costa Rican tarpon knot for heavy mono and striper flies. Be sure to seat all knots.

The Field Guide to Fishing Knots: Essential Knots for Freshwater and Saltwater Angling by Darren Brown has all the knots you'll need to know.

Flurocarbon has some significant advantages. The diameter per pound test of breaking strength is thinner than mono, it doesn't rot, and it's more abrasion resistant – a big benefit when fishing on beaches or around rocks. It costs an arm and a leg, but to scrimp on the fish-catching end of things never made any sense.

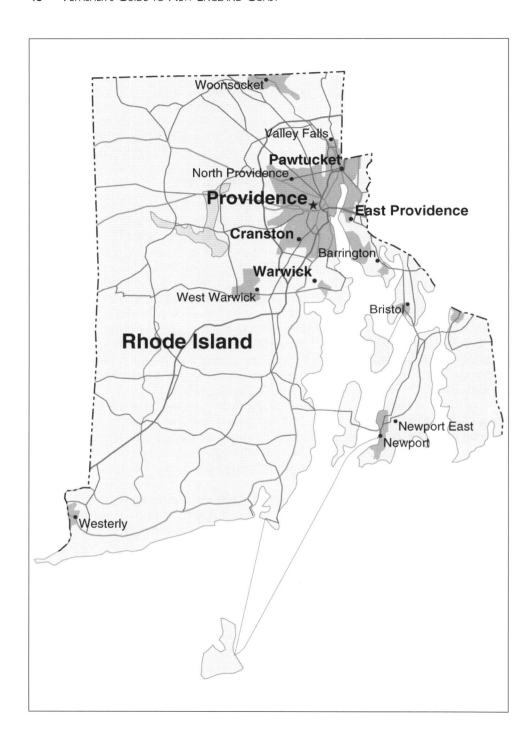

Rhode Island Coast

Rhode Island Waters Overview

Think of Rhode Island in three different sections. South County, the stretch from Point Judith to the Connecticut border would be one section. Here you'll find beaches, rock piles, saltponds, reefs, and breachways. Then there is the middle section, or Narragansett Bay. The West and East Passages split Narragansett Bay into two sections. You'll find rocks and ledges along Narragansett, Jamestown and Newport, estuaries and river systems, coves, and cobble bars. And it is all wrapped up in a bay with channels and edges galore. Eastern Rhode Island is a pleasant mix of river estuaries, rocks and ledges, beaches, rock gardens, and open ocean. There is a little something for everyone, all in very close in proximity.

REGULATIONS

Fishing regulations (especially saltwater fishing regulations) are constantly subject to change, and as such we cannot possibly keep up with the current regulations in this guide. Therefore, we can only provide you with a link to the website that will have the most current rules.

For Rhode Island, the website is: www.dem.ri.gov/programs/bnatres/fishwild/mfsizes.htm

RHODE ISLAND SPECIES AVAILABILITY

SPECIES	APR	MAY	JUN	JUL	AUG	SEP	OCT	NOV	DEC
Striped Bass	+	++	++	+	+	++	++	++	+
Bluefish		+	++	++	++	++	++	+	
Squeteague	+	++	++	+	+	+	+	+	
False Albacore					+	++	++		
Atlantic Bonito				+	++	++	+		
Spanish Mackeral				+	++	++	+		
Skipjack Tuna				+	++	++	+		
School Bluefin Tuna	+	+	+	+	++	++	++	+	

+ = Available, ++ = Prime Time

The whitewater that comes from the sea surge creates turbulence along rocks. Baitfish get disoriented in the turbulence, and are easy prey. Cast into the whitewater and begin your retrieve immediately as the surge falls back into the ocean. The rocks off of Newport's Ocean Drive are a good place to look for big bass.

South County

South County runs from Point Judith/Galilee west to the Connecticut border. It's hard to find one area that has beaches, saltponds, reefs, rocky points, jetties, and coves combined with all species of northeast saltwater gamefish spread out across a season that extends from April through December. Striped bass arrive in late April, bluefish in May and with its close proximity to the Gulf Stream, July through October brings in pelagic species such as bonito, false albacore, skipjack, and Spanish mackerel. The majority of the fishing occurs by foot or by boat, but kayaks are becoming more popular, particularly in the saltponds and river systems, and two beaches – Charlestown and Westerly – allow for seasonal 4x4 use. Tides are easy to chart in the ocean, but remember when fishing the saltponds that there is a delay in high and low tides. Depending how high in the ponds you go, it can be as much as a three-hour difference. The same holds true on the dropping tides, so plan accordingly.

The following sections go from west to east.

WESTERLY/NAPATREE POINT

Napatree Point is the end of the road. It is a peninsula that is connected to Watch Hill and the mainland by about a 1.5-mile stretch of beach, appropriately named Napatree Beach. To the north of Napatree Beach/Point is Little Narragansett Bay. The Pawcatuck River runs south along Watch Hill and enters into Little Narragansett Bay. To the south is the historic Watch Hill Lighthouse. Napatree Point is accessible from two paved parking lots on Bay Street. And as all anglers know, something about the end of the line captures our attention. Napatree Point's reputation is easily deserved.

Due to storms and erosion, a rock garden has formed at the western and southwestern ends of Napatree Point. What is interesting to flyfishers is how the point cuts back to the northeast, thereby creating a large cove. Depths change quickly, from a mean low tide of 1 to 6 feet, perfect when fish are moving into a dropping tide and a stiff southwest wind. When the alewives, herring, and silversides arrive in the spring/early summer, you'll find them moving into the bay and the river, spread along both sides of the beach and all along the point. There are a lot of fish in a relatively small space.

Boaters should plan their entrances into Little Narragansett Bay around the tides. With Sandy Point to the north and Napatree Point to the south, there has been a lot of erosion that has filled the area. Average low-tide depths are between a half and 2

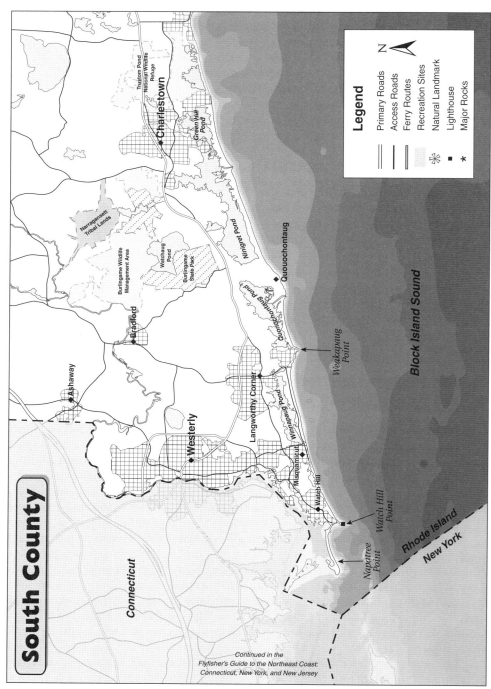

South County

Legend

N

Primary Roads
Access Roads
Ferry Routes
Recreation Sites
Natural Landmark
Lighthouse
Major Rocks

Truston Pond
National Wildlife Refuge

Charlestown

Green Hill Pond

Narragansett Tribal Lands

Burlingame Wildlife Management Area

Watchaug Pond

Burlingame State Park

Ninigret Pond

Quonochontaug

Quouochontaug

Block Island Sound

Bradford

Ashaway

Quonochontaug Pond

Weakapaug Point

Langworthy Corner

Winnapaug Pond

Westerly

Misquamicut

Watch Hill

Watch Hill Point

Napatree Point

Connecticut

Rhode Island

New York

Continued in the
Flyfisher's Guide to the Northeast Coast:
Connecticut, New York, and New Jersey

feet, so it's easy to run aground. Move into the upper reaches around the higher water marks to take advantage of the dropping tide and you'll be able to drop out before the depths get too shallow. Watch the fish on the edges and on the flats – sight fishing is a possibility. On flood tides, you'll see fish move on to the flats in good numbers.

Watch Hill Cove is on the northern side and at the eastern end of Napatree Beach. What makes Watch Hill Cove a good fishing spot is the dramatic drop-off in depths and the channel on the northwestern side. While the edges may only be between 2 and 4 feet deep, the middle is 10 feet deep. In the fall, you'll see some bonito and albies along the edges. Floating and intermediate lines are best. Currents move quickly, so make sure that your cast isn't in the same direction as your drift. You'll find that you can't retrieve fast enough, and while you haul in a bunch of line your fly doesn't move. Cast on a 45-degree angle to the boat.

Above Watch Hill Cove is Foster Cove that is formed by Rhodes Point. There are rocks at the point and it runs foul in close. Night fishing during the early summer can be good in Foster Cove, and because it's so protected by land, it makes for good kayak fishing. The cove and point are easy to navigate, and floating or sink-tip lines work best. When silversides and sand eels are in, you'll hear fish popping on the surface.

Rhodes Point is at the mouth of the Pawcatuck River. The Connecticut/Rhode Island stateline basically splits the river in half, the west side belonging to Connecticut and the east to Rhode Island. The importance here is that as of 2010, Connecticut and Rhode Island have two totally different sets of regulations for keeping striped bass, with the former running a slot limit and the latter working off of a legal-length limit.

After you've accounted for the legality of your fishing, know that the Pawcatuck River can be a great spot. There are some rocks spread along the western edge, and the current moves on the dropping tide. Depths drop off quickly, from 2 to 10 feet, and the water clarity can be somewhat murky. There are a good number of rocks scattered from Rhodes Point to Graves Neck that are great for bass, but bad for lower units. Kayak anglers can cast into the rock gardens at mid-tide from the landside, while boaters will run the channel edge and cast into the rocks, towards shore. The Main Street Boat Ramp is located on the Pawcatuck River between Union Street and School Street. This state-owned concrete boat launch is in excellent condition and located upriver from the Margin Street Launch. Ample parking is available for vehicles and trailers. Another ramp is located at the Viking Marina off Margin Street on the tidal portion of the Pawcatuck River. The marina is privately owned but has one small boat ramp available for public use. The ramp is 10 to 12 feet wide and public parking is located a half mile away.

Graves Neck is on the northern side of Colonel Willie Cove. There is a salt marsh at the back of the cove, which makes for excellent night fishing on a dropping tide, particularly when the current pulls the shrimp into the cove. Some rocks are on the western end of Graves Neck, and the channel that moves into the Pawcatuck River creates depth and speed. You'll find bass and bluefish moving into the Pawcatuck River, and the area is good for wade, kayak, or boat anglers. The diverse combination of water moving in a variety of directions makes for phenomenal fishing. Use a combination of floating lines to keep from fouling in the rocks, to sink tips along the beaches. Flyfishers favor the north side during the spring and summer months, mostly due to the prevailing south/southwest winds, and will shift over to the south side as the winds shift to prevailing north/northwest in the early fall.

Again, this area is an all-season, all-species fishery. You'll find some of the earliest striped bass arriving in New England as well as the last departing fish during the fall migration. An early push of bluefish arrives in the beginning part of the season, and then disappears. They return in the summer and stay until the water cools in the fall. Some weakfish arrive in the spring, but their numbers are not that significant. Bonito, false albacore, and the occasional skipjack make their way into town in late July and depart in early October. You'll also see a lot of Connecticut and New York plates in the parking lots, for the close proximity to those states make it attractive to anglers. Odds are you'll see Charles George and his crew from Bedford, New York's Bedford Sportsman.

As if that's not enough, the fishing will only get better. On the Pawcatuck, the Lower Shannock Dam was removed in 2010. In 2011, a fish ladder is being built at Horseshoe Falls in Shannock and then the Kenyon Mills Dam will be removed. As baitfish stocks improve, look for this area to be an even better spring and fall location.

WATCH HILL

Watch Hill is one of Rhode Island's most recognized fishing locations. There are three parts to the area, and they typically get interchanged by anglers to the point of confusion. I have been one of these anglers.

The first part is Watch Hill Point, which is the rocky area on the mainland, just below the lighthouse. A long walking path off of Bluff Avenue leads to a stretch of sandy beach. This path is due east of Watch Hill Lighthouse. Here you'll find rocks and ledges – excellent striper water. When you see it you'll also recognize it as big fish water. The best tides to fish along the rocks are mid-incoming or high-outgoing. The water is clear, which makes for a great night-fishing spot, particularly on the full and new moons when the current is sharp. Korkers are a staple item, as the rocks are very slick. All anglers have a tendency to want to hike out as far as possible, but exercise caution, particularly at night. Scope out your area during the day, particularly on a full moon low tide. The rocks are very slick.

Watch Hill Passage is below the point, accessible by boat. What makes this area great is the change in depth from 17 to 18 feet into 45 to 60 feet. When the tide is moving, concentrated bait washes through the dramatic current, and the fish move high up into the current line to feed. The combination of bait is incredible. From alewives and herring in the spring to squid in the mid-season to menhaden in the summer to bay anchovies, butterfish, and mullet in the fall, there is usually no shortage of bait. The fish will move higher or lower into the passage based on the tide.

The rocky Watch Hill Reef is below Watch Hill Passage, and creates an even more dramatic effect than the Passage. Here, the reef formation runs just under water at low tide, with equally deep adjoining depths as the Passage. Most boaters will use one of two approaches: either drift with the tide, being cautious about how close they get towards the reef, or stem the tide. Positioning your boat just above the drop-off enables casters to make a reach cast with a mend and swing a fly down to the fish that are on the current and depth edge. Most anglers favor extra-fast-sinking lines for the Passage through the Reef, and will increase tippet and leader strengths to 20- or 30-pound flurocarbon. You'll also want to make sure you have plenty of backing because fish that run with the current are tough to stop.

Striped bass will move into the reef and the rocks when they move into the Napatree Point area. After the herring runs are over, those fish will also move in due to the change in arriving bait. As spring moves towards summer, squid move in to feed on the silversides, and Watch Hill Reef comes alive. The current blows across the reef on the dropping tides, sweeping both silversides and squid into big schools of concentrated striped bass. Water temperatures are such that you'll also see decent concentrations of bluefish moving in. The current and surge make for better boat and wade fishing. When the tides are higher, many anglers will favor extra-fast-sinking shooting heads or sink tips. Sinking lines also help offset the current speed. When the bite is hot, floating lines with a pinch of lead will work best. If you're looking to hang a really good striped bass, June is the time. Night fishing on the moons is when you'll see many anglers fishing from shore.

As spring and early summer are great times to fish from Napatree Point through Watch Hill, so too is the fall. As the bait stages on the quarter moons, Little Narragansett Bay fills up. Napatree Point gets hot as the staged bait moves on the

Tim Shields wades off Charlestown Beach in Rhode Island. Charlestown Beach is great for stripers, bluefish, bonito, false albacore, squeteague, and shad.

full and new moons, and with the northern winds the casting gets a bit easier on the western and southern sides. When all of the bait dumps out of that area, it hits Watch Hill, which makes for a feeding frenzy.

Part of what makes Watch Hill such a tremendous fishery is that it's the end of the road that starts all the way east at Point Judith/Galilee. The current sweeps along the entire beach and either ends, or begins, at the rocky reef outcropping. Waves can be significant. Fall fishing illustrates that point very clearly, and in September, Watch Hill is one of the targeted areas for a Northeast grand slam of striped bass, bluefish, bonito and false albacore.

Watch Hill is also receiving stimulus monies for habitat improvement. For years, a variety of government agencies and advocacy groups have wanted to remove dams and build fish ladders. Their common goal has been to increase the baitfish populations that in turn will support better gamefish stocks. They have struggled for funding but that has all changed now. Three million dollars in stimulus money provides funding for six projects on the Ten Mile and Pawcatuck Rivers. The size and scope of this project is incredible, and when it is all said and done, herring, alewives, shad, and other fish will be able to migrate through the Pawcatuck River from Watch Hill in Westerly all the way to Worden Pond, in South Kingstown. This is a tremendous victory for the area. According to Chris Fox, the executive director of the Wood-Pawcatuck Watershed Association, the funds would open access to Worden Pond by 2011, instead of 2018 as originally planned. Lisa Cavallaro, a habitat restoration specialist for NOAA in Narragansett, said the projects were ready for initiation, with design and permitting far along. Cavallaro added that a series of fish ladders are to be constructed at a variety of spots, namely Omega Pond, Hunts Mills, and Turner Reservoir on the Hunt River.

WEEKAPAUG

Weekapaug consists of three parts moving from west to east: the breachway, the point, and the beach. Winnapaug Pond is at the top of the breachway.

Weekapaug is a small jetty and is a top bass spot in the early and late seasons. In the spring, many bass filter off the beach, around the breakwall and into Winnapaug Pond. There is a hard current that runs off the east end of the breakwall that fishes well on the dropping tide. The pond fishes fairly well in the early season, and a kayak is invaluable for getting around. Most of the current is soft, and nighttime is better as the beach crowds will have diminished. Floating or extra-fast-sinking lines work best for either the pond or at the mouth. As the jetty is small, space is a commodity. You'll find squeteague in the spring, and albies in the fall. Weekapaug is one of the better areas in Rhode Island for a wade angler looking for a grand slam as bluefish arrive in late May, bonito in late July/early August, and false albacore in late August/early September. The occasional spring squeteague arrives in May.

Striper diehards favor Weekapaug Point. The one-third-mile rocky shoreline features point and coves. A rock garden is towards the western end of a small cove. There is a strong current line just beyond the rocks in which fish stage during the lower water marks. As the tide floods, you'll find the fish pushing closer to shore and the action heating up. Weekapaug Point gets a big surf during storms or heavy wind, and during those times you'll find the fish even closer to shore. Floating or sink-tip lines are fine in this clear water, and a few pinches of split shot are all that is needed to get your fly down. The floating line will help with line control.

QUONOCHONTAUG

This state-owned 49-acre parcel runs parallel to the east side of the Quonochontaug Breachway. Parking for cars and boat trailers is available at the end of West Beach Road, and can hold about 50 or so vehicles and trailers. There is no float (dock) which is important to note because of the swift current.

When fishing down here, anglers should know that while Quonny is a great fishery, public access has become hotly contested. The Quonochontaug Beach Conservation Commission (QBCC) spearheads the management of the private sections of the beach, and strives to balance needs and usage demands of both the public and the private sectors. The QBCC allows for open-to-the-public parking during specified times. Most of these times are during the shoulder seasons and off-seasons which is of zero consequence for anglers. We like the non-peak beach seasons as the fishing is best then, namely in late April and May and after Labor Day through Thanksgiving. In 2008, there were a series of boards with 3-inch nails buried in the sand with the nails exposed. Perhaps this was to deter resident vehicle traffic, but kids also run along the paths and could easily get badly injured. Access to the beach and pond are through well-marked sand trails and anglers are encouraged to stay on those trails. As the QBCC is aligned with the Weekapaug Fire District and the Shelter Harbor and Shady Harbor Fire districts – you can also check with them.

Quonny can get crowded, but Rhode Island anglers are good natured and helpful. It is one of the earlier spots for striped bass to arrive, and it is one of the deepest and cleanest of the several ponds in South County. Mostly small fish arrive in mid- to late April. The water warms very quickly here, so you'll also see an early push of bluefish. Big schools of bass will move into the pond in the early season. While you'll find stripers in the pond during the summer months, their numbers are smaller than in the spring. Bluefish arrive in good numbers in late June and will stay through the fall. Most of the time, they will be found along the beach, in the current seams at the mouth, and in and along the jetty. Sometimes they will move into the pond, and finding a blitz of bluefish in the calm water at first light is about as fun as it gets. Bonito arrive in late July and false albacore follow in mid- to late August. They'll stay through the end of September and into October. Then the fall migration starts, with a mix of bass and bluefish. Bass will continue to push down the beaches through Thanksgiving.

One way to fish Quonny is to work your way out on the jetty towards the ripline at the eastern end. Most anglers will work the outside edge and move back up towards the beach. The corner where the breakwall and the beach meet is a good spot to find fish. Watch the current. Sometimes the fish will move down the beach to the corner and then along the breakwall to the rip current. Other times, the fish move up the rip current, along the breakwall, and then along the beach. It's common to see a mix of bass, blues, and albies running along the beach at the drop-off (20 feet from shore) in September. There are private cottages to the east of the breakwall, so getting through to the beach is difficult. There is a parking area near East Beach, but it's a long walk down to the breakwall.

A second approach is to work the pond, and you'll see boat, kayak, and wade fishermen. The pond fishes really well in the early season at night. On full moons in the spring and early summer, you'll find good worm hatches. The fish can be very selective, and dropper rigs fished on floating lines help increase hook ups. Worm hatches can be the most exciting and the most frustrating of experiences, and the dominant hatches are in the spring.

The edges of the pond are wadeable. Just shuffle your feet and slow down when you encounter the mud higher up in the pond, so you don't sink in too deeply. The pond is surrounded by land and trees which provides a degree of shelter from the early and late season winds. There are numerous coves spread throughout the pond which will hold bait, and you'll find the occasional squeteague and shad as well. On a quiet summer's night, the fish pop and are easy to find.

You'll see every type of common bait in Quonny Pond, from silversides, sand eels, shrimp, and crabs as well as some that are not as common. Quonny Pond is a popular place for one of Kenney Abrames' free Tuesday-night fishing classes. The events are posted on his website: www.stripermoon.com. One of the best parts – the class involves NO FISHING. Abrames leads students around the pond with dip nets and they study baitfish so as to develop flies for future fishing. With so much bait in the ponds, Quonny is a virtual aquarium.

CHARLESTOWN

At the east end of East Beach Road, is a 3-mile long beach called East Beach. East Beach separates Ninigret Pond from Block Island Sound and is open to 4x4s. The outer beach is open from April 15 through October 31, from 7:00am until 11:00pm. Cost is $50 for residents and $100 for non-residents. Permits are obtained at Burlingame State Park or through the state park website: www.riparks.com/eastbeach.htm. Nearby Burlingame Campground offers tent campsites, RV hookups, cabin rentals and yurts, all of which is spread out across 3,100 acres (www.riparks.com/burlgmcamp.htm). It's a perfect way to get in a lot of fishing.

East Beach runs all the way down to the Charlestown Breachway, and the fishing is good in the spring and the fall. Floating, sinktip, or intermediate lines all work well. Erosion has taken its toll over the years, and you'll find rocky points along the way. The best time to fish East Beach is half flood through half ebb tides. You'll find bluefish in the mid-season, with some epic blitzes occurring at first and last light. Bonito and albies also run along the beach and concentrate along the breakwall.

Charlestown Breachway is the entrance to Ninigret Pond. Located just off Route 1 (bordering the northwestern side of Ninigret Pond), this federally maintained site consists of grasslands, brush and shrub, uplands, freshwater ponds, salt marsh, and a barrier beach. There is a 75-tent campground that is open from April 15 though October 31. For more information, go to www.riparks.com/charlesbreach.htm. There is a public boat ramp on the east end of the park and a second one at Ocean House Marina, on the north end of the pond. Located off Town Dock Road on Fort Neck Cove, Ocean House Marina is privately owned, but offers a public boat launch for a nominal fee. The marina is situated in a well-protected cove of Ninigret Pond in a picturesque setting. When you launch here, you start fishing immediately. In addition to a boat ramp, Ocean House also has a bait shop, boat repair, and trailer parking for customers.

On the east side of the breachway and off of Charlestown Beach Road is a section of the beach that is owned by the town and is open to the public. Pay parking is available for approximately 300 cars, and the beach is about 500 feet away. As with the other two breachways, there is an easterly current swing as the tide drops. You'll find bass and blues working into the current as silversides, sand eels, and bay anchovies drop out. You'll also find bonito and albies running along Charlestown Beach, hitting the tide line, and moving into the breachway. Along Charlestown Beach, you'll see a stand of five cottages, a place where there is a recess in the ocean floor, and a rocky point jutting out. "The 5 Cottages" is a great place to fish in both the spring and in the fall.

Striped bass, bluefish, shad, and squeteague trickle into Ninigret Pond in April and May. Water temperatures warm significantly by June, but that just means that the fishing shifts to nighttime. There are some tremendous clamworm hatches around the full moons in May and June, and fish in the 40-pound class are caught every year. There are channels, flats, points, and coves. You'll also find bonito and false albacore in the fall. When the bite is hot, anglers are spread all along the jetty for good reason; the fish get into the pond through the channel. However, the beach is also a great spot to fish, and many times the larger fish hang in the rip current or in the deeper water.

Perry Creek is a small tidal creek that connects Ninigret Pond to Green Hill Pond. There is a small dirt road that extends north from the town beach parking lot (off Charlestown Beach Road) to a sandy shoreline area bordering Perry Creek. Because of the shallowness of the creek, only shallow draft boats and kayaks are accessible. Green Hill Pond is a saltwater pond and has a great worm hatch. You'll find bass, squeateague, and bluefish.

DEEP HOLE AND MATUNUCK BEACH

Located near the end of Matunuck Beach Road, this small pocket of sandy beach is set-aside for Rhode Island anglers. However, surfers also use the beach. Parking is available for approximately 30 cars. The first striped bass of the season always seem to arrive at Deep Hole, which is about a third of a mile southeast of Mantunuck Point. There is a rocky bottom, which runs into the deeper drop-off of Deep Hole. The best way to wade fish Deep Hole is to work your way out over the rocks to get to the drop-off on a dropping tide and then to work your way back on the incoming tide.

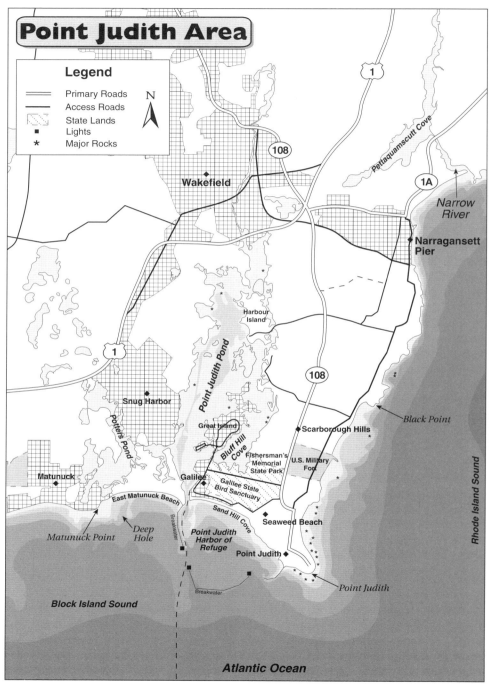

Point Judith Area

Legend

≡ Primary Roads
— Access Roads
▨ State Lands
■ Lights
★ Major Rocks

N

Wakefield

Pettaquamscutt Cove

Narrow River

Narragansett Pier

Harbour Island

Point Judith Pond

Snug Harbor

Black Point

Great Island

Scarborough Hills

Bluff Hill Cove

Fisherman's Memorial State Park

U.S. Military Fort

Potter's Pond

Matunuck

Galilee

Galilee State Bird Sanctuary

East Matunuck Beach

Sand Hill Cove

Seaweed Beach

Rhode Island Sound

Matunuck Point

Deep Hole

Breakwater

Point Judith Harbor of Refuge

Point Judith

Point Judith

Block Island Sound

Breakwater

Atlantic Ocean

© 2010 Wilderness Adventures Press, Inc.

The rocks are slippery, so Korkers are a great idea. You'll also see some surfers around Matunuck Beach, but they mostly prefer the fall when the surf is higher.

Many anglers move on to other areas in Rhode Island after catching their first fish of the season at Matunuck, but that's a mistake. Matunuck fishes well in the summer and it can get red hot in the fall when the mullet, blue backed menhaden, and peanut bunker arrive. Bluefish, squeteague, shad, bonito, and albacore all run the tideline from Deep Hole to the West Wall.

Carpenter's Bar is a long, rocky bar that runs parallel to Matunuck Beach. When the tide floods, the fish will hold on the outside edge and then move over the bar towards the beach or follow the bar in an easterly or westerly direction, depending on the current and the wind.

POINT JUDITH

There are a few towns that overlap in this area. Jerusalem is to the west and Galilee to the east. Point Judith Harbor of Refuge is smack dab in between and it is a working harbor. You'll see charter boats, head boats, draggers, and trawlers heading out before dawn. There is a large fleet of recreational boaters who sail out of Point Judith too. As if that's not enough traffic, the Block Island Ferry departs from the harbor. When the harbor is busy, the fishing can be slow. But when the boat traffic slows down, it can be hot.

There is a public ramp that is located off the Galilee Escape Road at the southeast end of the Great Island Bridge. This state-owned fishing access site has a boat ramp with parking for cars and trailers. There are floats for boat tie-ups.

Rolling surf is a part of every beach. Tuck your rain jacket outside your waders and cinch it with your wading belt and the water will run outside of your boots

Point Judith and Potter's Pond are excellent spots for year-round fishing. They are protected from the breachways and inshore islands like Little Comfort Island and Great Island. The inshore islands provide splits between the main channels and muddy flats, with some rocks thrown in for good measure. Point Judith Pond is big, and it runs from nearly 3.2 nautical miles to the town of Wakefield. Potters Pond connects to Point Judith Pond on the west side. Both ponds are relatively shallow, with small boats and kayaks the best form of transportation. You'll find worm hatches in the spring, all forms of bait in the spring through fall, and excellent fish through December. Bass, bluefish, squeteague, and shad move into higher reaches of the ponds in the early season. Floating and intermediate lines work best. In the summer, the night fishing in both ponds is excellent, and a kayak can get you to bass popping on the surface.

Three walls form the outside of the Point Judith Harbor with one on the inside: the West Wall, the Center Wall, the Short Wall, and the East Wall. The West Wall is well known for two reasons: early striped bass and a place to catch bonito and albies from shore. There is a tremendous current line that runs in close proximity to the West Wall, and the depths drop off very quickly. The hard edge provides the perfect drop-off for pelagic species, particularly with copious amounts of bait dropping out of the harbor. Bluefish and squeteague are also frequent visitors, and they typically arrive in the early spring, moving into Point Judith and Potter ponds (both good spots).

The West Wall gets a lot of attention from all anglers – fly, conventional, and bait alike. It's an easy jetty to walk out on and there is ample room for all types of anglers. That said, boat fishing affords a little more flexibility. Most of the time you'll see bass and bluefish moving up the western side of the wall and into the current along the beach. Moving with them in a boat is a good idea, or move off the breakwall and on to the beach. When the albies and bonito arrive they'll race up and down both sides of the wall. You'll typically see them splashing the surface on the western side of the wall. That's not to say they're not on the inside, only that the ample boat traffic keeps them deeper.

On a dropping tide, the current also streams off to the west that creates a current parallel to the beach. Many times the fish run the current edge perpendicular to the bar. Most fly rodders think that standing on the breakwall is the only slot for wade fishermen to have a shot at a hardtail, but schools of albies and bonito will run the beach, and on calm days they'll run along the drop-off all the way down to the Charlestown Breachway.

One note: the West Wall has a lot of obstructions. There are numerous lobster pots and lines and commercial fish traps. False albacore are used commercially for pet food and fertilizer, so the issue isn't so much in hooking a fish as it is in landing a fish. A good rule of thumb is to increase tippet size so as to steer the fish around the buoys, lines, and nets.

The Short Wall is in Galilee. Due to its small length, it fills up quickly. The current isn't as hard, so the fishing tends to be more focused on the time of year when there are big schools of fish. On windy days, you'll get lots of weeds coming down from Point Judith and Potter Pond. It's an ok spot for fly rodders, but it gets more baitfishermen.

That said, the Short Wall is adjacent to Sand Hill Cove. In the spring and fall, enormous amounts of mullet, silversides, sand eels, bay anchovies, and peanut bunker fill the area. Heading to the east is Seaweed Beach and some rocky areas, perfect for bait. The rocks are a good place for spring and fall bass and summer and fall bluefish. Floating and intermediate lines are best.

The Center Wall creates nearly a perfect barrier. Its U-shape flattens strong seas, and there is a natural gap between the end of the West Wall and the East Wall. All species of fish filter in and out between those two openings. When the bait is in, you'll find all kinds of predators. One year, while looking for bass or bonito, I caught none. But I had a heyday with shad to about 4 pounds.

The East Wall fishes better in either the early or the late season. It's a spot where some of the first bluefish arrive in the late spring/early summer, and it's a quiet night fishing spot. You'll also find bonito and false albacore in the fall. Of particular note is the fall fishing, for the area between Point Judith and the East Wall is the southern corner for fish heading from Rhode Island to points south. The wall runs on a southwest line from shore, so odds are you'll get seas and wind in your face.

Point Judith Lighthouse is to the east of the East Wall. There are rocky points, off-shore bars, big boulders, and a sweeping current that makes for great fishing. You'll find all sorts of bait moving through, from squid to silversides to mullet to butterfish and large and small menhaden. With so many rocks in the area, floating or sink-tip lines work best. Rig terminal gear with heavier tippets, even up to 40-pound-test in the fall. Rocks are spread all along the shoreline, and a half through flood tide is best. As you're walking along the point you'll be able to see how the current pushes back and forth off the rocks. Head out at low tide and look for the structure, for when the tide starts running you'll see seams and hard edges forming which is where the fish will be. It's slippery.

WEST NARRAGANSETT BAY

As South County is filled with long, sweeping beaches, Narragansett is that familiar seaside New England landscape where agrarian meets coastal. After centuries of storms, hurricanes, and the pounding surf, what remains is long sweeping rocks, with boulders and ledges in the water. Gaps are hollowed out, and there is whitewater where the waves smash against the ledges. Long casts are usually not required, as the fish will be at your feet. As with all rock fishing, Korkers or studded boots are important for staying upright. And if you're fishing in a big sea after a storm it may be a good idea to wear a horsecollar-type PFD, just in case. You'll find big bass in the rocks, and runs of bonito and false albacore on the tide seams.

BLACK POINT

If the Department of Environmental Management creates a parking place for fishermen, you know you're in a good spot. There is one at Black Point. Black Point is due north of Stinky Beach, known for the stench caused by decomposing seaweed

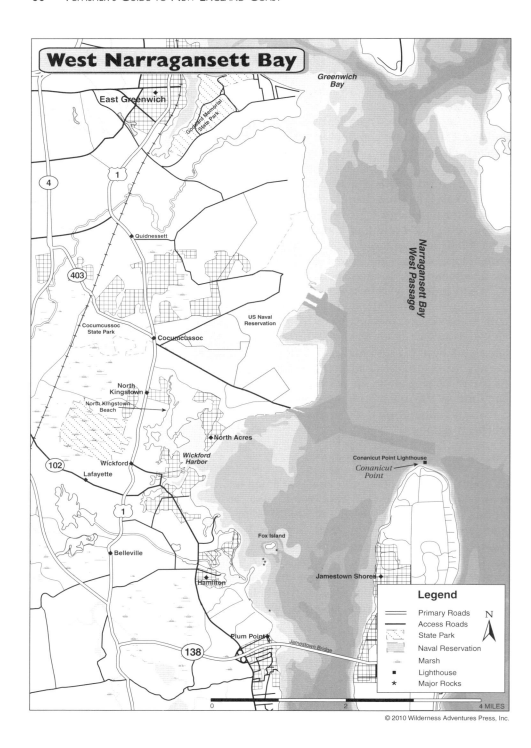

© 2010 Wilderness Adventures Press, Inc.

that routinely washes on shore. There is a cement retaining wall around the point, and large rocks and boulders that extend past the wave line. There is a long offshore bar that runs to the south, and from Black Point you can cast to the edge of the current line. The fish will also move north along the rocks, which means that even when anglers have a head wind they don't need to cast far in order to catch fish. Because of all the rocks, floating lines and poppers or streamers are favored. In the event that you need to get deeper, add a pinch or two of lead to your leader. The water drops off quickly, from 3 to 4 feet into 40 feet. Just south of Black Point are the League Rocks, which are best fished by boat. On the ocean side, the depths drop from foul (rocky, exposed, unable to sail or motor through) to 46 feet, perfect even in the summer.

Look for the area where the whitewater and the suds form, mostly due to the waves crashing into the rocks. Striped bass like the white water, mostly because it makes for easy pickings as the bait gets disoriented.

A few tips for fighting fish in the rocks:

- Fish heavier tippets, 25- to 30-pound flourocarbon is ideal.
- Consider using a non-mono tippet, like PowerPro or Spyderwire.
- Use double lines, like bimini twists, five-turn surgeon's loops, or spider hitches. Many times, line will break on a rock but you'll still be able to land the fish.
- Consider using shock tippets, tied with an Albright knot and a Homer Rhode loop knot.
- Pick a spot to land your fish. A good spot should be a flat area that gently drops to the sea or a recess in the rock formation that is protected. When the tide surges onto the rock, guide your fish up and on to the flat area with your rod. Don't try to pull the fish out of the water and up to the rock; if you don't break off the fish you'll probably wind up breaking your rod.

HAZARD AVENUE THROUGH BASS ROCK ROAD

Running along Route 108 is a series of perpendicular roads that connect with a path that leads to the ocean. Here you'll find a few miles of rocks and ledges that is classic striper water. The coastline juts in and out, and there are ledges and boulders not far from shore. Move up and down the rocks and focus on any white water. Also, drop your flies or plugs into any of the breaks in the rocks. These passages, while small, may hold fish. You'll also find the stripers in the rocks in June rooting out lobsters that have shed their exoskeleton. A dead-drifted lobster pattern with an occasional twitch can be deadly.

In the fall, you'll also see false albacore running the tideline just off shore. Most of the time they're reached more easily from a boat, but they'll move close enough to shore often enough to make the fishing worthwhile. Bass Rock Road is a right-of-way extending east of Ocean Road. This site is difficult to find because it is unmarked and can be easily confused with the many private driveways in the area.

NARROW RIVER

Just north of the rocks and the pounding surf is a pleasant little river system – the Narrow River. One of the state's most popular tourist attractions is at the upstream end, the Gilbert Stuart Homestead. Stuart's father operated the first snuff mill in the family's basement, and his son became a famous portrait painter. What makes this spot interesting for fishermen is the gristmill. Yes, it was used for grinding corn for the famous Rhode Island Johnny Cakes, but for us there is a more important reason for visiting the pond just above the mill: think herring and alewives.

In the spring, herring move up the Narrow River to the pond. With the river's close proximity to the ocean, the Narrow River has freshwater at its headwaters and is thoroughly tidal throughout the rest of it. You'll find shad, squeteague, and bluefish in the river, and at the mouth there are albies in the fall. The river winds down past numerous mosquito ditches and upriver, the bottom is mud. As it gets closer to the ocean you'll have rocks all along the north side, and a long cobble bar that runs southward and parallel to Narragansett Beach. You'll find bait all year long in the Narrow River, from herring and alewives in the spring to silversides, sand eels, bay anchovies, crabs, and worms during the rest of the year. Dropping tides concentrate the bait, and a kayak can be a great asset.

Located at the end of Walmsley Lane off Tower Hill Road/Route 1, is a 5-acre parcel that offers limited access to the Narrow River as well as access to the adjacent URI boathouse. It's a dirt road with limited on-road parking but you can launch kayaks and canoes up here. Just east of Sprague Bridge, on the south side of the Narrow River inlet is a small parking area and a path to the tidal waters of the Narrow River. This site offers access to a popular fishing site underneath the bridge and an excellent place to launch a kayak.

NORTH KINGSTOWN TOWN BEACH

Right off of Route 1A at the end of Beach Street is North Kingstown Town Beach, a quick and easy spot to fish. It is a bowl-shaped beach that basically serves as a cove, has soft currents, and is sheltered from the elements. Early spring is a good time for striped bass and squeteague that are moving, and just about the time the sand eels show up, so do the crowds. Summer fishing is limited to early mornings or evenings, and the beach can get very crowded (flyfishermen, watch your backcasts). The natural configuration, though, makes it a perfect spot for post-Labor Day fishing. Bait, from silversides, sand eels, and peanut bunker stage in the cove on the quarter moons and move on the full or new moons. Fish the points at either end of the beach around the full and new moons and the beach on the quarter moons. When the bait is staging, you'll find it, striped bass and bluefish at the drop-off, an easy cast away.

WICKFORD

With a main street with stores and restaurants and a harbor with boats and dock fingers, Wickford is a nearly perfect coastal town. You'll see fish popping in the

Wickford Harbor as well as in the cove behind the harbor, which are two good areas for kayak fishermen. Boat anglers will launch at near by Wilson Park. Wilson Park is owned by the town and sits just above Wickford Harbor. Anglers head straight to the boat ramp and parking area which is at the end of Intrepid Drive. Kayaks can be launched from here, too.

Fishing around Mill Cove, Cornelius Island, and Fishing Cove is pretty good. Mill Cove has two sections. The first is a series of coves along shore that run around long Route 1. These coves are best fished from a kayak or by boat, but you can access the coves from shore, too. Rabbit Island is a small island just north of the boat ramp that breaks up the water. To the north is a small tidal river, and you'll find bass and bluefish with the occasional squeteague in the coves.

Cornelius Island is to the east and is an island that separates Mill Cove from Fishing Cove. Fishing Cove is a good early-season spot for striped bass and also is good in the summer for bluefish. Mid- to high tides are best.

NARRAGANSETT BAY

With a state as small as Rhode Island, it is easy to move from remote, open and natural within a short period of time and distance. As anglers move higher up into Narragansett Bay, they can expect the following:

- More crowds. Providence, the state's largest and capitol city, is at the northernmost end of Narragansett Bay. The population density is the highest in the state, and Rhode Islanders love to fish. You'll see a good amount of angling pressure in the northern parts of the bay.
- Warmer water. The dark bottom with lesser current exchanges means the water warms up early and stays warm for a longer part of the fishing season. You'll see early school bass high up in the bay, squeteague feeding on worms, shrimp and silversides, and you'll see the first run of bluefish (and corresponding blitzes) in May. Pack your bag for a variety of species.
- Heavy non-sporting usage. Some of the areas, such as Goddard and Colt Parks, attract a wide variety of visitors. Parking areas fill up quickly after sunrise and stay full throughout the day. No matter, with the warmer water temperatures you'll want to fish pre-dawn and post-sunset, so you should be fine. Just be cautious of roller bladders, runners, and picnickers.

GODDARD MEMORIAL STATE PARK

Warwick's Goddard Memorial State Park technically is in Greenwich Bay. It's a peninsula, perfectly surrounded by water. Located on Ives Road, the park has a public boat launch ramp that can only be used on high tides, and there is a fishing area with plenty of parking for trailered vehicles at the west end of the park. The 500-acre park is state owned, and hours of operation are a half hour before sunrise to a half hour after sunset.

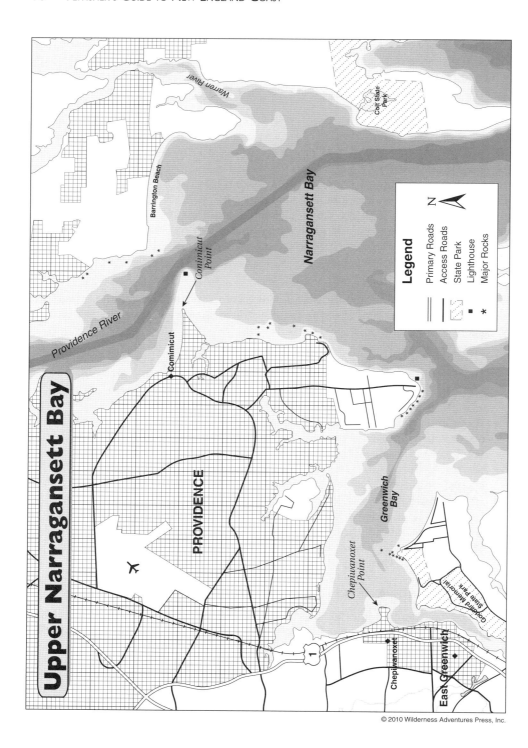

Upper Narragansett Bay

On the northwest end of the long neck is Greenwich Cove. The cobble and sand beach makes for easy walking and wading. Floating and intermediate lines are best. A rock garden at the northernmost end holds schoolie bass, and Greenwich Cove gives anglers a good shot at squeteague. Floating and sink-tip lines get the nod. There are early season bluefish, too, and they typically arrive in early May. The gradual sloping beach means higher water marks are better for fishing. If the bite is slow, you can always play a round of golf or go for a horseback ride, or your family can do that while you fish some more. Though there are some bigger fish caught, the park is best in the early season for schoolie bass and blues. Kayaks can be launched here as well.

CHEPIWANOXET POINT

At the northern end of Greenwich Bay in Warwick is Chepiwanoxet Point. It's a relatively small area and is owned by the state. When combined with Goddard State Park, you can hit two spots in a tide. The shoreline is small and rocky, but it's protected area and makes for easy casting and fishing. The point sticks out into Greenwich Bay, so depending on the wind and the tide, you'll find that one side of the point fishes better than another (as in dropping tide, south side, flood tide, north side, east side on full moons). After the initial push, most of the larger bait moves through towards the Providence River, so Chepiwanoxet Point is a better early-season spot. It's also a good spot for schoolie bass, and the action can be hot. There are bass in the summer, but usually later in the season the bait drops out of the area, thereby making the higher reaches quieter. But, there have been some years with excellent fishing, provided that the bait moves that far north.

CONIMICUT POINT

Conimicut Point is reminiscent of Connecticut's Penfield Reef. Both have long cobble and sand bars that run for a long way out to a lighthouse. The shipping channel that runs into Providence is on the eastern end of the lighthouse. Providence is still a working port, and though you may stay inside of the lighthouse, the area is similar to Boston Harbor: big wakes accompany big ships.

When small bait is in, you'll find the fish stacked up on the down current end of the bar. Conimicut Point has good fishing on the higher water marks, but that also can make for difficult wading, particularly on a full or new moon tide. No matter, bring a kayak, for the sheltered area is an excellent kayak spot. Early season is best, and night fishing in the summer can be good. You'll find both early and late season bluefish. On a high/dropping tide, you can begin your fishing above the parking lot on the peninsula, and as the tide drops you can work in an easterly direction onto and out on the bar. Pack a floating and an extra-fast-sinking line, for the current moves swiftly and after you pass the edges, the water is deep.

Conimicut Point Recreation Area has boat access to the Shawomet Boat Ramp. This sandy boat ramp is suitable for hand-carried boats or for trailered boats with four-wheel-drive vehicles. There is parking available for approximately 15 trailered vehicles, so when the fish are in, get there early.

Fox Point Hurricane Barrier and Providence River

The Fox Point Hurricane Barrier was completed in 1966, and was built after multiple hurricanes struck the coast in the early and mid-1900s, causing significant damage.

The Providence River and the hurricane barrier resemble another urban fishery – the Charles River Locks in Boston. The similarities are strong, and both dams were created to regulate water flows in and out of these major urban river systems. As a result, there are tremendous amounts of gamefish at the entrance points to these waterways, particularly when the alewives are moving in to spawn in the spring. A floating or sink-tip line will get your fly to where the fish are.

Most anglers will park in the South Water Street lot, and work their way down to the Hurricane Barrier. On-street parking is available, on South Water Street, too, and many anglers will begin by the walls. Lining the banks is a walkway with a rock retaining wall. The water speeds will change dramatically, depending on rain/runoff and whether one, two, or all three doors are open. The fishing is best after the doors have been closed for a little bit. The striped bass, shad, and bluefish will stage just below the dam. When the doors open; those same fish will move into the current and up above the dams. While the doors are closed, you'll find consistently growing numbers of fish feeding on the alewives.

An easier access point is a bit farther to the south towards Fox Point. Fox Point extends into the Providence River, and is a spot where fish hang, either moving towards the bridge or into the river.

Note that the Providence skyline and Route 195 pass by not far above this spot. The fishing is thoroughly urban, but there is something refreshing about catching fish within sight of a major New England city. Sinking lines are best, and larger herring flies in the spring work well. When the bluefish roll in, you can catch them on poppers and sliders on floating lines.

Bold Point is just upstream and across the river from the dam. It is a small part that is near the mouth of the Seekonk River. The Seekonk River is the tidal extension of the Blackstone and the Ten Mile Rivers, and is known locally as the Pawtucket River. The beach is a rocky/cobble combination, and there are some old piers that can create obstructions if you hang a good fish. The Seekonk is a freshwater river, so you'll find herring and alewives in the spring. Conditions deteriorate in the summer, with low flows and higher water temperatures.

Across the river from Bold Point is the India Point Park. Named for the East India Company, the park has been recently overhauled, with a new $9.5 million footbridge that channels some 75,000 visitors annually from the Fox Point neighborhoods. The park is close to the channel, so the drop-offs are quick – in some places to 20 feet at mean low tide. As the India Point Park is at the junction of the Providence and Seekonk Rivers, there are many old pilings that can foul casts. Again, spring striped bass and shad runs are good, with summer fishing slowing down.

The East Providence Bike Path has a rocky stretch with a few points that jut out. There are a few points working southeast from India Point Park, and the shoreline ends at the entrance to Watchemoket Cove. The cove begins at the river. A Conrail train track runs along the southern end of the mouth of the cove, just above Kettle Point. In the fall, the cove holds decent numbers of baitfish. On the northern side is a big saltpond that tends to hold smaller baitfish such as silversides, mummichaug, and shrimp. There is a rock wall that enables two or three anglers to walk down to the water's edge. Paddling a kayak from India Point Park (the dock for the Block Island Ferry is also located here) to the cove can be a great idea, for the cove is large enough for a small boat. Flyfishermen also carry down float tubes to get into the deeper center or to work the edges. There is a bridge that runs over the entrance to the cove and several points that stick out into the river. Fish down above or below the points, right where the current seams form.

As part of the economic stimulous plan, East Providence fishing is set to improve. For the past 30 years, volunteers lifted spawning herring one bucket at a time over the Omega Dam. In the fall they would lift the juvenile herring back over the dam so they could head out to sea. It was a tremendous amount of work and due to the stimulous plan it looks like it will come to an end. A fish ladder will be built there and at two other locations upstream.

Oftentimes, you'll find albies running beaches. They favor sharp drop-offs. This morning, Ben Ardito found them on the 12-foot line off of Rhode Island's Charleston Beach.

BARRINGTON BEACH

Barrington Beach is a gently sloping, cobble and sand beach that gradually slopes into deeper water. It's on the northwestern side of the peninsula of Barrington. Early season striped bass cruise the drop-off, and work their way into the adjoining river systems (the Warren and Barrington Rivers), and it's a great night fishing spot. With its proximity so high up in Narragansett Bay, the temperatures can get warm, so early morning is a good time as well. The current is softer and kayak fishing, particularly at night, can be very good. Casting while drifting is a sound approach, for the bass can get skittish with a lot of commotion. A kayak provides a perfect amount of stealth. On full moons, focus your night fishing on the grassy area toward the eastern end. As the tide drops, it pulls shrimp into the current and striped bass line up in the deeper water. A surface popper with a shrimp dropper can be deadly.

Late summer is a good time to fish Barrington Beach as well. Bluefish move into close range on the quarter moons in August, particularly when the baitfish begin to stage. Sometimes you'll even find false albacore running the drop-off when the smaller bait, like bay anchovies and sand eels, are in. Floating or sink-tip lines work best.

During the summer, the municipal beach is restricted to town residents who have paid the permit fee. You can get in to fish at night. The beach is open to anyone in the off-season.

WARREN RIVER

As you move into the slow moving Warren River you'll find that the bottom becomes particularly muddy. While typical of the higher reaches in tidal estuaries, the easy way to fish them is by kayak. There are two common put-ins, Rumstick Point which will require a short, three-quarters-of-a-mile paddle, or at the Crescent Street Parking area. Plan your fishing around the tides and you'll have an easier experience; float upriver on the flood tides and down river on the dropping tides.

At the upper reach of the Warren River you'll find a mud flat. Around high tide, striped bass move in and feed on silversides, mummichaug, and shrimp that drop out with the current as the tide ebbs. They'll concentrate below the bridge pilings, and the bass will use the pilings as structure. Hard currents form as well.

In the spring, you'll find herring and alewives, and with the surrounding landmass you'll get protection from the winds (which makes casting easier). Paddling a kayak works well, and casting along the banks into the mosquito ditches, or in the deeper recesses where the mosquito ditches join the marsh works well. As the tide drops, look for indentations in the marsh bank and note them with a land-based range. You'll want to target them on another day, as small baitfish such as silversides, will tuck into the slower current that adjoins the recesses. Striped bass will cruise those edges as the bait concentrates, particularly on the dropping tide.

Another way to fish the marsh is to pull your kayak on shore and wade fish. You can cast up and across and dead drift your fly or you can cast across and down and swing your fly along the bank. Using a dropper rig with clam worms, silverside patterns, and a big herring/alewife fly helps hook more fish.

The Warren River splits into two river systems: the Barrington River and the Palmer River. Fishing high up in the Barrington isn't allowed, so most folks will fish by the White Church Bridge. To the east is the Palmer River branch, and most anglers will fish along the bike path bridge which is Route 114 and Route 103. The bridge goes over the Barrington River and is where the Palmer River meets the Warren River. The river bottle necks and gets narrow, and the hard current is a good spot for schoolie bass and early season bluefish. By mid-summer, the water temperatures are warm and more of the bass drop out while the bluefish remain.

MILL POND

Located off the south side of Poppasquash Road, at the inlet to Mill Pond on Bristol Harbor, this site is a small pull-off parking area. Mill Pond is a moderate-sized pond

Tom Gabel and Captain Dan Wood with a Watch Hill albie.

due north of Bristol Harbor. Current flows are good and due to limited parking there never are too many anglers. Sink-tip lines are good choices. The terrain can be soft and muddy but it is wadeable. There are cuts and mosquito ditches, and it's a good spot in the early season for bass and for bluefish. The East Bay Bike Path runs along the eastern side of the pond, and some anglers will ride their bikes to the upper reaches. If you have a kayak, bring it. You'll be glad you did.

COLT STATE PARK

Colt State Park was once the property of the nephew of the famous Connecticut pistol manufacturer. Colt the younger was also a visionary; he shaped the future not with weapons but with the world's emerging new product: manufactured rubber products. Colt cobbled together three farms to form his one, all along Rhode Island's Poppasquash Neck, with Mill Gut towards the east. There is a fishing pier/boat dock in the northwest corner, and a boat ramp next to the Bristol Town Beach. Daytime fishermen walk and cast along the rock wall that runs along Narragansett Bay, and Colt State Park is located on a peninsula that separates Narragansett Bay from Bristol Harbor.

Early-season striped bass move along the shore, and the Mill Gut saltpond fishes well. Squeteague also move into the saltpond. As Colt State Park is owned by the state of Rhode Island, it is open only from dawn to dusk for land-based visitors.

Enterprising fishermen will access the pond or the shoreline along the park by kayak, putting in at the boat ramp. They'll even fish down through the gut after night fall. On a dropping tide, the gut and the mouth fish very well, even in the summer. Most of the fish caught are striped bass, but bluefish arrive in the late summer and early fall. Occasional schools of false albacore run the shoreline. Bristol Town Beach, which is adjacent to Colt State Park (off of Asylum Road), features a sandy, gravelly beach fronting upper Narragansett Bay. Plenty of on-site parking is available and there is an admission fee during the summer. Use a floating or intermediate line, and look for summertime bluefish at half flood through half ebb tides.

MOUNT HOPE FISHING ACCESS

Located off Annawamscutt Drive, this access has a single-width concrete boat ramp into shallow water, with a breakwater facing Mount Hope Bay. Adjacent to the boat ramp is a cobble beach and a fringing marsh. Walk along the shortline in either direction with a floating or sink-tip line. There is parking for about ten vehicles with trailers. You can also park along the entrance road and walk in. Early season stripers and mid-season bluefish are the common species caught. Night fishing is very popular up here. Mount Hope Bay gets lots of attention from the large schools of big bluefish that move up into the area. In the early season, you'll also find lots of small to medium-sized bass and some squeteague.

BRISTOL NARROWS

At the junction of King Philip Avenue and Platt Street is a set of concrete stairs and a path that leads down to a grassy area. Another set of stairs leads to the cobble beach below. When they reach the beach, most anglers will move to the left (north) towards the point that juts out and skinnies down the volume of water. The current picks up here and the fish move in to feed on the baitfish drifting past. You can continue walking beyond up current where it opens up and there is more water to cover. Bristol Narrows gets some good concentrations of striped bass and bluefish, but false albacore also wind their way up into current seams. Most of the time, a floating or sink-tip line will suffice, and the walking is easy.

MIDDLE BAY

Rhode Island bears another striking similarity with Boston Harbor: from the open ocean there is an archipelago of islands that is separated by two main channels. Rhode Island Sound enters into Narragansett Bay through the west and the east passages (in Boston it is President and Nantasket Roads). Another similarity is that some smaller islands are accessible only by boat. There are rocks, ledges, deep-water channels, and a variety of species of fish to catch.

There are some significant differences, though. Many of the islands in Narragansett Bay are fully inhabited. Several of them are accessible by vehicle and are a host to a series of quaint, seaside communities. These islands offer hotels, motels, and cottage rentals as well as dining and cultural opportunities, all within a short reach of some of the best fishing in the state. They bear easily recognizable names like Jamestown, Portsmouth, Middletown, and Newport, well known throughout history for their maritime history, their position during the turn-of-the-century extravagances, and more importantly for their significant contribution to outstanding saltwater fishing.

Conanicut Island to Newport

CONANICUT ISLAND

Jamestown is broken down into two sections: Jamestown (which is an island) and Conanicut Island (the island off the island). Beaver Neck is the southwestern section that runs off of Beavertail Road. The two sections are separated by a body of water known as Mackerel Cove. The two sections are separated by a body of water known as Mackerel Cove. On Beaver Neck, you'll find several different spots, and moving from south to north they are Beavertail, Hull Cove, and Fort Getty. On Jamestown, you'll find another several spots, and moving from south to north they are Southwest Point, Bull Point, Fort Wetherill, and Potter Cove.

BEAVER NECK

Beavertail

The southernmost part of Jamestown is Beavertail State Park. The rocky shoreline with ledges has historically been one of the best fishing areas in the state. The water drops off quickly, and Beavertail fishes great during the summer months and the fall. The terrain is very slippery here, and surges can be significant, particularly around a storm when the fishing gets hot. In addition to common baitfish, anglers will find stripers feeding on lobsters, crabs, mackerel, and pollock.

Currents are very strong as they sweep past the rocky ends. With all the nooks and crevices that have been carved into the shoreline, there is no shortage of spots to fish. The tendency is to go out on the rocks as far as possible, just be sure that as you're dreaming about a 50-pound bass, the tide doesn't cut off your way back in.

The fish in the rocks move around until they find a concentration of bait. Then, as the tide rises and the baitfish move up the rock ledges, the fish follow. Casting in and

Sgt. Major Tim Didas, USMC, lost the battle but won the war with a bogey in the perimeter. Based on the bite mark, the odds are a sand shark made short work of this short bass, but it could also have been one of the 15-pound bluefish that were nearby in Narragansett, Rhode Island.

around passageways where the current is allowed to push through is a good bet for finding fish. Beavertail is a common scuba diving spot, so watch for the "diver down" flags.

Fall is a great fishing time at Beavertail. In addition to the bass, you'll find bluefish, bonito, and false albcore. The latter two species hang on the significant depth changes, which are about 40 yards from shore.

Anglers will use a variety of lines here. Some like a floating line for better control, and will add a few pinches of split shot to sink their fly. Others like an intermediate as it'll get a progressive depth without hanging the fly on the rocks. Still, others like an extra-fast-sinking line to hit the deeper water drop-offs and get down to the fish lurking below. Line management is important, and stripping baskets and Korkers are a good idea – watch the wavelengths. Beavertail can be a hazardous area to fish, so pick your days to match your ability.

Hull Cove

Hull Cove is located on the eastern side of Jamestown, right where the island bottlenecks on its way to the end. It's a rocky beach, common with scuba divers who favor easy entrances, and good current. Hull Cove fills with bait in the fall, and it's a good spot for both bass and bluefish. Floating and intermediate lines are good calls.

Fort Getty Recreation Area

Fort Getty is another state-owned park, with an adjoining campground. The camping season begins about a month after the first stripers have arrived and ends before the last of the migration ends (May 20 through Oct. 1). That said, for $20 a night you can set up a tent and fish to your heart's content. Located on Fort Getty Road off Beavertail Road, this recreation facility is the former site of a fortification that was used during both World War I and II to guard the entrance to Narragansett Bay. There is a total of 115 campsites available – 15 spots are designated for tents and 100 for trailers. There is a fee to use the ramp during the camping season.

Fort Getty State Park is on Jamestown's northern-most point. Fox Hill is to the west, and Dutch Island sits across the water to the northwest. Narragansett Bay and Dutch Island Harbor intersect at the state park.

From here, you have lots of options, particularly if you bring along a kayak. The Fox Hill Salt Marsh sits in between the Fox Hill peninsula and the park. It's a quiet tidal estuary system, and provides a lee during the strong southern winds. There are channel offshoots, mosquito ditches, and all the bait you could ask for: from alewives in the spring to silversides, clamworms, shrimp, and the like. Squeteague are also common catches in the marsh, and you'll also find summer bluefish. On a dropping tide, the mouth can be an excellent night-fishing spot, and you can retreat to your camp very easily.

The channel between Dutch Island and Fox Hill has a diverse current that stems from the harbor and the marsh, which concentrates the baitfish. There are pockets and coves which jut in and around on the northwest corner, known as Beaverhead (opposite end of the island from Beavertail).

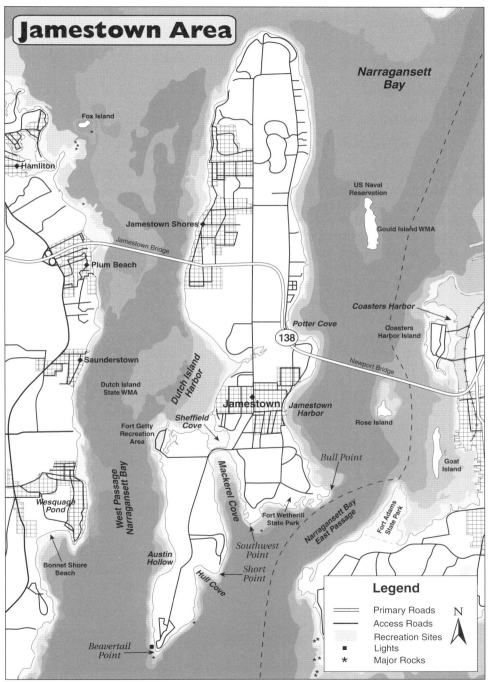

Jamestown Area

Narragansett Bay

Fox Island

Hamliton

US Naval Reservation

Gould Island WMA

Jamestown Shores

Jamestown Bridge

Plum Beach

Coasters Harbor

Potter Cove

Coasters Harbor Island

138

Saunderstown

Dutch Island Harbor

Newport Bridge

Dutch Island State WMA

Jamestown

Jamestown Harbor

Rose Island

Sheffield Cove

Fort Getty Recreation Area

Bull Point

Goat Island

West Passage Narragansett Bay

Mackerel Cove

Wesquage Pond

Fort Wetherill State Park

Narragansett Bay East Passage

Fort Adams State Park

Bonnet Shore Beach

Austin Hollow

Southwest Point

Hull Cove

Short Point

Beavertail Point

Legend

═══	Primary Roads	N
───	Access Roads	
▨	Recreation Sites	
■	Lights	
✳	Major Rocks	

Sheffield Cove is on the eastern end of Fort Getty, and also fishes well. Striped bass, bluefish, and the occasional weakfish fill the cove in late spring, and bluefish again in the fall. A kayak makes for excellent fishing at the mouth through the middle of Sheffield Cove, but the upper reaches get pretty muddy.

JAMESTOWN AREA

Fort Wetherill State Park

Another popular state park, Fort Wetherill, is located on Fort Wetherill Road off Walcott Avenue. Fort Wetherill is also used for open-water certification dives. There is an old Volkswagon Bug sunk off of the cobble beach for student's to dive on (I was one of them in a younger era), and during the day, it is common to see a dozen divers where you want to fish. The shoreline runs east to west, with Mackerel Cove on the western side. The rocks and ledges are significant, and there are tremendous opportunities for anglers. Across from Fort Wetherill is Newport.

You'll see where the water line starts by the bladderwort that hangs from the rocks. The drier rock above the vegetation should provide some clues for rock hopping along the shoreline. Fort Wetherill is a bit more protected than Beavertail, and it benefits from its northern proximity. Still, rogue waves and big swells can knock you down or worse. Be careful.

Low-light conditions are great times for fishing. Find some current and swing a fly. The long bar off of Conimicut Point in Rhode Island is in the background.

The points that are on either side of the eastern parking lot surround the cove where divers put in. They can fish well on the higher water marks, but there is a long and large cove on the western side where baitfish stack up. There is a second big gap on the eastern side. If you're not catching fish at either point, begin moving to the west or to the east. The coastline holds fish, particularly in the summer when the bay warms up. As with Beavertail, it's your call on the floating, intermediate or extra-fast-sinking lines. More natural patterns tend to work better, and don't be afraid to fish big patterns.

Potter Cove

Located on the east-central side of the island and just north of Route 138 to Newport is Potter Cove. Two different parking areas located just north of the Newport Bridge, off Bayview Drive, provide a very scenic view of the East Passage. A long, narrow beach wraps around Potter Cove. Stairs drop down to the beach from a small parking lot. Here you have a shot at catching most northeast species of fish, from bass and blues in the early and late seasons to bonito and false albacore during the late summer/early fall. The gentle slope on the beach is a mix between sand and cobble that extends out into a long flat. At low tide, the fish hold off the edge of the flat, and as the tide rises they filter on and around the flat. The cove's position makes for easy fishing, as the tailwinds keep the seas relatively flat. There are rocks at the eastern end of the cove, and you'll find striped bass cruising around them at night. The cove fills up with bait on the quarter moons in the fall, and here you'll find herring fry, silversides, squid, peanut bunker, and bay anchovies. On a dropping tide, bass and blues from the East Passage drop down and invariably wind up in Potter Cove.

NEWPORT AREA

FORT ADAMS STATE PARK

Around the corner from the Ida Lewis Yacht Club is Fort Adams State Park, a former Naval Academy during the Civil War. Located off Ocean Drive, this state facility is one of the largest seacoast fortifications in the United States, containing a visual record of military history from the 1820s to the end of World War II. Now a state park, complete with boat ramp, Fort Adams gets a lot of attention from fishermen, partly due to its location at the northwestern point of Newport Neck. To the east of Fort Adams lies the historic port of Newport Harbor. Incidently, the park was named for our former U.S. President, John Adams.

A rock retaining wall lines the harbor, and large rocks and boulders separate the retaining wall from the sea. Striped bass and bluefish cruise the harbor. Fort Adams is a spot you can fish without waders, and with the ramp nearby it's perfect for kayaking. The close proximity to Narragansett Bay means strong currents on a dropping tide. You'll see the tide lines forming very easily, and bass and bluefish moving into them between the tide lines and the shoreline.

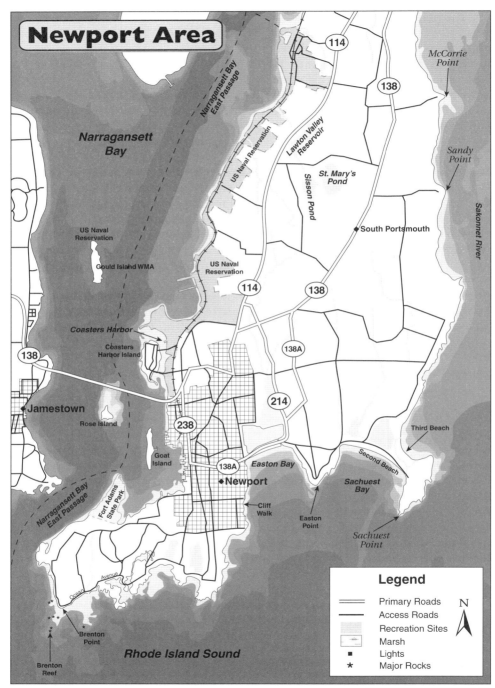

Newport Area

Narragansett Bay East Passage

McCorrie Point

Narragansett Bay

Sandy Point

US Naval Reservation

Lawton Valley Reservoir

St. Mary's Pond

Sisson Pond

South Portsmouth

Gould Island WMA

US Naval Reservation

Sakonnet River

Coasters Harbor

Coasters Harbor Island

Jamestown

Rose Island

Third Beach

Goat Island

Second Beach

Easton Bay

Newport

Sachuest Bay

Cliff Walk

Easton Point

Sachuest Point

Fort Adams State Park

Narragansett Bay East Passage

Ocean Avenue

Brenton Point

Rhode Island Sound

Brenton Reef

Legend

═══	Primary Roads
───	Access Roads
	Recreation Sites
	Marsh
■	Lights
★	Major Rocks

N

In the spring, you'll find striped bass filtering into the harbor. Boat traffic is light at this time of year, so daytime fishing can be very productive. As Newport has a working harbor, you'll find that the depths drop off very quickly and close to shore, thereby making for an easy spot to fish. During the summer, night fishing tends to be better, mostly due to the reduced summer boat traffic. Bonito and albies are occasionally found on the Narragansett Bay side of the state park, where there is also a state beach. There are rocks at the southern end and sand and cobble in between. In the fall, Newport Harbor can be full of bait which range from peanut bunker, silversides, bay anchovies and the like. You'll also find a lot of squid in the harbor.

BRENTON POINT/BRENTON REEF

At the southwestern corner of Newport is the shorebound Brenton Point. Brenton Reef extends on that same southwestern tack, and three markers, a gong, can, and bell buoy mark the rocks where the reef runs foul. Hazardous for boaters? Sure, but Brenton Point and Reef and all the rocks that run westward from Hancock Ledge create big striper water. From shore, there is about a mile of land to fish. Big swells crash all along the shoreline, and the uneven terrain makes for complex currents. On the northwest side is a jetty that is best to fish on the dropping tide, but be careful to avoid being trapped on the jetty as the tide floods. The rocks farther out on the jetty lead to a picture perfect rock ledge and are higher than those close to shore. Continuing westward, the terrain flattens out and makes for easier casting and fishing.

Bluefish and false albacore also come into the corner to feed on the baitfish, and boaters will see them spread throughout the reef structure, particularly on the dropping tide. Stemming the tide is the preferable way to fish the reef, and if you're drifting, be sure to keep your outboard running and a watch for the rocks. The water depths vary throughout the reef, and you'll find 20-something-foot mean low tide depths dropping down to 70- to 80-foot mean low depths – perfect for summer bass.

Fishing along the southern side of Newport – and all the stately mansions – requires getting close enough to drop a fly in the wash. The good part is that as you cast your fly into the whitewater that crashes against the rocks, you have a good opportunity at hooking a tremendous fish. Striped bass in the rocks are some of the prettiest you'll ever see, with pitch-black markings and lines, and vibrant purple with hints of green. As you cast with stately homes in the background you'll also see upside-down metal 'u's, which are bass stands from the turn of the century. Anglers would night fish along the rocks with lobster tails for bait, and hang lanterns and gear on the metal stands. Oftentimes they would lean against them to pass time, and during heavy seas they may have grabbed hold of them to avoid being dragged into the pounding sea.

You'll need to get close to the rocks, but be vigilant for rogue waves that come out of nowhere and can push your boat on the rocks.

The stormier the seas, the better the fishing. Brenton Point and Reef give up some of the biggest bass of the year, and in the late summer early fall it's a great spot for a bass-bluefish-albie slam. That said, it's a spot that deserves respect from both shore and boat anglers.

FIRST BEACH AND THE CLIFF WALK

I think you'd be hard-pressed to find a prettier spot to fish anywhere in the Northeast than First Beach (also known as Easton Beach) in Newport. First Beach is on the northern cove of Easton Bay, the end of the famous Newport Cliff Walk. It's a mostly sandy beach with some rock and is an early-season striped bass and bluefish spot. First Beach gets some early season bluefish and later season false albacore, and can be a good fishery until the prevailing west/southwest winds start to form. There is a quick drop-off, and kayak fishing can be good when winds are light. After the initial spring run of fish, First Beach slows down and can get crowded.

That said, the historic Cliff Walk has plenty of rocks and ledges to fish, with the Newport Summer Cottages as a backdrop. Beginning at Memorial Boulevard, this 3.5-mile scenic walkway overlooks the rocky bluffs and the Atlantic Ocean as well as the adjoining famous Newport summer mansions. The seas can be stiff, so pick your days carefully. Striped bass and bluefish move in to feed on silverside, pollack,

The rocks off of Jamestown, Rhode Island hold good bass in the summer. On calm seas, anglers can pick pocket their way through the entire coastline.

mackerel, and squid. When the bay anchovies and the peanut bunker arrive the albies can be found moving in and out of the area. There is access from the southern end, too, which is off of Ledge Road. Located near the southern end of Bellevue Avenue, before Ocean Drive, this right-of-way provides access to the end of Cliff Walk. Unlike the other parts of Cliff Walk, this end of the walkway is not paved, and consists of boulders, dirt paths, and narrow passages along the bluffs. Ruggles Avenue also ends at the Cliff Walk, just south of the Breakers off Bellevue Avenue. Located at the eastern end of Narragansett Avenue is an area called Forty Steps. This site provides access to the mid-point of Cliff Walk. Forty granite steps lead sharply down the face of the rocky bluffs above the ocean.

Easton Point

Easton Point is the large rocky point that separates First and Second Beach and Easton Bay (First Beach) and Sachuest Bay (Second Beach). Rhode Island Sound runs perpendicular to the point. With all of the beaches and bays, Easton Point is surrounded by structure and current. And, you've got options on windy days.

Easton Point isn't as easy to navigate by foot as other rocky areas; it's more of a riprap structure. Korkers are necessary if you're staying on shore, but another way to go is by wearing a wetsuit and walking out to the rocks on the low tide and casting into deeper water. There are two off-shore depth changes, one to 26 feet and then another to 36 feet. On the coming tides, the significant depth changes bring fish closer to the offshore reef and then further into casting range.

Second Beach

Sandwiched in between Sachuest and Easton Points is Second Beach. It runs on an approximate east/west parallel, with protection from all but a straight southern wind. There is a long parallel bar about a hundred yards from the water's edge. As the tide floods, early season stripers move up and over the offshore bar, chasing silversides and squid in close to shore. The fishing, oftentimes, is right at your feet.

The main parking lot for this beach is located off Sachuest Point Road. This site has a wide, long, sandy beach that faces Sachuest Bay. Second Beach gets somewhat crowded during the summer days, but after dark the crowds leave and the fishing improves. It's a mile-long stretch of sand and, depending on the wind, you may find the fish at either end of the beach. Fall is a good time for Second Beach, particularly after the crowds have thinned out. The bookend terrain makes for a natural cove, gathering bait as well as predators. The beach can be an excellent bluefish, bonito, and false albacore spot during the day and an even better striper spot at night.

From September through November, bass migrating from Buzzards Bay naturally hit Sachuest Point, Second Beach, and Easton Point before moving down past Newport and Breton Point and on towards Point Judith and South County. The area offers good fishing for several different species throughout the season.

To the west of Second Beach are two other spots worth checking out. Purgatory Chasm is located on Tuckerman Avenue just south of the junction with Purgatory Road. There is a rocky cliff that overlooks Sachuest Bay and a bridge over a deep natural rock chasm (hence the name). You can also access this spot from the next spot, which is Hanging Rock. A parking area is located at the end of Hanging Rock Road, which is at the western end of Second Beach. These areas are popular with surfers, and night fishing in the rocks with sink-tips and large flies around the higher tides can be outstanding.

SACHUEST POINT

The 242-acre Sachuest Point National Wildlife Refuge in Middletown is located off of Sachuest Point Road. Sachuest Point was originally a sheep farm, and in the 1940s it was used as a rifle range for the U.S. Navy. Since the 1970s, it has been a wildlife refuge, and offers some of the best fishing in southern Rhode Island for all species.

The refuge spans the eastern side of the peninsula and covers three dominant fishing areas. Flint Point is at the northeastern end and it fishes better on a coming tide. Here you'll get the sweep from Third Beach down to Flint Point, a great place for baitfish and current. In the middle of the refuge on the eastern side is a cluster of rocks and a tidal flat called Island Rocks. There are a few different rock formations and ledges which provide great structure and a break up of the currents, and they tend to fish better with more water, namely from mid-flood tide through the first half of the dropping tide. Further south, you won't find many landmarks until you get to the end of the road; there you'll find Sachuest Point, a few coves and lots of rocks and ledges. Because of its southernmost position, all tides can fish well.

The Sakonnet River meets Rhode Island Sound on this eastern edge, and the currents are strong on the dropping tide. All along this face you'll find a mix of boulders, rocky shores, coves and cobble, perfect ambush sites for striped bass and bluefish. It's more flat, though, and on a southwest wind (which is the dominant summer wind), the seas are manageable. Floating, sink-tip, or intermediate lines get the nod, and the diversity of the structure and the rocky drop-offs make for excellent bass fishing. Bluefish also like this area, particularly as the Gulf Stream pushes closer to shore in the summer. The summer brings bonito, false albacore, and skipjack. All sorts of bait concentrates along the point, and the three areas can be accessed through a series of roads and trails that are maintained by the refuge. The refuge's hours of operation apply, and if you're hiking watch for ticks and mosquitos.

With a western, southern, and eastern face, anglers can easily pick their fishing areas based on the wind and the seas. Headwinds often will push fish closer to shore, but the waves get pretty big when they crash on the rocks. Long casts are not necessarily needed, and Sachuest Point is a place where caution should be exercised. It sometimes can get a lot of weeds from offshore storms, but with so many currents it clears up pretty quickly.

THIRD BEACH

Heading north past the Sachuest Point National Wildlife Refuge is Third Beach in Middletown. Third Beach runs along, well, Third Beach Road, and faces the Sakonnet River. It's basically a letter 'c' made entirely of beach sand with drop-offs. The beach gathers bait and also bass, blues, bonito, and albies. It's a good spot with the exception of the peak of summer when there are a lot of folks swimming and sunbathing. No matter, fish for bass at night. There are additional rocks at the northern end of the beach and Flint Rocks at the southern end of the beach, so you have somewhat of a bookend. Floating and sink-tip lines are most common, and the flood tide tends to fish the best. Waves don't get too high over here.

Third Beach is broken down into four beaches: the Third Beach Boat Ramp, the East Middletown Town Beach, the semi-private Peabody Beach, and the Third Beach Club. Gardiner Pond is to the west of the beach.

What makes Third Beach appealing is the natural bowl that it forms. Baitfish will concentrate on the tide seam on the dropping tides, thereby bringing striped bass, bluefish, bonito, and false albacore into close range. The current is stronger at the northern end and you'll probably want to fish this section during the dropping tide. Then, you can work your way down towards Flint Point and fish your way back up on the coming tide. No fees are charged at in the offseason and there is ample parking.

Located at the end of Third Beach Road is a town boat ramp that will accommodate boats up to 18 feet. Kayaks can also be launched here.

PORTSMOUTH AREA

Heading north out of Newport, you'll run into the historic town of Portsmouth. Home to the Melville Nature Preserve, this former Navy land is part of the 92-acre Melville Recreation Area, which includes the town-operated Melville Pond Campground. A place to camp near good fishing is always welcome.

WEAVER COVE

Across from Dyer Island is Weaver Cove, a long, bowl-shaped recess that has Coggeshall Point at the north and Carr Point at the south. The sandy cove has some cobble and rocks scattered in various positions, and drops off very quickly into depths of around 20 feet. The currents here are fantastic for fishermen. The two points, Dyer Island and Prudence and Gould Islands, create a terrific flow.

Think of Weaver Cove as a 'j', for at the southern end by Carr Point there is a tremendous bar that shelves up as it extends to Dyer Island. Depths on the north side of the 'j' are in the 20- to 30-foot depth, but on the south side they are in the 40- to 50-foot depth. On a dropping tide, you'll find bass and blues on the edge of the drop-off, and the deeper water makes for a good summer location. The cove concentrates the bait, and on a dropping tide in the fall, the edge around Carr Point can offer some of the best fishing anywhere. You'll also find bonito and albies running the drop-offs. Located off Burma Road, a mile south of Stringham Road, is a concrete public boat ramp that offers plenty of vehicle and trailer parking.

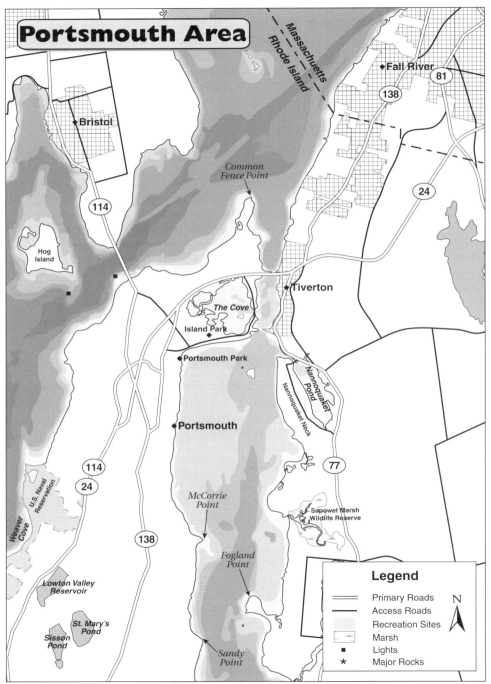

Portsmouth Area

Massachusetts
Rhode Island

Fall River

81

138

Bristol

Common
Fence Point

24

114

Hog
Island

Tiverton

The Cove

Island Park

Portsmouth Park

Nannoquaket
Pond

Nannoquaket Neck

Portsmouth

114

24

77

U.S. Naval
Reservation

McCorrie
Point

Sapowet Marsh
Wildlife Reserve

Weaver
Cove

138

Fogland
Point

Lowton Valley
Reservoir

St. Mary's
Pond

Sisson
Pond

Legend

═══	Primary Roads
───	Access Roads
	Recreation Sites
	Marsh
■	Lights
★	Major Rocks

N

Sandy
Point

McCORRIE AND SANDY POINTS

There are two points on the eastern side of Portsmouth that deserve a look. The northern point is McCorrie, and the southern point is Sandy Point. McCorrie Point extends into the Sakonnet River on a northeast line where as Sandy Point is more gradual and rounded. Fishing the northern section of the McCorrie is a good bet on a dropping tide. The current sweeps baitfish along the extensive cobble beach shoreline until it blows off the point. There is a long sandbar that allows for easy walking so that you'll be able to cover a lot of water efficiently.

Located at the end of Sandy Point Avenue, off Route 138, this is a wide, sandy beach about a half mile long, forming a point in the Sakonnet River. Don't let the name kid you, but there are a lot of rocks around Sandy Point, too. The average depth close to shore is less than 3 feet at mean low tide, but it drops off quickly into the mid-teens. You'll find a sandy terrain on the northern end of the point, and more rocks as you move south. Current seams are easy to spot, and bonito and albacore will race up the drop-offs in the summer.

With so many port cities receiving harbor clean ups, it's becoming increasingly common to catch fish in the presence of tankers. Providence, New Bedford, Fall River, Boston, Portsmouth, and Portland are some major cities near terrific fishing. Boston Harbor's Peddock's Island is in the background.

Eastern Rhode Island

There isn't much left to Rhode Island, for the Massachusetts border is just east of Quicksand Pond. No matter, there is still plenty of water to fish around the Sakonnet River and the Tivertons and Little Compton. Incidentally, Little Compton is the birthplace of the famous chicken, the Rhode Island Red (which is what Foghorn Leghorn was named after).

Sakonnet Point and South Shore Beach

As previously stated, the end of the line always gets the attention, and the jetty at Sakonnet Point at the mouth of the Sakonnet River is no exception. To be sure, you'll find many species of fish off the point: striped bass, bluefish, weakfish, bonito, false albacore, and skipjack.

Sakonnet Point starts farther north, at Church Point and Church Cove. Church Point has a shallow shoreline that is adjacent to a deeper drop-off. Rocks run foul at Church Point, making for a great fishing spot on its own.

But it gets better. Church Cove runs south to Sakonnet Harbor. The harder drop-off runs much closer to shore, and there is a series of rocks and boulders throughout the cove. So here, on the dropping tide, is where you'll have enormous concentrations of baitfish.

Sakonnet Harbor is at the lower end, and a state ramp makes for an easy launch for boaters to continue south to Sakonnet Point. Shore bound anglers flock to the breakwater for shots at all fish but in particular for albies and bonito. There is excellent water all along the west side of the point, right past the Sakonnet Light and a series of rocks, ledges, and islands at the base. West and East Island are on respective sides of the point, with a varying depth of between 12 inches and 45 feet at mean low water. The incredible variety of terrain makes for tremendous current flows and seams, and it is perfect for all species of fish. In total, the nearly 3 miles of water from Church Point to East Island is some of the best in Rhode Island.

Peckham's Creek

Peckham's Creek and the adjoining Donovan's Marsh have one of the best herring runs in the state. The creek is on the southeast side of the marsh, and extends northeast into Nonquit Pond and through Pachet Brook into the Harold E. Watson Reservoir. The entrance to the creek is a combination of rock and cobble with mussel beds. Early spring is certainly the best time to hit the creek.

Fall is also a tremendous time to fish at Peckham's. Glass minnows, or herring fry, drop out of the pond and the reservoir in fall, and the bass move in to feed. The dropping tide is the best time to fish in the fall, and you'll also find bonito and albies cruising the edge of Peckham's and the Sakonnet River. Silversides are also around and squid move in when the fry moves out.

FOGLAND BEACH

Northwest of Peckham's is the Fogland Beach peninsula. Fogland Beach is on the southern end, and Fogland Point is on the northern end. One of the big benefits to this area is its proximity into the Sakonnet River and shallow, wadeable water. On the southern beach side, you'll find a cove formation that extends all the way down to High Hill Point and a marsh system. The big cove is an outstanding fall spot, particularly with its close proximity to deeper water. The low tide depths of 1 or 2 feet quickly drop to 11 feet. Sinking lines work best around here.

There is also a cove on the north side, but the water is generally shallower, typically 1 or 2 feet deep for a longer period. On the incoming tides, you'll find stripers and bluefish moving out of the 10- to 12-foot water onto the sand to feed. The main river is close to the point, which makes for great boat fishing. Depths step down again into the 25- to 40-foot mark. Use a floating or intermediate fly line in the shallow beach water, and alternate between a floating and sinking line if you're boat fishing.

There is an abundance of bait around here, and good tidal seams that concentrate the silversides, bay anchovies, peanut bunker, and more. As a result, you'll find bonito and false albacore working into the current on the dropping tides in the fall. The public boat ramp is a big help, but when the fish are in, the area can get very crowded. Off of the end of Fogland Road at the junction of High Hill Avenue is a boat ramp on the Sakonnet River.

SEAPOWET MARSH

Seapowet Marsh is part of a wildlife management area, and this entire area is fishy. To the north is Nannaquaket Neck with drops down into a river estuary system. Moving west, you'll find the first pond that is called Rueker Pond. A little farther down is another saltpond/cove. You'll find all types of bait in the marsh, and you'll find squid, menhaden, mackerel, herring, silversides, shrimp, crabs, you name it. The marsh is a perfect area for squeteague as well as bass and bluefish. Bonito and albies come here in the fall, too.

The shoreline is completely wadeable, but the best way to work the marsh is with a kayak. Here, you can paddle and fish without getting stuck in the soft muck. Sepowet Cove is on the south side, and there is a bridge that runs over Sapowet Creek north into Sepowet Pond, which makes for a terrific paddle. There is a parking area on

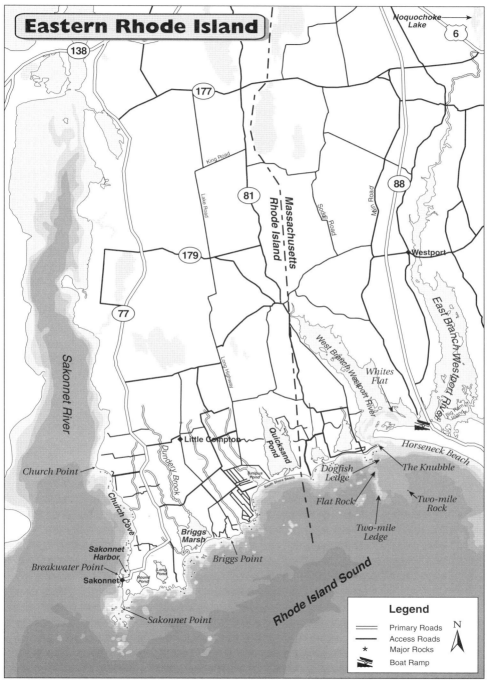

Eastern Rhode Island

Noquochoke Lake

138

177

King Road

Lake Road

81

Massachusetts
Rhode Island

Soule Road

Main Road

88

Westport

179

77

Long Highway

East Branch Westport River

West Branch Westport River

Whites Flat

Sakonnet River

Dundery Brook

Little Compton

Quicksand Pond

Tunipus Pond

South Shore Beach

Dogfish Ledge

Horseneck Beach

The Knubble

Church Point

Flat Rock

Two-mile Rock

Church Cove

Briggs Marsh

Briggs Point

Two-mile Ledge

Sakonnet Harbor

Long Pond

Breakwater Point

Round Pond

Sakonnet

Rhode Island Sound

Sakonnet Point

Legend

N

	Primary Roads
	Access Roads
★	Major Rocks
	Boat Ramp

the southern side, which is off of Seapowet Avenue. You'll have easy paddling into the creek or along the shoreline and into the coves/saltponds. The Emily Ruecker Wildlife Refuge is a 50-acre parcel of land off of Sepowet Road.

NANNAQUAKET NECK AND POND

Just south of Tiverton is Nannaquaket Neck and Nannaquaket Pond. Depths around the shore are mostly deep which makes for more of a boat fishery. Nearby Gould Island is to the west of the Neck, and it splits the river. What happens here is a little bit of magic; within 200 yards you'll go from 2 feet to 81 feet in depth. The striped bass will stage in the deeper water and move into the shallows, particularly at night. The area between the Neck and Gould is particularly good, as it creates a bottleneck and cuts the amount of water to fish in half.

The increased drop-off also makes for a great edge for bonito and albies. The 15-foot line drops down to a 33-foot edge and fishes well on a dropping tide. The baitfish concentrate in the slower, shallower water that is adjacent to the deeper water. On the eastern side of the Neck is Nannaquaket Pond. A similar pattern forms in here, which is a shallower edge around the shoreline followed by a dramatic depth change, mostly from 1 or feet to between 16 and 26 feet at mean low water. The pond is good for squeateague, bass, and blues. Sometimes an errant pod of bonito and albies finds its way into the pond, but the fish mostly stay in the tremendous current exchanges around the Sakonnet River, the Neck and Gould Island.

Fall is a good time anywhere, and the cool mornings and warm days make for outstanding fishing.

To the northwest of Gould Island is Island Park. To anyone who has fished Newburyport's Joppa Flats, you'll find more of the same. Basically, there is a deep river channel on one side with a giant flat that varies in depth. Around the edges you'll find a depth of 1 to 3 feet close to shore, which increases to 8 feet and more. There are some grassy areas near shore, and the water is usually very clear, making for sight-fishing opportunities. On the dropping tides in the summer, look for pods of bluefish on the surface, particularly at first and last light. There is a small parking area for 20 cars on the west end of the bridge.

THE COVE

The Cove is to the west of two points: Almy Point to the south of the cut and Hummock Point on the north side. There are three inshore islands: Tommy, Spectacle, and Hen. Directly west of the channel mouth you'll find deeper water, and as you move throughout the cove you'll find shallower water, right down to a foot at average low tide. There are sand bars, points, and coves. A right-of-way exists in Island Park at Pole 6 that consists of a narrow path that extends northeast from the intersection of Cedar Avenue and Beach Street to a cobble area bordering the cove. A second spot is just off the Coral Street intersection; this very narrow right-of-way runs off Green Street to a grass path leading to a set of concrete steps to a salt marsh and tidal flat area at the south end of Blue Bill Cove.

The Cove tends to fish better in the spring, for the water warms in the summer. Bass and squeteague move in to feed on shrimp and crabs, and when the menhaden stage in the Cove you'll find pods of bluefish. Sometimes albies and bonito crash the mouth. ConRail runs along the north end of the cove, thereby making for urban-like fishing. Here too is the Gull Cove State Boat Ramp, which is just before the Hummocks Road and Common Fence Point exits on Route 24/138. The state ramp offers boaters easy access to both the Sakonnet River and Mount Hope Bay. Many anglers head down Point Road to the Stone Bridge Ramp, which is next to Stonebridge Marina. This ramp provides access to upper Sakonnet River.

COMMON FENCE POINT

With Bristol to the northwest, Mount Hope Bay to the north and Tiverton to the east, Common Fence Point is where all of the Mount Hope Bay water moves to join Narragansett Bay or the Sakonnet River. The point is shaped somewhat like a spearhead, the shallow depths of 1 to 3 feet close to shore with deeper water in the 10- to 30-foot range and long sweeping curls at the base. The point is an excellent spot for bait that moves in and out of Mount Hope Bay, and the bass and blues take advantage. You'll find big pods of early bluefish that move into the bay, and when they do they'll have to pass by Common Fence Point. Mount Hope View Road is located at the Common Fence Point area at Pole 56S, at the northernmost end of Anthony Road. The path starts between a picket fence and a fire hydrant. A second way to access it is off of Narragansett Road.

Kenney Abrames' Fly Box

Kenney Abrames is a native Rhode Islander and is a naturalist, an artist, a writer, a lecturer, a fly designer, a teacher, a retired charter boat captain and a sometimes freshwater bass tournament fisherman. Abrames is also one of the early members of the Rhody Fly Rodders, a flyfishing group which began in Rhode Island in the early 1960s. Abrames relies on observations of baitfish and gamefish and while he knows the scientific principals, say, of light diffusion at depth, he also knows that a yellow and red swimmer fished at a depth beyond the limits of those definitions still puts fish in the boat. His flyfishing roots began with trout and stripers and later spread to salmon and steelhead, and he comes from a long line of Yankee fishermen out of New England.

Some of his best-known patterns are the Razzle Dazzle, the Eel Punt, Ray's Fly, Flatwing, the L&L Special, and the RLS Bullraker.

BAITFISH IDENTIFICATION

It is common among most saltwater flyfishers to capture a baitfish, remove it from the water and tie a fly based on its size, silhouette, and color. One of Abrames' lifelong fascinations has been observing baitfish in their natural surroundings. He has designed his flies to imitate their size and silhouette, but more importantly, he has factored into their construction the way that baitfish change color according to the light. In recent years, his long-time friends Mark and Carol Archambault offered to help him document this ability of baitfish to alter their appearance by photographing baitfish on-site and in natural light to document their fascinating ability to change appearance. He is using these slides in his new books, upcoming articles, and slideshows. If you ever have the opportunity to see Abrames' slideshow of baitfish at any of the consumer flyfishing shows or the seminars, it will open up your eyes as to why his flies have lots of blended colors. As an artist, Abrames' detects subtle nuances of color. Instead of tying in a pre-packaged green, he creates it by blending primary, secondary and tertiary colors to get to get a tone that has a wider spectrum with tints, shades and formed hues that imitate the way natural baitfish can alter their appearance. His slideshows are excellent and he has also categorized these slides in the 'Baitfish Gallery' on his website. I find his silverside slide most interesting because it shows how light affects baitfish; one silverside shows the dominant lateral stripe while nine others in the same group show various hues of yellow, lavender, or pink. As a result, Abrames is credited with color blending as a tool for imitating particular baitfish in saltwater fly patterns.

PATTERN DESIGN

Abrames' fly patterns are traditional. He is credited with incorporating the flatwing fly design into Northeast saltwater fly patterns. While he didn't develop flatwings (they were first used for Scottish spey flies a long time ago), he modified them for the Northeast saltwater. A flatwing has its hackle tied in at the tail and parallel (horizontal) to the hook shank which allows the fly to suspend naturally in the water. Abrames' has spent a decade working with a hackle supplier to develop a long- and thin-stemmed hackle that moves with a natural side-to-side undulation in the water better than thick-stemmed hackles that are used in standard feather wings. His flatwings feature these thin-stemmed hackles as well as sparse amounts of flash, tinsel bodies, bucktail wings, cheeks, long, sparse, and mixed-color collars tied from blending long bucktail and jungle cock eyes. The length of the hackles corresponds to the length of the baitfish and the way he spreads his bucktail mimics a wide, translucent profile of a living baitfish without added weight or bulk. Abrames also uses all-natural materials because they have a spine which offers support whereas synthetic materials do not.

Abrames is a prolific fly designer who has outlined over a hundred template patterns, many of which are in his second book, A Perfect Fish, and has directly influenced a lot of fly tiers. One of the country's most respected saltwater fly designers, New Jersey's Bob Popovics, has long favored indestructible, bluefish-resistant flies tied with synthetics. He recently spent a lot of time with Abrames at a series of Northeast consumer flyfishing shows and enhanced his Bucktail Deceiver to the Hollow Fleye Eye by using natural materials and a sparsely tied, color-blended in the round, blended bucktail construction.

Block Island

Dutch Explorer Adrian Block first found the island in 1614. It wasn't until 1661 that Captain John Underhill of the Massachusetts Bay Colony landed on this nearly 10-square-mile island that is located just about 13 miles south of Point Judith. And while Nantucket and Martha's Vineyard became known as toney islands, mostly due to their wealth generated from whaling endeavors and whale oil, Block Island was a dowdy, agrarian stepsister. Block Island produced one heck of a lot of peat, but that's what burned in the winter (peat was used in the fireplaces).

With its proximity so close to the Gulf Stream, Block Island has been known mostly as a spring and fall striped bass fishery. Early-season striped bass hit the island in April, and are some of the last bass to leave New England pass by in November. Some squeteague are in the coves as well, but the population has been small in recent years.

If you turn your sights to warmwater species, then you'll probably find Block Island to have a good number of fish in the summer. Striped bass are around in the rips and in deeper water, oftentimes too tough to catch with a fly rod, but so are bluefish, bonito, false albacore, skipjack, and school tuna.

There are two harbors on Block Island. Old Harbor is on the east side of the island, with ferries arriving from Rhode Island or Massachusetts. New Harbor is in the Great Salt Pond on the west side, with ferries arriving from Connecticut and New York.

North Rip/Sandy Point/Cow Cove/Grove Point

The Block Island National Wildlife Refuge encompasses the northern tip of Block Island (Sandy Point) and includes the historic North Lighthouse. The shoreline of the refuge consists of a sandy/cobble beach that extends from the Settler's Rock parking area to Sandy Point, and a sandy/cobble beach that extends several miles along the west side from Sandy Point to Great Salt Pond. They are great for wade or boat fishing, they are good in the spring, summer, and fall, and they are outstanding for big bass and bluefish. They are also some of the most dangerous spots on the island.

Sandy Point is the absolute northern most tip of the island. The North Reef, also known as North Rip, extends on a north/northeast tack towards the mainland. At low tide, anglers can wade very far out on the sand bar. You'll also see charter boats fishing the edges and drop-offs, particularly on the dropping tide as baitfish wash over the sand. On the eastern end of the bar, the water depths are shallower, and on the western end of the bar the depths drop off significantly faster. As the tide begins to move, the current is strong and it can and does sweep anglers off the bar. Sandy Point is an interesting mix of cobble and sand, excellent holding water for striped bass. Wade fishing is for the experienced angler, only. An extra-fast-sinking line gets the nod unless there is some surface action.

Adjacent to Sandy Point is Cow Cove, a rocky/sandy basin. Average depths close to shore are around 5 feet at low tide, but they drop off very quickly to a dozen feet or so. Running on a northwest-southeast coordinate is an ocean hole that runs down to Grove Point Rock, and serves as a catch-all for bait. There are rocks and ledges all through Grove Point. With a dominant west/southwest wind, the north side stays pretty flat. That said, on a quarter moon with a northern wind, the fishing can be epic.

You'll also hear the area referred to as Settler's Rock, which is where the original founders landed and swam their livestock to shore (hence the name Cow Cove).

CLAY HEAD (POTS AND KETTLES)/BALLS POINT

Clay Head is typically the area that you see from the Block Island Ferry, and it's known by locals as Pots and Kettles. There are three points along this northeastern stretch of the island: Balls Point North, Balls Point, and Jerry's Point. Each contains rock gardens and ledges, which are perfect for striped bass. You'll see bass in and around the rocks as the water temperatures warm, and also cruising back and forth on the tide line, which is at the 7-foot mark. In between the points is a combination of sand and cobble. Korkers or studded boots are a good idea, and an intermediate line is the best choice.

CRESCENT BEACH

After you see Pots and Kettles from the ferry, you'll next see Crescent Beach. The beach got its name as it resembles a crescent moon, which is actually a great time to fish it. There are three smaller beaches that comprise Crescent Beach: Fred Benson Town Beach (locally referred to as State Beach), Scotch Beach, and Mansion Beach. Believe it or not, there was a mansion at Mansion Beach – it just washed away.

All three beaches are packed in the summer, which makes for better early- and late-season fishing, as well as night fishing. They're flat and mostly sandy, with a shallow drop-off. Fish cruise by during the day, and a floating or intermediate line works best. You'll also see migratory fish running the beach in the fall. East/northeast winds are the favorable time to fish here (which makes for difficult casting). But, the fish are usually at your feet.

OLD HARBOR JETTY AND BALLARD'S BEACH

There are two rock jetties that make up Old Harbor. The smaller rock wall is at the southern end of Crescent Beach. There are a good number of rock boulders and mussel beds, which make for good night fishing. The area is relatively shallow, and

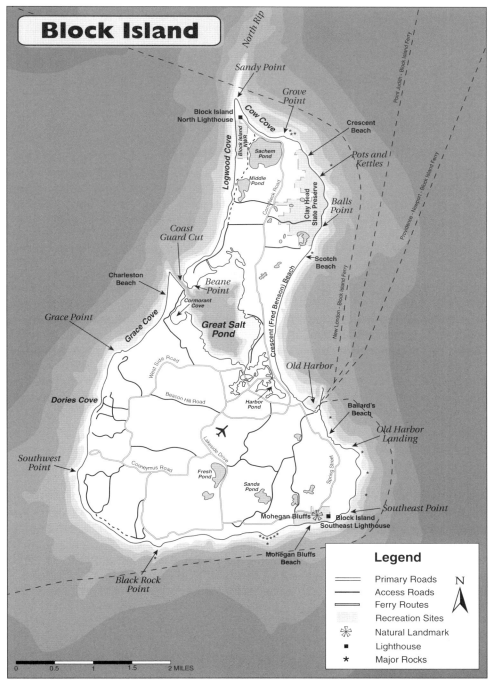

Block Island

North Rip

Sandy Point

Grove Point

Block Island North Lighthouse

Cow Cove

Crescent Beach

Logwood Cove

Block Island NWR

Sachem Pond

Pots and Kettles

Middle Pond

Corn Neck Road

Balls Point

Coast Guard Cut

Clay Head State Preserve

Scotch Beach

Charleston Beach

Beane Point

Cormorant Cove

Grace Point

Grace Cove

Great Salt Pond

Crescent (Fred Benson Beach

Old Harbor

West Side Road

Dories Cove

Beacon Hill Road

Harbor Pond

Ballard's Beach

Old Harbor Landing

Lakeside Drive

Southwest Point

Cooneymus Road

Fresh Pond

Sands Pond

Spring Street

Southeast Point

Mohegan Bluffs

Block Island Southeast Lighthouse

Mohegan Bluffs Beach

Black Rock Point

Point Judith - Block Island Ferry

Providence - Newport - Block Island Ferry

New London - Block Island Ferry

Legend

	Primary Roads
	Access Roads
	Ferry Routes
	Recreation Sites
✳	Natural Landmark
■	Lighthouse
★	Major Rocks

N

| 0 | 0.5 | 1 | 1.5 | 2 MILES |

© 2010 Wilderness Adventures Press, Inc.

mid- to higher water marks are better for fishing. It's a good spot for a kayak as the area is close to shore and protected from three sides. The main jetty runs northeast off of Ballard's Beach. You'll find bass and bluefish on the ocean side, and in August and September you'll find the occasional bonito and false albacore buzzing by. Ballard's Beach can be a good spring and fall fishing spot. There is a quick drop-off close to shore that runs into about 5 feet at mean low tide and you'll find some big bass around Lantern Rock. Along shore are a lot of rocks and kelp. Most of the fishing here is done with topwater poppers and lures.

SOUTHEAST POINT AND SOUTHEAST LIGHTHOUSE

The epic relocation of Southeast Lighthouse to keep it from falling into the ocean is well known, and the erosion that had claimed many rocks and boulders over the centuries has created a terrific fishery. With rocks, ledges, and cobble bottoms, Southeast Point and adjoining Southeast Lighthouse are classic striper water. Heavy seas kick up and pound the coast when the fishing is best, so any wind from southeast to northeast drives the fish in tight to the rocks. That said, a west wind can be great as it's on an angle which moves fish in close without stacking up the seas.

MOHEGAN BLUFFS AND BLUFFS BEACH

With the prevailing west/southwest winds, you'll find a lot of summer anglers on the south side of the island, particularly when the gusts get to 15 knots or more. There is a sharp drop-off and a 140-or-so stair walkway down to two beaches that sit in between rocks and ledges. Bluffs Beach is first and Vail Beach is second. There are a few points, and Great Point is on the southwestern side of the bluffs. If you continue southwest for about a quarter to a half mile, you'll come to Barlows Point. The coastline is irregular, it's rocky and slippery with sandy areas, and the water averages around 5 feet at mean low tide. Fishing the higher water marks is best, and flood tide with an intermediate line can make for a good day.

BLACK ROCK POINT

Anglers flock to this area for good reason. The piece of land that extends from Black Rock Point to Black Rock (which is in between mean low tide depths of 10 to 18 feet deep), accounts for some of the biggest fish of the year. On shore, the structure is a series of small rocky coves with rocks and ledges on either side. Extending out to Black Rock, though, is a pocket where the current moves quickly and changes depth irregularly. It makes for perfect striped bass and bluefish conditions. Black Rock is also a popular surfing spot. Seas can be very big on a dropping tide and an opposing wind, so be careful.

SOUTHWEST POINT

Bluff Head/Southwest Point is another excellent spot. What makes the area great for fishing is the foul-through-2-foot depth that extends halfway to the bell buoy. There are rocks all along shore, but there is a big clump about 100 yards south of the point that extends to about the 14-foot line. What you have, therefore, is a bookend, with the sandy spit, a recess, and a rock garden. Perfect when the tide is moving, particularly on a dropping tide. Use an intermediate line and big flies without too much flash.

DORIES AND GRACE'S COVES

On the western side of the island are two coves, Dories and Grace's. Dories Cove is a true cove, a recess in the land. Grace's Cove is formed at Grace Point, which is where the island's southern curve begins. Both are littered with rocks and make for excellent fishing. If the swells aren't too high, try a kayak. The water drops quickly from 5 to 12 feet at mean low tide. Take a plastic gallon jug, fill it with sand, and hang if off the kayak to use as a drift sock. You'll slow your drift enough to work through the entire rocky coastline. You'll find early season bass and bluefish, but you'll also find a lot of summer striped bass, and big ones, too. Sinking lines work best during the summer months, as do big, natural flies.

CHARLESTOWN BEACH

The long sweeping sand that connects Grace's Cove with the rock jetty entrance to the Great Salt Pond and New Harbor is Charleston Beach. The first fish of the season typically arrive at Charleston. It's a very easy place to fish during the spring or at night, but it can get crowded during the day. The current is soft, with the exception of the ends (by the breakwall and the rocks by Grace's Cove). You'll find some rocks at the southwestern side of the beach, and there are three quick depth drops. What makes Charlestown Beach a good fishing spot is that the drop-offs are gradual. As a result, fish move through the depth changes very easily and come in close. Summer red weed can clog the beach, but a northern wind will blow it out as fast as it came in. You'll also find early bluefish hitting the beach, and the beach and the breakwall are two of the most reliable wade spots on the island for bonito and false albacore.

WEST BEACH/LOGWOOD COVE

The vast stretch of turf between the Coast Guard Cut and Sandy Point is West Beach, and toward the north end is Logwood Cove. In the section just north of the cut are a bunch of rocks and a cobble beach, with some rocks running foul a few hundred yards from shore. The terrain makes for a better corridor for fish that are moving up island, but the fishing in the spring on the full moons can be good, as can the fishing on the quarter moons in the fall. The average depth is 4 to 6 feet at low tide. The current moves up and down the cove, and it's a quiet place to fish. Use a floating line out here with a pinch of split shot for depth.

GREAT SALT POND

The Great Salt Pond is a busy place. It's the first stop for pleasure boats hailing from Connecticut, New York, and New Jersey, and ferries that run from Montauk and New

London. Still, there can be some great fishing in a few different areas. A lot of bait hangs in the Great Salt Pond, particularly silversides, sand eels, and shrimp, but also a tremendous amount of squid. Rent a kayak or bring your own, and paddle throughout the pond. You'll find squid along the dock fingers at night, and paddling the shoreline after sundown can provide some action. Watch for boats entering and exiting the pond – they may not see you in the low-light conditions.

Coast Guard Cut

The cut is one of the easier places to fish, which makes it popular as a daytime spot as well as a night-fishing spot. As with all channels, the drop-off goes from 2 feet to 27 feet at mean low tide. Along the breakwall is a long sand flat that runs out to the end, and a rocky point extends slightly beyond land's end. Anglers will find striped bass in the deeper water, but due to the daytime boat traffic, the night fishing is better. It's particularly good on the dropping tide, as the bass will move onto the flat pop bait at the surface. On a coming tide, the east end of the cut fishes well, particularly as the water shelves and turns to enter Cormorant Cove.

The cut is a popular shore wade spot, perhaps one of the best on Block Island. The bonito and false albacore favor the sharp drop-off, and on a dropping tide the current flow sweeps out, thereby creating a rip for these fish. You'll find bluefish moving from Charlestown Beach into the cut, and they'll move all the way into the Great Salt Pond.

Cormorant Cove

Adjacent to the Coast Guard Cut is Cormorant Cove, a shallow, sandy area that abruptly drops off into 20 feet of water. There is one channel in the middle with two flats on either side. Sometimes you'll find bonito in the cove, but most of the time you'll catch striped bass, bluefish, and squeteague. At low tide you can walk all around to Cormorant Point, or take a kayak. The rocks around Cormorant Point are a good early-season spot for bass.

Beane's Point

The north side of the cut is Beane's Point. There is a breakwall that extends to the west, and a rocky, shelly, cobble stretch of land that runs into the deeper water. The cut wraps around and flattens on the eastern side where it runs into sand and a few rocks. This side of the cut fishes well for bass and blues on both tides, and it's also a good shore bonito and false albacore spot. In the spring, you'll find bass wrapping along the inside of Beane's Point. The sandy flat fishes well, and you'll find squeteague as well.

Rhode Island Saltwater Public Boat Ramps

BARRINGTON

Haines Memorial Park on Bullock's Cove, off Metropolitan Park Dr. Concrete slab. Depth - 4 ft. Parking - Yes.

BRISTOL

Bristol Harbor State Street and use is restricted to permitted Bristol residents. Concrete ramp. Depth - N/A. Parking - No.

Independence Park at the foot of Church Street, off Rt. 114. Depth - N/A. Parking - Yes.

Colt State Park off Hope St (Rt. 114). Concrete ramp. Depth 4 ft. Parking - Yes.

Annawanscutt to Mt. Hope Bay Annawanscutt Drive, off Metacom Avenue (Re. 136), past Veteran's Home. Linked concrete planks. Depth - 2 ft. Parking - Yes.

CHARLESTOWN

Charlestown Breachway at west end of Charlestown Beach Road. Linked concrete slabs. Depth - 3 ft. Parking - Yes/fee when park is open.

Quonochontaug Breachway off West Beach Road. Concrete plank ramp. Depth - 3 ft. Parking - Yes/north lot for trailered vehicles.

Town Dock Road. Depth - N/A. Parking - Yes.

CRANSTON

Pawtuxet Aborn Street. Depth - N/A. Parking - No.

EAST GREENWICH

Greenwich Cove Pole #6, Crompton Avenue. Depth - N/A. Parking - Yes.

EAST PROVIDENCE

Bold Point off Veteran's Memorial Parkway via Mauran Avenue at the end of Pier Road. Concrete slab. Depth - 4 ft. Parking - Yes.

Sabin Point Park off Bullock's Point Avenue. Hard-packed sand. Depth - N/A. Parking - Yes.

Haines Memorial Park on Bullock's Cove, off Metropolitan Park Drive. Concrete slab. Depth - 4 ft. Parking - Yes.

JAMESTOWN

Fort Getty Recreation Area off Beavertail Road. Concrete. Depth - N/A. Parking - Yes, fee when the park is open.

Fort Wetherill at southeast end of Ocean Street, off Walcott Avenue (Rt. 138). Linked concrete plank. Car-top only. Depth - 2.5 ft./steep. Parking - Yes.

LITTLE COMPTON

Sakonnet Point on Sakonnet Point Road (Rt. 77), north side of Town Landing Road. Linked concrete planks. Depth - 2 ft. Parking - Yes.

MIDDLETOWN

Third Beach Road. Concrete ramp. Depth - N/A. Parking - Yes, fee when beach is open.

NARRAGANSETT

Galilee at corner of Galilee Road and Great Island Road, southeast side of Great Island Bridge. Linked concrete planks/double ramp. Depth - 4 ft. Parking - Yes.

Monahan's Dock at east side of Ocean Road, at South Pier Road. Concrete - steep drop. Depth - 3 to 4 ft. Parking - Yes.

Scouting for new spots is best accomplished at low tide. Only then can you see what lies below the surface. As the water covers the rocks and boulders, you'll know where to find the fish, particularly around the corner from Southwest Point on Block Island.

NEWPORT

Off Washington Street. Two locations: Elm Street and Poplar Street. Depth - N/A. Parking - limited.

Kings Beach directly off Ocean Drive. Natural rock and cement. Car-top only. Depth - N/A. Parking - Yes.

Fort Adams State Park off Harriston Avenue. Concrete slabs. Depth - 3 ft. Parking - Yes.

NORTH KINGSTOWN

Wickford at east end of Intrepid Drive, off Post Road, Rt. 1, near fire station. Linked concrete plank - moderately steep. Depth - 3 ft. Parking - Yes.

Wickford on Pleasant Street. Depth - N/A. Parking - limited.

Allen's Harbor, Rt. 1 (Post Road), to Quonset Point/Davisville. Depth - 3 ft. Parking - Yes/Fee.

PORTSMOUTH

Sandy Point Road off Rt. 138. Concrete ramp. Depth - N/A. Parking - limited.

Weaver Cove on Burma Road, south of Melville complex. Concrete ramp. Depth - 4 ft. Parking - Yes.

Stone Bridge off Rt. 138 at junction of Park Avenue and Point Road at Teddy's beach. Concrete planks. Depth - 3 ft. Parking - limited.

Gull Cove on Rte. 138. Linked concrete planks. Depth - 2 ft. Parking - Yes.

SOUTH KINGSTOWN

Snug Harbor at foot of Gooseberry Road. Depth - N/A. Parking - No.

Narrow River off Pettaquamscutt Road between Middle Bridge Road and Bridgetown Road. Concrete planks. There are several bridges on Narrow River with fishing access. Depth - 3 ft. Parking - Yes.

Pond Street at the end of Pond Street. Paved asphalt. Depth - N/A. Parking - No.

Marina Park Exit on Rt. 1. Concrete slabs. Depth - N/A. Parking - Yes.

TIVERTON

Sapowet Point off Rt. 77, southwest side of Sapowet Avenue off Lafayettee Avenue. Ramp is hard beach cobble with natural slope ramp. High tide only. Depth - 2 ft. Parking - Yes.

WARWICK

Goddard State Park via Rt. 1 and East Greenwich. Linked concrete planks ramp. Depth - <2 ft. Parking - Yes.

Conimicut Point at northeast end of Shawomut Avenue off Symonds Avenue. Linked concrete ramp. Problematic ramp, frequently sand covered. Depth - <2 ft. Parking - limited.

Passeonkquis Cove at southwest end of Gaspee Point Drive off Narragansett Parkway. Concrete and asphalt ramp. Closed 8:00pm to 6:00am. Depth - 2 ft. Parking - limited.

Oakland Beach at Warwick Cove. Oakland Beach Avenue, take last left and proceed to east side of Oakland Beach. Concrete ramp. Depth - <4 ft. Parking - Yes.

Longmeadow at east end of Samuel Gorton Avenue off Warwick Neck Avenue. Linked concrete ramp. High Tide Only. Depth - <2 ft. Parking - Yes.

WESTERLY

Westerly Boat Ramp on Main Street. Concrete slab ramp. Depth - 4 ft. Parking - Yes.

Hub City Information: Rhode Island

WESTERLY

Population - 22,966 Area Code - 401 County - Washington

Hotels and Motels

Andrea Resort Hotel, 89 Atlantic Ave / 888-318-5707 / www.andreahotel.com
Breezeway Resort, 70 Winnapaug Rd / 348-8953 / www.breezewayresort.com
Sandy Shore Motel, 149 Atlantic Ave / 596-5616 / www.sandyshore.com
Shelter Harbor Inn, 10 Wagner Rd / 322-8883 / www.shelterharborinn.com
Villa Bed & Breakfast, 190 Shore Rd / 596-1054 / www.thevillaatwesterly.com
Weekapaug Inn, 25 Spray Rock Road / 866-322-0301 /
    www.weekapauginn.com

Restaurants

Up River Café, 37 Main Street / 348-9700 / www.uprivercafe.net
Vertrano's Italian Restaurant, 130 Granite Street / 348-5050 /
    www.vertranorestaurant.com
84 High Street Café, 84 High Street / 596-7871 / www.84highstreet.com
Dylan's Restaurant, 2 Canal Street / 596-4075 / www.dylanssteakhouse.com
Maria's Seaside Café, 132 Atlantic Avenue / 596-6886 /
    www.mariasseasidecafe.com

Fly Shops/Bait and Tackle Shops

Weekapaug Bait & Tackle, 660 Atlantic Ave / 322-8058 /
    www.weekapaugbaitandtackle.com
Watch Hill Outfitters, 157 Main Street / 596-7217 /
    www.watchhilloutfitters.com

Marine Supplies

Hall's Marine Supply, 103 Bay Street / 348-9530
In Motion Marine Repair, Inc., 106 Cross Street Ext., Unit 8 / 596-5884 /
    www.inmotionmarine.com

Hospitals

The Westerly Hospital, 25 Wells Street / 596-6000

Airports

Westerly Airport (WST), 56 Airport Road / 596-2357
T.F. Green Airport (PVD), 2000 Post Road, Warwick / 888-268-7222
Newport Airport (UUU), Forest Road, Middletown / 846-9400

Trains

Westerly Amtrak Station (WLY), 14 Railroad Avenue / 800-872-7245
Providence Amtrak Station (PVD), 100 Gaspee Street, Providence /
800-872-7245

Other Activities

Flying Horse Merry-Go-Round, Bay Street / 348-6007 / The only flying-horse
carousel surviving in the country and the oldest merry-go-round in
America, built in 1876. Horses are hand-carved from wood and have real
tails and manes, leather saddles, and agate eyes. Children only.
Westerly Armory, Railroad Avenue & Dixon Street / 596-8554/
www.westerlyarmory.com / Declared an American Treasure by Congress in
2003. Tour the collection of military and community artifacts.

POINT JUDITH
Population - 17,443 Area Code - 401 County - Washington

Hotels and Motels

Blueberry Cove Inn, 75 Kingstown Road, Narragansett / 792-9865 /
www.blueberrycoveinn.com
Anchor Motel, 825 Ocean Road, Narragansett / 792-8550 /
www.theanchormotel.com
The Richards B&B, 144 Gibson Avenue, Narragansett / 789-7746 /
www.therichardsbnb.com
Village Inn-Narragansett Pier, 1 Beach Street, Narragansett / 783-6767 /
www.v-inn.com
Scarborough Beach Motel, 901 Ocean Road, Narragansett / 783-2063 /
www.scarboroughbeachmotel.com
Ocean Rose Inn, 113 Ocean Road, Narragansett / 783-4704 /
www.oceanroseinn.com

Restaurants

Spain of Narragansett, 1144 Ocean Road, Narragansett / 783-9770 /
www.spainri.com

Basil's Restaurant, 22 Kingstown Road, Narragansett / 789-3743 /
www.basilsri.com

Crazy Burger Café & Juice Bar, 144 Boon Street, Narragansett / 783-1810 /
www.crazyburger.com

Cheeky Monkey, 21 Pier Market Place, Narragansett / 788-3111 /
www.cheekymonkeynarragansett.com

Ocean View Chinese Restaurant, 140 Point Judith Road, Narragansett /
783-9070

Fly Shops/Bait and Tackle Shops

Maridee Canvas-Bait & Tackle, 304 Point Judith Road, Narragansett /
789-5190

Captain's Tackle, 33 State Street, Narragansett / 783-8513

Marine Supplies

All Points Marine, 83 State Street, Narragansett / 284-4044

Wilcox Marine Supply, 330 Great Island Road, Narragansett / 789-1890 /
www.wilcoxmarine.com

West Marine, 91 Point Judith Road #14, Narragansett / 788-9977 /
www.westmarine.com

Hospitals

South County Hospital, 100 Kenyon Avenue, Wakefield / 782-8000 /
www.schospital.com

Kent Hospital, 455 Toll Gate Road, Warwick / 737-7000 /
www.kenthospital.org

Airports

Westerly Airport (WST), 56 Airport Road, Westerly / 596-2357

T.F. Green Airport (PVD), 2000 Post Road, Warwick / 888-268-7222

Quonset (OQU), 210 Airport Street, North Kingstown / 295-5020

Trains

Kingston Amtrak Station (KIN), 1 Railroad Avenue, West Kingston /
800-872-7245

Westerly Amtrak Station (WLY), 14 Railroad Avenue, Westerly / 800-872-7245

Other Activites

Point Judith Lighthouse, 1460 Ocean Road, Narragansett / 789-0444

PROVIDENCE
Population - 171,557 Area Code - 401 County - Providence

Hotels and Motels

Hotel Providence, 311 Westminster Street, Providence / 861-8000 /
www.hotelprovidence.com

Radisson Providence Harbor Hotel, 220 India Street, Providence / 272-5577 /
www.radisson.com

Renaissance Providence Hotel-Marriott, 5 Avenue of the Arts, Providence /
919-5000 / www.renaissanceprovidence.com

Hampton Inn and Suites Providence Downtown, 58 Weybosset Street,
Providence / 608-3500 / www.hamptoninn.com

Edgewood Manor Bed and Breakfast Hotel, 232 Norwood Avenue, Providence
/ 781-0099 / www.providence-lodging.com

Providence Biltmore, 11 Dorrance Street, Providence / 421-0700 /
www.providencebiltmore.com

Restaurants

Blue Grotto Restaurant, 210 Atwells Avenue, Providence / 272-9030 /
www.bluegrottorestaurant.com

Cav Restaurant, 14 Imperial Place, Providence / 751-9164 /
www.cavrestaurant.com

Hemenway's Seafood Grill, 121 South Main Street, Providence / 351-8570 /
www.hemenwayrestaurant.com

Café Paragon, 234 Thayer Street, Providence / 331-6200 /
www.paragonandviva.com

Walter's Restaurant, 286 Atwells Avenue, Providence / 273-2652 /
www.chefwalter.com

Fly Shops/Bait and Tackle Shops

Ocean State Tackle, 430 Branch Avenue, Providence / 714-0088 /
www.oceanstatetackle.com

Hospitals

Rhode Island Hospital, 593 Eddy Street, Providence / 444-4000 /
www.lifespan.org

Miriam Hospital, 164 Summit Avenue, Providence / 793-2500

Butler Hospital, 345 Blackstone Blvd., Providence / 455-6200 / www.butler.
org

Airports

T.F. Green Airport (PVD), 2000 Post Road, Warwick / 888-268-7222

Trains

Providence Amtrak Station (PVD), 100 Gaspee Street, Providence /
800-872-7245

Other Activites

Roger Williams Park Zoo, 1000 Elmwood Avenue, Providence / 785-3510 /
www.rogerwilliamsparkzoo.org

Museum of Art, Rhode Island School of Design, 224 Benefit Street,
Providence / 454-6500 / www.risdmuseum.org

JAMESTOWN
Population - 5,473 Area Code - 401 County - Newport

Hotels and Motels

Wyndham Newport Overlook, 150 Bayview Drive N / 800-989-1574 /
www.extraholidays.com

East Bay Bed & Breakfast, 14 Union Street / 423-0330 / www.eastbaybnb.com

Restaurants

Trattoria Simpatico, 13 Narragansett Avenue / 423-3731 /
www.trattoriasimpatico.com

Tricia's Tropigrille, 14 Narragansett Avenue / 423-1490

Chopmist Charlie's, 40 Narragansett Avenue / 423-1020 /
www.chopmistcharlies.com

Slice of Heaven, 32 Narragansett Avenue / 423-9866 /
www.sliceofheavenri.com

Boathouse Waterfront Dining, 227 Schooner Avenue / 624-6300 /
www.boathousetiverton.com

Fly Shops/Bait and Tackle Shops

The Saltwater Edge, 1077 Aquidneck Avenue, Middletown / 842-0062 / www.
saltwateredge.com

Marine Supplies

Conanicut Marine, 20 Narragansett Avenue / 423-7158 /
www.conanicutmarina.com

Hospitals

Newport Hospital, 11 Friendship Street, Newport / 846-6400 /
www.ribiobank.org

Airports

T.F. Green Airport (PVD), 2000 Post Road, Warwick / 888-268-7222
Newport Airport (UUU), Forest Road, Middletown / 846-9400

Trains

Kingston Amtrak Station (KIN), 1 Railroad Avenue, West Kingston /
800-872-7245

Ferry

Jamestown Newport Ferry, 20 Narragansett Avenue / 423-9900 /
www.jamestownnewportferry.com

Other Activites

Clingstone – famous "House on the Rocks", A privately-owned home perched
on top of a rock called Dumplings Island in Narragansett Bay.

NEWPORT
Population - 23,523 Area Code - 401 County - Newport County

Hotels and Motels

Francis Malbone House, 392 Thames Street / 846-0392 / www.malbone.com
Vanderbilt Hall Hotel, 41 Mary Street / 846-6200 / www.vanderbilthall.com
The Chanler at Cliff Walk, 117 Memorial Blvd. / 847-1300 / www.chanler.com
Pelham Court Hotel, 14 Pelham Street / 877-735-4261 /
www.pelhamcourthotel.com
Castle Hill, 590 Ocean Avenue / 849-3800 / www.castlehillinn.com
Spring Street Inn, 353 Spring Street / 847-4767 / www.springstreetinn.com
Newport Marriott Hotel, 25 America's Cup Avenue / 849-1000 /
www.marriott.com

Restaurants

Mamma Luisa Italian Restaurant, 673 Thames Street / 848-5257 /
www.mammaluisa.com
Tucker's Bistro, 150 Broadway / 846-3449 / www.tuckersbistro.com

Fly Shops/Bait and Tackle Shops

The Saltwater Edge, 1077 Aquidneck Avenue, Middletown / 842-0062 /
www.saltwateredge.com

Marine Supplies

Harbor Supply of Newport, 547 Thames Street / 848-2228 /
www.harborsupply.com

Hospitals

Newport Hospital, 11 Friendship Street / 846-6400 / www.ribiobank.org

Airports

T.F. Green Airport (PVD), 2000 Post Road, Warwick / 888-268-7222
Newport Airport (UUU), Forest Road, Middletown / 846-9400

Trains

Kingston Amtrak Station (KIN), 1 Railroad Avenue, West Kingston /
800-872-7245

Ferry

Jamestown Newport Ferry, 20 Narragansett Avenue, Jamestown / 423-9900 /
www.jamestownnewportferry.com

Other Activites

Old Colony & Newport Railway, 19 America's Cup Avenue / 849-0546 /
www.ocnrr.com
Fort Adams, 90 Fort Adams Drive – Fort Adams State Park / 841-0707 /
www.fortadams.org
Newport Mansions Tour, 424 Bellevue Avenue / 847-1000 /
www.newportmansions.org

BLOCK ISLAND

Population - 1,010 Area Code - 401 County - Washington

Hotels and Motels

The 1661 Inn, One Spring Street / 466-2421 / www.blockislandresorts.com
Spring House Hotel, Spring Street / 466-5844 / www.springhousehotel.com
Atlantic Inn, High Street / 466-5883 / www.atlanticinn.com
Rose Farm Inn, High Street / 466-2034 / www.rosefarminn.com

Restaurants

Ballard's, 42 Water Street / 466-2231 / www.ballardsinn.com
Beachhead, Corn Neck Road / 466-2249 / www.thebeachead.com
The Oar, 221 Jobs Hill Road / 466-8820
Eli's, 456 Chapel Street / 466-5230
Sharky's, 596 Corner Neck Rd / 466-9900

Fly Shops/Bait and Tackle Shops

Block Island Fishworks, Ocean Avenue / 466-5392 / www.bifishworks.com

Marine Supplies

Boat Works, Corn Neck Road / 466-2033 / www.littlebuildings.com

Hospitals

South County Hospital, 100 Kenyon Avenue, Wakefield / 782-8000 / www.
schospital.com
Rhode Island Hospital, 593 Eddy Street, Providence / 444-4000 / www.
lifespan.org
Newport Hospital, 11 Friendship Street, Newport / 846-6400 / www.ribiobank.
org
The Westerly Hospital, 25 Wells Street, Westerly / 596-6000

Airports

Block Island State Airport (BID), New Shoreham / 737-4000
T.F. Green Airport (PVD), 2000 Post Road, Warwick / 888-268-7222

Trains

Providence Amtrak Station (PVD), 100 Gaspee Street, Providence /
800-872-7245

Ferry

Block Island-Montauk Ferry, Viking Fleet, 462 Westlake Drive, Montauk, New
York / 631-668-5700
High-Speed Ferry to Block Island, State Pier in Point Judith/Galilee,
Narragansett / 401-783-7996

Other Activities

Block Island North Lighthouse, Sandy Point, north end of Block Island /
466-3200 / www.lighthouse.cc/blockinorth
Mohegan Bluffs, off Southeast Light Road, New Shoreham / 466-5009

*For flats fishing, and particularly on calm days with spooky fish, it's sometimes easier to
get out of your boat and wade to the fish in Rhode Island's Ninigret Pond.*

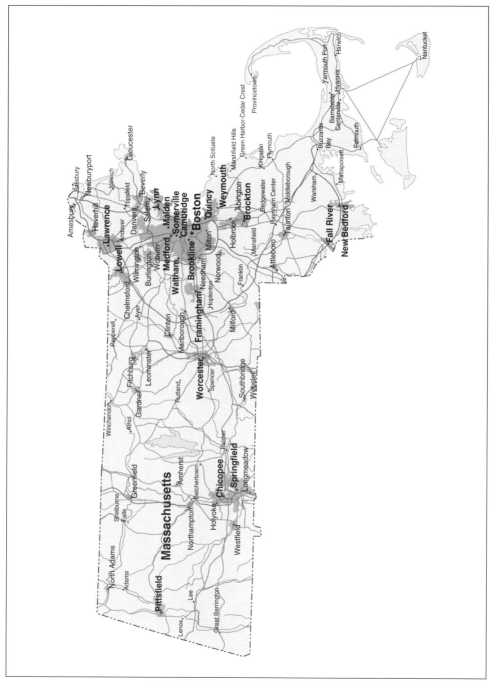

Massachusetts Coast

Massachusetts Waters Overview

Massachusetts is the most popular choice among recreational saltwater anglers. Of the estimated 1.5 million anglers who fish in New England coastal waters, some 548,691 (Southwick Study Road Map) fish in Massachusetts. Some come to fish the southeastern coast that runs from the Rhode Island border to the Cape Cod Canal. Others like island life and frequent Cape Cod, Martha's Vineyard, or Nantucket. In each of these areas, the Gulf Stream runs close by, which means that pelagic species like bonito, false albacore, skipjack, school bluefin tuna, and the occasional mahi mahi are caught in addition to striped bass, bluefish, squeteague, and shad. The South Shore gets a lot of action for striped bass, bluefish, and shad, and is oftentimes accessed by anglers stopping over to fish while on their way to the Cape and islands. In the past decade, Boston Harbor has become a popular destination fishery. It particularly does well for the businessman-angler who likes to catch a bass or blue before the market opens in the Financial District. The North Shore varies from urban to truly coastal. A densely populated area like Lynn stands in sharp contrast to Newburyport. Still, each area represents a fantastic opportunity for its fish catching.

The southeastern coast of Massachusetts, or from Westport to Buzzards Bay, is probably the unsung hero of Massachusetts. Part of it may have to do with the industrial origins of the region, which featured Fall River as epicenter of the world's most productive textile mills from 1847 to 1937. Maybe it was the story of Lizzie Borden, or the Pequod that sailed out of New Bedford in search of Moby Dick. For some reason, places like Cape Cod, Martha's Vineyard, and Nantucket get the historical nod partly for the romance of island life, while places like Boston Harbor get a lot of current attention. No matter, locals know what southeastern Massachusetts has to offer: outstanding fishing from April through December for over half a dozen species.

Buzzards Bay is wide open to the winds coming from the south/southwest. These winds are typically spring through fall winds. What you also get due to the landmasses from the continental side as well as the island sides (Cape Cod and the Elizabeth's) is a funnel. So, on a southwest wind you'll find that wind speeds increase and are often double the farther east you go. A light wind in New Bedford can be honking at Onset.

Boaters should know, too, that they will experience a larger chop towards the eastern side of Buzzards Bay.

Fishing along the Southeastern Coast is both a blessing and a curse. The close proximity to the Gulf Stream means that the water temperatures warm quickly and striped bass and bluefish arrive early. It also means that as the Gulf Stream pushes closer to shore that the water continues to warm and the bass move out for colder water. That's ok, it just means that the bluefish fishing remains strong and that bonito, false albacore, skipjack, and school tuna move in closer.

Wet suiting begins with a swim to that extra-sweet-looking ledge that you can't cast to. A Farmer John wetsuit offers buoyancy as well as warmth, and Tevas or wetsuit booties keep your feet from getting cut on barnacle-covered rocks. Rockport, Massachusetts offers great wetsuiting opportunities..

REGULATIONS

Fishing regulations (especially saltwater fishing regulations) are constantly subject to change, so we cannot possibly keep up with the current regulations in this guide. Therefore, we only provide you with a link to the website that will have the most current rules.

For Massachusetts, the website is:

www.mass.gov/dfwele/dmf/recreationalfishing/rec_index.htm

Massachusetts is the only state covered in this guide that requires a saltwater fishing license as of press time. From the Massachusetts Division of Marine Fisheries website: "Massachusetts anglers who fish in federal waters, or target or catch anadromous species (saltwater fish that spawn in freshwater) like shad, striped bass or smelt in any tidal or salt waters must register beginning January 2, 2010. Some individuals are exempt from this registration requirement, including, anglers who are under 16; only fish on permitted charter, party or guide boats; hold a Highly Migratory Species Angling permit; are fishing commercially under a valid permit; or are already registered through an exempted state. Starting January 1, 2010, you can register online at www.countmyfish.noaa.gov or by calling 888-MRIP-411 (888-674-7411)."

Starting in 2011, anglers must purchase a state permit .

MASSACHUSETTS SPECIES AVAILIBILITY

SPECIES	APR	MAY	JUN	JUL	AUG	SEP	OCT	NOV
Striped Bass	+	++	++	+	+	++	++	+
Bluefish		+	++	++	++	++	++	+
Squateague	+	++	++	+	+	+	+	+
School Bluefin Tuna	+	+	+	+	++	++	++	+

Only from Westport through Chatham, MA

False Albacore					+	++	++	
Atlantic Bonito				+	++	++	+	
Spanish Mackeral				+	++	++	+	
Skipjack Tuna				+	++	++	+	

+ = Available, ++ = Prime Time

Southeast Coast

WESTPORT AREA

WESTPORT RIVER

There are two sections of the Westport River – the East Branch and the West Branch. Both branches fish well at different times of year, but the East Branch gets more of an angler's attention for a variety of reasons.

First, there is a public boat launch and ramp by the Route 88 bridge. Second, the East Branch continues north and gets progressively smaller until it reaches Noquochoke Lake; what that means is the East Branch is an excellent spot in the spring when the herring are in. Third, the river is very protected, right down to the mouth, and it makes for an excellent place to fish out of a kayak. Fourth, there are a number of islands in the river.

The launch is at the Route 88 bridge, at Point of Pines. As you move upriver, you'll find a mixture of mud flats such as Halfmoon Flat with islands like Big Ram and Little Ram. On a dropping tide, most of the bass and blues will drop off the mud flats surrounding Big and Little Ram Islands and back into the river channels. Similarly, as the tide floods, those same fish will move right back and into the marshy areas. As you move farther north, you'll find a few more islands: Gunning Island, Great Island, and Big Pine Island. On the full moons in April and early May, herring move into the East Branch in big numbers. The water is brackish and gets muddy. On the higher water marks you can get by with sinking lines, but floating and intermediate lines are fine choices too. Silversides arrive in May, and you'll find squeteague, shad, and bluefish as well.

The river deepens and widens below the bridge as it gets close to the mouth. Water depths run from 12 to 20 feet, and there are several flats scattered around the mouth and into the West Branch. You'll find Bailey's Flat at the mouth, and Whites, Great, and Sandford Flats in the West Branch.

The mouth of the river features Acoaxet on the west side. The Knubble extends far out to the west of Acoaxet and directly south of Horseneck Point. Here you'll find a tremendous depth change – from 20 to 25 feet ramping up to between 5 and 7 feet at low tide. These seams and current flows are what attract seasonal bonito, false

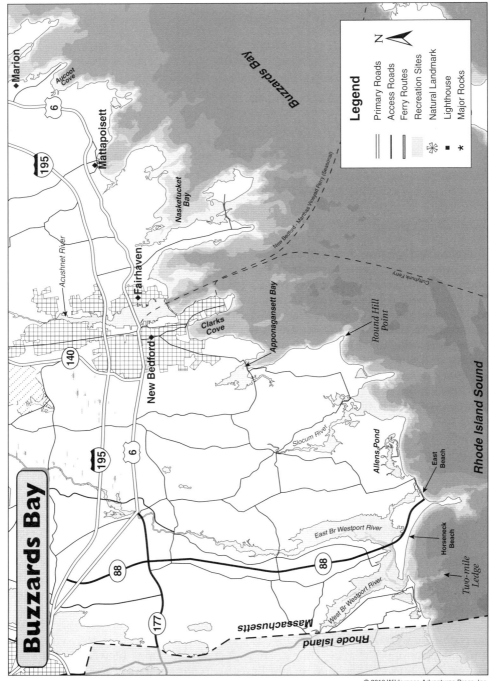

Buzzards Bay

Legend

N

	Primary Roads
	Access Roads
	Ferry Routes
	Recreation Sites
✳	Natural Landmark
■	Lighthouse
✳	Major Rocks

Marion

Aucoot Cove

6

195

Mattapoisett

Buzzards Bay

Nasketucket Bay

Acushnet River

Fairhaven

New Bedford — Martha's Vineyard Ferry (Seasonal)

Apponagansett Bay

Round Hill Point

Cuttyhunk Ferry

Clarks Cove

New Bedford

140

Rhode Island Sound

195

6

Slocum River

Allens Pond

East Beach

88

East Br Westport River

88

Horseneck Beach

Two-mile Ledge

Massachusetts

Rhode Island

West Br Westport River

177

© 2010 Wilderness Adventures Press, Inc.

albacore, and skipjack. These pelagic fish will run up into the lower stretches of the river mouth, particularly on the dropping tides.

For boat anglers, make sure to continue south for a half to three-quarters of a mile. There are a series of ledges and rocks that create ideal striper-holding water. Dogfish Ledge, Flat Rock, Two-mile Ledge, Markham Ledge, and Two-mile Rock create great structure that holds striped bass and blues (see Eastern Rhode Island map). You'll also find bluefish, bonito, and albies running the edge drop-offs.

A note of caution: boaters should not try to enter the Westport River during strong southerly winds as heavy seas break over the entrance bars. Southerly winds and dropping tides are probably the most dangerous, as the river mouth is crooked and narrow. There is an excellent public boat ramp.

HORSENECK BEACH

Running southeast along the Horseneck Beach State Reservation is a sliver of land that creates a peninsula complete with a 600-acre, 100-site campground and a boat ramp. The 2 miles of beach is the demarcation point: Rhode Island Sound is on the west side and Buzzards Bay is on the east side. On the west side, you have one giant bowl that slopes down all along the reservation. At the top end, which is where the campground is, is Gooseberry Neck.

The water around Gooseberry Neck is a combination of large boulders and rocky cobble, perfect for early-season striped bass. Fish it on mid-tide through high tide with an extra-fast-sinking line. The reservation gets crowded during the summer, but in the shoulder seasons the fishing is excellent and the only crowds you'll see are other anglers.

EAST BEACH AND ALLEN'S POND

Gooseberry Neck is marked by several large towers. Where the land and the neck meet is very bony; the many rocks around Gooseberry Neck are great for fishing, and they continue east and line East Beach, the entrance to Allen's Pond. The rocks around the beach are great for striped bass and bluefish, with some bonito and albies in the later season. You'll also find early-season squeteague. Allen's Pond is a perfect kayak spot, with moderate current exchanges. It's a large pond, and working with the incoming and outgoing tides is important so you can keep fishing instead of paddling. At the mouth, Allen's Rip pounds out on a dropping tide, with a sandbar on either side. The current is strong and fish will hold on the edges and drop out quickly as the water dumps fast.

SLOCUM'S RIVER AND THE LITTLE RIVER

One great early-season spot is the combination of Slocoms Neck and Mishaum Point. Splitting those two landmasses are the Slocums and Little Rivers. The two rivers are separated by Potomska Point, a peninsula that creates lots of current when the water is moving. There is a long bar at the entrance of Slocums that is exposed at low tide, and the channel is narrow and unmarked. Slocums is the larger of the two, and they are classic estuaries, with cuts, banks, coves, and pockets throughout. The basins are mud, and you'll occasionally find squeteague and shad.

On the west side of Slocums River is 1,800 feet of oceanfront beach that is part of the Demarest Lloyd State Park – one of the best-kept secrets on the Southeast Coast. The beachfront fishes well for early-season bass and mid-season bluefish, and upstream is Giles Creek. The rivers are great for kayak fishing, and you'll occasionally find bonito and albies at the mouth. The summer months get warm for striped bass, but it's good for bluefish.

Towards Mishaum Point, you'll find lots of rocks on the central-west side through the southern tip. Early-season bass will stage in the rocks and move along the point into the river systems, and then drop back out. About a half mile west of Mishaum Point is Slocums Ledge, which runs between 2 and 7 feet in depth – a good spot on a mid-dropping tide. Pawn Rock and Barney's Joy Point are on the west side of the river entrance. Floating and sink-tip lines are fine.

SALTERS POINT THROUGH ROUND HILL POINT

Salters Point, also known as Salt House Point from back in the salt-codfish-packing days, is a cove with a small saltpond. Rocks run foul along the coast to the point, and by the saltpond the depth increases and the terrain gets sandy. Early-season fishing is good, and the drop-off to 10 to 15 feet of water is dramatic. The better fishing is to the south and east of the point, basically on the 12-foot line from Salter's Rock to the breakwall. The combination of rock in shore and consistent drop-offs means there is a natural edge for fish to run. In the fall they will move up the line and into the cove that is formed by Salters and Round Hill Points. Use an extra-fast-sinking line in the deeper water.

Round Hill Point comes by its name honestly; it's a round hill on the point of land. The spot is easily detected by the white tower and radar installation. There are a lot of rocks and boulder fields surrounding Round Hill Point. Close to shore on the east side are the Barekneed Rocks which run foul at low tide, but offers good passage on both sides. Drop-offs on the ends are 22 feet, perfect holding water for big bass. Heading south are two areas that run foul – White Rock and Ragged Rocks. Again, the water on either side is deep, and the current blows in between them and the point.

The point runs foul most of the way out to the Dumpling Rocks, where, again, the water drops off into 35 feet. The water stays deep all around the point, and the bowl is a perfect spot for congregating baitfish. There are two ledges that hold bass and also get occasional bonito and albies racing around them – the Sandspit and Great Ledge. Depths skinny up from 50 feet to 10 feet at the Sandspit which is a good spot on either tide, just so long as the water is moving. Great Ledge shelves up from 32 feet into 12 inches. It's shallower on the northeast side and a bit deeper on the southwest side. Both ledges are good on moving water when the bluefish are in.

West Shore of Buzzards Bay

Apponagansett Bay and Padanaram

If you have Nonquitt and Bayview Villages to your south and South Dartmouth to your north, you're in Apponagansett Bay. You'll find the Padanaram Breakwater is on the southern end, and Buttonwood Brook dumping into the northeast corner of the bay. There are a lot of toxins coming from nearby New Bedford, so there isn't much of a herring/alewife run.

In the early season, fishermen will find bass with some herring and alewives moving out in front of the brook. There is one small island named Little Island, and a recently dredged channel runs up to the island. There are numerous coves and pockets as well. The marsh and estuary at the southwest side attracts some squeteague and shad, and is a small but good kayak spot.

On both sides of the channel entrance to the bay are rocks and ledges, with a short sand flat on the west side of the channel. As the season moves on, the bay fills with moorings and boats, so your fishing season is limited to early and late. At that point, move down towards the Padanaram Bridge for more action and moving water. Head south along Smith Neck Road for good shore fishing. Floating or intermediate lines are fine, and it's a better early- and late-season spot or when there is lighter boat traffic (as in during the week or at first light).

Clarks Cove

From Moshers Point through Clarks Point is a horseshoe shaped cove called Clarks Cove. Jones Park is on the west side and Rodney French Park is on the east side. The anchorage is between 12 and 22 feet deep, so there aren't a whole lot of boats moored in the area. By early May, you'll see bass moving into the cove, and bluefish throughout the summer off of Fort Rodman Military Reservation, Clarks Point, and an old granite fort. Off of the point on the southwest side the rocks run foul, which is good hold water. Depths drop off quickly to around 25 feet, and either a floating or extra-fast-sinking line is best.

New Bedford and Fairhaven

Fishing in New Bedford and Fairhaven is difficult. These ports have been working harbors since long before Moby Dick's era. You can tell the two ports very easily: smoke stacks in New Bedford, church steeples in Fairhaven. For centuries, many folks lived in Fairhaven and commuted to New Bedford.

Some of it is a work in progress. The Acushnet River forms the harbor in between New Bedford and Fairhaven. In 2007, there was a $1.4 million river restoration project to return a herring run to the Acushnet. This is good news for springtime fishermen, particularly since there is a major harbor clean up slated for 2010 and beyond. While the fishing in the harbor isn't so great now, look for it to be one of the dramatic recovery stories in a few years.

The bottom in and around the harbor is broken. Depths around the channels are typically deep, and there are four islands inside. Pope's Island is the largest, with Fish, Crow, and Palmer Islands being inside the hurricane barrier. The barrier, combined with upstream dams, reduces the strength of the current in and out of the harbor.

The northeast side of Pope's is 7 to 8 feet deep, with a 3- to 4-foot-deep perimeter. In the early season, striped bass and some shad will hold in the deeper water and make their way up onto the flat. The New Bedford-to-Martha's Vineyard and the New Bedford-to-Cuttyhunk Ferries depart from the State Pier Ferry Terminal.

Outside of the hurricane barrier, there are a lot of boulders, rip rap, shoals, and ledges. You'll find some bonito and albies in the channel, but what's of more interest to anglers is Fort Flat, which is off the south end of Fairhaven's Fort Phoenix. Bass and bluefish will move up on to the flat, and with all the rocks that run foul off the south side, there is plenty of structure. Bluefish in the late spring and summer, and bonito and albies also run along Fort Phoenix in the summer and in the fall.

West Island and North Cove get a lot of attention as well. Here you'll find early-season bass, and blues throughout the year. The terrain is perfect with two points and a 'u'-shaped cove, and has excellent bluefish blitzes – it's also a popular spot during the fall run. In addition, bonito and albies can be caught from shore during the late summer/early fall.

MARION AREA

Sippican River/Sippican Harbor is the main body of water in the town. Marion is a boating community, and from Black Point to Allen's Point you'll find moored boats. There are a few different boat ramps – one at the Island Wharf Town Dock and one at Wings Cove, both of which are free and residents only. Aucoot Cove offers launches and Burr Brothers offers use for a fee. Kayaks can go in, too, and head down to Planting Island Cove and Meadow Island. Dropping tides are good choices. Work the coastline, too, particularly around the cliffs. Boaters will fish in between Butler Point and Bird Island Lighthouse. Silvershell Beach off of Front Street is open to the public and is a white sandy beach directly across from Allen's Point. Here the river bottlenecks and the current exchange speeds up. Spragues Cove and the Sippican Marsh are good places to fish, too. Floating or intermediate lines and higher water marks are the best bets. There is also access at Bayberry Lane to the north. The rocks, cobble, and sand hold fish.

Marion hosts a race to Bermuda and is a big sailing city, so boat traffic can be heavy.

NASKETUCKET BAY AND MATTAPOISETT

Some 5 miles northeast of New Bedford Harbor is Mattapoisett Harbor. When you look at the area from the south, you see a strange similarity. Between Nasketucket Bay, Brant Island Cove, and Mattapoisett Harbor there is a series of necks interspersed by coves. There are a number of rocks and ledges and a few inshore islands and coves as well. The proximity farther east makes for less urban fishing.

To the east of Mattapoisett Harbor is an area called Ned's Point – most folks recognize the famous lighthouse that overlooks Buzzards Bay. To the east is Pico Beach. Ned's Point is a good early-season bass and bluefish spot, and with the lighthouse, it's easy enough to find, especially at night. Work the area along the landing off of Ned's Point Road with a floating or intermediate line. You'll find bluefish from Memorial Day through mid-October, with snappers coming in around late August or September. The eastern side of beaches, rocks, and coves also fishes well. Mid-incoming through mid-dropping are good bets for finding fish.

WEWEANTIC RIVER

From spring stripers to summer bluefish to fall bonito and albies, the Weweantic River is a good spot. The river runs all the way up to Horseshoe Pond, but there is a dam. Therefore, you'll find herring and alewives in the spring below the dam and they don't stay around for very long. The feeder streams that drain into the river contribute all the usual suspects of mummies, crabs, shrimp, and silversides. Bass arrive early in the river and then tend to move out shortly thereafter. Some head into the deeper, cooler water around the Elizabeth Islands, some move through the canal. Fall fishing is strong, particularly on dropping full-moon tides when the bait mixes with the migrating bass. In the summer you'll also find bluefish, bonito, and albies running around. Great Hill Drive runs in between Great Swamp and the river. If you work your way downcurrent toward Warren Point, you'd do well to head west and fish Great Hill Point and Wing's Cove. Bait stages in the fall and can provide some of the best fishing around. Summer bluefish blitzes are strong, too.

BUTTERMILK BAY

Taylor Point is the end of the road on the west end of mainland side of the Cape Cod Canal. Just north of Taylor Point is Buttermilk Bay – a terrific fishing spot. The bay is home to one of the last remaining native sea-run brook trout fisheries in the eastern United States. The 4.5-mile-long Red Brook is off of Head of the Bay Road and is part of the Theodore Lyman Reserve. The Reserve is popular today with flyfishers, and is catch-and-release only as the Trustees (a non-profit of over 100,000 members that works to preserve public land in Massachusetts) work to restore more habitat.

If you enter the Bourne Marina and go straight to the end of the lot, you'll arrive at the Cohasset Narrows. The current moves quickly, so an extra-fast-sinking line works well. Indian Mound Beach on the west side of the bay offers public wade access. Toss in a kayak and also hit Miller Cove. Both spots have good early-season bass and bluefish. Seasonal albies and bonito will work up through the narrows. There are shoals, channels, and flats to fish. The upper reaches and coves fish better on the higher tides, and the lower stretches at the lower water. Buttermilk Bay can get you out fishing during nasty spring and fall weather. It's a good ace to have up your sleeve, and if yours is Buttermilk Bay then you're a lucky angler.

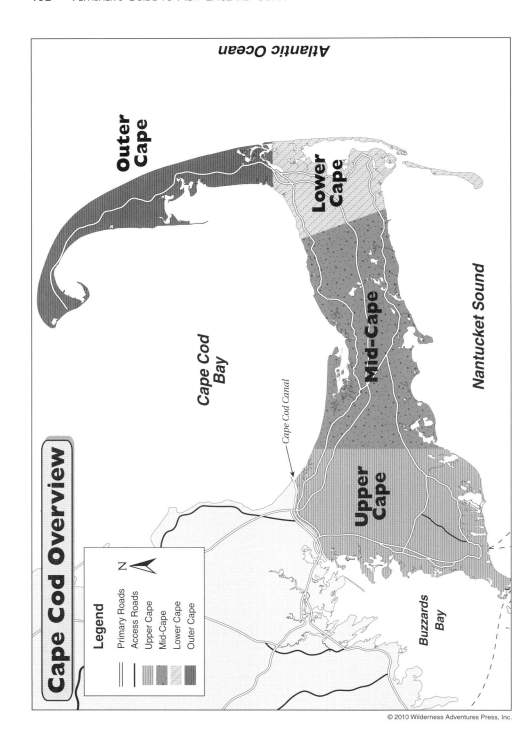

Atlantic Ocean

Outer
Cape

Lower
Cape

Nantucket Sound

Cape Cod
Bay

Mid-Cape

Cape Cod Canal

Upper
Cape

Buzzards
Bay

Cape Cod Overview

Legend

N

Primary Roads
Access Roads
Upper Cape
Mid-Cape
Lower Cape
Outer Cape

Cape Cod

Historically, Cape Cod had been attached to the mainland. Discussions beginning during the late 1800s resulted in two common understandings about the region. First, going around the cape to compass headings to the west took too long, and second, two many ships were lost along the way. Both claims were true, so a canal project was begun to link Massachusetts and Buzzards Bays through a 7-mile project. Construction began in 1909 and concluded in 1914, and in the 1920s, the width increased significantly. For the past 100 years, the arm-shaped island is still thought to be a peninsula.

An important point to remember about Cape Cod: As the first landing spot of the Pilgrims (they landed on the bayside in the Outer Cape, somewhere between Wellfleet and Provincetown), the towns were oriented around harbors. Towns such as Falmouth, Chatham, and Orleans were organized around the maritime industry. Towns that lacked harbors, such as Eastham, were more agrarian, and did not feature an organized downtown. The reason that is important is that many of the towns that do not have an organized town center are not as commonly known for good fishing. Those sleeper towns do, in fact, have some of the best fishing, you just need to work a bit harder to get there.

There are four parts to Cape Cod: Upper, Mid, Lower, and Outer. The Upper Cape is the section of Cape Cod closest to the mainland and this portion of the cape includes the towns of Bourne, Sandwich, Falmouth, and Mashpee. Part of the town of Barnstable is located on the Upper Cape, it is more commonly considered to be in the Mid-Cape area. Falmouth is the home of the famous Woods Hole Oceanographic Institution and several other research organizations, and is also the most-used ferry connection to Martha's Vineyard. Falmouth is composed of several separate villages, including East Falmouth, Falmouth Village, Hatchville, North Falmouth, Teaticket, Waquoit, West Falmouth, and Woods Hole, as well as several smaller hamlets that are incorporated into their larger neighbors (such as Davisville, Falmouth Heights, Quissett, Sippewissett, and others).

The Upper Cape is where various bodies of water come together and form an incredibly fertile fishing ground. The Cape Cod Canal is on the north side and it empties on the west end into Buzzards Bay, north of the Elizabeth Islands. Vineyard Sound extends from the south side of the Elizabeth Islands all the way to Martha's Vineyard. With all the moving water there is a tremendous amount of current as well as a close proximity to the seasonal Gulf Stream.

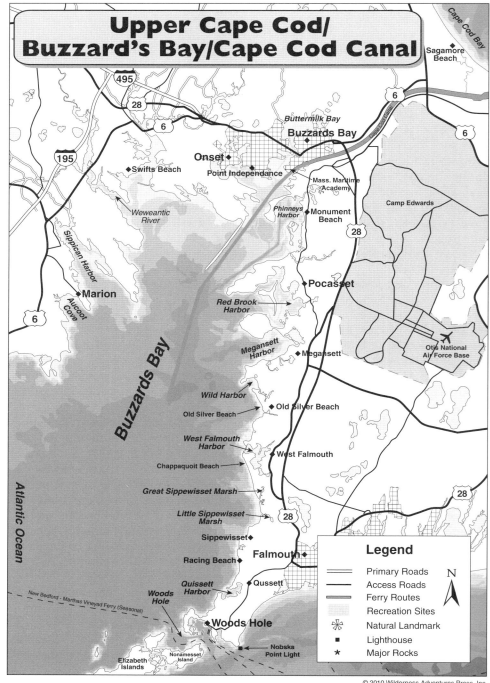

Upper Cape Cod/ Buzzard's Bay/Cape Cod Canal

Cape Cod Bay

495

28

6

Sagamore Beach

6

6

6

Buttermilk Bay

Buzzards Bay

195

Onset◆

◆Swifts Beach

Point Independance◆

Mass. Maritime Academy

Camp Edwards

Weweantic River

Phinneys Harbor◆

Monument Beach

28

Sippican Harbor

◆**Marion**

Alcoot Cove

6

Pocasset◆

Red Brook Harbor

Megansett Harbor

◆Megansett

Otis National Air Force Base

Buzzards Bay

Wild Harbor

Old Silver Beach—

◆Old Silver Beach

West Falmouth Harbor

◆West Falmouth

Chappaquoit Beach—

Great Sippewisset Marsh—

28

Little Sippewisset Marsh—

Sippewisset◆

28

Racing Beach◆

Falmouth◆

Atlantic Ocean

Quissett Harbor

◆Qussett

Woods Hole

New Bedford - Marthas Vineyad Ferry (Seasonal)

◆**Woods Hole**

Nonamesset Island

Nobska Point Light

Elizabeth Islands

Legend

═══	Primary Roads
──	Access Roads
═══	Ferry Routes
�	Recreation Sites
✳	Natural Landmark
■	Lighthouse
★	Major Rocks

N

UPPER CAPE COD

CAPE COD CANAL TIDAL FLATS

Much of the fishing in the Cape Cod Canal is better suited to forms of fishing other than with a fly, but the tidal flats off of Bell Road near the railroad bridge is a good spot. Next to a large parking lot is a large cove that can be very good in the spring and at night. The bottom is hard enough for wading, and there are always mummies, shrimp, crabs, and silversides in the cove. Poppers and sliders make for great top-water action. On the dropping tide you can work the drop-off that is parallel to the canal with an extra-fast-sinking line. Big fish move in and around the sharp drop-off. There is a bar on the west end of the flat that you can wade. Watch for the rising water and current speed if you're wading along the edge. When fishing this area, it's always important to plan how to fight and land your fish with the light fly tackle. If a good bass gets into the canal's current, you may actually land the fish some 50 yards from where you began. That means you'll be working past other anglers, so introduce yourself when you arrive, chat a bit, and they'll wind up helping you get your fish to shore. Extra-fast-sinking lines are best for the deeper drop-offs and floating lines for the cove.

MASSACHUSETTS MARITIME ACADEMY

Nearly directly across from the tidal flats is the Massachusetts Maritime Academy. The Academy has a sand beach with a rocky, slippery edge. At the western end is a large sand flat and channel that is one part of the entrance to Buttermilk Bay. The combination of deep and shallow water makes for a lot of different depths and current speeds, perfect for baitfish and predators. The MMA area is better for fly rodders on a dropping tide; there are several current seams where the bottom terrain changes depths, and room for casting is pretty good. Floating or sink-tip lines are best, but you'll also see your fair share of extra-fast-sinking shooting heads. Most of the time you'll find bass and blues around the academy, but in the late summer and early fall, you'll have shots at bonito and albies as well. The MMA is a good shot for a slam.

SANDWICH CREEK

There are several spots to fish along the east end of the Cape Cod Canal, and they're all in the vicinity of Sandwich Creek. The first is the breakwall that is on the cape side of the canal. The tide coming through the canal is fast, but at the end of the jetty there is a bowl that backs around to the beach. The breakwall, bowl, and beach are usually pretty good during the spring, but they tend to fish better in the summer and best in the fall. Migratory fish tend to move quickly through the area until they settle into their respective regions. You'll find fish here all year long, but you're in for a treat in the fall, as all striped bass that remain inside of Cape Cod Bay must go through the canal. In order to make that passage, they usually stop off around Sandwich Beach, particularly on the quarter moons in the fall when the bait concentrates in the cove.

There is a bar that extends farther out into the bay, and there is a hook off the point which offers plenty of casting and fishing room on both sides of the bar. When the water is particularly warm, you may find bonito and false albacore buzzing the breakwall, right on the edge of the drop-off.

Sandwich Creek is the first estuary on the east end of the Cape Cod Canal, and it is reminiscent of a medium-sized trout stream. Most anglers can cast across nearly the entire creek. There is a long bridge that spans the entire marsh and a long estuary that splits a few hundred yards from the mouth. Higher up, the bottom is a mix of sand and mud, and there are some cobble areas with current seams and deeper water. Sandwich Creek is a perfect spot for a kayak, and many anglers will paddle and then get out of their boat and wade the banks.

On the west side of the mouth is a breakwall and deeper water that swirls around. Fish will stage on the lower water marks, particularly on the dropping tide, and wait for the bait to wash down to them. They do the same on the east side of the mouth, but instead of a jetty there is a long, sweeping cobble bar. Around low tide it's easy to wade across the river to access the current seams that pull bait out into the bay. Most of the bait that you'll find are silversides, sand eels, shrimp, and crabs, so swinging flies is a great approach. To the east side you'll find a short sand flat and deeper water. Sandwich Creek can also be a good late fall and winter spot, not just for holdover striped bass but also for sea-run trout. The population of salters is small, but they are there if you're looking to get out and fish. Extra-fast-sinking or floating lines are commonly used depending on the water height.

Scorton Creek

Moving east you'll find Scorton Creek, another estuary. Due to its proximity away from the canal, Scorton Creek experiences different current flows and its terrain is less sandy and more muddy/marshy. There is a gravel bar on the east side of the mouth, and the sand protrudes straight out on the west side, creating a hard edge and current. The east end is more of a rounded bull-nose bar, with deeper drop-offs on the edge. The water to the west is shallower than the water on the east side, which has deep troughs and pockets, perfect for concentrating baitfish. The water is deep at the mouth, and fishing a dropping tide or the first phase of the flood tide is best. Anglers will find stripers and bluefish, some shad, and there is a possibility of sea-run trout. Scorton runs far inland, which means that there is an abundance of bait that washes throughout the river system. You'll find silversides, sand eels, shrimp, and crabs, just like with Sandwich Creek. Many anglers favor kayaks for they can drift with the tide and fish the banks and ditches.

Cautionary note: Be careful when wading along the banks. While the ground may seem firm, there are tremendous amounts of moving water that can weaken it.

Bournes Pond and Green Pond

Two good, early-season ponds in Falmouth are on the south side, just west of Waquoit Bay. They are narrow sliver ponds with breakwalls at the mouth, have lots of trees

lining east and west sides to block the wind, warm up quickly in the early season, and are full of fish all season long. The ponds are not tremendously deep, and floating and intermediate lines work best. Most anglers will work the areas to the inside of the mouths of the ponds. The jetties outside the mouths are good spots to look for bonito and albies in the late summer and early fall, and hold bass and bluefish on the the the dropping tides. If you're coming on a fishing trip you may want to check out the Green Harbor Waterfront Lodging (www.go.greenharbor.com) which offers a free boat ramp and dock as part of their overnight efficiency-style lodging. From there you can fish your way up or down Green Pond and be in close proximity to hit Bournes Pond and Waquoit Bay, or move west to fish the Elizabeth Islands.

NOBSKA LIGHT

One of the most well-known lighthouses on the eastern seaboard also is a spot for some of the best fishing. Nobska Light is located at the southern most tip of Cape Cod. Tips are always good, but this one is interesting in that there are off-shore parallel and onshore perpendicular bars on the west side and rocks on the east side. A strong current forms at this juncture on both phases of the tides which makes for great fishing all around. The proximity of the light is also significant because of the combination of structure and water. While Nobska Light is in Vineyard Sound, Buzzards Bay and two of the Elizabeth Islands, Nonamesset and Uncatena, are just northwest. The current moves quickly here which means that later in the season, the warm Gulf Stream water and hard tide seams makes Nobska Light the first passage way of bonito and albies along the west side of the Upper Cape. There is a lot of boat and ferry traffic coming through the passage way, with both the New Bedford and Woods Holes Ferries steaming towards Martha's Vineyard. You'll have a shot at a grand slam during September.

WOODS HOLE AND NORTH

With the combination of the Oceanographic Institute and the stately homes, there isn't much public access around the waterfront. Penzance Point, which was the outermost point, is now a private community, so you'll need a boat to fish Great Harbor or Little Harbor. There are two inshore islands on the east end of the end of Penzance Point which are absolutely worth fishing around. Water passage and strong current flows run all around the islands and the peninsula, with rocks and shoals in between. The combination of recreational and commercial boat traffic makes for tricky fishing, so focus more of your attention around the end and to the west side. Bonito and albies are frequent visitors in the late summer and early fall, and tempers can flare with boat rage. That said, late August through late September is a good time for a slam.

QUISSETT HARBOR, RACING BEACH AND SIPPEWISSETT CREEKS

There are three popular spots in Quissett Harbor: Gansett Point on the southern point of the harbor, the Knob on the northern point, and the beach off of Quissett Harbor

Road. Gansett Point is sandy with lots of rocks and boulders scattered along the water's edge. It's a good spot on northwest winds. Fish the outside on the dropping tides and the inside on the coming. There is a lot of boat traffic in this small harbor, but paddling a kayak at first or last light or at night produces a lot of bass. The irregular coastline on the inside of the Knob is an excellent place to look for them, particularly since it's close to the parking area and town dock. The Knob is the northern peninsula, with a rock seawall surrounding the small land mass. The sharp turn from the beach forms a terrific cove, an excellent spot for finding fish in the fall on the quarter moons. Most of the time, you'll catch bass and blues. The beach on the Buzzards Bay side of the Knob has a sandy parallel offshore bar, which gathers bait. You'll occasionally find bonito and albies running the outside edges.

Due north of Quissett Harbor is Racing Beach. Here you'll find a series of parallel offshore sand bars, with funnel-like entrances at both head and tail, and rocks at those points. The diverse structure makes for good fishing, and an intermediate or floating line works best.

Farther north above Racing Beach are Little and Great Sippewissett Creeks. These river systems are not large, but as they connect with Buzzards Bay they get striped bass and bluefish. Both have sandy/muddy bottoms with sections of marsh – perfect for a kayak. In the spring, the fishing tends to be better, particularly when the sand eels and silversides are in. As the water warms, you'll find more action at the mouths of the rivers which connect to Buzzards Bay. These areas are sandy and offer some good fishing on the lower tide marks. You'll find worm hatches during the full moons.

Chapoquoit Beach and West Falmouth Harbor

West Falmouth Harbor sits in between two bodies of land and two roads: Little Island Road and Chapoquoit Beach Road. Breakwalls on both ends dramatically reduce the waves and current from Buzzards Bay, provide structure that holds fish, and focuses the current through the mouth. As a result you'll find some deep water as well as shoals on the inside of the passage way and a soft bottom.

There are three marshy coves in the harbor, and careful wading is required due to both the mud and the private homes. You'll find all types of bait here as well as a worm hatch on the full moons in the spring. A kayak is a great asset for working the coves, and there is a town landing for launching boats. The peninsula that separates the harbor in half (off of Snug Harbor Lane) runs parallel to the breakwall. As a result, you'll find many fish concentrated in the northern reaches of the coves. Floating, intermediate and sink-tip lines are best.

Old Silver Beach/Wild Harbor

You can't miss the beach with all the signs directing you there. That said, there are a few parts that are worth noting for focusing your fishing. The first area is Herring Brook, which is off of Quaker Road. You'll want to wade or kayak fish this area in the spring when the herring arrive and in the fall when the glass minnows drop out. At the mouth is a breakwall and you'll get occasional shots at bonito and albies in the late summer and early fall. Bluefish are also popular during the summer. The beachfront is gently sloping, and there are no bars to speak of. You'll find fish in the deeper troughs. Just north of the Old Silver Beach is Wild Harbor and the Wild Harbor River. The peninsula formed off of Point Road creates one giant cove, with a feeder river (the Wild Harbor River) on the southeastern side. At the mouth of the river is a sandy shoal that is a good spring and fall spot. There isn't much protection from the dominant southwest winds, but it does push the fish in close to shore during the spring. Bait naturally stages here during the fall, and when most of the boats get hauled you'll have plenty of room to work the shoreline. Floating and intermediate lines are most commonly used, but pack an extra-fast-sinker for the deeper troughs.

MEGANSETT THROUGH POCASSET

There is a lot of interesting structure in this small region. Scraggy Neck, Lawrence Island, and Squeteague Harbor form Megansett Harbor. With points, shoals, coves, beaches, channels, and jetties, there is enough texture to last an angler for a long time. Spring and fall are great times to fish for bass and blues, and you'll have shots at bonito and albies as well which mostly run along the jetty and the drop-offs on the south side of Scraggy Neck. There used to be a good squeteague population but it's pretty sparse nowadays.

Pocasset and Red Brook Harbors are separated by Bassetts Island. With the land masses arranged on an east-west orientation, Bassetts runs north to south and splits both harbors in half. Ideal protection for boaters seeking safe haven, perfect for anglers. The currents all around Bassetts run hard on both tides. Most of the water is deep with rocks and ledges, but on the south side at Hospital Cove you'll find more sand and shallow water. There are a lot of private homes in the area, and access can be difficult.

PHINNEYS HARBOR

Phinneys Harbor is the last area to fish on western Cape Cod before they start to run the canal. Mashnee Road runs through the middle of the peninsula that creates the harbor, and Eel Pond is at the northeast corner. Bait, particularly herring, menhaden, and silversides, enters the harbor on the flood tides and washes down along the outside beaches on the dropping tide. You'll also see some worms hatching on the full moons. The hatches aren't thick, and they are spread out over about a week. If you notice fish being selective at night, try a dropper rig with a cinder worm pattern on it. To the southeastern part of the harbor is Toby's Island. Toby's is basically a harbor-within-a-harbor, and with flats at the southern end, channels in the middle and coves at the northern end, it's a perfect place to get out of the heavy currents.

The Gray Gables section of Bourne is where President Grover Cleveland summered. There are two coves that are directly west of the entrance of the canal that break up some of the current along the shoreline. The current ranges between 4.5 and 6 knots coming from the canal, and bass and blues will move out of the current and into the lee of Phinneys' beaches. With that current comes hard edges, just the sort of terrain bonito and albies love. You'll see them racing all along the drop-offs along the outside of Phinneys as well as up into the canal.

WAQUOIT BAY

Waquoit Bay is one of the prettiest bays on the eastern seaboard. Compared to bays like Narragansett, it is small in size and scope, the water is clear, and there are lots of species to catch and places to catch them.

At the mouth is a long, rock jetty, with the typically sharp drop-offs into the channel. You'll find some of the earliest Cape Cod bass in here in late April and early May, and the first runs of racer bluefish around Waquoit. A tide seam forms on both sides of the jetty wall that concentrates bass and blues in the spring and summer, and bonito and albies in the late summer and fall. The fish move into the channel along the edge and follow the turn. There is good fishing around the sandy beach and bar. Typically, that is about as far as pelagic fish will go.

Bass and blues are a different story. On the rising tide, some will move up into the shallow water that adjoins Washburn Island, so wade, boat, and kayak fishing is a good way to find them. Most of the time, an intermediate line will be best, but for the

Kenney Abrames casting to a pod of cruising striped bass in a foot and a half of water. Controlling your line, as Abrames successfully does, enables quick and proper casts that reach fish.

deeper edges you may want to use a sink tip or an extra-fast-sinking shooting head. Other fish will filter along the eastern edge and move into the shallower water that is parallel to the beachfront. The fish move along towards Sage Lot Pond and will then head up and into two river systems: the Little River and the Great River. At the top of the Little River is Hamblin Pond and at the top of the Great River is Jehu Pond, both excellent spring spots when herring, silversides, and sand eels are in. There is a boat ramp in the Great River and the entire eastern section of Waquoit Bay is excellent for kayak fishing.

The north cove of the bay fishes well in the early season, but the water warms quickly, thereby making for slow fishing in the heat of the summer. You'll find bluefish here, and you'll also find the Seapit River, which connects Waquoit Bay with the Childs River. The Childs River runs south and connects to Eel Pond which connects to the ocean, thereby making for another good early-season spot for bass and blues and a good fall spot for bonito and albies.

An interesting way to fish this area is either on a clockwise or a counter-clockwise pattern. Start at the mouth of Waquoit Bay, work your way higher up in the bay, maybe into the two river systems and ponds. Then, at high tide, migrate towards the Seapit River and fish your way down the river through Eel Pond and to the mouth. You can also work the format in a clockwise pattern by beginning at the mouth of Eel

Cloudy days reduce the wariness of many animals, and striped bass are no exception. This bass was feeding on lobsters in June when their exoskeletons were soft.

Pond and working your way up to the Childs and the Seapit and then down through Waquoit Bay. The possibilities are endless, but Eel Pond has many moorings during the summer months.

The water can get discolored during heavy winds or full and new moon tides. If sight fishing gets difficult, cast into the fishy-looking areas.

SOUTH CAPE BEACH / POPPONESSET BEACH / POPPONESSET BAY

To the east of Waquoit Bay is an interesting and historic fishery – South Cape Beach. There are always anglers working the beach, but from mid-April through mid-June and from mid-September through mid-November, there are times when you'll see a line of anglers for as far as the eye can see. The depths are relatively shallow, with gradual drop-offs, so floating or intermediate lines work well. The bars run parallel to shore, and the South Cape area is where anglers typically see the first racer bluefish of the season in early May. The racer bluefish are fresh off of their migration. In season, they may weigh 15 to 18 pounds and tape out at 36 to 38 inches, but these fish may weigh a scant 7 to 9 pounds for the same length. Oftentimes anglers will see these trophy fish finning on the surface, and since they are not actively feeding (due to their migration) they are incredibly hard to catch. After a week or so, look out, you'll want to be around when they put on the feedbag. South Cape Beach continues to around the New Seabury community, and around that point, the mainland turns on a northeast tack.

Popponesset Beach begins after the turn past New Seabury. What makes the fishing interesting up here is the series of bars that run perpendicular along the entire 6-mile beach, right up to the entrance to Popponesset Bay. The interesting part is that in the spring and fall, large schools of migrating bass and blues hit the ends of the bars and follow the bait right up to your feet. The dominant southwest wind runs right up the beach and there is no lee, so right-handed casters may have a tough time casting, so you may need to turn around and release on your back cast.

The entrance to Popponesset Bay is at the top of the beach. The bay is smaller than Waquoit; there is a rock jetty on the east side and a long, sandy flat on the west end that is separated by a channel. Anglers will find swift-moving current that gains speed when the tide falls below the sandy shoal in the lower bay. Once the current is focused on the two channels, it moves quickly. Here, you'll want to fish a sinking line or extra-fast-sinking shooting head to get down to the fish. And when you're swinging flies and your line comes tight on the down current drift, the fly raises quickly out of the strike zone. Kayaks and shallow draft boats are great for the bay, and there are a few coves to explore. Two favorite spots are the south end of Popponesset Island on a high dropping tide and the mouth of Ockway Bay on the west side. Night fishing can be good inside the bay, but parking is limited. You'll find seasonal shad and bluefish in the bay, but overall the fishing is secondary to Waquoit and is better in the early season.

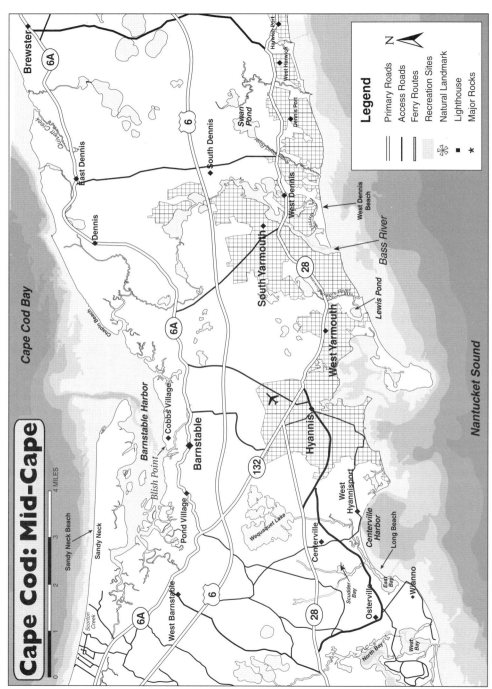

Cape Cod: Mid-Cape

Mid-Cape Cod

The Mid-Cape includes the towns of Barnstable, Yarmouth, and Dennis. The Mid-Cape area features many beautiful beaches, including warmwater beaches along Nantucket Sound. There are seven villages in Barnstable, including Barnstable Village, Centerville, Cotuit, Hyannis, Marstons Mills, Osterville, and West Barnstable, as well as several smaller hamlets that are incorporated into their larger neighbors (like Craigville, Cummaquid, Hyannisport, Santuit, Wianno, and others). There are three villages in Yarmouth: South Yarmouth, West Yarmouth, and Yarmouthport. There are five villages in Dennis including, Dennis Village (North Dennis), East Dennis, West Dennis, South Dennis, and Dennisport.

In recent years, the area around Barnstable has been getting a lot of attention. There have been strong runs of bass, bluefish, bonito, false albacore on the ocean side in Cotuit and outstanding fishing on the bay side in Barnstable Harbor. Barnstable Harbor has been getting a tremendous amount of attention, and for good reason. The fishing has been terrific, and there is a combination of flats, beach, and estuary fishing.

Cotuit Area

The peninsula of Cotuit has terrific structure and current. There are three beaches on the eastern side that benefit from the current dropping out of Cotuit Bay: Oregon, Loop, and Riley's. The current funnels down past Sampson's Island and enters Nantucket Sound, pulling all the baitfish with it. Stripers and bluefish work the shoreline. Whereas South Cape Beach offered no lee from the southwest winds, Cotuit is protected. As you walk along the beaches, you'll see jetties and docks, all of which are private. In the spring and fall, the fishing is daytime, in the summer the fishing is more at night.

The beaches are all sandy with gradual drop-offs, and there are some offshore perpendicular bars. Off of Oregon Beach, best known for outstanding spring and fall bluefish fishing in May and then from August through early October, these bars disappear as you move up the coast. Near the Loop Beach parking area is a large shoal that runs parallel to Dead Neck. This shoal was formed from eroding sand, and creates the channel to enter into Cotuit Bay. What you have in essence is a cove within a cove, which makes Cotuit an excellent fall quarter moon spot. Lots of bait concentrates around here.

You'll also find several other species of fish roaming the area in the late summer and fall. There are bonito, false albacore, and Spanish mackerel that will run the beaches and along Dead Neck. Intermediate lines are best from shore, and extra-fast-sinking lines are an option, too. When the fish are on the surface shift to a floating line and add a pinch of split shot as needed and toss in a few mends.

The peninsula of Osterville separates three bays: Cotuit, North, and West. There are two bodies of waters that connect them: the Seapuit River connects Cotuit Bay with West Bay, and the Narrows connects West Bay with North Bay. Each bay is protected, and you'll find sand shoals with adjoining deeper water and channels. The bays fish really well in the spring and get warm in the summer. There is a lot of boat traffic during the summer, but with so much water it's easy to find a quite place to fish. In the spring, anglers can go anywhere they want, and in the summer, predawn and last-light fishing is best. If you're using a kayak, watch for the bigger vessels – they probably don't see you.

The Narrows is the bottleneck between North Bay and Cotuit Bay, and it offers increased current and deeper water. You'll find a parking area off of Cordwood Road, and it's a popular spot for bass and bluefish. The sandy shoals around the mouth shortens the water column and adds structure and current that bass and bluefish like.

The Seapuit River that connects Cotuit Bay and West Bay is small and is on the north side of Dead Neck. It's a good early-season bass spot, particularly as it connects with Nantucket Sound on the east end breachway. While fishing this river and the breakwall, it makes sense to continue working the shoals and the channels going into West Bay. You'll find some bonito, albies, and Spanish macks in the late summer and early fall.

SANDY NECK

The 7-mile spit of land called Sandy Neck forms Barnstable Harbor. On the inside of the harbor are a few islands, some flats, and marshy river systems. The water moves well, and with Barnstable Harbor's proximity on the inside of the Cape's arm, there is a great current wash into the protected harbor.

To access Sandy Neck, you'll need a couple of items. First is a permit for your four-wheel-drive vehicle, which can be picked up at the gate. Next, camping is allowed, but it is only in self-contained rigs, meaning if you're planning on spending the night, you'll need to have a camper, not a tent. Anglers can walk into Sandy Neck, and should check in with the guard at the gate. There is a Marsh Trail that runs parallel to the beach, and there are six trails that will connect you with the beach.

Trails 1 through 4 connect anglers to the barrier beach that has a gently sloping beach and a few ocean holes. Most of the water is between 1 and 5 feet at mean low tide, and it serves as a passageway for fish. Where Sandy Neck gets particularly interesting is off of Trail 5 where two contrary actions occur. First, the sand bars run from tight-to-shore to a 45-degree northeast tack that extends far from shore. There are numerous bars and cuts that are created by the current, and the current blowing over the bars is perfect for predators picking off baitfish. This shoal forms the western entrance to the harbor. Second, the land mass curves on a southeasterly tack, forming somewhat of a beak of land. Beach Point is the end of the line.

And what an end of the line it is. The entrance to the harbor is between 11 and 16 feet at mean low tide. The cove is on the inside and sits northwest of Horseshoe Shoal and northeast of Moon Shoal. Both areas skinny up and two channels run on either side. You'll find a number of tidal creeks that dump into the harbor, with baitfish moving in and out on every tide. On the eastern side, you'll find Chase Garden Creek, Lone Tree Creek, Mill Creek, Short Wharf Creek, and others. On the western side you'll find Bass, Wells, Scorton, Spring, and Brickyard Creeks. Each of the creeks will hold fish and is an outstanding kayak spot. Get a small boat and gunkhole around.

In the spring, herring and alewives move into most of the creeks. With the surrounding marshy areas, you'll also find mummichaug, shrimp, crabs, and some worms. Squid, sand eels, and silversides are found throughout the harbor. Summer fishing can be outstanding at night, either from a kayak or from shore, particularly on the higher water marks. You'll find bass moving into the grassy areas to feed on shrimp and other baitfish.

Maraspin Creek separates Slaten Point from Blish Point, which is where you'll find Millway Marine as well as a public boat launch. A series of trees mark the way out from Millway Marine to the harbor. Fog can roll in very quickly and thickly in the spring and fall, so make sure you pack at least a compass, particularly if you're kayaking. Fly rodders favor the last few hours of the dropping tide as well as the first few hours of the flood tide. You'll see large schools of bass concentrate on the edge of a flat or bar, waiting for the tide to rise so they can chase sand eels and silversides onto the flat. Most of the time, a floating line will work around the lower water marks, and an extra-fast sinking line will work better as the tide rises. Take ranges of where the edges are, and as the tide floods you'll find fish moving up and down the edges.

BARNSTABLE HARBOR BY FOOT

Public parking is somewhat limited to three points: Scudder Lane, Blish Point, and Bone Hill Road. What most anglers do is park in one area and follow the channels to the east or west. Most of the wading is very easy with a hard sand bottom. If you move higher up into the marsh the sand gets traded in for a typically muddy bottom. Fishing the last part of the dropping tide and the first part of the flood tide is best.

Scudder Lane

You'll pass Hinckley Pond on your way in to Scudder Lane (on Route 6A) that offers an easy park-and-fishing place. You'll find a deep channel a few hundred feet in front of you. There are some small boats moored here, and on the other side of the channel is a shoal/flat. The channel runs on an east-west line, and fishing out in front is a good option. Bringing along a kayak is a great idea.

Moving to the east you'll find a harbor at the end of Pine Oaks Drive. This deeper water splits around a shoal, with one section moving down past Scudder Lane and into Brickyard Creek, and the other moving northwest towards the mouth of Spring Creek. You'll find fish in the deeper water all along the edge drop-off, but again, having a kayak is a tremendous idea for following the fish as the tide floods. If you have limited space, bring a floating line with an extra-fast sinking spool.

Blish Point

Blish Point is off of Millway Road and there is a large parking lot at the end. The west side is the channel that runs from Millway Marina into Barnstable Harbor, and the north side has sand flats that connect with Barnstable Harbor. The shallow water and the sandy bottom make for a perfect spring and summer sand eel spot, but you'll also find silversides, squid, herring, alewives, and menhaden as well. Walking past the beach, you'll find deeper water that parallels Sunset Lane. On the northern side of that deeper water is a shoal. This terrain makes for a perfect low-water mark on either tide, dropping or flood. The bass and bluefish will stage on either side of the bar, picking off baitfish as it washes over the sand. There is a town landing in between Blish Point and Bone Hill Road. Another great kayaking spot, but be careful when the tide starts to flood for it moves very quickly, and swimming in your waders isn't much fun.

Bone Hill Road

Located on the eastern end of Barnstable Harbor is Bone Hill Road. You'll walk on hard sand fishing the edge drop-offs, channels, and bars. On the lower water marks, you can wade very far out and access deeper water along the way. Sometimes the fish stage longer than other times, so plan your exit carefully. The tide rises quickly here.

Use a hint of green in your flies when fishing in shallow water with eel grass bottoms, like this spot in Barnstable Harbor.

My experience is that moving back towards shore at about an hour and 45 minutes after the tide turns is best. Sometimes the fish don't start moving in until after that time, so having a kayak makes for an easier and drier experience. What you may do is tether the kayak to your wading belt and walk and wade. When the water begins to flood, you can get in your boat and catch more fish. Use floating or intermediate lines for the shallows, and extra-fast-sinking lines in the dropoffs.

Mill Creek is to the east of where you put in, and is an equally good wade or kayak spot on either the flood or dropping tides. The creek is also good at night, and bass will move along the edges looking for sand eels, mummichaug, and shrimp.

BASS RIVER

With a name like the Bass River, you can expect to catch fish here. The Bass River is the longest estuary system on Cape Cod and runs from the ocean-side towns of South Yarmouth and West Dennis to above the Mid-Cape Highway. The river follows a north-south orientation from the public ramp and breakwall at the mouth to the saltpond at its northernmost end. A cranberry bog is to the west of the salt pond.

There are two beachfronts to fish. One is the Bass River Beach and it is on the South Yarmouth side. The beach is just below a large parking lot and public boat ramp, with a walk to the beach taking about ten minutes. There also is another parking lot off of South Shore Drive as well and it is closer to the beach.

As the current drops it creates a very strong flow and current which can make for some tricky hauling and launching. That said, the current flows hard around the point and along the beach. There are a series of parallel offshore bars, and you'll find bass and blues on the beach in the spring.

West Dennis Beach is on the east side of the Bass River, and is well known as a windsurfing beach. In the fall, you'll find bonito and false albacore working baitfish on a dropping tide on the jetty, and there is usually a 60-plus-pound bass taken on the inside of the jetty at some point during the fall.

From the east side of the jetty for about a mile you'll find a sandy shoal that fishes best on the higher water marks. About a mile or so out the shoal ends and there is an inverted 'v' of deeper water that concentrates fish. That location is on the beach about even with Uncle Steven's Pond. The spring run of bass and blues as well as the fall run is an excellent time to fish the beaches. Nighttime is also a good time, particularly around the high-tide mark. There is a breakwall off the beach that can be a good spot for boat anglers, and the breakwall is right at the end of the shoal.

The river moves inland and splits at Stage Island. The deeper water is on the west side of the split and a shallower offshoot runs parallel to the beach. You'll find bass and blues in the deeper water around Stage Island and you'll also find them all the way up into the channels and fingers that run into Weir Creek Pond.

Northwest from the Route 28 bridge is a giant cove that is adjacent to a golf course, and the cove holds fish on the higher water marks. Farther upriver you'll find Grand Cove on the eastern side of the river. Grand Cove can be an excellent night fishing spot, particularly around full moons and out of a kayak on a dropping tide.

Above the Route 6 bridge, the Bass River splits into three bays and ponds: Kelley's Bay connects with the top of the river, to the west is Dinah's Pond, and farther north from Kelley's is Follin's Pond. Each of these areas fishes well during higher water marks and at night, but one of the best worm hatches occurs on the full moons in the spring. During those times you'll want to be in one of these three areas. Wade fishing spots are a premium, but the slow water makes for great kayaking.

There is a tremendous amount of bait all season long, but there is heavy boat traffic in the summer. Shift your fishing times to either first light, last light, or at night. Use floating or extra-fast-sinking lines in the deeper waters, and intermediates along the beaches and in the flats.

PARKERS RIVER / LEWIS AND SEINE PONDS

At the west end of the Bass River Beach is Parkers River. Parkers River pales in comparison with the reputation of the Bass River, but it still fishes well in both the early season as well as the late season. There is less fishing pressure, too. In front of the river is a tremendous sand flat, where you can sightfish for bass and blues. You'll find seasonal bonito and albies along the flat and especially along both breakwalls. As you move inside the river you'll find a small salt pond called Lewis Pond. With its proximity so close to the mouth there is some great early-season bass and blues and decent amount of bait. The pond is moderate sized and is a good kayaking spot. Farther up Parker River is Seine Pond which is situated above Route 28. As at Follin's Pond, you'll find worms hatching during the spring full moons. If you're fishing at night or in a kayak, pay attention to the boat traffic, as there is a marina just below the Route 28 bridge.

Big flies, small fish.

SWAN POND RIVER AND SWAN POND

The Swan Pond River is a good early-season spot for bass and bluefish. It is a small river, easily paddled with a kayak. The Swan winds back and forth repeatedly which slows the current flow. At the northernmost end, which is just above Route 28, you'll find Swan Pond, a giant saltpond. Most of the time a floating and an extra-fast-sinking line will do. The water can get discolored during the summer, and there is oftentimes heavy traffic during the summer months.

HERRING RIVER/EAST AND WEST RESERVOIRS

There are a number of Herring Rivers on Cape Cod and like all the other ones this one gets a good herring run. The reason for the strong herring population lies at the top of the river, particularly where it splits and moves to the east and to the west and into the East and West Reservoirs. This moderate-sized river fishes well in the spring and also in the fall when the glass minnows (herring fry) drop out of the reservoirs.

The mouth has an extra long jetty wall that extends very far out. It makes for a good bass and bluefish jetty and you'll also get shots at bonito and albies in September and October. A long sandy beach hooks to the west on the western side of the breakwall, and is a good area for staging fish at the lower water marks. There are some bonito and albies.

CHAPIN BEACH

Chapin Memorial Beach is on the Dennis/Yarmouth line, and at the west end of the beach is Chase Garden Creek. These two spots work well when fished together, and they are due east of the mouth of Barnstable Harbor.

Begin your fishing in the creek at high tide. There are a number of winding turns in the river, most of which create solid current seams that will concentrate the current on the dropping tides. There are a few shoals in the middle of the creek as well. You'll find stripers and bluefish moving along the banks looking for herring in the spring, silversides, crabs, and shrimp in the summer and menhaden in the fall. The creek is great on a high dropping tide, and fishing either a floating line and a popper or slider will work well, or a sinking line. Bring along a kayak – you'll be out of the wind and can drift down to the mouth. There is deeper water on the southwest side of the creek, a perfect staging place for stripers and seasonal bluefish, particularly when the bait dumps out on a dropping tide or the wind shifts direction to west/northwest.

Out at the mouth are a series of perpendicular bars, each of which gets the fish to run in tight to shore. About where Fox Hill Road runs into Chapin Beach Road is where the bars begin to run parallel to shore. Here you'll find the fish passing through on either an eastern or western tack. The bars will continue to run parallel all the way to Sesuit Harbor, with deeper water adjoining the outer edges. The terrain is almost exclusively sandy, and has large concentrations of sand eels. There is a parking area to the east of the river mouth. Floating or intermediate lines are best, and natural patterns without too much flash are good choices.

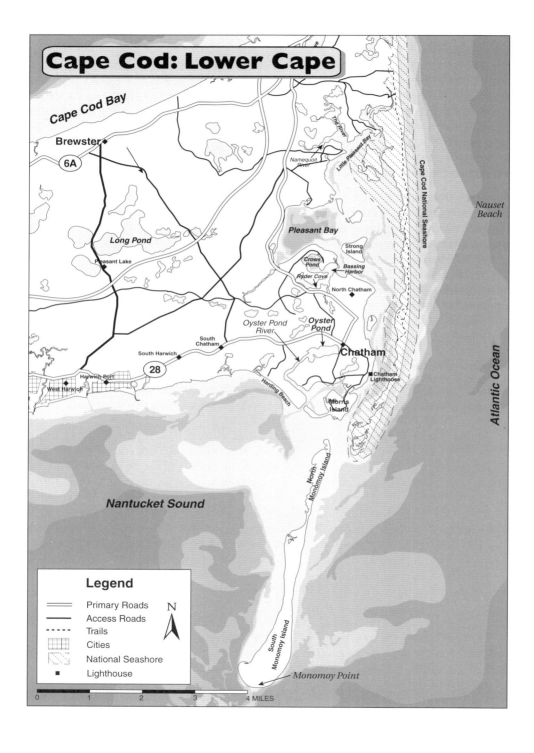

Cape Cod: Lower Cape

Cape Cod Bay

Brewster

6A

The River

Namequoit River

Little Pleasant Bay

Cape Cod National Seashore

Nauset Beach

Long Pond

Pleasant Bay

Pleasant Lake

Strong Island

Crows Pond

Bassing Harbor

Ryder Cove

North Chatham

Oyster Pond River

Oyster Pond

Chatham

South Chatham

Chatham Lighthouse

South Harwich

28

Harwich Port

Harding Beach

Morris Island

West Harwich

Atlantic Ocean

Nantucket Sound

North Monomoy Island

Legend

	Primary Roads
	Access Roads
----	Trails
⊞	Cities
▨	National Seashore
■	Lighthouse

N

South Monomoy Island

Monomoy Point

0   1   2   3   4 MILES

LOWER CAPE COD

The Lower Cape is the narrower portion of the cape, where it bends sharply to the north. This section includes the towns of Harwich, Brewster, Chatham, and Orleans. When many anglers think of Cape Cod they typically think of the Lower Cape region, mostly because of the famous Monomoy Island Flats. There is some other renowned water as well.

BREWSTER FLATS

If you needed a rough coordinate for the Brewster Flats it would be sandwiched in between Sesuit Harbor in Dennis and Rock Harbor in Orleans. The flats run on and on, and have a very interesting combination of parallel and perpendicular bars, which seem to keep the fish concentrated in an area around the low-tide marks. As the water rises above the bars, the fish are usually in close to shore. Just west of Orleans is a recess in the flat, and the deeper water is one area that concentrates the fish that move on and off the flat around the lower water marks. The water is very clean, and you'll find fish on the flats starting with the herring in late April and early May and staying throughout the season. Sand eels are the dominant bait in the summer, and the deep water edge of the flats load up with fish in the fall. There are a lot of public/private turf wars going on with the Ocean Edge community and public right of ways, so check to see what the current rulings are. Make sure you have a bunch of Kenney Abrames' L&L Special, probably the best flats fly going.

QUIVETT AND PAINE'S CREEKS

To the east of Sesuit Harbor are two creeks: Quivetts is first and Paine's is second. In addition to being two of the prettiest creeks on the cape and perfect for kayak fishing, they have significant spring herring runs. What makes them particularly interesting to flyfishers is the alluvial river mouth which opens up to one expansive flat. Anglers typically go into the creeks at high tide and fish their way down to the mouth and then flats fish as the water runs low. After the herring runs thin out, you'll find bass and, later on, bluefish chasing silversides in the lower stretches of the river systems, and sand eels out in front. The flats extend for quite a ways out, so there is ample fishing time and place.

If you tether a kayak to your waist then you can get the best of both worlds. The bars at the mouth run perpendicular to the beach. Far to the east side you'll find deeper water and several shoals that are exposed at lower tide. There are several cuts that go through the shoals, and these passages are perfect areas to look for both baitfish and bass and blues. You can wade fish on the dropping tide and then hit the flats, and when the tide turns you can get into your boat and fish the entire flood tide. Many times you'll see the fish hit the end of the bars and follow one side all the way up to the beach as the tide floods.

The creeks are small and they get warm during the summer months, but that's ok for daytime bluefish. You'll find them cruising the mouth of both creeks, particularly on the dropping tide. If you're looking for bass in the summer, shift your game to the nighttime. You'll find some bass popping sand eels on the higher water marks, and the crowds will have thinned out so you'll be able to move around. Floating lines are best at night and a split shot will get you deep (if you need to get deep). Fall fishing is great, particularly when the glass minnows are dropping out of the creeks.

Hardings Beach

To the west of Harding's Beach are a series of bars that are positioned on a northeast angle. On the east end of Harding's Beach is the entrance to Stage Harbor and the Oyster Pond River. In between those two ends is a sandy and eelgrass bottom with channels and guzzles.

With the bar configuration, Harding's Beach is basically one giant cove. There is a parking area off of Hardings Beach Road, and from there you can go east or west. If you go to the west you'll find three distinct offshoots: Mill Creek (which runs in to Taylor's Pond), Cockle Cove (an inverted 'v'-shaped bowl), and Sulphur Springs (a saltpond that connects to the beach). Each of these areas is quiet and protected and gets early runs of bass and bluefish, particularly when the herring are in. Sand eels, the main game in town, arrive in mid-June. Anglers will find seasonal bonito and albies. Most of the time these fish will hang off the edge of the bars, but with a strong southerly wind, they may be within reach of shore casters. Kayakers will enjoy fishing Mill Creek and Cockle Cove.

Stage Harbor is at the east end of Hardings Beach. It's one of the prettiest lighthouses and overlooks three good pieces of water. On the north side is the mouth of the Oyster Pond River, on the northeast side is the channel that runs into Stage Harbor, and on the south side is Nantucket Sound and North Monomoy Island. With all the water moving in and around the point the fishing can't be beat. Stage Harbor is an active harbor, with dozens of draggers, trawlers, and charter boats heading out to sea. Combined with an active recreational boating fleet there is a tremendous amount of traffic. While kayaking in the Oyster Pond River and Stage Harbor is excellent, it's not recommended due to the volume of boat traffic. It's a good spot for a slam in September.

Make sure that you venture forth with a compass. Chatham is well known for fog that blows in during temperature changes, and it is very easy to get disoriented. The water around here is very clear and combinations of floating, intermediate, or extra-fast-sinking are helpful. Many anglers prefer blue or clear mono lines and flurocarbon.

Morris Island

Morris Island is a freestanding island that is surrounded by Stage Harbor to the west, Little Mill and Mill ponds to the north, Chatham Harbor to the east, and Nantucket Sound to the south. Main Street in Chatham runs into Morris Island Road, and runs all the way to the southern end of the island. The sand spit continues all the way to the mouth of Stage Harbor and is known as Harding Beach Point. Sand eels are popular baitfish here, and there is a lot of excellent sightfishing.

CHATHAM LIGHT BEACH

Walking down the long staircase puts you on a barrier beach where Pleasant Bay dumps out into Chatham Harbor. Across the harbor is the end of the world famous Nauset Beach. The beach used to run continuously from Nauset Cut in Orleans/ Eastham down to Chatham, but a new cut broke through which has changed the current flow, thereby making Chatham Light Beach less popular these days. Sand eels are a common baitfish on the beach.

The channel and associated bars are excellent on the dropping tides, and the current seams and pockets disorient baitfish from the spring until the fall. Most of the sandy shoal is on the opposite side of the channel, a good thing on the dropping tide as it concentrates the fish close to a wade fisherman's side. From here, there is quite a long stretch of beach to cover, and several bars and ocean holes. Fishing is best around the lower water marks, and the water clarity can get somewhat murky on full moon tides. Fog can roll in very quickly in this area, particularly in the spring and in the fall, so be sure to pack a compass. You also may want to use a heavier sinking line to offset the strong current. Whereas you'd normally swing a floating or intermediate line you might want to use an extra-fast-sinking shooting head. Toss a reach cast into an up current cast to get some depth. You'll find bonito and false albacore from time to time in the late summer and early fall, and all sizes of bluefish throughout the year.

MONOMOY ISLAND

From looking at the large number of Florida Keys-style flats boats, you can be sure that sight fishing on North and South Monomoy Islands is popular. The water is clear, the current is strong, and there are a few ways to fish the two islands.

You can wade fish Monomoy by hitching a ride from the Rip Ryder, a shuttle service that will ferry you and your party across the channel to the island. The cost is minimal, and it's a great way to spend the day. Families will pack up and sun bathe and swim, with fishing all around. Kayaking is also a great way to fish Monomoy, and putting in from Morris Island makes for the shortest paddle. From there you can move along the northern channels across from Hardings Beach. The west side of the island is shaped like a backwards 'j', a perfect structure for gathering baitfish on the dropping tide.

South Monomoy Island has one of the most significant rips which fishes great in the summertime. As the water temperatures warm, it seems as if every striped bass and bluefish moves in to feed on squid, sand eels, silversides and bay anchovies. Most boats will position up tide and stay on their motors so as to stem the tide. Anglers will use extra-fast-sinking lines. In the fall, big bluefish, bonito, and albies cruise the rips, and skipjack and school tuna will also move into the area. During the summer, sand eel and crab patterns are most popular. Use an extra-fast-sinking shooting head in the rips to get down to the fish.

STRONG ISLAND AND THE COVES

Tucked in the lower stretch of Pleasant Bay is the triangular shaped Strong Island. To the east side of Strong Island are a series of sandy flats that extend all the way to the lower stretch of Nauset Beach and the new break. You'll see bass and blues moving in and out on the second and third hours around low tide. The channels around the island are what they use as passageways in and out of Pleasant Bay. There is no shortage of baitfish in Pleasant Bay, and there are some interesting coves on the west side of Strong Island.

Bassing Harbor, Crow's Pond, and Ryder Cove are three interconnected bodies of water that are great fishing spots. They are protected by land masses on all sides which can significantly reduce the wind, are calm, and are excellent for kayak fishing. The terrain varies and is a combination of sand and mud. You'll find more silversides, shrimp, crabs, mummies, and worms in these three reaches. Fishing the coves on the higher tides is the best, and at night you'll hear fish popping bait. High dropping tides are best. Floating or sink tips are good choices.

SOUTH SIDE OF NAUSET CUT

The south side of the Nauset Cut is more manageable for wade fishermen during the day. It's pretty much a park and walk. At the mouth, anglers will find several sand shoals that change with the winter storms. The entire mouth is sandy, which makes for difficult passage at low tide, and Nauset Cut is one of the more challenging and aggressive harbor entrances on the Eastern Seaboard.

The beauty of running the beach in a 4x4 means that you can wade out and fish without crowds. This fish was caught off of Nauset Beach.

It is quite possibly one of the best kayak fisheries on the Eastern Seaboard. Most of the time at the mouth, you'll find piping plover nesting areas, but anglers will begin fishing the mouth on the incoming tide. This area is known as the Main Channel. As the water increases, they'll move around on the inside of the Main Channel and also work along the inside edge of Nauset Beach. There are several main channels that wind past islands, bars, and flats, and they are worth exploring. A kayak really is a great asset here, for you can work down with the current and back up when the tide turns. You're also not frustrated when you see fish breaking on the other side of the channel. Striped bass will arrive in May and follow herring and alewives into the waterway, and there are always fish when the sand eels and silversides arrive. Nighttime is a great time to fish Nauset, and with all the bait plus shrimp and crabs you'll oftentimes hear the fish popping on the surface. Nauset hasn't fished as well lately as it has in the past, but that shouldn't discourage anglers from heading out. Odds are another world record may be a few feet away.

NAUSET HARBOR

The first sharp bend in the Main Channel is Nauset Harbor. There is a 'u'-shaped shoal that fishes well at high dropping tide, particularly as the fish are hanging in the deeper water along the edge. The harbor is filled with boats during the summer and there are numerous mooring balls, so fishing can get tricky. As this area is a sharp bend, it tends to be a catch-all for bait and for bass and blue fish. The bottom alternates between sand and mud, so watch your footing.

In the back of Nauset Harbor you'll find three coves that are worth checking out. The higher you go, the smaller they get. Robert's Cove is first, Mill Pond is second, and Little Cove is third. The best area to fish is off of Mill Pond Road which is the intersection of Robert's and Mill. The passage way between the two is deeper and there is structure on all sides with a spit of land splitting up the two bodies of water. Kayak fishing on the higher water marks can be good, and spring is a good time to be up here. Later on in the season the water temperatures warm significantly.

THE COVES: WOODS, RACHEL, ROBERTS, AND TOWN COVES

As you move higher up the Main Channel you'll see two repetitive structures: coves and offshoots. The coves are shallow areas, mostly with muddy bottoms, and lots of shrimp, some worms, silversides, mummies, and crabs. They'll fish better on the higher water marks, and at night you'll find bass moving in and out of the coves. There are some rocks around them that have fallen down from erosion, so watch your props.

The first one is Woods Cove. Sandy at the mouth, there is a long bar that extends into the cove from Weeset Prop Way. To the right side of the bar is a deep trough that concentrates some fish during the early seasons and sometimes at night. The shallow, muddy cove is always worth a short look as some big bass can get in there on a full moon tide.

Rachel Cove is higher up into the Main Channel and is more of a true cove. Spits of land on both sides create one relatively narrow entranceway to the cove, and there is slightly deeper water on the Causeway Road side and stronger current.

After passing Rachel Cove you'll pass over a shoal that is mostly exposed at low tide and into the deeper water of Town Cove. Bass and some bluefish will most around the edges of Town Cove, and you'll find them popping up on the higher water marks and at night. The Goose Hummock tackle shop is located on Town Cove, and if you're looking for a kayak rental you'll find one here, too. The staff is thoroughly knowledgeable about all facets of fishing and their selection is immense. In addition, you'll find a public ramp at the top of Town Cove.

NAUSET BEACH

Wade anglers typically will access Nauset Beach where parking moves close to the sand. Around the Cut and out in front is a good area, particularly on the last phases of the dropping tide when the baitfish and therefore fish move out and along the beach. From there south there are parallel bars which make for good early-season and fall-run fishing areas. Lots of bait will push past Nauset and the fishing is hot. Most of the bars are parallel off-shore, and the troughs in between the two, fish well at mid-tides.

The best way to access the miles and miles of national seashore is to get an Over-sand Permit and drive. A few years ago, anglers could drive all the way to the point where Pleasant Bay passes by the end of Nauset Beach and Chatham. Back in 2007, the Patriot's Day Storm opened a section of Nauset Beach. It caused damage to a number of the beach shacks and anglers can no longer drive to the end. Still, there is plenty of excellent water to fish; in fact, Tony Stetzko, the resident Nauset Beach guide, caught his one-time world record 73-pound fish on Nauset Beach.

A perpendicular, onshore bar off of Nauset Beach creates a bowl that gathers bait. Fish the points on full moons and coves on quarter moons.

Outer Cape Cod

The Outer Cape is the outermost part, containing the towns of Eastham, Wellfleet, Truro, and Provincetown. This area includes the Cape Cod National Seashore, which is a John F. Kennedy-created national park that comprises much of the outer cape, including the entire east-facing coast.

The farther you go towards the end, the skinnier the land mass becomes. That is a good thing for anglers, for it becomes a short ride from either the ocean side or the bay side. The current blows around the tip of the cape, and every striped bass that does not pass through Cape Cod Canal passes by the Outer Cape, thereby making an exquisite fishery.

Outer Beaches

There are two beaches on the ocean side that are next to each other, Coast Guard Beach and Nauset Light Beach. Coast Guard Beach is well known for two reasons. First, it is the access point to the northside of the famous Nauset Cut. Second, it provides access to Nauset Marsh from the Outer Cape. Coast Guard Beach has a long sweeping offshore parallel bar that extends down to the rounded point. It is easy to access, with a reasonable parking lot. The dunes are relatively flat, so it's easy to get in and out without huffing and puffing. Best times of year for fishing here is in the spring when the striped bass arrive, at night, and in the fall. Coast Guard Beach was rated one of the Top 10 beaches in the world by Doctor Beach, so it's crowded during tourist season. Many anglers will work their way south towards the mouth, fishing the points of the offshore bars, the rip currents, and the ocean holes until they wind up at the northside of the Nauset Cut. There is fee parking during the day, and free parking at night. Floating or intermediate lines are best, and if you're fishing around the cut during higher water you may want an extra-fast-sinking shooting head.

On the inside of the cut is Nauset Marsh. There is a long sand flat and bar that sweeps around throughout the first turn of the mouth. The sand and cobble bottom fishes well on the first phases of the flood tide and again later in the dropping tide. The current is particularly strong at the mouth, and a dropping tide with an east wind makes the mouth one of the most treacherous entrances on the Eastern Seaboard. It's a perfect kayak spot, particularly if you like to get out of your kayak and wade. There are flats, guzzles, channels, and feeder streams throughout the marsh, with mussel and oyster beds and a salt pond. To access the marsh high up in the system (as in on a high tide) take Hemenway Road off of the Mid-Cape Highway. Herring arrive in the spring and silversides and sand eels are the dominant bait. You'll always find crabs, shrimp, and squid in the marsh.

You can't miss Nauset Light Beach, for the Nauset Light gives it away. As you speak with other anglers, be sure to differentiate Nauset Light Beach from Orleans' Nauset Beach. The banks are a bit steeper due to the dune erosion, and you'll find a few rocks scattered along the parallel offshore bars. Nauset Light Beach is a good night fishing beach, as there are some deeper ocean holes that concentrate bait. The current flow is a bit slower than around the mouth of the cut, and on an east wind in the fall you'll oftentimes find the fish right at your feet. There is fee parking during the day, and free parking at night. Floating and intermediate lines, and first part of the coming tide fishes best.

Bay Beaches

There are several bayside beaches, and the best ones for fishing are First Encounter, Campground Landing, Cooks Brook and Sunken Meadow.

First Encounter Beach is where the Pilgrims first met the Native Americans. In the general area are three particular aspects that make it good for fishing. The first is the long parallel bars that are broken throughout the end of the beach. As the beach runs south towards Orleans, there is an alluvial mouth that runs into the second dominant feature, the Herring River. The Herring River is a short, narrow estuary, with a combination of sand and mud. At the southern end of the Herring River is Boat Meadow Creek, an even smaller river system that runs deep into the town of Eastham. With the combination of bay tides as well as the ebb and flood of the Herring River and Boat Meadow Creek you get a bottom terrain that is broken. You'll find striped bass and bluefish frequenting these areas because they are likely pausing places, where the bait will move along the bar and then stop in the deeper adjoining water.

A tremendous shift occurs between Campground and Cooks Brook Beaches, and that change dramatically affects Sunken Meadow. The bars at Campground Landing run either parallel or on a 45-degree angle to shore, and there is an ocean hole at the north end of the beach. As with all bayside beaches, the water temperatures warm in the summer, and the beaches are narrow, with some sand and cobble mixtures, and shallower towards shore. After the deeper hole, the bars change at Cooks Brook and become perpendicular onshore bars. There are numerous fingers that have deeper water slots in between the bars. The way to fish Campground Landing and Cooks Brook is to fish them together. When the fish are in, you'll find them running parallel to shore on the coming tides. Then, they hit the ocean hole and stage, moving into the current (which is coming from deeper water) and then hit the end of the point bars and follow them along into the shallower water. Sand eels and silversides are the dominant bait, and you'll also find squid in the deeper adjoining water.

The bars get progressively wider, with a few high spots, until they create a dramatic end that dovetails into a 45-degree angle that basically funnels fish into Sunken Meadow. The Meadow is surrounded by land on three sides, Eastham to the south and east and Wellfleet's Lieutenant's Island on the north. At the top of the meadow is a ditch that connects Sunken Meadow to Blackfish Creek. So here you have bars that move into deep water with a consistent flow on both the east and the west sides of the Meadow. Outstanding fishing, particularly when the double-digit bluefish move in. Campground Landing, Cooks Brook, and Sunken Meadow will fish well throughout the year, and are especially good in the spring and summer. You'll find Sunken Meadow to be an exceptional kayak spot. Use floating and intermediate lines for the lower water marks or for surface activity, but pack a sinking line for when the tide is high.

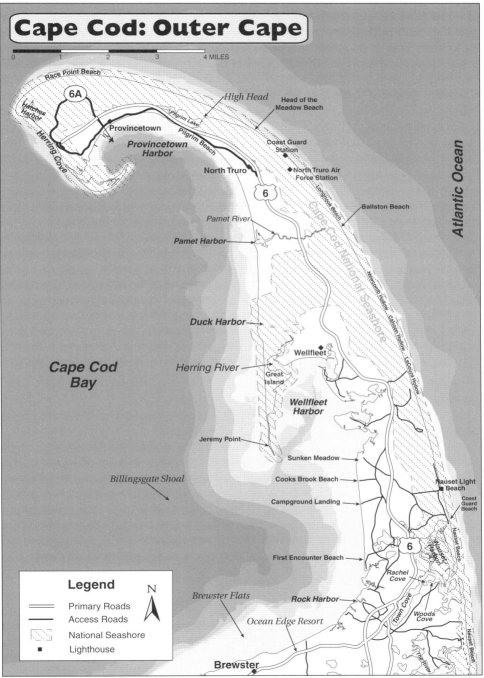

Cape Cod: Outer Cape

0 1 2 3 4 MILES

Race Point Beach

6A

Hatches Harbor

Herring Cove

Provincetown

Provincetown Harbor

Pilgrim Lake

Pilgrim Beach

High Head

Head of the Meadow Beach

Coast Guard Station

North Truro

North Truro Air Force Station

6

Longnook Beach

Ballston Beach

Atlantic Ocean

Pamet River

Pamet Harbor

Cape Cod National Seashore

Newcomb Hollow / Cahoon Hollow / LeCount Hollow

Duck Harbor

Wellfleet

Herring River

Great Island

Cape Cod Bay

Wellfleet Harbor

Jeremy Point

Billingsgate Shoal

Sunken Meadow

Cooks Brook Beach

Campground Landing

Nauset Light Beach

Coast Guard Beach

6

Nauset Beach

First Encounter Beach

Town Cove

Rachel Cove

Woods Cove

Brewster Flats

Rock Harbor

Ocean Edge Resort

The River

Nauset Beach

Brewster

Legend

N

—— Primary Roads
— Access Roads
National Seashore
■ Lighthouse

© 2010 Wilderness Adventures Press, Inc.

OUTER BEACHES

Lecounts Hollow is on the southern side of the ocean side of Wellfleet. It's a good early-season beach that features a combination of offshore parallel bars, rip currents, ocean holes, and bull-nosed bars. Most of the fish will hold in the rip currents in between the bars, and others will hold on the outside of the outer bars. As the tide rises, fish will move closer to shore and follow the current line along the beach. Whitecrest has a similar configuration, but the offshore bars are shallow and generate a tremendous swell that makes it a popular beach for surfers. Fishing close to shore on the higher water marks is best at Whitecrest, but don't neglect some of the low-tide fishing when the sand eels are in. Cahoon Hollow, home of the famous Beachcomber Restaurant, is one giant bull-nosed bar on the north side of the parking lot, and on a coming tide on a west wind the fish will move in tight to shore. Anglers need to move around the edges of the bar to find fish, and when there is an abundance of bait you'll find the two corners of the bar that work great. Newcomb Hollow is the last of the Wellfleet oceanfront beaches, and is the more popular among fishermen. The beach is long, with several offshore parallel bars and slots with rip currents. In the spring,

Launch times vary by boat ramp. Check with your local ramp to see if there are any nuances that may affect your launch or haul times. This clock in Wellfleet Harbor is meticulously maintained.

the striped bass hold in the water in between the shore and the bar, and cruise back and forth. Of all the beaches, Newcomb is the best for summer night fishing. Bluefish arrive in July and stay through October. The morning and evening bite is typically the best, and a first light/incoming tide can be outstanding. Floating and intermediate lines are good bets.

Bay Side Beaches

On the bay side are two beaches that are worth fishing. The first is at Duck Harbor and the second extends south past Great Island down to Jeremy Point. Duck Harbor has a series of finger bars, all onshore point bars that extend hundreds of yards out into the bay. The point bars also flatten out into parallel offshore bars, and the summer water is warm enough for wet wading. Anglers typically will move out to the point bars and then across the parallel bars, fishing the adjoining deeper water as they move. Striped bass and bluefish will frequent these areas, and most of the fishing is sight fishing to cruising fish. If you hike out to the end of Great Island, bring a sinking line for the high-dropping tide.

Walking south along the beach you'll find a rocky cobble cove with a sandy point bar. The cove holds striped bass in the eel grass when they move into the grass beds to feed on silversides and grass shrimp. The water drops off quickly, but folks can move along shore and then out into the bay on the point bar. For the shallow water and the flats, a floating or intermediate line is best.

Herring River and the Gut

To get to these beaches, you'll pass over the Herring River and an area called the Gut. Water floods and ebbs from the Herring River on the rising and falling tides, respectively. The bottom is soft and mucky, so move around the sides where it is firmer. There is also a bridge to fish that positions anglers just above the water. You can also wade along the tidal seams when the water is moving, but the Gut is a perfect place for a kayak fishing jaunt. Just over the river is a drive on your left that puts you in a perfect position for launching your craft – you'll be right near the water's edge. The fishing in the Gut is excellent when the herring move in, and the circular cove is protected from the wind on three sides. Occasionally you will find summer bluefish and school bass feeding on silversides, mummichaug, shrimp, and crabs. There are discussions about a river restoration to bring back the natural flow and improve the herring run, but that hasn't happened yet.

Wellfleet Harbor

On the harbor side of Great Island are three worthwhile spots: Smalley Bar, Lieutenant Island, and Blackfish Creek. Smalley Bar is a crescent shaped bar that separates the Inner Harbor from the Outer Harbor. There are several rocks on the north side of the bar that will hold fish, and on the dropping tide a terrific current seam concentrates bait. Most of it is sand, so herring and sand eels are common baitfish. In the spring you'll find striped bass and in the summer, the inside will fill with bluefish. The channel that leads to the harbor separates the end of Smalley Bar from Lieutenant Island and the entrance to Blackfish Creek.

The west end of Lieutenant Island is a combination of large boulders, rocky cobble, sand, and mud. The inside of Lieutenant Island is one of the early school spots, with fish moving into Blackfish Creek on the flood tide and dropping out into the rocks and cobble on the drop. The water warms too much in the summer to hold striped bass, but bluefish do move out front of the island and into the mouth of the creek in the summer. Intermediate lines are good choices.

OUTER BEACHES

Some of the biggest bass on Cape Cod are caught on the Outer Beaches. Historically they are caught on live eels at night, but nowadays, fly rodders do well on 20- to 30-pound bass from shore. The beaches are long with white sand. As they are part of the Cape Cod National Seashore, parking permits are needed during the daytime from Memorial Day until Labor Day. Permits are not needed for night fishing. Due to erosion, some of the beaches have significant drop-offs, and should be limited to anglers in reasonably fit condition. Other beaches are closer to the water, and the walks down to the edge aren't so bad. During the summer season, the beaches are particularly crowded during the day, which makes for difficult fishing. Fishing out here is terrific at night. The off-season is quiet, so getting around isn't too difficult. Anglers stop coming to the Outer Cape in October, but there are still schools of fish migrating through until just about Thanksgiving. In recent years, possibly due to the warm fall weather, the fishing in October has significantly eclipsed that of the traditionally best month, September.

Hint: On a coming tide, the fish move left to right and on a dropping tide, the fish move right to left.

HIGH HEAD

Four-by-fours are the only way to get to High Head. At this section of the cape, you'll find a turbulent area on the Head of the Meadow side, with a sweeping push of an offshore sand bar farther from shore. What this creates is deeper water along the sand, and a giant catcher's mitt. The fish moving into the current often will move into the slot and stay for an extended period. The deeper water stays cool, even in the summer. As you move towards Provincetown, you'll find some outstanding changes in the terrain that keep bait moving.

HEAD OF THE MEADOW

The biggest bass of the fall run historically come off of Head of the Meadow Beach. Head of the Meadow is the last beach before the dramatic end of the cape change. Here, the current strength flattens out the smaller onshore bar systems and creates more of a longer offshore bar. The bars are not parallel, but instead are on an angle so they get closer to shore. Deeper adjoining water forms somewhat of a cove/bathtub, and the fish are either on the outside bars or at your feet. The bars are long, wide and sweeping, and the current moves quickly. Intermediate lines work best.

COAST GUARD BEACH

The limited parking area makes for a relatively quiet beach. There is 4x4 access on the right side of the parking area that allows anglers to drive south towards Long Nook. Out here, you'll find that the onshore bars form a similar reverse 'c' configuration,

Gentle winds and gentle seas along the beaches of the Cape Cod National Seashore. Note the silversides spraying out in the wash, possibly from a bass underneath.

with a slight difference. As the towns move around the outside of the cape, the current gains speed, and cuts troughs on the inside of the 'c'. The deeper water is a perfect staging area for bass, and anglers who fish downstream from the bars do very well. Depending on the tide, you'll either find the fish in tight to shore, in the middle of the bar, or at the outer edge. During calm seas, I like to paddle a kayak to the outer edge of the bars, but that's only to be done on calm seas and soft winds.

Long Nook

As the current runs around the outside bars, they change into onshore bars, usually at a 45-degree angle, but some hook and form what looks like a backwards letter 'c'. The result is a series of bars that you can get way out on, fish the outside, and then fish the inside. You'll need to do that at mid- to lower water, and you'll also need to pick your tides based on the winds. A west wind that is stronger than the current phase is an absolutely great time to be on the beach, as the fish will move into the wind and tight to shore. It's a long drop down the dunes to Long Nook, so it's probably not a good spot for anglers who aren't in good physical condition. There is a nude beach down here as well.

Ballston Beach

At one point in time, the Pamet River ran all the way from bayside to ocean side. It now ends just about at the beach. Most of the bar configuration at Ballston is parallel bars. At the southern end, though, the bar runs closer to shore which creates somewhat of a funnel for bass and blues, particularly on the dropping tide. Begin your fishing at the top of the tide and work south. On the north side is a deeper hole where the end of the bar is cut sharply and forms a rip current. You'll find fish moving around here as well, and moving in to shore along the rip current.

Bay Beaches

Probably one of the most popular areas in Truro is on the bay side, the Pamet River. The river estuary is shallow, probably should be dredged, and it features a public boat ramp. With the natural tidal exchanges, there is what looks like a rounded bull-nosed bar at the mouth. Water covers it at low tide, but not much. The edge surrounding the sand drop-off is deeper, and there are eel grass beds on either side. Striped bass and bluefish will enter the Pamet River on the higher water, and drop out to the mouth as the water column gets skinny. They'll move up towards Provincetown or down towards Wellfleet.

Provincetown

The artistic exuberance that has characterized Provincetown for years makes it a high-energy place that is not for everyone. It's the end of the road, which makes for terrific fishing all season long.

THE BREAKWALL

At the west end of Commercial Street is a breakwall that extends all the way across the top of Provincetown Harbor to Wood End. Water flows through the breakwall and into a series of river systems that form a marsh. The fishing isn't bad on a coming tide, and striped bass and bluefish will move along the harbor edges and up onto the shallower water. The dropping tide is the preferable time to show up on the Breakwall, particularly at night. The water flowing out of the marsh and through the rocks brings shrimp, krill, and crabs into the harbor. Combined with the baitfish of silversides and sand eels, you'll have good fishing for the entire dropping tide. Adventurous anglers will pack some food and water and hike out to the end of the cape. Fishing around the absolute tip, which actually hooks back around, you'll find a deep recess that concentrates fish. Work your way around the outside towards the Wood End lighthouse and you'll find bass and blues moving into the harbor. The entire end of the cape is called Long Point. Use floating lines during low water, and extra-fast-sinking lines on the higher water.

HERRING COVE AND HATCHES HARBOR

There is a tremendously long parking lot that runs along Herring Cove Beach. The sandy beach drops off quickly, and with the proximity to the open ocean there is plenty of current exchange. Striped bass and bluefish move along the beach, and school tuna usually move close to shore. During the spring and summer, you'll have a variety of bait moving in and around, but for the most part, the dominant bait are silverside and sand eels. In the fall, you'll find a smorgasbord of bait, from silversides, sand eels, tinker mackerel, menhaden, peanut bunker, herring, squid, mullet, and butterfish. A half-mile walk towards Race Point is Hatches Harbor. Hatches Harbor is a moderate-sized saltpond. The depth of the pond at high tide is 10 to 14 feet deep, but at low tide the water might be a foot. There are two entrances (and therefore exits) of the water into the pond, and fishing around them is a good idea. Fishing the pond with a kayak can make for outstanding fishing, particularly at night. Seas are usually calm except in the fall when the winds blow from the north.

RACE POINT

Anyone who has read any literature about striped bass fishing, particularly during the fall run, has heard of Race Point. Frank Daignault is renowned for his years spent running the beaches in a 4x4 in pursuit of 'old pajamas' (stripers). You can get to Race Point by foot, but it's a few-mile hike in the sand, so it's best to get an Over-sand Permit. Race Point is the northernmost point of Cape Cod. What makes it interesting is that the bars push very close to shore on both sides of land, thereby creating a natural bowl that concentrates baitfish and predators. Bass and bluefish are the standards, with school tuna making their seasonal appearances. Night fishing is allowed and Race Point has been a historic hotspot for the fall run. Some of the biggest bass of the year are caught around Race Point, and intermediate lines are best.

Martha's Vineyard

The ferry ride from Cape Cod to Martha's Vineyard lasts for an enjoyable 45 minutes. Because of the short distance, there are numerous ferries per day, the cost is affordable even if you're towing a boat, and having a 4x4 vehicle means you can access some of the most historic striper water on the Eastern Seaboard. With its proximity along the Gulf Stream, you'll find abundant pelagic species, from bonito to albies to skipjack and small tuna. The first bonito arrive off of Hedgefence, a reef on the northside of the island.

Martha's Vineyard is about 20 miles long and 10 miles wide with summer water temperatures that climb into the high 60s to low 70s. There are 124.6 miles of tidal shoreline, and it's located 7 miles off the southeast coast of Massachusetts.

Most of the fun is in exploring the island, and here are a few pointers to jumpstart your trip.

- There are six towns on Martha's Vineyard and they are broken down into two classifications: Up Island and Down Island.
- Up Island is basically the western half of the Vineyard, characterized by more wooded and farming areas. The three Up Island towns are West Tisbury, Chilmark (which includes the fishing village Menemsha), and Aquinnah, formerly known as Gay Head.
- Down Island is basically the eastern half of the Vineyard, characterized by more sea-faring towns. The towns are Tisbury (which includes Vineyard Haven and West Chop), Oak Bluffs (which also includes East Chop), and Edgartown (which includes Chappaquiddick and Katama).
- Vineyard Haven is the primary port of entry for visitors and cargo.
- Oak Bluffs is a secondary port of entry for visitors and cargo, and is operated seasonally.
- The Martha's Vineyard Striped Bass and Bluefish Derby was founded in 1946, and is one of the island's best events. The derby begins after Labor Day, and runs until the middle of October. All four species – bass, bluefish, bonito and false albacore – are eligible in a variety of divisions: boat, wade, fly, and conventional, among others. Offseason rates make for a more affordable outing.

- Ferries run to the island from a variety of locations. From the west, the New Bedford-Vineyard Haven Ferry is the quickest route. From the north you've got lots of choices. You can pick from the Falmouth-Edgartown, Falmouth-Oak Bluffs, Woods Hole-Oak Bluffs, or the Woods Hole-Vineyard Haven Ferries. From the east, grab the boat from Hyannis-Oak Bluffs.
- The island's oldest continuously functioning herring run is on tribal land in Aquinnah. It runs from Squibnocket Pond to Menemsha Pond. Another ancient run is at Mattakessett in Edgartown. A herring run at the head of Lagoon Pond and a smaller one at the head of Lake Tashmoo are in operation, too.
- Edgartown has a number of inactive runs. Many are targeted for restoration, so keep an eye out for progress, as they'll develop into excellent fishing spots.

One confusing part is the opening and closing of shoreline ponds. Anglers visiting Martha's Vineyard and Nantucket probably scratch their heads when friends mention spots. The opening and closing of ponds is a long-standing tradition in coastal New England. Early Colonists may have learned the practice of opening shoreline ponds to the sea from local Indians. Anadromous fish were able to move into the saltwater ponds and access the freshwater sections of rivers, streams, and seeps for breeding purposes. I don't know that this was an early "green" movement, as the rationale was two-sided: baitfish and gamefish were easily caught in weirs, nets, or hooks-and-lines in the summer. In the case of the American eel, a common bait of striped bass, Indians cut through the ice in the winter and speared them. These brackish ponds supported oyster beds and low salinities caused by closing the ponds back up helped control oyster predators. These fish and shellfish provided a handy year-round supply of bait and food.

JOSEPH SILVA STATE BEACH, SENGETACKET POND, AND STATE BEACH

One of the consistent year-round fishing spots for a variety of species is the combination of two beaches, two channels, and Sengetacket Pond. In the early season, anglers find striped bass along both beachfronts, in the channels along the jetties, and all the way into the pond. Many bass will filter through the channels and into the pond, thereby making for perfect kayak fishing. Inside the pond you'll find marshes on the northern end, sand/mud shoals in the middle, and pockets on the southern end.

As the water warms, you'll find bluefish moving along the same patterns, and then in August and September, bonito and false albacore will move in. These three species tend not to go all the way into the pond, but instead will stay out along the beachfronts and along the current seams and drop-offs created by the dropping tides. Floating or intermediate lines are best for the area, with maybe an extra-fast-sinking line for working the jetties on a dropping tide. The water is crystal clear and because of its protected position, it doesn't get hit as hard as other parts of the island.

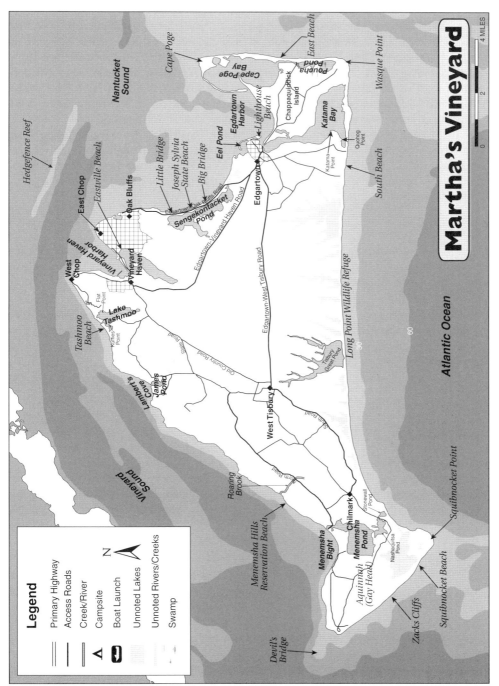

Martha's Vineyard

Legend

Primary Highway	
Access Roads	
Creek/River	
Campsite	N
Boat Launch	
Unnoted Lakes	
Unnoted Rivers/Creeks	
Swamp	

Nantucket Sound

Hedgefence Reef

Cape Poge

East Beach

Cape Poge Bay

Poucha Pond

Wasque Point

Katama Bay

Chappaquidick Island

Quohog Point

Lighthouse Beach

Edgartown Harbor

Eel Pond

Little Bridge

Joseph Sylvia State Beach

Big Bridge

Eastville Beach

East Chop

Oak Bluffs

Edgartown

Katama Point

South Beach

Sengekontacket Pond

Edgartown-Oak Bluffs Road

Edgartown-Vineyard Haven Road

West Chop

Vineyard Haven Harbor

Vineyard Haven

Flat Point

Lake Tashmoo

Tashmoo Beach

Kuffles Point

Sisson Road

Edgartown-West Tisbury Road

Long Point Wildlife Refuge

Tisbury Great Pond

Atlantic Ocean

Lambert's Cove

James Pond

Vineyard Sound

West Tisbury

Old Country Road

South Road

State Road

Roaring Brook

Menemsha Bight

Menemsha Hills Reservation Beach

Chilmark

Menemsha Pond

Stonewall Pond

Nashaquitsa Pond

Squibnocket Point

Aquinnah (Gay Head)

Zacks Cliffs

Squibnocket Beach

Devil's Bridge

0   2   4 MILES

30   60

LITTLE BRIDGE

A popular spot with some local anglers who just want to grab a few minutes of casting before work, this spot – where outgoing water flows into the sound from Sengekontacket Pond – holds plenty of small stripers, especially from May through early June. It's not too crowded, and bonito and albies will sometimes show up in August and September, too. Work your way into the pond on an incoming tide as bass follow the channel and move up onto the shoals and flats on the pond side.

The fishing is getting better as town officials in Oak Bluffs and Edgartown have been working together to find a way to get a pond-dredging project on the southeastern end of the pond underway, in order to improve pond circulation. Nearly 60,000 cubic yards of sand will be taken from the channel between the bridges to refortify town beaches that suffer from erosion.

BIG BRIDGE

Also known as Anthier's Bridge, this is the spot that was featured in the film *Jaws* where the shark goes into the pond. The pond here is Sengekontacket Pond on the Edgartown/Oak Bluffs town line. In the summer, teenagers jump from the bridge into the water, and that can make for tough daytime fishing. However, not many folks are jumping into the early or late season water, which are good times to fish. Night is also a good time to come.

Plenty of big fish are taken here each year. Small bait patterns fished on a floating or sink-tip line work well as there are always sand eels and silversides in there. You'll find a lot of fish on the ocean side of the bridge on an outgoing tide in the spring; the warm water from the pond flows out into the sound. Later in the season, both tides are good. If you are here on a bright afternoon, you may be able to see fish swimming around under the bridge, especially if you stoop low, wear polarized glasses, and shade your eyes.

EEL POND

Eel Pond is where the coastline drops down into Edgartown Harbor, a moderate early-season area. Sand shoals are scattered off of the sand spit that forms the harbor, and the seasonal boat traffic makes for very difficult in-season fishing. Still, when the bait arrives in late April and May, you can have some good wade and kayak fishing for schoolies. You'll also find bluefish in the summer, mostly working along the boats and feeding on silversides at first and last light.

FULLER STREET AND LIGHTHOUSE BEACHES

There is a lot of texture at the mouth of Eel Pond and along Fuller Street Beach and Lighthouse Beach, and you'll find some type of fish around here throughout the season. Schoolie bass and bluefish arrive in April and May, you'll find a mix of bass and blues (more bluefish) in the summer, and then bonito and albies running the edge from Middle Flat into Edgartown Harbor from August to October. If you're fishing along the beaches you'll probably use a floating or intermediate line, and if you're working the deeper water edge going into Edgartown Harbor you may want an extra-fast-sinking line.

CHAPPAQUIDDICK ISLAND

A ferry runs from Edgartown to Chappaquiddick Island. The ride is just across the channel and more time is spent docking and launching than sailing. Regardless, once you get onto the island you have several different places to explore. Fish it by boat, by kayak, or run the beaches with an Over Sand Permit.

Chappaquiddick Island's eastern edge is a barrier beach formed thousands of years ago by offshore currents that deposited tons of sand. Longtime visitors to the Vineyard will remember this area as the Cape Poge Wildlife Refuge. Today this beach extends for 7 miles from Wasque Point past the Cape Poge Lighthouse to the Cape Poge Gut. Tidal waters support extensive salt marshes, especially around Poucha Pond. The Cedars is a grove of century-old, low-growing eastern red cedars sculpted by salt spray and wind. Cape Poge Elbow is home to a gull rookery and nests of piping plovers, least terns, and oyster catchers. West of the dunes lies Cape Poge Bay, where calm, clear waters serve as a nursery for finfish and shellfish. Powerful currents push through the gut, flushing Cape Poge Bay with oxygen-rich water and attracting striped bass, bluefish, bonito, and false albacore.

CHAPPAQUIDDICK BEACH

Chappaquiddick Beach is a great spot for false albacore and an occasional bonito. There is plenty of room here for lots of anglers. In the early and late seasons you'll catch bass and bluefish, and the crowds aren't that packed. Once the funny fish – the pelagic species like bonito, albies, skipjacks, and Spanish macks – arrive, the beach gets very congested, and a little courtesy goes a long way. To avoid the crowds, get to the beach early for the 'first-light bite'. Boat traffic gets heavy around mid-morning, an important point to remember when you're fighting a hard-running fish. Larger patterns match the early-season baitfish and are replaced by smaller patterns during the mid- to late season. You can paddle a kayak from Edgartown Light or take the Chappy Ferry across the Edgartown Channel, and walk to the left.

CAPE POGE / CAPE POGE GUT / CAPE POGE BAY

Cape Poge can be reached by 4x4, boat, or kayak. The ebb and flow of the tides has created shallow shoals at the mouth, and the beach runs seemingly forever on the north side of the island. Neck Road ends at John Oliver Point. The fish trade back and forth on the tide and follow the structure into the bay. Around the gut, you'll find bass, blues, albies, and bonito during the late summer and fall. It's a good spot to get a slam, and floating lines are good choices. Inside the bay, you'll tend to find stripers and bluefish – the bass during the early through mid-season and bluefish later in the season. Off of Lighthouse Road is Shear Pen Pond, a small pond that connects with the bay and the landmass below it, called Little Neck. Cape Poge Bay runs south and under Dyke Bridge and forms Poucha Pond. You'll find some flats around here which offer good sight-fishing opportunities. Other productive flats lie off of Cape Poge, to the east of Edgartown at Cape Poge Bay, on the inside of Chappaquiddick Harbor, and off of Chappaquiddick Beach. There are others in the area too, and a floating or sink-tip line will work well on the flats.

Cape Poge Gut is a very popular spot for both flyfishers and surfcasters alike. There is a blend of deep water with sloping structure, and combinations of fast currents, back eddies, and slow currents. Cape Poge Gut is a natural inlet to Cape Poge Bay and is a great conductor of bait that drains off the flats on both sides of the inlet. In the early and mid-season, you'll find striped bass and bluefish. As the water temperature warms, target striped bass at night. Many anglers will work the flats and the edges on the inside of Cape Poge Bay. Incoming tides bring the fish out of the deeper water and onto the flats to feed, and you'll also find them dropping off the flats into the deeper water on an ebb tide. Bring an extra-fast-sinking shooting head for the deeper water.

Many flyfishermen and light-tackle enthusiasts head to the gut in mid- to late August when the warm water brings bonito and false albacore into the area, and it's a good spot for a slam. First light, particularly on an incoming tide, is a good time

Bonito have a bright green stripe that runs from their neck to their tail, and stripes that run from their back to their belly. This one was taken off of Martha's Vineyard's Cape Poge.

and tide for the spot. The fishing can be so consistent that some anglers call it 'Albie Alley'. Small silversides, sand eels, and anchovy patterns are good, either tied flatwing style or Deceiver style. Mushmouths are also popular patterns. Floating or extra-fast-sinking lines are the most popular selections. Techniques vary between straight cast and retrieve with dead drifting or greased-line swings. Winds can complicate the spot, with west/southwest being ideal and east/northeast being difficult as there is no lee. The water is clear and if bonito or albies aren't hitting your fly, change or fish a dropper rig to find out what they're eating.

To get to Cape Poge, take Chappaquiddick Road to Dyke Road. There is a tire inflation air station here, and you'll be able to head to the north to fish all the outside ocean water up to Cape Poge Lighthouse, round the corner and head along Cape Poge Elbow, and even continue south to the end at Cape Poge Gut. You can also work on the inside of Cape Poge Bay, and head past Shear Pen Pond, Little Neck, and Drunkard's Cove.

A second way to go from the airstation is south toward Wasque and Wasque Point. Most of the driving is along the beach, basically because of the marshy areas along Poucha Pond.

Admission Fees & Permits

From May 30 to October 15: Trustees members free. Nonmembers: adult $3, child (15 & under) free. Free to pedestrians at other times of the year. Over-sand vehicle permit fees: $180. One Trustees of Reservations complimentary family-level membership is included with your Over-sand Vehicle Permit purchase. Permit is valid April 1 to March 31 and can be purchased from patrolling ranger or gatehouse attendant May 30 to October 15, daily, 9:00am-5:00pm. Membership in the Trustees of Reservations is not transferable, and member cards may not be used by nonmembers.

SOFT SIDE

Cape Poge Pond empties through this sluiceway. Most anglers will fish this area on an incoming tide, but it can also fish well on a dropping tide. The sluiceway bottlenecks and concentrates the current (thereby making for an excellent flow) while the depth changes give fish an edge to follow. In the early season you'll find bass that then get replaced by blues that then are joined by albies and bonito. First and last light are good times to fish. If you don't catch a fish, no matter; you'll be in one of the prettiest places on the Eastern Seaboard.

NORTH NECK (HARD SIDE)

North Neck/Hard Side is accessible by taking a left on North Neck Road which is about a mile after you get off the ferry. If you follow it to the end, you'll find a small parking lot that holds about ten properly parked cars. From there, you can walk up and over a small cliff where you'll find a stairway. Take the stairway down to the beach.

With such limited parking, this spot fills up quickly...and stays filled up for the day. If you really want to fish here, the best plan is to get up early and get your place. Both tides fish well, and you'll find striped bass in the early-mid-season, then bluefish, then bonito and albies. The bass seem to favor the dropping tide while the other fish respond to both tides. Try heading out to the deeper channel on the east side of the dock. This property is owned by the Martha's Vineyard Land Bank. No fees are charged, no permits are required, but please make sure you leave it cleaner than you found it so that fishing access isn't lost.

East Beach/Dyke Bridge/Poucha Pond

Dyke Road is the one route to East Beach. At Dyke Bridge, you'll find the top of Poucha Pond. Wade fishermen can get around the pond easily enough, but the best way to cover the deeper water middle, the sand shoals and points near the bridge, and get to the main section of the pond to the south is by kayak. In the early season through the end of June, you'll find striped bass moving around the pond. Most of the fishing is in shallower water or on the surface, so a floating line is ideal. Add a split shot for an increase in depth. If you're fishing out of a kayak on a bright sunny day you may want to bring along a sink tip for the deeper water. There are creeks, ditches, and grassy banks, and night fishing on a dropping tide can be a good time.

Across the sand from Poucha Pond and extending to the north is the renamed East Beach. The beach is well known for all four species of fish, and is a great early-season bass and bluefish spot and a solid summer season bonito and albie spot. You'll be hard pressed to find a prettier area on the eastern seaboard. Towards the southern end, you'll find sand spits running perpendicular to the beach, perfect for bringing the fish in close to your feet. Floating and intermediate lines work best, and the water is clear enough to sight cast around low tide.

Wasque Point

There is a big rip at Wasque Point that stems from the current dropping down from along East Beach. You'll find that rip on the dropping tide. Bass show up when the herring arrive, and you'll also find a lot of squid in May. June brings smaller bait, sand eels, silversides, and also bluefish. While some areas hold bass and blues together it seems as if the bass move out along Wasque when the blues move in. As the water warms in August and September, you'll also find bonito, Spanish mackerel, and albies working the rip current along the drop-off. You might like a sinking line to offset the current speed.

Katama Bay

Back in 2007, the Patriot's Day Storm that opened a section of Nauset Beach also broke open a section of Katama Bay. The 300-yard-wide, 20-foot-deep break in the barrier beach at Norton Point that appeared April 18 brought improved water quality, fishing, and shellfishing to Katama Bay. The new break sends cold, clean water shooting far up into the bay at three times the speed of water coming through the tiny opening at Chappaquiddick Point. There had been a number of flats and sandy shoals in the area where the beach break occurred, but they have been purged due to the increased current. That's not a bad thing, for there are still other flats that are easily reached by kayaks and by wade fishing that offer great early-season sight-fishing opportunities. Bring along a sink-tip line for the channel edges and a floating line for the shallower water.

SOUTH BEACH

South Beach is known interchangeably as Katama Beach, or sometimes it's called South Beach at Katama. Down here you'll find one of two beaches that is open to the public for 4x4 driving. There are 3 miles of barrier beach located on the island's south shore at the end of Katama Road with a big saltpond up inside.

You'll find excellent surf on the south side with views of Katama Bay. As with most beaches that have parallel offshore bars, the fishing can be really good on the first few hours of the flood tide when there is a lot of current moving in between the bars and the beach. Strong winds make for a big sea, and for that very reason, you'll share South Beach with surfers. During those winds, head to the inside of the pond. There are a number of flats from Quohog Point to the cut and they extend north to Katama Point. Water clarity is usually very good. Channel cuts run in the bay. It's a good place to fish from a kayak, too. Floating and extra-fast-sinking shooting heads will get you on most of the fish in most spots. During the fall you've got a good chance for a slam.

South Beach is a very popular summertime beach, which makes it a better early- and late-season daytime spot, or a full-season night-fishing spot. Parking is usually available at South Beach.

LONG POINT WILDLIFE REFUGE

At more than 600 acres, Long Point is one of the largest publicly accessible properties on Martha's Vineyard. Hours of operation are from mid-June to mid-September: 9:00am to 5:00pm (last admission at 5:00pm; gate closes at 6:00pm). Mid-September to mid-June: daily, sunrise to sunset. There are 2.1 miles of trails that run through the refuge, but of interest to anglers is the amount of excellent water to fish. At Long Point you'll find several ponds surrounding the refuge: Tisbury Great Pond and its coves, Town Cove, Tiah Cove, Deep Bottom Cove, Middle Point Cove, Long Cove Pond, and Big Homer's Pond are within the refuge but don't connect with Tisbury Great Pond and therefore don't have saltwater gamefish (but if you have a freshwater license you can catch a largemouth bass and a striped bass in approximately the same area). With freshwater seeps in the saltwater coves, you'll find herring and alewives in the spring, American eels, sand eels, shrimp, and whole host of other baitfish. Look for striped bass in the early through mid-season. As the water temperatures warm, the swimming is good but the fishing slows down and becomes more of a night game. Floating lines fished out of a kayak are a great combination, and if you arrive by vehicle be sure to head out at sunset. Tisbury Great Pond is opened to allow anadromous fish to enter for breeding purposes. The pond may open and close multiple times during the year, and when the bait and fish dump out in the fall you can have epic fishing.

SQUIBNOCKET POINT

Squibby is one of the historically favored fishing spots on Martha's Vineyard. It's not an easy place to fish for two reasons: access due to private property and the strong currents blowing over a tough terrain.

There are several different parts to this southwest corner of the island, and you can get to Squibnocket by taking State Road to South Road. Once at the beach you'll find parking for about fifteen cars, so getting there early or late is a good idea. There are three clusters of rock piles which is ideal striped-bass structure. Some large coves run in between them. In the fall the bait stacks up in the coves and makes for some of the best fishing on the island.

What makes the fishing so good is the combination of rocks, coves, and constant surf. The footing along those rocks can be precarious in the dim light of night, what with the mossy, seaweed-coated rocks. When the surf's up, the footing can be tricky, so Korkers are essential, as is a fishing partner and a headlamp – the partner to keep an eye on you, you to keep an eye on him or her. Some of the very best striped bass fishing takes place here at night, so make sure you arrive before sundown to get a good lay of the land.

At high tide there isn't much beach. The water just beyond the rocks drops off from 6 feet to 15 feet at low tide, so the temptation is to go far out and to stand on a rock at low tide. If you're a rock hopper, dress for the occasion and wear a wet suit and swim out. Spring and summer's prevailing southwest winds can stack up the seas quite a bit, so exercise caution, particularly at night. Incoming tides bring fish closer, but wade anglers can't stay far out for very long. Intermediate or extra-fast-sinking lines are ideal.

Between the rocks at the point and the rocks along Zacks Cliffs is Squibnocket Beach. Squibnocket Beach, on the south shore, is a narrow stretch of boulder-strewn coastline that is part smooth rocks and pebbles, part fine sand. The area has good waves, and it's popular with surfers. During the season, this beach is restricted to residents and visitors with passes. The dunes drop down quickly, and there are some large boulders in the water that drops off quickly. Change is constant due to the strong currents, and the beach erodes at a foot and a half per year.

Squibnocket is not for the faint of heart as it's a tough spot to fish and the surf can be strong. Night fishing is the best time to fish here, and you'll see lots of surfcasts tossing Danny Plugs. Some anglers do well in front of the parking lot while others head to the mussel bar to the right around low tide. Many anglers head to the well-known Squibnocket Bass Stand which is best fished with a friend. The shoreline makes for tough walking.

AQUINNAH (GAY HEAD)

Gay Head Lighthouse was authorized by President John Quincy Adams to mark the treacherous offshore shoal, Devil's Bridge, at the entrance to Vineyard Sound. Many anglers know the area as Gay Head, but the name was officially changed to Aquinnah, from the Wampanoag language meaning "the shore or end of the island below the cliffs." And that is where the best fishing is, particularly at night.

The cliffs rise some 150 to 200 feet above the ocean. Through erosion there are large boulders, rocks, bowls, holes, and beach all on this southwestern tip of the Vineyard. In May and June, you'll find striped bass and a mix of bass and blues in the summer and early fall. Look for deep water in between the sand and rocks. As you walk under the cliffs, start fishing as soon as the lighthouse comes into view. It's a long walk, but worth it. Intermediate lines are good, but if you're fishing the higher water tides you might want to get more depth, and a sinking line will do the trick. Big flies out here are good, and Devil's Bridge is a good place to fish a Razzle Dazzle.

Boat fishermen like Devil's Bridge for bass and blues during the early through mid-season, and will also find bonito and false albacore running the edges of the shoal in the fall. The shoal is about a half mile off shore, with lots of rocks and current in between. The shoal closest to shore runs at 2 to 3 feet deep at low tide, while at the opposite end the depth is about 17 feet. Watch your lower unit as the depth of the shoal varies, and fishing it at the high dropping tide is great.

As with all types of fishing, fly selection is sometimes tricky. It's a mystery how a fish will attack a bait that is nearly as large as itself, but sometimes that is the case off of Devil's Bridge on Martha's Vineyard.

LOBSTERVILLE BEACH

Lobsterville Beach can be standing room only from the time that the striped bass arrive in June until they depart in October. As the season progresses, the fishing gets better with bluefish, bonito, and false albacore adding to the mix. Most anglers will hit the beach and walk to Dogfish Bar that is to the left of the Town Beach. Or, they will walk to the right for about a mile or so to the jetties. The beach is one large bowl that serves as a catcher's mitt for any of the variety of baitfish. The water is clear, and the drop-offs are gradual, making for a good spot for floating or intermediate lines.

One of the interesting parts of Lobsterville Beach is that you can catch all four species in one day. From bass at night to bluefish at first light to bonito and albies during the day, the spot is a good one if you're trying for a slam. September is the month to do it. Stripers and bluefish arrive here beginning in late May, and continue on through the summer. June is the best month for consistent action and the reason is the arrival of the sand eels. You'll see a mix of 1.5-inch-long juveniles to 4- to 6-inch adults. First and last light or night fishing are the best times to head to Lobsterville Beach, but the fishing can also be good during the day time. The water is so clear that sightfishing frequently occurs. False albacore run the beach starting in mid- to late September, and with bluefish on the beach it's a good spot for a slam. Bonito also run the beaches and into the jetty at the east end of the beach. A good way to start fishing is at the middle of the bowl formed by the curve of the beach and then move up to the jetty. Both sides of the jetties get a lot of play, but you'll have to access the east side from Menemsha. They're hot spots for wade anglers when the bonito and the albies are in. The dropping tide sets up a hard current that the speedy fish love, and the sand eels, anchovies, and silversides concentrate along the drop-offs. It's standing room only and can get a bit tricky when multiple fish are hooked. Add to the mix the occasional mixed bag of bluefish and you can have quite show on your hands.

You'll see the first fish moving along the beach and into Menemsha Pond when the herring arrive. The island's oldest continuously functioning herring run is on tribal land in Aquinnah. It runs from Squibnocket Pond to Menemsha Pond, so early season is an excellent time to look for stripers along Lobsterville Beach and into Menemsha Pond. The converse is true, too, so when their herring fry drop out of the ponds in the fall (glass minnows) you'll find the fish feasting on the inch-long bait. The herring run is on the southwest corner of the pond.

The fishing really heats up in May with the arrival of silversides and more significantly in June with the arrival of the sand eels. Crowds tend to pack up along the beach when the word gets out, but the feeling is one of a fishing fraternity more than that of a combat zone. First and last light are great times and fishing up the moon at night is excellent.

Menemsha Pond is excellent if you have a kayak. On the east side you'll see dock fingers with boats. At night there are striped bass popping on the surface, usually spraying silversides all around. There is an old creek on this side called Mememsha Creek.

There is a boat basin that separates the beach from the pond, and as you pass around it you'll see the remains of a boat. That boat is the Orca, and was used when filming the ledgendary movie *Jaws*. There is a sandbar that is perpendicular to the point which makes for accessible wade fishing on both phases of the low-water marks. You'll find bass popping at night, particularly on a dropping tide, and squid also fill the harbor. If you're fishing the flood tide then remember there is a deep trough near shore that you'll need to cross.

At the southeastern end of Menemsha Pond there are two other ponds, Nashaquitsa Pond and Stonewall Pond. You'll find a lot of boat traffic in Nashaquitsa Pond, as there are a number of moorings on the northeastern and southwestern points of the pond. The boat traffic can make for difficult fishing, but take a poke in the evening, particularly from a kayak. It's a protected area and makes for a good spring spot, but it gets warm during mid-season. A floating line is sufficient up here. Use a kayak - much of the land is private.

MENEMSHA HILLS RESERVATION

If you're looking to combine hiking and fishing, then the Menemsha Hills Reservation is for you. There are 234 acres of conservation land that is part of the Trustees of Reservations, and room for 20 cars in the parking lot. You can pass by Prospect Hill, the second highest elevation on the Vineyard at 300 feet above sea level while en route to a beach that virtually no one fishes, even during tourist season. The southwest corner of the reservation is one expansive, cobble beach, with a sharp drop-off. On the northeast corner you'll find boulders and the Great Sand Cliffs are near Roaring Brook. Steeple casts work best, and floating or intermediate lines get the nod. The reservation attracts some anglers during the fall when baitfish stages. No night fishing is allowed. The last three or four hours of either tide produce well here.

LAMBERT'S COVE

There were some parking changes in 2008 that negatively impacted Lambert's Cove. The net is that the cost went up and the number of spaces went down. Nowadays, a limited number of night-fishing parking permits are issued for fishing at Lambert's Cove Beach. The passes are free and anglers can park in the lot from 9:00pm to 7:00am. It goes without saying that the regulations will get more strict if the area gets abused. Applications are available at the new Park and Recreation shed at the West Tisbury School tennis courts on Monday through Friday from 9:00am until 12:00pm and on Friday, Saturday, and Sundays from 4:00 to 7:00pm. Inspite of all the commotion, Lambert's Cove is one great place to fish. It's popular in the off-season, particularly because that's when the fishing is best. Staying in one of the bed & breakfasts, inns, or renting a house solves the access issue.

Lambert's Cove is formed by Makonikey Head to the northeast and Paul Point at the southwest. During the quarter moons in the fall, you'll find great concentrations of baitfish in the cove. There is a pond, James Pond, that has a narrow and winding opening to Vineyard Sound at Lambert's Cove beach. It has been managed for herring, which makes for good early and late season fishing. You'll find a host of baitfish in the cove, from silversides, sand eels, and squid throughout the season to peanut bunker and anchovies in the fall. Floating and intermediate lines are ideal, and you'll find all four species of fish around during August and September. From Makonikey Head to Norton Point is a nice stretch of sand mixed with boulders and rocks.

TASHMOO BEACH AND LAKE

Lake Tashmoo is a tidal pond with a depth of up to 12 feet below mean sea level. Fresh water enters the pond at its southern end, as well as from groundwater-fed springs, the pond connects to Vineyard Sound through a man-made channel. There is a breakwall on either side of the channel.

The inlet is a popular spot, mostly because it holds a lot of small bass and blues. When the winds are blowing from the south, the inlet is protected which makes for easy casting, too. There are flats on both sides of the entrance and then as you move into the pond the depths increase. On a flood tide, they'll move onto the flats and then closer to the shoreline edges. Around Kuffies Point and Flat Point the water gets deeper. Floating lines with a pinch of shot are enough. In the spring you'll find alewives and herring, silversides and shrimp. Tashmoo also has a strong worm hatch that begins in mid-May and lasts for as long as two weeks. You'll see the worms begin to swarm in the late afternoon and continue until dusk. The hatch tapers off when the sun goes down, but then it picks up again and goes for a lot of the night. Bring many different worm patterns, for the fish can be selective. Cast around the edges of the worms so your fly will stand out a bit more. If you cast into the middle of the worms your fly will usually get lost. Dropper rigs with several patterns fished on a floating line are the best idea for finding what the fish want. Wade anglers typically fish to either the right or to the left of the boat ramp and kayak anglers are able to get better access to the fish and have better success.

Tashmoo is another wade spot where anglers can catch a 'Vineyard Slam'. Around the end of July you'll see bonito showing up at the inlet. You'll see them on either tide, dropping or coming, and they typically are eating smaller bait and squid. False albacore usually show up in mid-September. Hardtail junkies like the last three hours of the incoming tide when it coincides with first light, but that doesn't always hold true. You'll find bluefish outside of the inlet from the mid-season until the water cools off in the fall. Poppers and sliders are good choices when they're blitzing on the surface.

WEST CHOP

The Sheriff's Meadow Foundation owns a small parcel of land around the east side of West Chop called West Chop Woods. Anglers can access the shoreline just below it. Parking is just off of Franklin Street. Most of the property around West Chop is private and heavily monitored, so you'll need to work the average low-tide reaches. There is some structure that is worth fishing. First and last light coming tides are good times to fish, and a floating or intermediate line works well.

EASTVILLE BEACH

Across the way on East Chop is Eastville Beach and its jetty. The jetty is not that popular for bass and blues, but it does get a lot of attention from shore anglers looking to catch bonito and albies in the fall. Higher water marks such as the last few hours of the flood tide through the first few hours of the dropping tide seem to fish better than the lower water marks. The jetty slows down currents so there usually is a lot of bait along the edges.

Anglers targeting bass and blues tend to fish Eastville Beach more than the jetty. The small beach tends to hold smaller fish and good numbers of them. So if you're looking for lots of action or you have some kids who need to catch some fish, Eastville Beach is a good spot. Most of the bass will feed on smaller bait like silversides and sand eels, and floating or sink-tip lines work well. The spot holds fish from spring through fall. This area is a good place to try for a slam in the fall, with bass and blues on the beach and albies and bonito on the adjoining jetty.

Using a kayak as transportation makes sense to access hard-to-reach areas. Cabe Loring finds a legal striped bass along a grassy cove in Martha's Vineyard's Tashmoo Pond.

Spotlight:
The Martha's Vineyard Derby

One of the most celebrated fishing events on the East Coast occurs during September and October, the Martha's Vineyard Striped Bass and Bluefish Derby. It began in 1946 and was the creation of the late Al Brickman and Nat Sperber. The concept was to bring more visitors to the Vineyard during the offseason, to celebrate the phenomenal fall fishing, for commeraderie, and for fun prizes. Headquartered at the Martha's Vineyard Rod and Gun Club, the derby is a mixture of islanders and off-islanders and has been the subject of many articles and books. The competition is open to boat and wade, adults and children, fly and all tackle, for striped bass, bluefish, bonito, and false albacore. Top prize is a Boston Whaler boat, motor, and trailer. In that first year, the largest striped bass was caught amid the surf by Thomas L. Flynn – a 35-pounder. Today's derby attracts fishermen from all around the world and participation in recent years has approached or touched 2,000, and over $70,000 in donations have gone to islanders for the purpose of educational scholarships. Trying to find a fishing guide during the Derby can be a challenge, so book a charter well in advance. Many of the charter captains fish the derby, too. To follow the action or more information, check out www.mvderby.com. The website also features an online Derby Board of daily winners through leaders.

Nantucket

Nantucket has a nickname – the Gray Lady. Visitors know that the gray comes from being socked in fog and the lady from her dignified status that stems from a rich, whaling heritage. The water surrounding the island is known as Nantucket Sound, which is basically a triangle that runs offshore from the continent. The boundaries are Cape Cod to the north, Nantucket to the south, and Martha's Vineyard to the west. It gets a bit confusing on the western end for Vineyard Sound adjoins Nantucket Sound. The easy way to remember the difference is that Nantucket Island through Hyannis is in Nantucket Sound, and points to the west are in Vineyard Sound.

Striped bass begin to infiltrate Nantucket Sound and Nantucket Island in late April/early May. They continue to arrive with each passing week, and the bluefish usually make their initial appearance during the middle to end of May. Fishing for bass and blues is terrific through the end of June. At that time, the Gulf Stream has pushed closer to shore and the bass fishing becomes a night game as well as a rip/deeper water game. The most popular rips are McBlair's Rip and Fishing Rip. The temperature of the water in these deeper rips generally stays in the low 60s, and they fish best on a dropping tide. This warmer water does carry a fringe benefit as the bluefish are joined by bonito which arrive in mid-July. Anglers on Nantucket always seem to have some species of fish to catch.

As the water continues to warm up throughout August, other pelagic fish arrive. Spanish mackerel, false albcore, school bluefin tuna, and mahi mahi all come close to the island. With the island's distance from the mainland, there is a robust offshore fishery for white marlin, yellow and bluefin tuna, blue, thresher, dusky, tiger and mako shark. Some fly rodders target blue sharks with chum slicks, but most of the fly rodders focus on the inshore waters as well as Nantucket's 82 miles of beaches.

As mentioned above, the opening and closing of the shoreline ponds is a common practice on Martha's Vineyard and Nantucket. The opening and closing of ponds is a long-standing tradition in coastal New England. Early Colonists may have learned the practice of opening shoreline ponds to the sea from local Indians. Anadromous fish were able to move into the saltwater ponds and access the freshwater sections of rivers, streams, and seeps for breeding purposes. I don't know that this was an early "green" movement, as the rationale was two-sided: baitfish and gamefish were easily caught in weirs, nets, or hooks-and-lines in the summer. In the case of the American

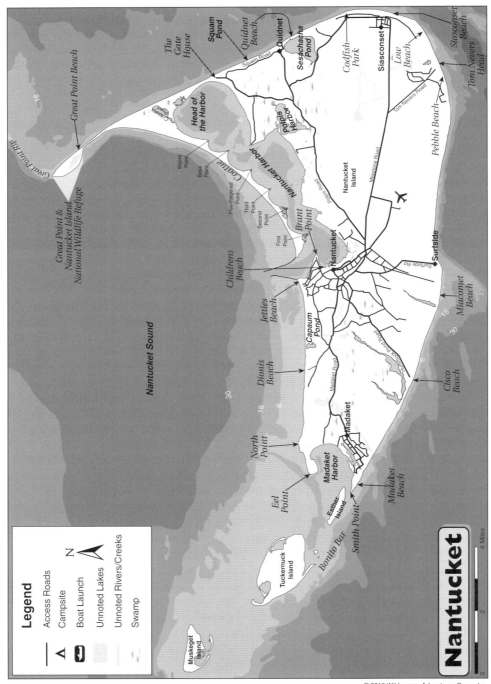

Legend

Access Roads

Campsite

Boat Launch

Unnoted Lakes

Unnoted Rivers/Creeks

Swamp

N

Nantucket

0   2   4 Miles

© 2010 Wilderness Adventures Press, Inc.

eel, a common bait of striped bass, Indians cut through the ice in the winter and speared them. These brackish ponds supported oyster beds and low salinities caused by closing the ponds back up helped control oyster predators. These fish and shellfish provided a handy year-round supply of bait and food.

With regard to Nantucket, the practice of opening ponds is well into its third century. In 1665, colonial settlers and Indians cooperated to dig a permanent ditch from Long Pond to the nearby saltwater at Hither Creek. Later, in the May 1876 issue of the Inquirer and Mirror there was the first mention of a pond opening during a storm which created a breach in a barrier beach. The six major coastal ponds on Nantucket (Squam, Sesachacha, Tom Nevers, Miacomet, Hummock, and Capaum) have all been opened to the sea on a more-or-less regular basis. Until 1933, pond opening was an informal process, accomplished by groups of fishermen working together to dig ditches when pond levels were high enough to provide sufficient "head" for eroding substantial channels. These days it is more mechanized, but there are a few pointers. First, if you're around during the opening of one of the ponds, expect large amounts of bait to push through and the predators to be waiting. Second, if you're around when the bait is draining out of the ponds, you'll find predators waiting at the entrances. Nature has a way of bringing baitfish and predators together, and your local island sources will be able to describe the process in greater detail.

If you're trailering a boat on the island, you'll head to one of two launch sites. The first spot is in town near the ferry dock at Childrens Beach. This is the best spot for accessing the northern side of Nantucket Island. If you're planning on fishing the south side of the island head to Madaket Public Landing, which is on the south end of the island. To save on confusion, the ramp is also known as the Walter Barrett Public Pier, and is on F Street off Madaket Road. The ramp accesses Hither Creek, which flows into Madaket Harbor.

Town of Nantucket Beach Permits

The Town of Nantucket requires stickers for driving on the beach. You can buy permits at the police department and they are valid on a calendar year from January 1 to December 31. Rules, regulations, and a map of beaches that are open to driving accompany every permit which makes getting out on to the beach an easy next step. During the summer, running the beaches is restrictive due to the increased traffic and the nesting shore birds. Most recently, anglers have had to contend with the closing of some of the best angling spots. Smith and Eel Points and Miacomet Beach have been closed due to erosion. No worries. Savvy anglers follow the traditions from the 1940s and add a kayak to their rig. For instance, drive as far as you can towards Smith and Eel Points, toss your boat in the drink, and paddle the rest of the way. Add a line to your kayak and you can get out and wet wade. The possibilities are endless, even if some beaches are closed.

GREAT POINT RIP, GREAT POINT BEACH, AND THE NANTUCKET NATIONAL WILDLIFE REFUGE

The Nantucket National Wildlife Refuge consists of the northeast tip of Nantucket, known as Great Point. The 24-acre Nantucket refuge's particular purpose is, "carrying out the migratory bird act". The refuge is open to the public for fishing and over-sand driving. Access ain't easy, and there are no roads to cross, just about 5 miles of sand. Four-by-four use requires a permit ($125 for the season) from the Trustees of Reservations since you must cross their property to reach the refuge. The Trustees of Reservations owns the land immediately adjacent to Great Point, known as the Coskata-Cotue Refuge. The sand on the way to Great Point is mostly firm, which makes for easy driving.

Once you finally get to the end, you'll notice that the terrain is similar to Block Island's North Rip. The strong and diverse currents have created a bar structure with deeper water on both sides with a long bar off the top that forms a rip during incoming and outgoing tides. You'll find bass and bluefish at Great Point from the time they arrive in the spring until the time they depart in the fall. You'll also find bonito and false albacore in late July through October. Their numbers are not as great as in other areas, and boat anglers fare better with the hardtails than shore-bound anglers. Great Point Beach runs along the eastern side. Extra-fast-sinking lines are commonly used when fishing the rip due to the strong currents.

THE GATE HOUSE

Squam Road runs along the eastern shore and ends at the Wauwinet Gate House. This is the only way in to the wildlife refuge, but also serves as an access point anglers who don't have a 4x4. You can leave your vehicle in the parking area and hike in to fish either the east side or the west side. Standard park rules and regulations are found on websites maintained by several land trust foundations.

Coatue is the barrier beach that runs southwest from Great Point and forms Nantucket's inner harbor. The sand at Coatue is far softer than it is at Great Point, which makes for trickier driving. If you're a novice at running beaches, it might make sense to cut your teeth elsewhere. On the ocean side, you'll find mostly beach break, with bass and blues around for the majority of the season, and albies and bonito buzzing the beach as well as the channel formed by Coatue and Brant Points. The current sweeping along the beach and down to the point makes for excellent fishing. Sand eels are common throughout the entire season. On the inside of Cotue in Nantucket Harbor are a series of points and over 1,000 acres of flats. Some of the points are conveniently numbered, with First Point beginning at Coatue Point and moving eastward to Second Point, Third Point, Five Fingered Point, Bass Point, and Wyers Point. At the end of the line is Head of the Harbor. Within most of these points is skinny water with sand flats that hold fish in the early through mid-season. Flood tides fish well as do the last few of the drop. Boat traffic and warmer water temperatures tend to slow down the mid- to late season fishing inside the harbor. At the northwestern corner of Head of the Harbor is Coskata Pond, which is a lagoon with a sandy/muddy bottom that holds bass in the early season. There is a long channel that connects Nantucket Harbor with the pond, so you'll find staged fish in the harbor on lower water and they'll move into the pond on the flood tide. The dropping tide is the best time to fish here, for the bait will be concentrated. You'll see a wide variety of bait, from herring to silversides, sand eels, and shrimp. For flats fishing the latter two hours of the dropping tide and the first few of the flood tide are best. Floating lines get the nod.

Across the harbor from Five Fingered Point is Pocomo Head and Polpis Harbor. Here you'll find a different terrain, with more grasses that are commonly associated with a marsh/estuary system. You'll find bass moving around the openings on the dropping tides, particularly during the early season and at night. Try some shrimp and crab patterns.

SESACHACHA POND

Sesachacha Pond, on the eastern side of Nantucket, is separated from the Atlantic Ocean by a narrow barrier beach. It is a large pond of about 280 acres that throughout history has been opened to the ocean. The pond is one of the areas targeted for research and improvement by the Mass Insight Corporate that seeks to improve water quality and overall habitat conditions. You'll see dramatic improvements in the fishing at Sesachacha Pond in the near future. The town opens Sesachacha Pond in the spring and fall to resalt, clean out, and re-oxygenate. Winter flounder, sea bass,

School fish, like this bonito off of Nantucket's Bonito Bar, swim quickly and feed aggressively along current seams and drop-offs. One fish splashes on the surface while a second one feeds below.

blueback herring, American eels, oysters, soft-shell clams, and other baitfish thrive in the pond. After the pond is opened and baitfish pour out is an excellent time to fish at the opening, which is Quident Beach. Quident Beach is a good early through mid-season spot and then again later in the season. The beach is popular among families so daytime fishing is tough, but first light and last light/night are good times to go.

SIASCONSET BEACH

To sound like you didn't just walk off the high-speed ferry, pronounce the town "scon-sit". There are about 70 or so houses along the beach, and the town was originally a fishing village. Located at the end of Milestone Road, this beach has heavy surf and faces erosion problems similar to other eastern shore beaches (like the Outer Beaches on Cape Cod). Early-season striped bass can be found along the beach break. Around mid-season, the first of the seasonal bluefish blitzes begin, and you'll find them at first and last light. There is a new beach initiative program called the Beach Nourishment Project that will cover less than five percent of the cobble habitat in the project area. The BNP includes plans to reduce erosion by building new reef habitat and supplying replacement cobble habitat directly offsetting the covered cobble. Stay tuned for more updates. While you're there, fish the last three hours of the dropping tide and the first three hours of the flood tide with an intermediate line. Switch to a floating line if the fish show on top.

CODFISH PARK

Just below Sankaty Head on the mid-eastern stretch of the island, Codfish Park has been subjected to erosion from the strong and sweeping currents. This area slated for reconstruction projects that could dramatically improve the terrain, and therefore the fishing. One project calls for three acre-sized plots of cobble rock and concrete reef balls, 2 to 3 feet in diameter, to be placed some 500 feet off shore. Three additional acre-sized plots of the same materials would also be placed about 1,000 feet off shore. The rock garden would significantly stabilize the beach and keep it from eroding. A second option is to rebuild 3 miles of beach which runs from Sankaty down to Codfish Park with 1.9 million cubic yards of sand dredged from about 3 miles from shore. These two initaitves are important to watch, for they could become the new island hot spots.

Currently the beach break and moderate depths attract striped bass and bluefish. The water moves quickly along shore, and whereas a floating or intermediate line would get the call, many fly rodders step to a sink tip or an extra-fast-sinking shooting head.

LOW BEACH

As with Codfish Park, erosion is a problem at Low Beach, with an average of 9 feet of sand per year disappearing. Currents are strong on Low Beach. You'll find decent early-season bass fishing and good summer bluefishing at Low Beach. Over here try a sinking line due to the strong currents.

TOM NEVERS

From 1955 to 1976, Tom Nevers was a submarine listening base that was owned by the U.S. Navy. Though originally used for bombing practice during World War II, this tract of land offers good access to the long, sloping beaches on the South Shore. Tom Nevers Road ends at Tom Nevers Head, and the best fishing is in the southwest corner of the old Navy Base. From the oceanfront work your way to the west, which is where you'll find Pebble Beach. The area is mostly sand, with deep water, strong currents, and heavy surf. Combined with the dominant southerly summer winds, you'll have big waves that may make for difficult casting but easy catching (with the fish at your feet). Line management can be an issue, so consider skipping the stripping basket and using a floating line with a few pieces of shot and a few mends.

SURFSIDE

Located at the end of Surfside Road, this is a very popular beach, mostly because it is reachable by bus or bike. The surf can be heavy. A popular strip of Nantucket's south shore that had been used for decades by beach drivers and fishermen was quietly closed to four-wheel-drive vehicles after a group of Western Avenue residents petitioned the selectmen to remove the property from the town-issued beach map. Although the town's beach map was altered to reflect the change, it was never formally announced that beach drivers were no longer permitted to drive between the access points at South Shore Road, Surfside, and Nobadeer. If you're looking to take a 4x4 on to Surfside, check with the fishing shops to see if any status updates were made. Until that time, walking on the beach or fishing from boat is the only way to fish Surfside.

MIACOMET BEACH

Located at the end of Miacomet Road and West Miacomet Drive, this beach has heavy surf and strong currents. The Miacomet Rip extends on a southwest tack from the beach and is an excellent place to find concentrated baitfish and fish. It would seem that an extra-fast-sinking shooting head would be too much for the shallow water, but when your line swings tight it lifts off the bottom. The rip is also a good place to find bonito from late July through September.

Miacomet Beach is a long beach that used to be open for 4x4 driving but has been recently closed due to beach erosion. It is doubtful that it will reopen any time soon. There is a large parking lot and anglers still can access the beaches to fish. In the early season you'll have the beach to yourself, but in mid-summer Miacomet is largely a family beach. As a result, fishing times tend to be in the morning or evening.

CISCO BEACH

Located on the western side of the south shore at the end of Hummock Pond Road, this beach is known for surfers and very soft sand. The surf is strong and is a good place to drop off the family and then to do a little fishing. Bring both a floating and an extra-fast-sinking shooting head. A late afternoon bluefish blitz at last light is a great way to close the day. Cisco Beach is one of the best spots to find a bluefish blitz from mid-May through October.

MADAKET BEACH

This is a huge beach and with its western exposure it gets a lot of traffic from folks interested in watching the sun set (watch your backcasts). This beach on the island's westernmost tip is only accessible by four-wheel-drive vehicle. There are some lifeguards and restrooms but not on the entire length of the beach. The surf is heavy. All along the edges of Madaket Harbor is a good place to look for albies during the months of September and October, and is a good bet for a shot at a slam.

SMITH POINT

This is the westernmost tip of Madaket and was only accessible by four-wheel-drive vehicle or by boat. Due to a new cut, this end of this classic spot can only be reached by foot, boat, or kayak. The entire area is now a combination of a series of flats and bars and a channel. The area is now a boat and kayak fishery. And what's wrong with that?

Albies follow the bait along the channel between Smith Point and Eel Point. You'll also find striped bass and bluefish in this same area and also spread throughout the entire Madaket Harbor area. Shorebound anglers can catch albies from the tip of Eel Point where the channel comes within a few feet of shore. When the sand eels arrive you'll find striped bass close behind.

One area that has gotten a tremendous amount of notoriety is the Bonito Bar. The Bonito Bar is south of the opening between Tuckernuck Island and Smith's Point to the west of the land-based Smith Point (the new Smith Point) and, on nice days in late summer or early fall, it gets super-crowded with boats. Most anglers and charter captains favor the incoming tide, particularly when it coincides with first light, and they tend to work the outer edge of the bar, right on the drop-off.

EEL POINT

At the end of Eel Point Road is Eel Point. The pensinsula at the northwest corner of the island is one of the best fishing spots. There is a marsh as you make your way out to the point and sand flats to the north and to the south. A deep water rip is on the western side, and you have all the ingredients for good fishing. Running north to south from the point is the channel, and fish will move up to the flats on the flood tide and then drop-off as the tide ebbs. Use floating or intermediate lines for the shallow water, sinking lines for the point. Due to erosion you can't drive all the way out, but that's ok, it's worth the hike. North Point is on the north side of Eel Point, and has a series of near-shore finger bars that adds structure and current.

DIONIS BEACH

Located east of North Point is Dionis Beach. There is a large parking lot at the end of, you got it, Dionis Beach Road. From the parking lot, there are two access points to the beach, one that is a sand path that runs to the west and one that is a sand path that runs to the east. Because of its proximity on the north side, the waves are generally small because the landmass slows down the dominant west/southwest winds. Dionis Beach is very long, and there is some good fishing at the eastern end. When the winds shift to west/northwest you'll oftentimes find fish on shore, particularly during the fall run.

JETTIES BEACH

Just a short walk from town, this beach has tennis courts, a skateboard park, and a playground which makes it more of a family beach. As with Dionis Beach, the waves are small in the summer during the west/southwest winds. Spring and fall are better seasons up here. Jetties Beach has a long jetty that creates two sand flats, one on the west side of the jetty and one on the east side of the jetty. In the early season, you'll see bass moving in along the beach, and along mid-season there are usually some bluefish. As the water warms, shorebound anglers can get shots at bonito and albies. Jetties Beach is not as reliable for them as the western/southwestern side of the island, but they do make their appearance. Floating and extra-fast-sinking lines are common. During the summer, the beach is best fished from last light through first light when the crowds are light.

BRANT POINT

You'll see Brant Point as you enter the harbor. It reminds anglers of Martha's Vineyard's Edgartown Harbor and is a good spot for a slam. Bring a sinking line to fish the drop-offs and watch for the wake left by the ferry. Boat traffic can be thick in the summer.

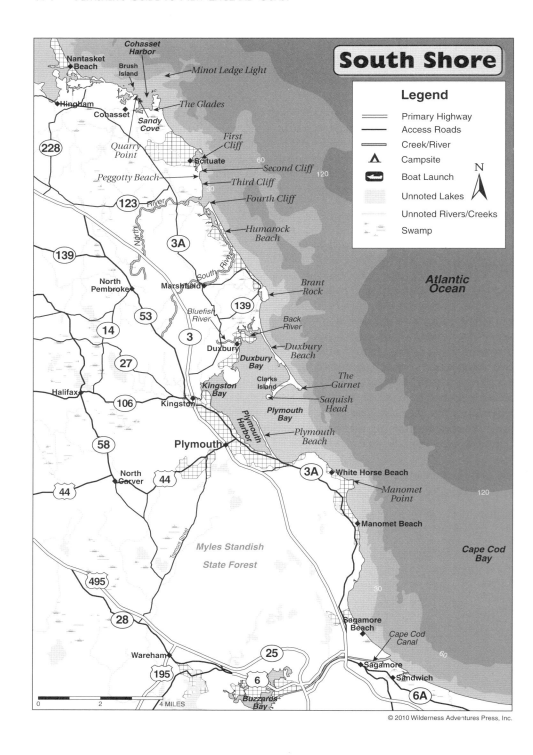

South Shore

Legend

═══	Primary Highway
────	Access Roads
═══	Creek/River
▲	Campsite
🛥	Boat Launch
	Unnoted Lakes
	Unnoted Rivers/Creeks
	Swamp

N

Nantasket Beach
Cohasset Harbor
Brush Island
Minot Ledge Light
Hingham
Cohasset
Sandy Cove
The Glades
228
Quarry Point
First Cliff
Scituate
60
Second Cliff
120
Peggotty Beach
Third Cliff
30
123
River
Fourth Cliff
North River
3A
Humarock Beach
139
South River
Brant Rock
North Pembroke
Marshfield
53
Bluefish River
139
Back River
14
3
Duxbury
Duxbury Beach
27
Duxbury Bay
Clarks Island
The Gurnet
Halifax
Kingston Bay
Saquish Head
106
Kingston
Plymouth Bay
Plymouth Harbor
Plymouth Beach
58
Plymouth
North Carver
44
3A
White Horse Beach
44
Manomet Point
120
Manomet Beach
Tremont Street
Myles Standish State Forest
Atlantic Ocean
Cape Cod Bay
495
30
28
Sagamore Beach
Wareham
25
Cape Cod Canal
195
6
Sagamore
60
Buzzards Bay
Sandwich
6A

0   2   4 MILES

© 2010 Wilderness Adventures Press, Inc.

South Shore

Running from the Cape Cod Canal to Braintree, the South Shore transitions as it moves from an adjunct of Cape Cod to an urban fishery. You round the corner from the east end of the canal and find beaches until you hit the Duxbury beaches and extensive flats, which adjoin America's hometown, Plymouth. Around Hummarock, a hamlet of Marshfield, you'll find the noteworthy North and South Rivers. There are the rocks and ledges from Scituate to Cohasset and the inshore islands around Hingham.

Depending on water temperatures and bait patterns, striped bass filter through the canal sometime in April. They chase alewives that move up and into the North and South Rivers. Silversides arrive in the shallower waters of Plymouth and Highham in May, and the fishing picks up dramatically. An early run of bluefish arrive in mid-May through June, with the big schools migrating with the warmer temperatures in July and August. Herring, silversides, shrimp, and crabs are hot baits beginning in mid-May, and sand eels arrive in June. And as with the North Shore, the fishing around Scituate and Cohasset heats up in June, July, and August. Here, you'll find mackerel, pollack, and lobsters as important food groups.

Public access is a hotly contested issue along coastal New England and the effects are felt in many seaside communities on the South Shore. Boat and kayak fishing allows anglers to thoroughly cover the water, but here are some of the common areas with enough beach access to get you started. A polite knock on the door to ask for permission can go a long way, too.

SAGAMORE BEACH

The beach that is located just north of the east end of the canal is known for two distinct times of year: spring and fall. In the spring, striped bass coming through the canal migrate along the shallow depths of Sagamore Beach and up the South Shore. In the fall, pretty much every fish that does not go around the tip of Provincetown goes near Sagamore Beach.

There is a tremendous amount of current that flows along the beach and ends abruptly at the breakwall by the canal. Because of that current, the bars are very different. Above the canal they are onshore and mostly bull nosed. A mile or so up the beach, they become offshore and parallel. And another mile up the beach they become parallel and onshore. Finally, about another mile up the beach they run perpendicular and offshore. Go figure.

What that means to fishermen is intermediate lines, heavy tippets, a variety of flies, and a lot of time in the spring and in the fall. In the spring you'll see big schools of fish moving in on every tide. There is a gradual slope from 1 or 2 feet in the wash to about 9 feet at low tide, so Sagamore Beach acts more as a corridor for these fish. After the initial three to six weeks of fresh arrivals, fishing will get quiet. Night fishing is ok, but mostly anglers will wait for the water temperatures to rise so bluefish will move into the area. In the fall the converse is true, and on the quarter moons the entire beach through a few hundred yards offshore is full of bait and fish staging to move through the canal. If you're ever looking to witness an act of nature, go to Sagamore Beach in the fall. You'll see blitzing fish for weeks, and then one day they are all gone. Leave your kayak home due to the current.

WHITE HORSE BEACH / MANOMET POINT

What is most interesting about White Horse Beach and the Manomet Point section of Plymouth is that the beach/knob protrudes far out in to the ocean, just before the dramatic descent to the canal. It's a straight shot south from Duxbury Beach, a close migration south from Plymouth Beach, and all moving fish wind up at White Horse Beach and Manomet. Bartlett Pond connects to the ocean, which makes for spring herring runs and fall glass minnow drops. There is a sandy flat where the river enters the ocean and it forms a bull-nosed bar. Running south the beach is curved until it forms Manomet Point. The small peninsula is cluttered with rocks and fishes well on a half coming tide. Seasonality is key to catch numbers of fish, and parking is difficult.

PLYMOUTH BEACH AND HARBOR

There are a lot of different sections of Plymouth, and each fish well during different times of year and tide. Plymouth has a lot of diversity, from beaches to flats, channels, and bars.

Plymouth Beach connects to Route 3A. There is a parking lot at the entrance. To the south is a cluster of rocks that fishes at mid-tides. In the spring it makes sense to work the beach, and you can pass over sand without an over-sand permit or deflating tires. The bars run parallel to shore and are very close until about two-thirds of the way toward the end. At that point they move offshore and run parallel to the beach. Starting at that point and working to the end is a good bet, particularly on a dropping tide.

There are a series of flats on the outside of the beach and also on the inside of the harbor. Most of these flats are moderate in size and have deeper channels (locally called guzzles) that allow for water, bait, and fish passage onto and off of the flat. What is most interesting in the channels is that some of them are quite deep at low tide, ranging between 10 and 71 feet deep. It's easy to shift from a floating or an intermediate line when the tide covers the flats, to an extra-fast-sinking line to catch fish on the lower water marks.

The channel into the harbor runs parallel to the inside of the beach and then makes a 90-degree turn. After fishing the end of the beach, anglers like to work in along

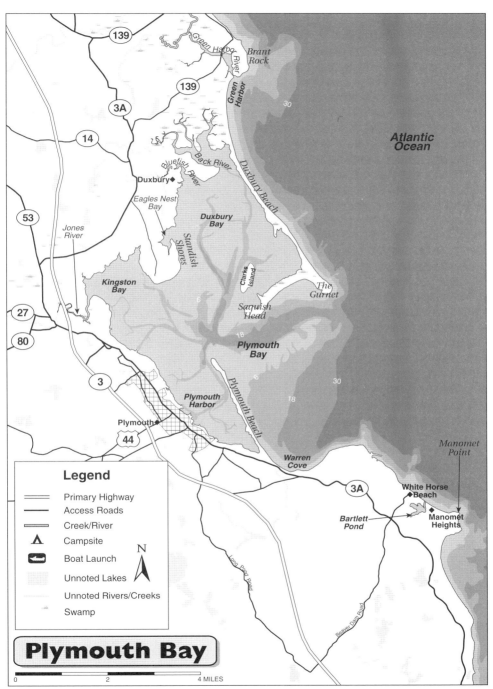

Plymouth Bay

Legend

≡ Primary Highway
— Access Roads
≡ Creek/River
▲ Campsite
🛶 Boat Launch
▨ Unnoted Lakes
— Unnoted Rivers/Creeks
⌇ Swamp

N

0   2   4 MILES

© 2010 Wilderness Adventures Press, Inc.

the harbor side. There is a long bar where the channel cuts inside of the breakwall, which fishes well through mid-flood tide and from mid-ebb to low tides. On the higher water marks, continue up to the confluence of the Eel River. Tremendous amounts of baitfish congregate in the Eel River, which continues upstream to two large ponds that are part of Plimouth Plantation. You can expect herring in the spring, menhaden in the fall, and silversides, shrimp, and mummies year round. The mouth of the Eel is also good at night, and don't be surprised if you catch a sea-run trout. They are escapees from the old Plymouth Rock Trout Company's raceways.

Stephens Field is a good fishing spot. It's good in the spring when the fish are moving around the harbor as bass will cruise the edges of the banks. It's also a good place for quiet night fishing in the summer, as there are plenty of shrimp and silversides. Hearing bass pop is common on the moving water, and a floating line and slider is a fun way to catch them. Kayak fishing on the higher water is also excellent here and the put-ins are easy, as you're far away from the motor boats.

There is a public ramp and parking at the Town Wharf, which is just off of Water Street. Some anglers will fish off the breakwall, and the end tends to be more productive.

Boat and kayak anglers like to fish the deeper water adjacent to the flats off of the Cordage Factory. The long, brick building used to make lines for sailing vessels during colonial days. Out in front are two flats and some deeper water with two channels – perfect for significant fish movement on the coming tides. When fishing along here, most anglers will use floating lines or sink tips. Note that when the water cranks over the bars the clarity can be significantly reduced.

Heading north you'll approach the neighboring town of Kingston, with most of the town still bordering on Plymouth Harbor. You'll see a similar configuration of flats, channels, and deeper water; and one good spot is where the Jones River enters the harbor. You'll find tons of baitfish in lower stretches of the river, and there is deeper water at the mouth and a flat on the outside. You'll find fish dropping out of the river and off the flat into the deeper water at the mouth and when they do, it's like shooting fish in a barrel.

Kingston Bay can fish well on the higher water marks. To access it you'll be in the land of Miles Standish. You'll take Standish Way and pass Miles Standish State Park which is near the beach called Standish Shores. Regardless, there is one deep channel that runs along the eastern side of Kingston Bay. It's about 12 to 15 feet deep at mean low water. The channel is typically full of boats, which makes for tough drifts in a boat or kayak. That said, there are several finger offshoots that cut into the sand flats that can make your day, particularly on a north wind in the fall on a quarter moon. Around to the east you'll find marshy areas interspersed with grass and flats, mostly from Goose Point past Standish Shores and out to Eagles Nest Point and Bay. At this point you're moving into Duxbury Bay, and the sand flats here fish better at about mid-tide.

Hooking up to bass and blues in Pilgrim-town means you might catch them off the bow of the Mayflower replica on the South Shore town of Plymouth.

DUXBURY

There are several parts to fishing in Duxbury: Duxbury Beach, the Gurnet, Saquish Head, Clark's Island, Duxbury Bay, Bluefish River, and the Back River. And that's not even all of 'em.

Duxbury Beach is like Plymouth Beach in that 4x4s can roll down it without deflating tires and getting an over-sand permit. The beach is long and sweeping, with a shallow and gradual drop-off. There will be fish moving up and down the beach most of the season, but spring and fall are the best times for numbers of arriving and departing fish. Bluefish show up in June and the first or last light fishing can be terrific. The ends of the beach are most noteworthy for consistency. At the bottom you'll find rocks and a jagged terrain as the beach moves into the peninsula called Saquish Head. On the east side is the Gurnet (where the lighthouse is) and on the west end is Saquish Head. The Gurnet has a rocky promontory that drops into deep water on the eastern and southern sides. There are good numbers of rocks and ledges as well. Along shore, the bottom shelves up and is a shallower sand/rock combination. The varying depths, rocks, and kelp make for perfect big-striper water. As you fish towards Saquish Head, you'll find increasingly deeper water with excellent visibility. Large patterns tend to work best, and moving water gets the fish to feed a little more easily than at the tops or bottoms of the tides. At the west end is a sand spit that runs to the west. Depending on how the tide is running, a position up- or down-tide from the bar is a good spot to find fish. And heading north you'll come upon Clarks Island, named after the mate on the Mayflower. Truman Capote wrote *Breakfast at Tiffany's* while staying on Clarks Island. You'll want to try the east side of the channel. There is a point bar that protrudes from Saquish Head and a small cove below it. Above the point is a flat. Either side fishes well, but be sure to move above the bar on the coming tide and below the point bar on the dropping. There is deep water that adjoins a flat on the northeast corner of the island, which is also a good spot, particularly as it moves in closer to shore and is surrounded by a flat on the north side. Two channels run north through Duxbury Harbor, and they are both on the west side of Clarks Island. The smaller channel runs in to where the Powder Point Bridge connects with Duxbury Beach. The second and larger channel is in the middle of Duxbury Bay and runs underneath the Powder Point Bridge and into the Back River.

Fish run the channels on the flood tide and move up onto the flats when the water is right. In the spring, they'll chase herring up the Back River and they'll feast on silversides and shrimp at night. A kayak is a perfect addition to that area. Fish the flats from mid-incoming through mid-dropping tides, and then drop back into the channels. The Bluefish River, in the northeast corner of Duxbury Bay, has a deeper channel in the center of the river and shallower banks on the sides. You'll find lots of bait and bass in the spring. The water warms quickly, and early bluefish runs appear. When the menhaden arrive, as they have in good numbers during the past few years, your fishing can be epic. Use floating lines on the flats and extra-fast-sinking heads in the deeper water. Due to the sand, the water clarity can get cloudy on full-moon tides and during storms.

BRANT ROCK, HUMMAROCK BEACH AND FOURTH CLIFF

Two Marshfield hamlets offer some outstanding fishing. Brant Rock is the town just north of Duxbury and is the home of Green Harbor on the Green Harbor River. The river will hold some bass in the early season and some bluefish in midseason. It's a working harbor and significant boat traffic can make the fishing difficult. From Brant Rock to Blackman's Point you'll find rocks, rocks, and more rocks – good striper water. Water depths range from a shallow depth of between 1 and 4 feet at mean low water to drop-offs of 7 to 10 feet. Striped bass will hang on the edges and move into the rocks on the flood through high tide. Brant Rock in the water is a spit of land with a perpendicular onshore bar, a perfect place for baitfish and also bass. Deep water is near the point, and the rocky/sandy point is a good spot for bass and blues.

Hummarock Beach is Striper Mike territory. Striper Mike landed a tuna from shore while plug fishing for bass. Not many men have accomplished that feat in their lives, so you know the beach is good for fishing. It's particularly strong in the spring when the herring and alewives arrive and also in the fall during the run. You'll find recesses in the beach break at 8th Road and at Oregon Road – two spots that are worth fishing around. The bars aren't pronounced at Hummarock, and instead the depth gradually drops off. Better fishing is on the mid- through higher water marks. As you move toward the end, you'll run into Fourth Cliff, which is at the end of Hummarock Beach. There is an Air Force recreation area right near the water. Here you'll find deeper water as you round the corner and move into the mouth of the rivers. Use intermediate lines out in front on the beach, and extra-fast-sinking lines as you move into the mouth of the river. The current is strong and consistent, a combination of two rivers.

NORTH AND SOUTH RIVERS

You can wade, boat, or kayak fish the North and South Rivers, just be mindful of the current. If you don't have a craft of your own, swing by Mary's Boat Livery at the junction of Route 3A and the North River. You can rent a skiff with a 6-horsepower outboard and be your own captain for the day. In the early season, herring will move up both rivers, but more so in the north. Several marshes and creeks run into the North and South Rivers, and the fishing is great. You'll also see early silversides, mummies, and shrimp. Night fishing can be good until the water warms significantly.

While the North River runs inland, the South River doubles back and runs nearly parallel to Hummarock Beach. It is broken up in a few points by islands. The basin is muddy, and you can cover more water from a kayak. With all the land and trees, you can find shelter from the early-season winds. Most of the fishing can be done properly with a floating line. When the water is low, look for indentations in the banks, then come and fish them later on. As the current increases in flow, you'll find baitfish congregating in those recesses and the bass won't be far behind.

The mouths of the rivers have some of the hairiest currents on the Eastern Seaboard, so exercise caution when fishing on a dropping tide. The north side of the river mouth is sandy with a long shoal heading out to sea. The sand and bars continue as you move north and, as you approach Third Cliff, you'll find rocks on shore and ledges in the water. Third Cliff is home to some large striped bass, particularly in the summer months when the water temperatures stay cool. You'll also find a sand/ cobble beach just north of Third Cliff which is called Peggotty Beach. Then it will make sense, because you have a river mouth with current on one end and a beach on the other with rocks and ledges in between. The waterfront burg of Scituate is residential and parking is difficult, so launching a boat at Mary's Boat Livery or a kayak at Peggotty Beach makes the most sense. You'll see a lot of herring in the spring that move around Third Cliff to get into Herring Brook at the mouth of the North River, and they'll drop out of Old Oaken Bucket Pond as glass minnows in the fall. There will be lots of bait out in front, and watch out for lobster pot lines when you hook a big bass.

SECOND AND FIRST CLIFFS

South of the entrance way to Scituate Harbor are two more cliffs. Second Cliff is the farthest south of the two and First Cliff is at the mouth of the harbor. Picture a dog bone with a long seawall connecting the two ends. There are tons of rocks in front of First and Second Cliffs, with not too many in between. It can get pretty bony on

Rent a skiff from Mary's Boat Livery in Marshfield and fish the North River as Ben Ardito shows.

the lower water marks, so stay offshore a bit and cast among the rocks and ledges on the higher water marks. Unless the fish are right on top, an extra-fast-sinking line will get you down, and shock tippets are a good idea. The water is very clear, so most flies tend to be natural patterns with less flash or bright colors. While you're fishing around the mouth of the harbor, be sure to take a few casts in and around the rocks and boulder fields of Cedar Point. You'll recognize Cedar Point because it's where Old Scituate Light was built. Spend some time around the north side of Cedar Point.

THE GLADES AND COHASSET

The Glades are on the eastern end of the mouth of Cohasset Harbor, separated by Bassing Beach and Briggs Harbor. The Glades are a series of rocks, ledges, outcroppings, and enough perfect big-bass water to make your hair stand on end. Fishing it on the higher water marks makes the most sense, and extra-fast-sinking lines with natural-colored flies is a good idea. Sheppard Ledges is off the northwestern side, and is a larger rock formation that gets the benefit of current moving between land and ledge. It's a great spot to fish when the tide is running. Be sure to work your way to the south along Glades Road. You'll see a bull-nose bar and rock formation that can hold good numbers of fish.

Pick pocketing your way through the minefield isn't easy, but when you hook a fish out here it's usually a good one. Cohasset is more of the same kinds of water, with rocks, ledges, and reefs. The fish show up in June after the water temperatures climb, and they'll hold fish all summer long due to the deeper depths, cooler temperatures, great structure, and ample bait. Mackerel, lobsters, pollack, squid, silversides, and menhaden are the popular baitfish, and there is also summer crab spawn as well. Rig with shock tippets, fight fish from the butt of your rod, and don't let them get into the rocks – they'll break you off for sure. Take some casts around Brush Island, Quarry Point, Sandy Cove (on the northwest corner of Cohasset Harbor) and Minot's Ledge Light.

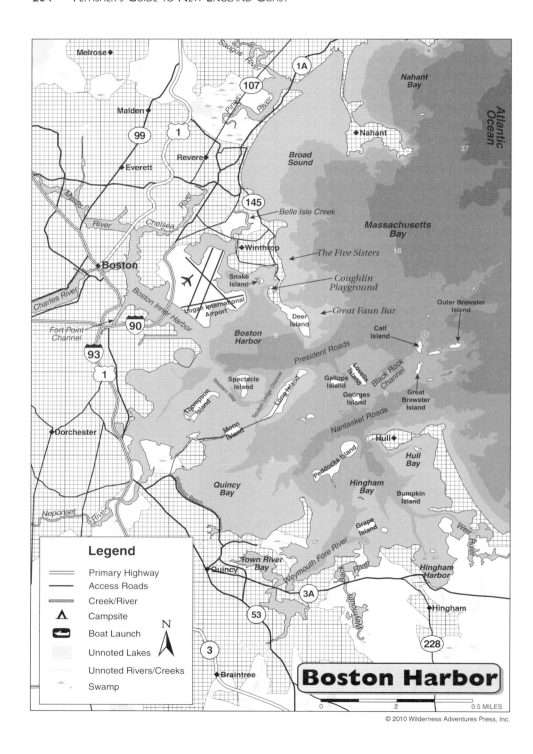

Legend

═══	Primary Highway
───	Access Roads
═══	Creek/River
⛺	Campsite
🚤	Boat Launch
	Unnoted Lakes
	Unnoted Rivers/Creeks
	Swamp

N

Boston Harbor

0   2   0.5 MILES

© 2010 Wilderness Adventures Press, Inc.

Boston Harbor

Several decades ago, which is the blink of an eye in Boston's historical terms, very few recreational anglers ever went fishing in Boston Harbor. The striped bass population was skinny, the bluefish fishing was hit or miss, and the most significant catches were, ironically enough, a seasonal shallow-water cod population in Quincy (Codfish are groundfish and typically inhabit offshore water that is a few hundred feet deep). Pollution, probably beginning when tea was thrown overboard during the 1773 Boston Tea Party, turned Boston Harbor into one of the most polluted harbors nationwide. By the time the 1960s arrived, the Standells were already working on their song, "Dirty Water", and sang: "'cause I love that dirty water, awwww, Boston you're my home." It couldn't get much worse.

Not long ago, when the sewage pumps simultaneously broke down at the waste treatment plants on Deer and Nut Islands, 4.3 billion gallons of raw effluent flowed into Boston Harbor and Quincy Bay. In 1982, the pumps broke down a whopping 144 times. Common shoreline features were shells, rocks, and debris. In 1985, 1,900 pounds of some of industry's worst by-products – namely chromium, PCBs, lead, and cadmium – were dumped into the harbor. What couldn't have gotten any worse actually did.

"There weren't many fish in the harbor in those days," recalled Bruce Berman, spokesman for Save the Harbor/Save the Bay, a shoreline conservation group. "How could they survive?"

Thirty years and $4.5 billion later, the rebuilt Deer Island sewage treatment plant solved many problems. Boston is now blessed with some of "the cleanest urban beaches in America," according to Berman. And he's right. With a strong urban striped bass and bluefish fishery, a thriving shellfish fishery, and regular triathlons, the Boston Harbor Clean Up is a modern success story.

Where else can you catch fish with L-1011s flying overhead? Many charter captains pick up their clients at one of the piers, take them out for a morning of fishing, and then drop them off in time for a breakfast meeting. With Boston's rich history, diverse sports teams, cultural activities, and fine restaurants – all a stone's thrown from great fishing – how can any angler go wrong?

There are technical ways to pick apart Boston Harbor. One way is to carve it up by the towns that are considered to be a part of Boston. A second way to set a boundary is by reviewing the county lines: Plymouth, Norfolk, and Suffolk, and sticking to that region (Boston is in Suffolk County). But the best way to view Boston Harbor is a practical one which is through a fisherman's eyes, and that is by the bays that an angler will fish. So for the purpose of this book, Boston Harbor will consist of the towns of Hull, Hingham, Quincy, Dorchester, Boston Proper, Chelsea, and Winthrop. Those towns will cover three bays – Hingham Bay, Quincy Bay, Dorchester Bay – and Boston Harbor.

INNER TO OUTER HARBOR ISLANDS

There are 34 islands in Boston Harbor wrapped up by two major land formations. The northern Winthrop Peninsula and Deer Island and the southern Nantasket Peninsula and Point Allerton create two arms that offer shelter to the Inner Harbor from Cape Cod Bay's Outer Harbor. Two deep-water anchorages, President Roads to the north and Nantasket Roads to the south (both water features), allow large ships and barges to pass. More importantly, they are the corridors that the striped bass and bluefish use. Both anchorages are separated by Long Island. Black Rock Channel connects the two anchorages and also sweeps from Winthrop to Nantasket.

The beauty is that you don't need a boat to fish Boston Harbor, for 11 of the 34 islands have visitor centers and allow fishing. Four of the islands allow overnight camping. You'll catch bass and blues near sea walls, forts, lighthouses, gun emplacements, concrete bunkers, cottages, and brick buildings. The architecture reflects the long history and changing character of the Boston Harbor Islands. What is neat, too, is how the islands increase in size during 10- to 12-foot tides. There are 1,483 acres on the islands at high tide and 3,067 acres at low tide. More spots to fish....

You'll see a wide variety of navigational aids that have provided safe passage to ships throughout the years. There are cans, nuns, bell bouys, hooter bouys – the usual markers. But some are unique. Boston Light on Little Brewster Island is a National Historic Landmark that is purported to include portions of the oldest lighthouse structure in the United States. Two lights even made the National Register of Historic Places: Graves Light on the Graves and Long Island Head Light on Long Island. Nixes Mate is a pyramidal black and white channel marker that has stood in the harbor since the early 1900s.

General fish passage into the harbor is through two main channels: the President and Nantasket Roads. As the tide floods, the body of fish move in different directions, mostly dependent on the time of year (bait), the wind direction, and the lunar phase. Many move northwest between Logan Airport and Deer Island, into Snake Island and Winthrop Harbor, and up into Belle Isle Creek. Others move due west past Long Island, Spectacle Island, Thompson Island, and Moon Island, and ultimately into Dorchester Bay and the Neponset River.

A different body of fish moves along Nantasket Roads, where they wind up in Quincy Bay. There they will pass Lovells, Gallops, and George's Islands, onward past Rainsford, Peddocks, and Hangman's Islands, all the way up to Wollaston Beach.

Some of the fish from Nantasket Roads back fill through Hull Gut and into the southern section of Boston Harbor. Here they will move into Hingham Bay and past

Sheep, Bumpkin, Slate, and Grape Islands and into Hingham Harbor. There are four islands in Hingham Harbor – Langlee, Sarah, Button, and Ragged Islands – and they are all west of World's End. Other fish will move towards Hewitts Cove or the Back River, particularly in the spring and summer when the alewives and silversides are in.

As the tide drops, the fish will filter back into the main anchorages and into deeper water and you can catch them again.

The Outer Harbor consists of several islands: Little Brewster, Shag Rocks, Great Brewster, Middle Brewster, Outer Brewster, Calf, Little Calf, Green, and Graves Islands. There are a number of channels that provide passage for the fish. There is the Boston North Channel, the Boston South Channel, the Black Rock Channel, and the Hypocrite Channel. Fish move out of the channels on the flood tide and filter into the rocks and current seams. They'll oftentimes wind up at the rock formation just past Green Island, called the Roaring Bulls, which is exposed only on lower water marks.

The Outer Harbor islands hold fish when the Inner Harbor water temperatures get warm. The way the current blows through gaps and along the rocks and ledges is perfect when the menhaden and mackerel are moving. They also fish well in mid-June when the lobsters shed their exoskeletons. Pollock attract the fish as well. Getting close to cast a fly into the rocks is key, and watching for ground swells is critical. The current is strong in the Outer Harbor, and lackadaisical boaters will find their boats onshore very quickly. With all the lobster buoys and hidden rocks, dinged propellers and damaged lower units are tough to avoid.

Boston Harbor's Quarantine Rocks at low tide reveals the structure that stripers and bluefish love.

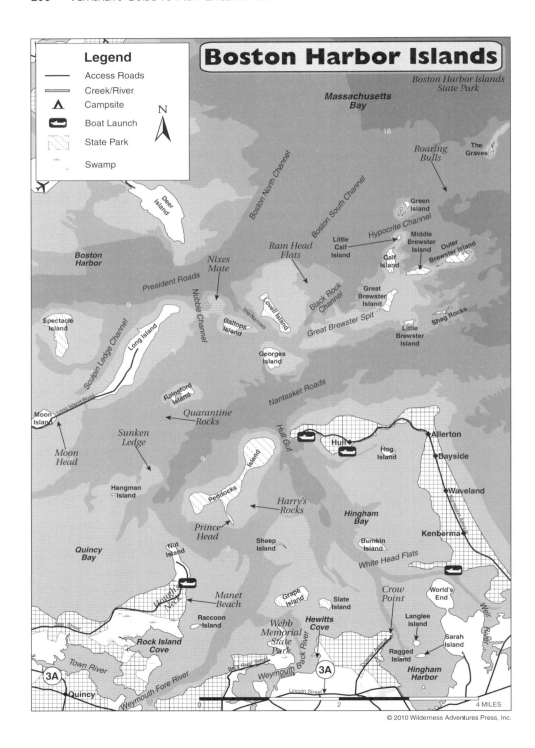

Boston Harbor Islands

Legend

— Access Roads

Creek/River

▲ Campsite

Boat Launch

State Park

Swamp

N

Boston Harbor Islands State Park

Massachusetts Bay

Roaring Bulls

The Graves

Deer Island

Boston North Channel

Boston South Channel

Green Island

Hypocrite Channel

Little Calf Island

Middle Brewster Island

Outer Brewster Island

Boston Harbor

Nixes Mate

Ram Head Flats

Calf Island

President Roads

Nubble Channel

Lovell Island

The Narrows

Black Rock Channel

Great Brewster Island

Spectacle Island

Sculpin Ledge Channel

Long Island

Gallops Island

Great Brewster Spit

Little Brewster Island

Shag Rocks

Moon Island

Long Island Road

Rainsford Island

Georges Island

Quarantine Rocks

Nantasket Roads

Sunken Ledge

Moon Head

Peddocks Island

Hull Gut

Hull

Hog Island

Allerton

Bayside

Hangman Island

Harry's Rocks

Hingham Bay

Waveland

Prince Head

Peddocks Island

Sheep Island

Bumkin Island

White Head Flats

Kenberma

Quincy Bay

Nut Island

Grape Island

Slate Island

Crow Point

World's End

Houghs Neck

Manet Beach

Langlee Island

Sarah Island

Raccoon Island

Webb Memorial State Park

Hewitts Cove

Ragged Island

Rock Island Cove

Back River

Weymouth Back River

Hingham Harbor

Sea Street

3A

Town River

Weymouth Fore River

Back River Street

Weymouth Fore River

Lincoln Street

3A

0   2   4 MILES

© 2010 Wilderness Adventures Press, Inc.

You'll notice a change in format, which will include a brief historical description of the islands. My experience with visiting anglers has been a curiosity about the islands that we're fishing near and around. As Boston Harbor was one of America's founding and busiest port cities, her history is rich. There are a number of excellent books that provide more detail, but this overview is a good starting point.

THOMPSON ISLAND

Originally hunting and fishing grounds for American Indians, Miles Standish and Squanto first landed on Thompson Island in 1621. Standish's trip from Plymouth took an entire day to make, but now it only takes 20 minutes. In the 1800s, Thompson Island became a teaching island. The brick Greek revival building that still stands once housed the Boston Farm School. It was founded in 1833 to teach boys farming, music, carpentry, blacksmithing, and printing. Now the school houses an Outward Bound program. You'll see young students climbing walls, working through ropes courses, and kayaking.

The east end of the island runs foul with rocks, which makes for a perfect fishing ground. The adjoining depth is 4 feet at mean low water, and alewives and silversides and then squid are abundant during the spring. There are mussel and grass beds at that end, too, which make for a perfect area for shrimp. On a summer's evening, you'll hear the bass pop. There is a deeper access that runs along the northern side of the island, where the depths drop sharply from 4 feet to 20 feet at low tide. The fish that have been pushing bait into the rocks and along the shoreline drop into the deeper water that lines up with the outflow of the Neponset River. You'll frequently see bass feeding on alewives and herring in the spring, particularly as the bait moves into the Neponset River. On the west end of the island is a tidal pond and marsh. On a high-dropping tide, you'll find fish in the pond as well as at the drainage out of the pond. A sand flat runs along the entire western side, nearly to the Squaw and Chapel Rocks across the channel at Squantum. On a flood tide, bass and blues will move on a north-to-south tack as the water washes over the bar. The current doesn't move so fast on the southside, but fishing can be good in the fall when the bass and bluefish are feeding on menhaden, silversides, and sand eels on the quarter moons. As you work back along the southside to the east end, there is a bowl that makes for a perfect holding spot for fall baitfish.

The buildings are available for rent for conferences, weddings, and special events. For more information and ferry schedules, visit www.thompsonisland.org. And if you attend a wedding on the island, be sure to bring a rod.

SPECTACLE ISLAND

For decades, the island named after a pair of eyeglasses, was a city landfill, horse rendering factory, and a quarantine station. Aggressive beautification projects ensued....and cost a staggering $170 million dollars. While families continued to live on Spectacle Island until the 1950s, the island now boasts 5 miles of walking trails, beaches, and a marina. A visititor's center provides a café, restrooms, rocking chairs, and island exhibits. Fishing rods and nets are available for rent and ranger-led toursare also available. Angler's can reserve space at the dock by contacting the Spectacle Island Marina at 857-452-7221 or VHF 69. Moorings are also available.

There are a series of rocks on the northern edge, and two large ones in particular on the northwest corner, that hold big bass, particularly when the alewives and herring have just arrived in the spring. The depths at mean low tide are still deep, typically between 7 and 8 feet. The edge of the adjoining President Roads drops to a depth of 25-plus feet. Typically, the fish stage in the deeper water, and as the tide floods they'll move up into the current and all around the rocks. If these fish aren't showing on the surface, use a sinking line and work the depth changes as well as the rocky shoreline.

As the current increases, some fish follow the rocky shoreline along to the east end and head south. They pause where the rocks run foul, and a rock garden protrudes and drops off into 5 feet of mean low-water depth. Casting around here with a floating or sink-tip line is a great idea. Another body of fish moves along Western Way toward the southern end of Spectacle.

MOON ISLAND

The stepping stone between Long Island and the Squantum section of Quincy is not for the faint of heart. From the 1870s through the 1970s, Moon Island was a sewage treatment plant. It's been completely overhauled and now has two recruit training grounds: Boston Fire Department's academy on the north side of the island and the Boston Police Department's shooting range and disposal of suspected bombs and explosives. Don't be surprised if you see smoke billowing from Moon Island or hear automatic-weapon fire.

The fish that pass from the south end of Spectacle will wind up off of Moon Head. There isn't much holding water off of Moon, and mid-flood or mid-dropping tide is best. A series of piles is on the sound end just underneath the Long Island Bridge, which then opens into Quincy Bay. Moon Head and the outer reach of Quincy Bay will fish well as the current is moving, and it is particularly good on quarter moons in the fall when the silversides and peanut bunker are staging. Sinking lines cast around the piles and along the current seams are good ways to find fish. It's a small area, so if you're not hooking up after a short time, move on – the fish are somewhere else.

LONG ISLAND

Long Island has had a distinguished military history. From raids on Loyalist prisoners during the Revolutionary War, to training and drilling maneuvers during the Civil War, to laying and controlling mines at the northern entrance to Boston Harbor during World War II, Long Island now houses boys and girls from ages 11 to 14 as a summer camp. Kids spend the summer in a renovated building that was originally purposed as a summer hotel in 1840 (www.campharborviewfoundation.org). The Farm at Long Island grows fresh produce for use in shelters and provides work opportunities for homeless men and women.

The west end of Long Island runs foul with lots of rocks, and these rocks continue on both sides of the island. When the alewives and herring are in, bass will hold all along the shore on half-tide through high-tide-through-half-tide. On the lower tides, use a floating line so you don't hang up, and cast as close to shore as possible. Fish will trail your fly as it moves into the deeper water, and this spot can hold big bass. Sculpin Ledge Channel runs on a northeast/southwest parallel on the north side, and bass and blues hold in the deeper water and move into shore as the tide floods. You'll find them on the edge of the drop-off and also moving in tight to shore. Depending on the wind speed, the fish will either be on the southwest end or the northwest end.

At the east end is a deep bowl with a rock formation that juts out toward Nixes Mate. The rocks are piled and then they fall off into a rock garden, perfect at mid/high tide. Some big bass come out of the east end. As you head south around Long Island, a mud flat juts far out into Nubble Channel, which causes boats to run aground on lower water marks. The water to about 100 yards to the south of Long Island is a great area to find fish in the spring and again in the fall. On the lower water marks you'll want to use a floating line to keep from hooking the rocks and ledges. On the higher water marks use a sinking line. Some big bass are caught here every year.

Be sure to fish your way from west side to east side; there are lots of fish that hold throughout both sides of the island. The currents are diverse enough for the fish to pick which ones they like, so watch for the changes and vary your position accordingly.

NIXES MATE

During the 1600s, Nixes Mate was a 12-acre island which pastured sheep. Now, all that remains is a black and white navigational pyramid and a rocky shoal. One yarn states that Captain Nix was murdered at sea by his mate. The mate professed innocence, yet was found guilty. His body was taken to the island and hanged. His last words were that the island would be washed away by an angry sea as proof of his innocence.

While Nixes Mate looks very fishy, the current doesn't move until the water is pouring over the rock bar at half tide. You'll find fish holding on the outside of the rocks on the eastern end toward the Narrows, and then on the southern end between Nixes Mate and Gallops Island. Towards high tide on a summer day you'll find bluefish moving all along Nubble Channel. Floating lines around the lower water marks work best, but most of the time anglers favor sinking lines around the edges.

GALLOPS ISLAND

French troops protected Boston during the Revolutionary War, and Gallops quartered as many as 3,000 Union soldiers during the Civil War. After the Civil War, Boston moved its quarantine station from Deer Island to Gallops. Immigrants were brought ashore and were disinfected prior to completing their journey to the New World. There are over 250 burial sites in an unmarked cemetery on the eastern end of the island – victims of smallpox, cholera, yellow fever, and leprosy.

The rocks along the northern edge of Gallops look like it would be a good spot, but the currents move slowly, mostly due to the shallow depths. You'll find more fish in the harder current, particularly on the western end through the breakwall that sticks out into the deeper water. The depth drops off very quickly, from a mean low tide depth of 4 feet to 28 feet. The fish will move on that edge, so positioning your boat in the deeper channel water and casting toward shore works well, or you can position yourself on shore and cast to the edge. On the east side you'll find fish along the southern point, and they'll hold either on the outside in the Narrows or on the inside toward Georges Island. Sinking lines are best when the herring and menhaden are in, and you'll find some blitzes during the summer – often a mix of bass and bluefish.

GEORGES ISLAND

Georges Island was originally formed as a Revolutionary War fortress, designed to protect the French fleet from the British navy while they made repairs to their boats.

Rock formations that support navigational markers are good areas to look for gamefish. The diverse current flows and varying depths creates good feeding grounds as shown here off of Gallop's Island in Boston Harbor.

During the Civil War, the below ground labyrinths transported Confederate prisoners to and from their cells. Twelve-inch cannons are still present on the island, and guided tours are available through the wooden archways to the old bakery, hospital, and living quarters. Moorings are available through the Spectacle Island Marina (857-452-7221) or on VHF 69. Private boaters may use the dock on a first-come-first-served basis.

Tremendous rock gardens run from the southeastern side to the northeastern side. While they run foul at low tide, they are excellent at half tide through high tide. Bass will move in and out of the rocks, but the water can get cloudy as the tide gains speed. The depths vary quickly, from a mean low tide of 11 feet to 4 feet, back to 11 feet, back to 3 feet. There are two large rocks in particular that seem to be bookends for big bass to move between. Use floating line, swim your flies, and use big flies. The rock gardens hold big bass. If you're working the channels, be sure to cast up-current and mend as you swing. Getting your fly deep is a good way to hook a big fish. Smaller bass and blues frequently feed on the surface in the deeper-water channels around Georges Island.

LOVELL ISLAND

When heading out to Lovell Island, it's best to chart a course different from the 74-gun French warship, Magnifique. In 1782, the ship ran aground on the island's western side. Treasure hunters continue to scour the shoreline with a dream of recovering the gold and silver coins said to be aboard the Magnifique.

What makes Lovell Island attractive to anglers is the fact that they can camp on the island. Don't worry about fishing near the Battery Burbeck-Morris; the 10-inch guns were used to protect the coast from German U-boats during World War II and were dismounted in 1943. But the campsites are scattered across Lovell Island – the most interesting ones are in the parade grounds, last used by soldiers in the 1940s. Reservations are required and can be made at www.reserveamerica.com or at 877-422-6762. Private boaters are not allowed to moor or tie up for extended periods of time, but can drop off passengers and provisions. The Inter-Island Ferry connects to Lovell Island either from Georges or Spectacle Island.

Lovell is positioned on a north/south tack. On the west end is a channel – the Narrows – on the south end is Black Rock, on the east end are the Ram Head Flats, and on the north end is the President Roads. What you have is shallow water that runs around the island and deeper water that adjoins the shallows. At half flood through high tide, you'll find that fish move out of the shallows and onto the flats and then back into the channel and back along the shoreline. Look for the current edge and that's typically where you'll find the fish. The current moves quickly. There are lots of rocks on the north end that provide structure, and the end of the Narrows – the sand spit that runs all the way to Great Brewster – acts as a funnel. Drifting big flies on a floating line between the rocks is a good way to find some big bass.

RAINSFORD ISLAND / QUARANTINE ROCKS

The island has a mixed history, from the dark days in the 1600s through the 1700s when it cared for quarantined Bostonians, to a reform school for wayward boys, to the lighthearted times in the 1820s when the Old Mansion House provided food and lodging for the guests of the island's doctor.

Rainsford is a lesser island that sits to the west of Gallops and Georges and south of Long Island. From the air it looks like a whale, with the tail at the west end and the body at the east end. The eastern end is shallow and fishes best with a floating line at mid- to high tide. As you get close to the island you'll find a mostly rocky shoreline that is better fished on half flood or half ebb tides. At the northwest corner, the island is directly across from Long Island's Bass Rocks – a great place for fish. The depths are shallow and then dramatically drop off. The north side had a big bowl that holds peanut bunker in the fall. The Quarantine Rocks are off the far west end, and should be fished on the higher water marks. Position your boat up-tide and offshore and cast into the rocks. Look for the breaks in between the rocks where the current blows through, and look at each end of the rock formations. Use big flies and sinking shooting heads when working the rocks. You don't usually find big concentrations of bass around Rainsford and the Quarantine Rocks, but the ones you find are usually good ones.

GRAVES ISLAND

At the entrance to Boston Harbor is Graves Light. The austere lighthouse gets far less attention than Boston Light. It's named after Thomas Graves, one of the early Puritan settlers. While the fish can be anywhere around the rocks, the northwest end of the island (on the Boston side) holds fish when the pollock are in, and the southeastern corner in the cove around the lighthouse holds fish for most of the season. On the northeastern end, there is another rock ledge called Northeast Graves that is worth fishing when the current is moving, but at low tide the rocks run foul. The current flow is good in between Graves and Northeast Graves and bass like it here. Sink-tip or extra-fast-sinking lines work well, and natural-colored flies and heavy terminal gear works best. Fish bigger fly patterns as the bait tends to be larger out here, and make sure to cast your flies into the white wash. The Outer Harbor fishes better from late May through the end of the season. Look for big schools of Boston mackerel and menhanden to pass by Graves on their northern migration. If you're on the water during those times, you'll find enormous pods of big fish.

GREEN ISLAND

North of Little Calf is Green Island, which is comprised of two connected islands. The Hypocrite Channel separates Green from the cluster of other islands due south. The island was the home of Samuel Choate, a recluse, who spent 20 years in a hut living on fish, lobster, and mussels. The rocky ledges prohibit landings, even in a kayak.

For fishing, the south side that faces the Hypocrite Channel offers more of a flat profile, with depths dropping quickly to 37 feet. On the northeast side is a cove that is about 20 feet deep and runs through Green Island to the channel. Striped bass trade back and forth through this channel, so be sure to cast on both sides. The Roaring Bulls are two rock formations that run foul at low tide and are due east of Green. If you're running from Green to Graves (or in reverse), make sure to take a few casts all around the Bulls; the water at the 50- to 60-foot depths stays cool in the summer and it's a good time to find bass down deep.

CALF ISLAND

Calf Island is known for the red brick chimney that once heated the summer house of railroad financier, Benjamin Cheney, Jr. Their home, the Moorings, was two stories, had 20 rooms, and would have been met with approval in Newport.

There are several ways to come ashore, but the best is the sandy cove on the northwestern shore. If seas are rough, the southeastern side, albeit rocky, will work

Check terminal gear for strength and and hooks for sharpness before approaching the rocks and ledges. Graves Lighthouse, in the distance, is at the entrance to Boston Harbor, and is so quiet that anglers would swear they were in Maine.

fine. Calf has a perfect amount of shallow ledges that surround the island, particularly on the southeastern side. With a couple of feet of water covering those ledges, try a floating line and drop a fly right on top of the ledge. Strip slowly and pause when your fly is on the edge where the depth drops off. You might need a pinch of split shot to get the fly down a couple of feet, but the cruising bass will rise to the pattern.

LITTLE CALF ISLAND

One hundred yards to the north of Calf Island is Little Calf Island. This tiny, desolate turf has never been used for much due to its lack of vegetation. At low tide there is a shallow passage with ledges and shoals that run almost down to Calf, and that connection to Calf typically has fish that trade back and forth between the two islands. Try the south side on the dropping tide and the north side on the flood. The northwest corner is also typically good, with a 3-foot to 26-foot drop-off. Calf and Little Calf are good places to dead drift lobster patterns in June.

GREAT BREWSTER ISLAND

Boaters easily recognize Great Brewster because of the 100-foot-plus high bluffs. The erosion is significant, and many of the island's rocks have fallen into the ocean, thereby creating an ideal fishery. The Brewster chain of islands is named after Elder William Brewster, the spiritual leader of the Pilgrims. You'll often see kayaks and flat-bottomed boats on the western beach, and staging a landing is well worth it. Only a shallow sandbar separates great Brewster and Little Brewster, and lighthouse keepers used to trade back and forth between the two islands in search of freshwater and grass for their goats. A dozen families had summer cottages on the island through the 1930s, and their foundations, asparagus, and Concord grape gardens still remain.

There are two long sand spits. Great Brewster Spit runs west to Black Rock Channel and nearly connects with Lovell Island. At low tide, most of the spit runs foul, but on the north side of the spit, the channel depths are between 20 and 30 feet. Fish dropping out of the ledges and sand flat wind up in the channel, and an extra-fast-sinking shooting head will get to them. From the north and southwest side of the island you'll find a tremendous amount of rocks, ledges, and shoals. The southwest ledge runs to Little Brewster Island. Fishing either side at half tide is a good time to find fish, and on either side of high tide is a good time to get in tighter to the island to work the rocks.

MIDDLE BREWSTER ISLAND

A peculiar stone archway that stands along the cliff of the island's southwest corner marks the entrance to this island. In the late 1800s the 10-foot-tall archway was the entrance to a white brick villa that was the summer resort of Proper Bostonians. One summer resident, Melvin O. Adams, Esq., achieved renown as the defense attorney for none other than Lizzie Borden, the daughter accused of hacking her father and stepmother to death with an axe.

The sunken crags and ledges caused by erosion make the island potentially hazardous for boaters. For fishing, the passageways between Calf and Outer Brewster on the moving tides are better. Off the southeast corner of the island is a long rock ledge that runs to 4 feet at mean low water, surrounded by between 19 and 37 feet. An extra-fast-sinking shooting head is best. The fish circulate back and forth, and move consistently closer to the island as the tide rises. There is a resident cod population so don't be surprised if you find a cod attached to your fly – an oddity for sure.

OUTER BREWSTER ISLAND

Rock for construction projects, such as the Austin Block at 92 Main Street in Charlestown (near the historic Warren Tavern) was the main business at Outer Brewster. But so were other activities that were frowned upon within Boston city limits. Illegal boxing matches, gambling, and rum running were common practices in this Las Vegas of Boston Harbor. In the 1940s, 6-inch gun emplacements, three barracks, and a mess hall were built to protect Boston during World War II. There is a rocky cove on the northern shore that allows dinghies or kayaks to come ashore. Pulpit Rock is just to the west of the cove and is a natural formation that looks like a minister's podium.

The western, southern, and eastern areas have lots of rocks and ledges, but also a significant amount of open water passing through. You'll be able to get long casts around the rocks but also in the deeper water in the between the rocks. While you're fishing Outer Brewster you'll want to head northeast to Martin Ledge. The ledge runs to 14 feet at mean low water, and the surrounding depth at low tide is between 70 and 80 feet. On a low incoming tide, the upwelling current brings bass higher up in the water column.

SHAG ROCKS

The fish-eating cormorant is known by the Brits as a shag, which is how the rocks got their name. Many a ship has been sunk on Shag Rocks.

The ledges make for great fishing, particularly on the western side where you have numerous pockets of deeper water and great current flow. On the southern side is a ledge that runs parallel to the rocks, with 17 feet of water separating the island from the ledge. There are two formations on the eastern side that fly rodders like, particularly since they can be approached from three sides. Extra-fast-sinking shooting heads are the best bet.

LITTLE BREWSTER ISLAND

You'll know Little Brewster Island because of the perfect New England lighthouse that sits on the southern end. In the 1670s, bales of pitch and lanterns were lit to mark the way into the treacherous harbor, but by 1716 Boston Light took shape. The lighthouse was a battleground for both Colonists and Loyalists, both of whom vied for control of passage in and out of the harbor. It was none other than John Hancock who rebuilt the lighthouse after the war ended; the reconstruction occurring in 1783. Sally Snowman who meets inbound ferries dressed in an 18th-century costume tends the lighthouse, and it was the first light station built in the United States.

Guided tours run from Thursday through Sunday between June and October. The ferry departs from the Fort Point Channel side of the Moakley United States Courthouse at Fan Pier in the South Boston Seaport District. For more information visit www.harborislands.org or call 617-223-8666. Private boaters are allowed to visit on Fridays, Saturdays, and Sundays between 12:30 and 3:00pm. There is no docking at Little Brewster, so boats must anchor offshore.

For fishing, working the south side is typically the best with the dominant southern wind. Start with the rocks on the western side, work up into the cove, and continue eastward to the split rocks. You'll also want to take a few casts around the ledges on the southern side of the island that rises from 26 feet to 12 feet. You'll also find a resident cod population that'll eat a fly. The best tides are half flood through half ebb.

HANGMAN ISLAND

Hangman Island got its name from the pirates that allegedly were strung up on the island. No true records document any such actual events, but the island was a seasonal home for lobstermen and fishermen. Erosion has taken its toll, and Hangman is now less than an acre at high tide. The surrounding rocks, ledges and shoals make for a difficult landing spot. The only place worth trying is the pebble beach on the southern side.

There are two parts to Hangman – the western rocks and the eastern rocks. At high tide, water flows through the two sections, but at low tide it's mostly exposed. Off of the southwest corner of the island is a spit of land that runs out into several rocks, a good spot to look for fish. Casting in between the two islands is great on the higher water marks. While you're fishing Hangman you should also check out Sunken Ledge – a good spot on either end of the half tides. Sunken Ledge is shaped like an upside down fishhook, and there is a vast amount of kelp, perfect for big feeding bass. Its proximity to the channel is good as well. Fish the spindle on the northwest side of the island, too. The bar drops off quickly and there are usually some big bass around it. During the summer, there is good bass and excellent bluefish fishing in Quincy Bay, and from Moon Head past Hangman is fantastic in the fall when the peanut bunker arrive.

PEDDOCKS ISLAND

While most islands in Boston Harbor are filled with forts, hospitals, and other buildings reminiscent of the city's unique history, Peddocks most closely resembles normal life. It is the only island to feature a collection of nearly 50 summer cottages, the last connection to summers past. Some of the cottages are dilapidated, but others are properly maintained. Some of the buildings were floated from Long Island to their new resting grounds, and local lore states that bootleggers and gamblers used Peddocks as a stopover during Prohibition. They hid their whiskey in between lobster pots and fishing nets. The island hosted many Revolutionary War skirmishes, and buckles, musket balls, and rusted sabers are still found on the island. The Peddocks Island chapel is one of the only churches that remains on the harbor islands and it was built according to a military template during World War II.

On the southern side is a 'u'-shaped bowl. Prince Head is the true land formation that connects to Peddocks, and is the closest to the channel. Bass will move up onto the flat and into the cove on the flood tides. There they will move high up towards the island and in and around the second formation, Harry's Rocks. Harry's Rocks is a long ledge that runs out to the channel. There typically aren't many fish around Harry's Rocks, but the ones that are there are usually big. Continue eastward and you'll fish through the famous Hull Gut. This area is better suited to conventional anglers, but if you are fishing an extra-fast-sinking line you'd do well to work from the northeast corner to Portuguese Cove. Dropping tides in the spring and fall are really good times to fish up here for the herring and menhaden that drop out of Quincy Bay stage in the various coves along Peddocks.

Private boaters can drop off guests and gear at the island dock and anchor offshore. They are advised to communicate camping trips with the Spectacle Island Marina at 857-452-7221 or channel VHF 69. Ferry service runs from the Hingham Shipyard and also from Boston's Long Wharf via Georges Island.

Al Wanamaker hooks up at Wolloston Beach, with the Boston Skyline in the background. Massachusetts residents are fortunate to have such outstanding fishing so close to a major urban city.

Hingham Bay

Sheep Island

This once-large island is mostly eroded, covered with scrub, sumac, and marsh grass. In the late 1800s, the Sheep Island Club, a group of prominent Boston politicians and businessmen, used the island for recreational outings.

The terrain around Sheep is pretty uniform. It's a combination of sand, mud, and rocks, and the uniformity doesn't allow for fish to hold consistently and regularly. On the flood tide, many fish filter in through Hull Gut and move up and past Sheep on the second or third hour of the flood tide. The water can get murky in the summer due to the sand and mud. Sheep Island lies on a predominantly north-south line, and there is a long sand spit that continues off the southern end, a good spot when the fish are in around high tide.

Raccoon Island

Two hundred yards off of Quincy's Hough's Neck is a bedrock outcropping that can be easily accessed by walking out at low tide – just bring a kayak for a paddle back on the high tide. The 3-acre island has been historically quiet, but the fishing is pretty solid. Raccoon sits on an east-to-west tack with the southern end adjoining Weymouth's Fore River. With its proximity so close to Hough's Neck, the current washing along Manet Beach and down to Rock Island Head makes for a good passage way into the Fore River. During the spring, the herring running into the river can make for excellent fishing at Raccoon. Later, silversides and menhaden make their appearance. Rock Island Cove, a short poke away from Raccoon, concentrates the baitfish so fall is also a good time to fish Raccoon.

Grape Island

The only grapes you'll find on the island these days are near the island dock, homage to the former vines that attracted Native Americans and early Europeans to the island. Tomahawk heads were routinely found in the 1800s, but Grape was routinely used for farming and the grazing of animals. Grape is close to the mainland, some 500 yards offshore from Weymouth Neck, with views of the John F. Kennedy Library in the nearby town of Dorchester.

Camping is allowed on the island, and reservations can be made at www.reserveamerica.com or toll free at 877-422-6762. The season is from late June to early September. Docks allow for drop-offs only by private boats, and the inter-island ferry rounds from Long Wharf to Georges Island to Grape, or directly from the Hingham Shipyard.

As if camping were not enough of a benefit, Grape Island is at the mouth of the Back River in Weymouth. What that means is that any fish going into the Back River (in the spring following the herring or later on following silversides) has to pass by one side of Grape. On the northern side you'll find shallow water and rocks and the southern side tends to be more sand and mud. On the southwest side is the channel that allows for boat passage into the Back River, and on the southeast side is Slate Island. Kayaking around Grape Island is good if you stay on the eastern side to avoid boat traffic. Floating lines around low water work well and use sinking lines during the higher water.

Slate Island

Located 250 yards east of Grape Island, Slate consists of slate outcrops. The rock was used for the construction of houses in Boston's distinguished Beacon Hill section in the 1600s. The rocky beach is preferable for landing a kayak or shallow-draft (and flat-bottomed) boat.

The water between Slate and Grape is shallow, and when the fish are following bait in between the structure, fishing can be fantastic. More often, the fish follow the deeper water on the east side of the island and then they filter back through on the south side. On the dropping tide, you'll see schools of bass and blues moving past Slate to pin baitfish against the bud flats that run from Crow Point to Hewitts Cove. The cove on the south side is a perfect spot for staging bait in the fall.

Bumpkin Island

On Bumpkin Island, you'll be hard pressed to know you're in the middle of a harbor. A grassy path through the woods leads you to the remnants of an old stone farmhouse from the 1800s. The home used to be a children's hospital and a World War I naval training center.

Native Americans traveled to Bumpkin in the summer months to dig clams, hunt waterfowl, and gather fruits and berries. The island's oval shape with a large, single sandbar that snakes back towards Nantasket Peninsula captures most anglers' attention. You can even sing the Bumpkin Island War Song, originally featured in the November 3, 1918 *Boston Sunday Advertiser*, written by Mrs. G.L. Camden for the Boston Naval Reserves.

Bumpkin is in the middle of Hull Bay, perfectly surrounded by the peninsula of Hull. To the southwest, you'll find a deep-water channel that marks the entrance to Hingham Harbor and the Weir River. The water shallows very quickly and runs into the White Head Flats, a perfect spot for shallow-water anglers. The White Head Flats run from the south side of the island all the way east to Nantasket. The protected area makes for good kayak fishing. Herring and alewives are the common spring baitfish, and silversides later in the year. You'll also see peanut bunker in the fall and sand eels along the flats.

Rangers lead edible berry walks, and camping reservations can be made at www.reserveamerica.com. Toll free number for campsites is 877-422-6762. Overnight guests will be assigned a campsite by an island ranger, and the camping season is from late June to early September, perfect for the fall run. Private boaters can only drop off passengers, and the inter-island ferry runs from Boston's Long Wharf to Georges Island and then on to Bumpkin. Direct-to-Bumpkin ferry service is available fro the Hingham Shipyard. Oh, and bring a kayak.

Hingham Harbor Islands

Hingham resident John Langley named the three northernmost islands in the harbor for his beautiful, but raggedly dressed, daughter Sarah. The innkeeper and boatyard owner's daughter turned out ok, and founded one of the oldest coeducational private schools in the United States after she became Sarah Langley Derby: Hingham's Derby Academy.

Four islands are situated in Hingham Harbor, with Crow Point on the western entrance to the harbor and World's End on the eastern entrance. A deep-water channel just off of Crow Point allows for safe passage on all tides. When north and east winds combine with a coming tide you'll find fish moving from the channel towards World's End, a good stopping point on your way in to fish the islands.

Langlee Island

There is a small beach on the northwest side of the island, just below a 40-foot-high cliff of Roxbury puddingstone. The southeast shore has a sweeping sandbar and sandy beach, noted mostly at low tide.

The channel runs along the northern sides of Ragged and Sarah that makes for good incoming tide fishing.

Ragged Island

There is a rocky cove on the northeast side of the island that holds fish at mid-tides. Also look to the southeast side of the island as Broad Cove empties into Hingham Harbor. This channel edge fishes well on a dropping tide, and fish can filter in and behind Ragged.

Sarah Island

There is a gravel beach on the north side of the island and 30-foot-high ledges on the south shore. Mudflats and tidal pools adjoin the gravel beach. The back side of the islands can fish better on higher water. Any fish that are inside of Hingham Harbor must pass by these two islands as the water drops. In the fall, the harbor acts as a giant cove and can fill up with baitfish, mostly silversides and peanut bunker.

Button Island

Higher up in the harbor is Button. Rock outcrops, boulders, sand, and mudflats surround the under-an-acre island. Button will fish better on higher water marks. There can be some good early season bass fishing and mid-season bluefish fishing, particularly at last light. That said, there is a lot of boat traffic from Memorial Day through Labor Day that makes for tough fishing.

Boston

Winthrop: Faun Bar / Five Sisters / Coughlin Playground / Belle Isle Creek

The oceanside town of Winthrop has several good wade-fishing spots, that also fish well out of a kayak, and some from a boat. There is a public boat ramp on Shirley Street which puts anglers in close proximity to Coughlin Playground, Snake Island, and Belle Isle Creek. If you continue down Shirley Street, you'll see a parking area next to the red, white, and blue water tower, which will give you access to the oceanside and the Five Sisters and Faun Bar.

There are two Faun Bars that are near each other, Great Faun Bar and Little Faun Bar. Both are on the west side of Deer Island. Great Faun Bar extends from the middle of the island while Little Faun Bar is at the southern end. Great Faun Bar is exposed at low tide, and is a mud, mussel, and rock bar. The surrounding water is around 6 feet deep which makes for good holding places for bass. A sand spit extends out the red nun and the water there is deeper, around 14 feet at low tide. What makes Great Faun Bar good for fishing is its close proximity to the main channel. Bass and blues will follow the channel in and then shift off to follow the structure which is where the baitfish are concentrated. Fall is a particularly hot time on the bar, particularly on the quarter moons when all the baitfish are staged. Floating lines are good around low tide, but try a sinking line on the higher water marks.

Little Faun Bar is smaller, with lots of rocks. On a dropping tide, the fish will move from the Inner Harbor, along the edge, and around Little Faun Bar. They'll typically move up and trade back and forth.

Five Sisters is a quick fishing spot which is usually combined with the two perpendicular bars at Winthrop Head. The Five Sisters are a series of breakwalls that are offshore and parallel to the beach. The gaps in between them allow current and fish to move closer to shore. Two sand bars connect to the third and fourth breakwall, and as a result, a cove on the inside has formed. It's a good kayak spot. While you're there, fish your way down along the beach to the two perpendicular bars that are below the water tower. You can wade far out on them. They are a combination of sand and cobble, and there is deeper water access. You'll also find fish on the quarter moons in the cove and along the beach to your right. A kayak is helpful for getting out a ways. East winds fish well, and the water is about 10 to 12 feet at low tide.

From Coughlin Playground you can fish all around the channel and the pilings. An intermediate line on a coming tide is a good time to fish over there. Then work your way back up the channel and wade all around the inside of the basin. Sometimes you'll find big schools of bass and blues when the bait is in, but mostly the basin is discolored and busy with boats that are launching. A great idea, though, is to bring a kayak. Paddling across the channel to Snake Island and either drifting while you cast or getting out on the island and wade fishing can be productive. At low tide, there are clammers digging steamer clams, but when the water is moving, there are fish around on the east side near the channel, off the rock garden on the south channel, and on the edge of the flat on the west side near the channel markers. The terrain is soft, so watch your step.

On your way out of Winthrop on Route 145, you'll pass Belle Isle Inlet and Creek. You'll typically see anglers fishing cut bait off of the bridge, and they can hook some big fish. Most of the time you'll find schoolies, and they'll move around the backwaters in between Logan Airport and Winthrop. In the spring and early summer, you'll find bass and blues chasing herring and silversides on the coming tides. The fish will move under the bridge and into the giant pond. Fishing in the basin near the bridge is one option, paddling a kayak around the pond is a second, or wading the banks with a floating line is a third.

Boston anglers can see the Boston Harbor Hotel up close while catching striped bass and bluefish. This is one pick up spot that is used by many Boston Harbor guides. What's remarkable is the harbor is so clean that anglers can leave a business meeting and catch fish within ten minutes of their conference room.

North Shore

Trying to determine where the North Shore actually begins is a matter of debate. Some say Lynnfield through Newburyport, and others include Winthrop, Revere, and Nahant. No matter, there is plenty of diversity up here. As you move out of the urban environment of Revere and Winthrop, you'll find rocks, ledges, and inshore islands in Cape Ann's towns of Marblehead, Beverly, Manchester-by-the-Sea, Gloucester, and Rockport. Continue on a northeast tack and you'll encounter many diverse river systems and barrier beaches from Ipswich to Newburyport. The North Shore is striper country.

Seasonality varies on the North Shore. You'll find alewives moving into the river systems as early as mid-April. The origins of many of the rivers are freshwater, a favorite of the anadromous baitfish. Shortly after the herring arrive you'll find squid, silversides, and sand eels. Adult menhaden arrive in the middle of June and juvenile menhaden stage in the fall. It's a veritable feast for stripers and bluefish.

Bass will arrive on the beachfronts and in the river systems shortly after the alewives arrive. I've caught them in the rivers as early as April 19, and I'm sure other anglers have caught them even earlier. They'll stay until the temperatures warm or the bait drops out. Not to fear, they're replaced by summer bluefish.

If you like to fish estuaries, you'll be in Hog Heaven. The major rivers are the Merrimack, the Parker, the Rowley, the Essex, and the Ipswich, and there are minor rivers off of most of them. With the 12-foot (give or take) tides, grass banks, and muddy bottom, you'll swear you're casting for smallmouths in some inland river.

Beach anglers are equally pleased. From Ipswich to Newburyport, you'll find mile after mile of some of the most beautiful beaches to wade. Some areas, like the mouths of the rivers, have moderate-sized flats on which anglers sight cast to cruising bass and blues. It's fisherman friendly, and few restaurants or tackle shops bat an eye if you walk in wearing waders.

Rocks abound in the Cape Ann stretch of the North Shore. Due to the colder water, the season around Rockport, Gloucester, Beverly, and Marblehead starts a little bit later than in the warmer river systems. You'll see a few different types of bait in these haunts – pollock, mackerel, and lobsters for starters. Make sure you pack a pair of Korkers as the rocks are slippery. And if you have a boat, the inshore islands off of Manchester-by-the-Sea, Beverly, and Marblehead are phenomenal in the summer.

Getting a strike on a streamer you just cast into the wash is almost as much of a rush as finding out how much the bass weighs.

As with the South Shore, it's tough to say exactly where the prestigious North Shore begins. The area from Boston to the New Hampshire border is known as Essex County or the "North-of-Boston" region. It's a historically rich region, with communities such as Salem, Gloucester, Lawrence, Ipswich, and Swampscott that played roles in the American Revolution. Marblehead, known as the Yachting Capital of the World (a title to which Fort Lauderdale, Florida also lays claim), is a model New England burg, replete with unique eateries and shops. The area was frequented by several U.S. presidents, including both Presidents Bush, who were educated at Phillips Academy in Andover.

In the more densely populated towns you'll find access is difficult, and that more spots are reachable by boat. Marblehead, Beverly, and Manchester-by-the-Sea can be difficult for shore anglers, and the rocks can be treacherous for kayak anglers. You're in luck if your buddy has a boat, and if he doesn't then hire a guide. The North Shore has some of the best water in the state.

REVERE BEACH / PINES RIVER

Home of the nation's first seaside bandstand and named for America's patriot Paul Revere, this beach can fish well in the spring and in the fall. This long beach runs for miles throughout Broad Sound, beginning just north of Winthrop and ending at the mouth of the Pines River. At the southern end is an 'L'-shaped breakwall. The area is mostly a sand and rock bottom, and you'll find early through mid-season bass in the rocks. They'll also be along the beachfront, and as you move toward the Pines River, the terrain gets increasingly sandier and less rocky. Some spectacular summertime bluefish blitzes occur off of the beach, and a floating or intermediate line works best. At the top of the Pines River is Pines Pond. Look for herring to move down Revere Beach and up the Pines River in the spring. You'll also find menhaden moving into the Pines during the summer months, and bluefish are not far behind.

NAHANT

The peninsula known as Nahant is a great fishery, but accessing it can be difficult. The thoroughly residential community does not offer ample public parking, but there is some. Long Beach runs down Nahant Road that connects the mainland with the peninsula. Little Nahant is the first outcropping before you hit the main island. Rocks are all along the north side and the water drops off quickly from shore. It's a good holding spot for big bass. South of Nahant is Short Beach (appropriately named), which forms a strong 'u'-shaped cove that runs into the main peninsula. You'll find bait staging here in the fall, particularly when the winds shift to their winter patterns. Moving south on the eastern side, you'll find a typically rocky terrain with ledges and boulder fields in the deeper water. On the eastern side is Saunders Ledge and Castle Rock – two areas with excellent current flow. Down by the twin towers is an extended boulder field that runs out to the Shag Rocks. When the fish are in, you'll

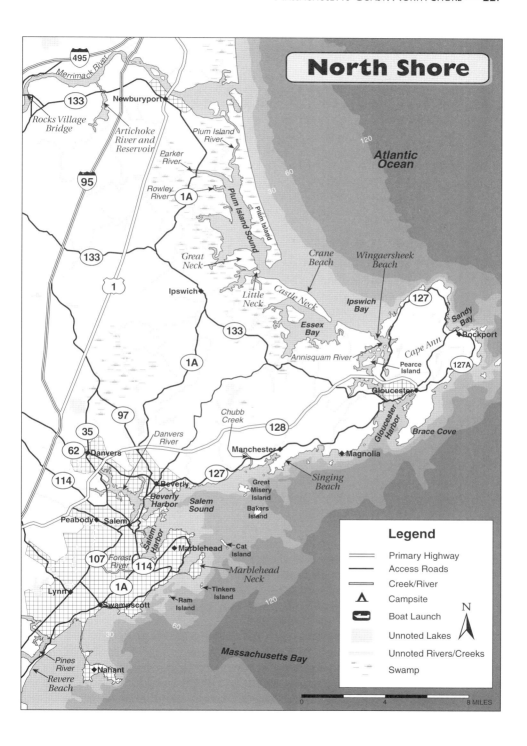

North Shore

Merrimack River
495
133
Newburyport
Rocks Village Bridge
Artichoke River and Reservoir
95
Plum Island River
Parker River
Rowley River
1A
133
1
Great Neck
Ipswich
133
1A
97
35
62 Danvers
114
Danvers River
Chubb Creek
127
Beverly
Beverly Harbor
Peabody Salem
107 Forest River
114
1A
Lynn
Swampscott
Pines River
Revere Beach
Nahant

Plum Island
Plum Island Sound
Little Neck
Castle Neck
Essex Bay
Crane Beach
Wingaersheek Beach
Ipswich Bay
Annisquam River
Pearce Island
Manchester
Great Misery Island
Bakers Island
Salem Sound
Salem Harbor
Marblehead
Cat Island
Marblehead Neck
Tinkers Island
Ram Island

Atlantic Ocean
120
60
30
127
Sandy Bay
Rockport
Cape Ann
127A
Gloucester
Gloucester Harbor
Brace Cove
Magnolia
Singing Beach
128

Massachusetts Bay
120
60
30

Legend

═══	Primary Highway
───	Access Roads
═	Creek/River
⋀	Campsite
⬭	Boat Launch
	Unnoted Lakes
	Unnoted Rivers/Creeks
	Swamp

N

0   4   8 MILES

find them moving through this area at mid-tides. Nahant Harbor is on the south side of the peninsula. It's classic striper country, with Pond Beach to the west that runs past a rock garden and into Dorothy Cove. Fish trade back and forth around mid-tide. You'll also find fish on the higher tide between Bass Point and Bailey's Hill on the southwestern end. Strong tippets are a must and Korkers are needed for wade anglers, while boat fishermen need to watch their prop and lower unit.

In the summer, boat anglers should head toward Egg Rock, off the coast of Nahant. There are sharp drop-offs with surrounding 50-foot depths. There are smaller rocks on the northeast side. Extra-fast-sinking lines and heavy tippets are standard fare. The fish pass by in late April through early May, and you'll find them around Egg Rock when the mackerel are in, when the lobsters shed, and when the water temperatures climb. Watch for diver-down flags around here.

MARBLEHEAD AND THE NECK

Marblehead has long been known for commercial fishing and sailing. Through the late 1960s, it was considered out of the way and difficult to reach. 'Headers like it that way, and the fishing is excellent. You should know that Marblehead is Marblehead, and the Neck refers to Marblehead Neck, the peninsula that forms Marblehead Harbor.

One spring and fall spot that fishes well is Devereux Beach off of Ocean Avenue. The beach has ample parking, and is a gently sloping sandy beach. Its crescent shape on the southern side makes it perfect in September and October, and one of the hot spots during the run. Most of the time, you'll find silversides as the dominant baitfish, and when the menhaden show up in the fall, you can expect a blitz at your feet. The current flow is moderate, and with the fall winds coming from the north (at your back) casting is a breeze. Most anglers favor floating or intermediate lines.

Access can be challenging, but remember that public access extends from the mean low tide mark (average low tide). A little kindness toward those in oceanfront homes goes a long way toward minimizing conflicts. I bring that up because one of the best areas to shore fish is Marblehead Neck, and it's an area that is heavily contested in the public/private debate.

From the Neck to Flying Point is an area of gently sloping rock, boulder fields, and ledges. It's a terrific area to fish, and some of the biggest bass of the year come from between Flying Point and Tinkers Island. What makes it so good is the ledge that runs between those two points and the deeper water on either end. The current moves quickly and the bait washes over. On lower water, a floating or intermediate line works best. When the tide floods, most anglers switch to an extra-fast-sinking shooting head.

While boat anglers will work the coastline from Flying Point all the way to Castle Rock, due to parking and access issues, wade fishermen will stop off at Castle Rock. This is a shared fishing/scuba diving spot. Water depths are deep, which makes it a popular summer fishing spot. Heading south you'll find a rocky cobble beach, steep in some areas, but if the water drops off fast, it creates a hard edge for anglers. It's a better summer spot, and sinking lines work well on the edge.

Chandler Hovey Park is at the end of the Neck, and it's where you'll find that skeleton of a lighthouse, Marblehead Light. The rocks all around the east end fish well on a half to high tide, and in particular the passageway between the Neck and Marblehead Rock. The east side of Marblehead Rock is the harbor entrance, so it gets busy with boats moving in and out of the harbor. Directly across the harbor from Marblehead Light is Fort Sewall. There is a cove on the southwestern side that is good for kayak anglers and also at mid- to high tide, and the entire harbor side of the fort can have good fishing. You'll want to get there to fish half flood tide through half ebb tide. Many times with the dominant south wind there are gentle seas on this north side, and it's possible to kayak around the rocks. When you can get in and around, be sure to concentrate on the area around Gerry and Brown Islands all the way to Peach's Point. There are coves, rocks, ledges, and drop-offs – perfect structure for summertime bass. That northern face is close to the South Channel that runs into Salem Harbor, and a dropping tide in the spring can be an excellent time to fish the rocks.

On the northwestern side of Marblehead is the Forest River, also known as the Lead Mills section that runs into Salem Harbor. You'll find the Forest River to be a good early season spot for bass (when the herring are in) and a mid- to late season spot for bluefish (when the menhaden are in). Fishing it on the dropping tide is best, and school fish will be here in the mouth of the river all season long. There is a newly rebuilt bridge above so you'll see runners and bikers, but they are high up and won't interfere with fishing. An intermediate or extra-fast-sinking line works best. Kayak fishing up here is good, too.

Bluefish are one of the hardest fighting fish in the salt, particularly when caught in shallow water. Tom Gabel hooks up off of Marblehead.

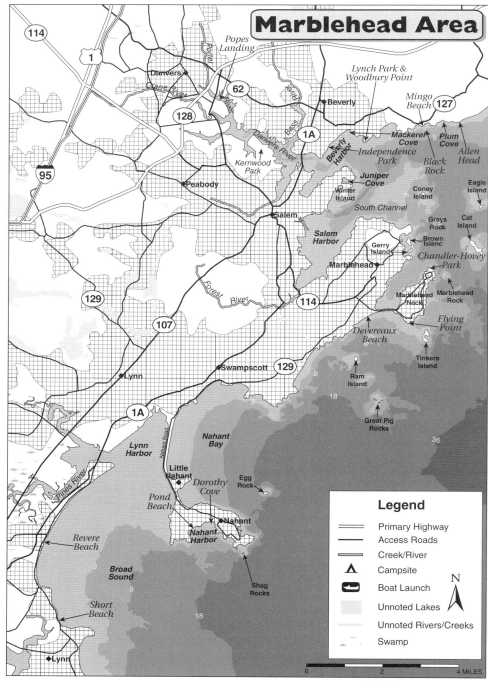

Marblehead Area

114

1

Popes Landing

Danvers

Crane River

62

128

Porter

Beverly

Lynch Park & Woodbury Point

Mingo Beach 127

1A

Mackerel Cove

Plum Cove

Allen Head

Beverly Harbor

Independence Park

Black Rock

Danvers River

Bass

95

Kernwood Park

Peabody

Juniper Cove

Winter Island

Coney Island

Eagle Island

Salem

South Channel

Grays Rock

Cat Island

Salem Harbor

Brown Island

Gerry Island

Chandler-Hovey Park

Marblehead

129

Forest River

107

114

Marblehead Neck

Marblehead Rock

Devereaux Beach

Flying Point

Lynn

Swampscott

129

9

Ram Island

18

Tinkers Island

1A

Nahant Bay

Great Pig Rocks

36

Lynn Harbor

Nahant Beach

Little Nahant

Dorothy Cove

Egg Rock

Pond Beach

Nahant

Pines River

Revere Beach

Nahant Harbor

Broad Sound

3

Shag Rocks

9

Short Beach

18

Lynn

Legend

≡≡≡	Primary Highway
—	Access Roads
—	Creek/River
▲	Campsite
⛴	Boat Launch
▒	Unnoted Lakes
	Unnoted Rivers/Creeks
	Swamp

N

0   2   4 MILES

© 2010 Wilderness Adventures Press, Inc.

Marblehead Islands

An archipelago of islands abounds around Marblehead, Beverly, and Manchester. Cat, Eagle, the Gooseberries, the Miseries, and Bakers Island are some of the spots worth fishing. Though some paddlers make their way out to these islands, flyfishermen typically fish them from a boat. From late May through October, these islands can fish well. There are many ledges as well, and if the fish aren't on the surface you'll need a sinking line to get down to them.

Salem/Danvers Area

Witch City was known for industry during the colonial days. Part of the reason for that was the large number of freshwater rivers that run into the ocean. As Salem Harbor is a working harbor, more of the fishing occurs from Winter Island, Salem Neck, and the Danvers River.

Winter Island connects with Salem Neck and is on the inside of the channel. There are a lot of rocks on the eastern side and Juniper Cove is to the north. Fishing here can be hit or miss. Boat fishermen will move more towards Middle Ground (between Salem Neck and Marblehead), particularly on dropping tides. There have been some tremendous spring and fall blitzes when the herring and the menhaden are in for both bass and bluefish.

One good way to fish the Danvers is on the high tide at Pope Landing at the Porter River. Starting on high tide, you can fish the dropping tide down through the Danvers River. From there you'll be able to hit the Bass River and the North River. There is a public ramp in the Bass River as well. The Crane River, which is next to the Porter River, was the site of a successful smelt restoration program. Obear Park is a good wade-fishing spot, as is Kernwood Park. Gillis Park at the mouth of the Bass River is also worth a shot. All three are good early season spots, with lots of school bass. Fish them on the lower water marks, as in the last two hours of the drop through the first two hours of the flood tides.

Independence Park along Lothrop Street/Route 127 offers public access along Beverly Channel and through Mackerel Cove. The depths are shallow at low tide, and to the south is the Beverly Channel that runs east into Beverly Harbor. The channel edge is the drop-off. Fish move up into the cove on the flood tide. In the spring you'll find herring, silversides, squid, and mackerel moving in to the shallows. Most of the fishing can be done with a floating or an intermediate line unless you're working the drop-off. Depths are in the 22- to 23-foot mark at mean low tide. There are a few rocks, but not many. Independence Park is a good kayak spot, just watch for boats in the channel.

Percy F. Lyons Park is known locally as the Dane Street Beach and is another spot to find seasonal striped bass and bluefish. Floating and intermediate lines are best. Fishing is better in the early and later seasons, and can be hit or miss. In the fall when the bait fill the beach, the fishing can be outstanding.

BEVERLY AREA

A good spot in Beverly is Lynch Park which is at Woodbury Point. From here anglers can access Mackerel Cove, Hospital Point, and Beverly Cove. Keeping in mind the tried-and-true adage of points on the full moon, coves on the quarter moon, you've got a good combination here. The water depths go through three-step increments until reaching the deeper water of Salem Sound. You'll find bass in the early spring and bluefish in the late summer and early fall, particularly when the menhaden are in. Floating and intermediate lines are good, and kayak fishing is convenient, too.

As you head east from a boat, you'll want to focus on two spots. The first is the rock ledge due south from Witch Lane, which is called Black Rock and is near Endicott College. Mingo Beach is to the northeast, and you'll find early season fish on the edge of the ledge. The water drops off very quickly here, and fish congregate off of Black Rock during the summer, too. The second area is from Smith Point to Allen Head around Plum Cove and Loring Beach. Access is by boat only, and fishing these areas during the higher water marks for big bass is a good bet. At the east end of West Beach (which is private) is a nice rock garden that is worth pursuing. One of two next steps is to continue east into Manchester or to head south to Great and Little Misery Islands. Many kayakers will head to the Miseries, too, and the fishing can be great. On the east end are deep drop-offs, and there is great structure in between the two islands along with good water flows.

MANCHESTER AREA

Chubb Island and Chubb Creek are on the western end of Manchester. If you want a river, rocks, ledges, shallow sandy areas, a marsh, a cove, and an inshore island all within the same area, this is your spot. As Chubb Creek dumps out into the ocean it creates a shallow river mouth with channels. On either side are rocks, ledges, and water that drops to between 10 and 16 feet at mean low tide. There are two coves within the rocks on the western end, all perfect structure for bass and blues. The area around Chubb Island is where Manchester Bay gets deep.

Off of Beach Street is Masconomo Park, which has a small bay adjacent to it. Better fishing times are spring and on higher water marks. There aren't a tremendous number of fish here but it's always worth a poke in the early season. Around the corner at Town Hall is a public boat ramp for powerboats and kayaks.

The water between Proctor and Gales Points at the entrance to Manchester Harbor is a good spot at half tide. Here you'll find shallow water with a combination of sand and rocks that run down to the rocks and ledges of Ram Island and House Island. The varying depths and rocky terrain make for excellent fishing, particularly during the warmer summer months. Extra-fast-sinking lines work well, and look for bluefish in the entire Manchester Bay when the menhaden show up in the summer.

Singing Beach is off of Beach Street in Manchester-by-the-Sea. The beach is rocky and stays cool, and the drop-offs are close to shore. It's one of the more popular beaches on the North Shore, particularly because it's accessible by the commuter rail and a walk from the train station. Parking is limited but you'll find fish out along the beach in the spring and at night in the summer. Ballarach Cove at the southwestern end of the beach is a small area, 5 feet deep at low tide, with a number of rocks at the mouth.

West Beach is long and shallow, and is a good morning and evening spot. Though the beach is private there is limited parking on Route 127 but in the early and late season it isn't much of a problem. To the east end is a large rock pile which is good on the medium to higher water marks. Floating or intermediate lines are best. The bars are parallel so the fish don't hold for long.

From a boat, head east and cast around the rocks at Eagle Head and hit Salt Rock, Rock Dundy, the Little Salt Rocks, and Boohoo Ledge. Each area offers structure adjacent to deeper water and fish well on the higher water marks in the summer months. You'll come upon Graves Beach and Graves Island.

MAGNOLIA AREA

There are three colors of beaches in Magnolia: White Beach, Black Beach, and Gray Beach. They move from west to east in that order, and they are similar in configuration. Odd, but the beaches run in a small, medium, and large size, too. What is similar about all three beaches is that they are coves, with sharp drop-offs, rocks, and ledges, with sand and shallows at the northern ends. The points fish well in the summer due to the colder water temperatures, and where they really excel is during the fall when the bait stages in the coves. White Beach gets a lot of scuba traffic, so watch for diver-down flags. Morning and evening are best bets during the summer, and all three beaches are popular with families. The beaches slope gently so a floating or intermediate line will work best. If you're fishing the rocky drop-offs around Crow Island (which is the point of land in between White and Black Beaches) or from Goldsmith Point through Mill Ledge (which is the point of land in between Black and Gray Beaches), you'll want to use an extra-fast-sinking line.

KETTLE ISLAND

Situated south of Grey Beach, Kettle Island is always worth a few casts. The western side is more consistent in its terrain while the eastern side has more texture in terms of more coves and recesses. Rock fishing in the summer for bass is good, and this island's close proximity to shore makes for good fall fishing, particularly close to the full moons when the bait that has staged in the coves prepares to move.

With its southern facing, Magnolia Point is a great fishing spot. It also gets a lot of scuba traffic due to the quick drop-offs. The rocks and ledges are slippery, so pack some Korkers. Survey the area for places to land your fish. To the east is Popplestone Beach, a classic rock beach with smooth drop-offs and rocks and ledges. Fish these areas on the higher water marks.

NORMAN'S WOE

There are three parts to Norman's Woe: Norman's Woe Island which is offshore, Norman's Woe Cove which is onshore, and Norman's Woe Reef which is offshore.

All three are worth fishing. Norman's Woe Cove offers parking in a fenced lot off of Hesperus Avenue. Here you'll find a few scuba divers making the quarter-mile hike in full gear to the waters edge. Anglers can move easily, but make sure you pack your Korkers. The fishing can be great, particularly on a heavy south wind, but the seas get high and dangerous as well. Extra-fast-sinking lines or floating lines work best. Norman's Woe Island and reef can be seen from land, and are the site of Longfellow's "Wreck of the Hesperus." The island runs on a mostly east-to-west pattern, and the rocky reef extends in a triangular shape on a mostly north-to-south tack. The south side of the island has lots of rocks and ledges with quick and dramatic drop-offs while the reef on the northern side is lower in altitude. There is a cove on the western side and a bulge on the eastern side. That structure means that if the fish are in you'll find them on one side or the other.

If you're boat fishing, the rocks to the northeast of Norman's Woe can hold some very large fish in the summer. Just watch for lower units and rogue waves. The stretch of land runs up to a cove which forms Mussel Point, a hook in the terrain. From the rocky beach to the rounded cove to the 'D'-shaped point, the area is very good for most of the season.

THE DOLLIVERS

Dolliver Neck, Dolliver Beach, and Dolliver Neck Marsh are on the west side of Gloucester Harbor and run into Freshwater Cove. In a short area, you'll have a marsh, a cove, a combination sand and gravel bar, a rocky beach, rocks, and ledges. Early and late seasons are good times to fish Freshwater Cove and Dolliver Neck Marsh (when the herring are in). You'll also find early mackerel and menhaden in the and around the harbor. In the summer months when the water temperatures warm, you'll want to fish out along the Neck where the average depth at low tide is between 17 and 33 feet. The pollack move in and you'll find stripers in and out all summer long. In the fall, the bait brings in the bluefish, and there can be some exceptional fishing on the western side.

STAGE FORT BEACHES

There are two beaches that are part of Stage Fort Park, Cressy's Beach to the south and Half Moon Beach to the north. Both have trails, fields, bathrooms, and small beaches which are a combination of sand and rock.

Cressy's Beach is the larger of the two and is underused because it's more of a walk from the parking lot, and the combination of sand and rock doesn't make for good lounging. It's good for fishing, and there is deep water access adjacent to shore. The beach is directly in front and fishes better on the coming tide. To the east is a knob of rocks and ledges, with coves and pockets. They are great spots during the higher water marks.

Half Moon Beach faces Gloucester Harbor and is a small sandy beach with a shallow, sandy beach set back in between two large rock outcroppings. Anglers can move to the south towards Cressy's Beach where they'll find large boulder fields and moderate to deep drop-offs or they can move to the north where they'll find sharper drop-offs, recesses, and clear water. Continuing north along the coastline you'll find enough boulders and drop-offs to keep you busy for a while. The farther north you go the closer you get to the top of Gloucester Harbor.

Gloucester Harbor is a working harbor, home of the Andrea Gale of *The Perfect Storm* fame. During the day, the significant boat traffic makes for difficult fishing. Along Stacy Boulevard, you'll see the Man Behind the Wheel, also known as the Gloucester Fisherman (a bronze statue of a fisherman at the wheel of his ship looking out over the sea, in memoriam to the fishermen who have been lost throughout the years). There is a public landing behind him and Pavillion Beach along the front. It's a mostly sandy beach that gets some early spring fish along the face. An intermediate line works best on the higher water marks. It's never crowded and when the fish are in, they'll be thick. An intermediate line is best.

The Annisquam River connects Gloucester Harbor with Ipswich Bay at Wingaersheek Beach. The river funnels baitfish and bass and blues back and forth all season long. When the tide is moving, you'll find fish somewhere along the route. There is a tremendous amount of boat traffic, but the confluence of the Jones River and the Annisquam is a good spot on a spring, high-dropping tide, as are the flats and channels below Pearce Island. Then there is the beach. Just off of Concord and Atlantic Streets is Wingaersheek Beach, a white-sand beach with lots of large rocks at the northwest edge. Fishing here is good before or after the crowds leave, and there are outstanding bluefish blitzes when first or last light match up with an incoming tide. The long sand bar enables anglers to walk pretty far out and access additional water.

IPSWICH AND ESSEX BAYS

When it comes to fishing Ipswich and Essex Bays, there is enough water here to last a lifetime. With beaches, river estuaries, creeks, flats, and inshore islands, any angler can find water that he or she loves to fish.

Ipswich Bay is all open ocean. Nothing protects it from the pounding Nor'easters, and the bay covers the ocean front section of Essex and the northwest part of Gloucester and Annisquam.

There are several beaches that are outstanding to fish. Crane Beach, which is part of Castle Neck, is the biggest draw. That's probably true because it is the longest beach. The 4-mile long beach and accompanying land were donated by the Crane Family and are now managed by Trustees of Reservations. Ipswich residents have free access, but non-residents must pay to enter. During the early season, you'll find bass filtering along the beach and moving into the river estuaries after herring or menhaden. When the sand eels and silversides arrive, you'll find them off of the bars and on the flats. The water here is very clear, and floating and intermediate lines are commonly used. If fishing from a kayak or a boat, pack along an extra-fast-sinking shooting head to get deep. Steep Hill is one section at the northwestern corner where Fox Creek and the Ipswich River are at the western end of Steep Hill. There are some clusters of rocks

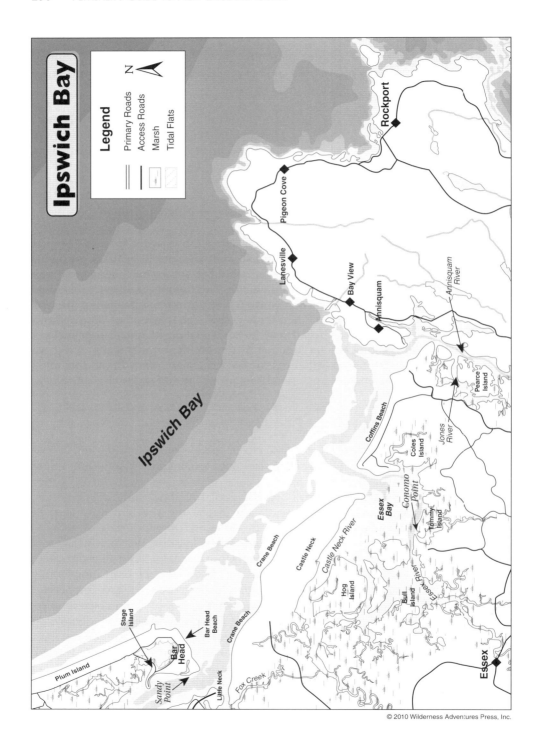

Ipswich Bay

Legend

N

Primary Roads

Access Roads

Marsh

Tidal Flats

Rockport

Pigeon Cove

Lanesville

Bay View

Annisquam

Annisquam River

Pearce Island

Ipswich Bay

Coffins Beach

Coles Island

Jones River

Conomo Point

Essex Bay

Tommy Island

Crane Beach

Castle Neck

Castle Neck River

Hog Island

Bull Island

Essex River

Essex

Stage Island

Bar Head Beach

Crane Beach

Bar Head

Plum Island

Sandy Point

Little Neck

Fox Creek

and it's the spot where Massachusetts author and fly tier Rich Murphy created his Steep Hill Special that is tied and sold by Umpqua Feather Merchants. That fly has caught a lot of fish and some big bass, all right, in the Steep Hill section. If you have a small boat or a kayak make sure to head up the creek with a paddle....and hit the Ipswich River, too. They fish well on the higher water marks.

Some anglers will walk south on Castle Neck to the cut which is where Essex Bay connects with Ipswich Bay. There are long bars and flats that lead all the way down to the channel that ultimately becomes the Essex River. During the summer there are a tremendous number of families on the beach, and that makes it difficult for daytime fishing. Most anglers will access the southern part of the beach by boat or kayak. You'll want to move slowly for the flats fish very well. Use natural sand eel patterns and floating or intermediate lines. You'll see Nat Moody and Derek Spingler who own First Light Anglers in Rowley fishing around here quite frequently.

Essex Bay runs on the inside of Castle Neck and Crane Beach. It is a diverse bay with several inshore islands, beaches, flats, and of course, the Essex River. The Castle Neck River runs on the west side of the beach, and this area has great fishing on both parts of the tide. It fishes well for bass in the early through mid-season, gets good bluefish runs, and also fishes well in the fall. On the inside are Hog Island (where the movie *The Crucible* was filmed), Conomo Point (a peninsula that Rich Murphy named another pattern after), Cole's Island, Tommy Island, Bull Island, and the Essex River marsh system. Inside fishes better on the higher tides and particularly on the dropping tide. Conomo Point Road runs to some of the prettiest fishing water around. There are bays, channels, flats, and rocks – perfect water. There is a boat ramp at Clammer's Beach but it is only a high water gravel ramp, good for small boats. There isn't much parking so get here early. It will put you in the action quickly. Kayaks can be launched here, too. Coffin's Beach is on the southern side of the cut, and can be a terrific fishery. As with Castle Neck/Crane Beach, a floating or intermediate line works best. Wingaersheek Road runs parallel to the beach.

Plum Island Sound covers the body of water to the west of Plum Island, and includes the towns of Plum Island, Newbury, Rowley, and Ipswich. The backside of Great and Little Neck open on to the Ipswich River, a perfectly protected spot for early season bass. Little Neck Road opens out to a parking area that is on Pavilion Beach, a good place to fish or to launch a kayak. The early season bass get replaced by bigger bass when the menhaden arrive and then lots of bluefish. It's a great fishery that is the mouth of several major rivers: the Plum Island River, the Parker River, and the Rowley River. A series of creeks and offshoots drain into each of these rivers, thereby creating a phenomenal fishery. When the larger bait like alewives and menhaden are in, you'll find big bass, and on a calm morning seeing bluefish erupt is outstanding. Floating or intermediate lines and casting against the banks and in the offshoots or creek mouths is a blast. The rivers are good kayak fisheries, too.

PLUM ISLAND

In between 27th and 29th streets on Northern Boulevard is a bull-nosed bar with ocean holes on either side. This area fishes well on half tides, and can be particularly hot during the spring when the fish arrive and in the fall when they're staging to depart. It's common to find several different types of bait mixed together, and a floating or intermediate line works best when fishing the higher water marks.

There is a restaurant at the end of the Plum Island Turnpike. Rather than turn left to head to the mouth of the Merrimack, head straight toward the ocean. There is a rock pile to the right and it's a good early season bass spot as well as a good spot for blitzing bluefish. Intermediate lines work well and you may have some company as it's a popular baitfishing spot.

If you want to fish the Parker River National Wildlife Refuge, you'll need a permit to fish the ocean-front beach between sunset and sunrise. Walking-on permits are not required, and you'll be able to fish around Stage Island and Nelson Island. Time of year is from July 1 to October 31. Four-by-four access starts September 1. There is a self sign-in/out book in Lot One with an air compressor station as well. Anglers can access through two areas. The North Beach Access is a half mile from the entrance

Rock Gardens, like these at the south end of Plum Island, Massachusetts, provide classic striper structure. As the tide rises and the currents move throughout the rocks, stripers can cruise through and pick off baitfish without exerting too much energy.

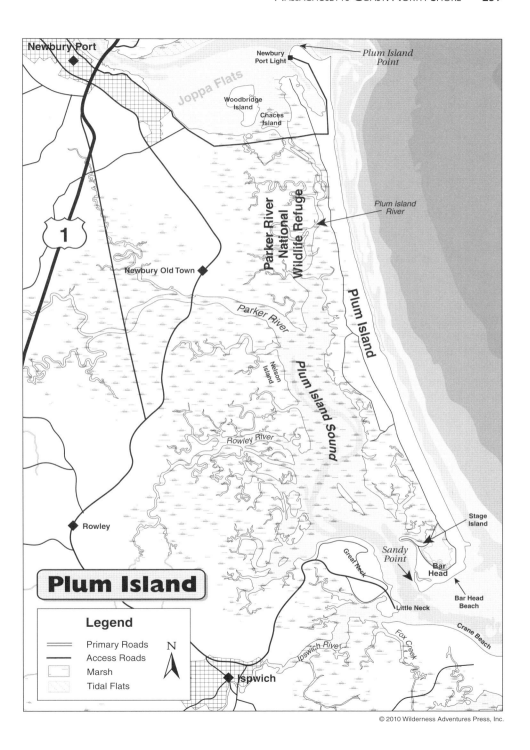

Plum Island

gatehouse, and the South Beach Access is 4.75 miles south of the entrance gatehouse. If you want to walk on, you can through lots 1, 2, 3, 5, 6, and 7 from September 1 through October 31.

You'll see a lot of texture all along the beach, with mostly beach break along the way. Toward the end of Plum Island, you'll find more interesting beach structure of parallel offshore bars and a long sweeping rock garden with a rock ledge called Emerson Rocks. The rocks are slippery but fish well throughout the lower water marks through the second hour of the flood tide. After that it gets a little dicey walking around on the rocks. Korkers are a must. The structure is great and an intermediate line is best. Heading farther south, you'll see sand and a bowl that runs for a few hundred yards down to the south end. Here is an enormous rock garden that fishes well year round. The nearby sand holds all types of bait from early season big bait to silversides and sand eels. The rock garden makes for excellent fishing. Intermediate lines are the best.

Bar Head and Bar Head Beach are all the way at the base. It's mostly beach break, but the southwest corner has a sweeping perpendicular bar that has deeper water on either side. From here to the northwestern Sandy Point, you'll find a long, sweeping crescent beach with deeper water. Sandy Point protrudes out and overlooks 'the spindle', a common boat fishing spot. From Sandy Point north to Ipswich Bluff is another crescent beach that has wadeable water with deeper water within casting range. Here's where you'll find fish moving into the area on both tides. Look for the drop-offs and the current seams and you'll find the fish. Intermediate or sink-tip lines are good, and the last three hours of the outgoing tide and the first three hours of the incoming tide are best.

NEWBURYPORT

The Merrimack River is one of those places that is just plain fishy. There is an Atlantic salmon stocking and restoration program in New Hampshire, and striped bass are caught high up in the river, with the city of Lowell being a place where you'll catch both smallies and schoolies. There are a tremendous number of places to target while wading, from a boat and from a kayak. Newburyport is an old working harbor, with lots of boats shipping out to sea every day. Like the Cape Cod Canal and the North River, the mouth of the Merrimack has incredibly fast currents and swift moving water. It's not an area for small boats and craft.

The first two obstructions on the river – the Essex Dam in Lawrence and the Pawtucket Dam in Lowell – have been equipped with fish-passage facilities since the mid-19th century. These ladders have been upgraded on several occasions, the latest being in the 1980s when fish lifts were installed at the two dams. So, the bait can get up river which means that bass will move high up into the river systems chasing them.

ROCKS VILLAGE BRIDGE

In the early season when all the bait arrives (from alewives to herring and silversides), you'll find another baitfish worth catching: the American shad. You'll catch 3- to

6-pounders throughout the river from mid-April through mid-May, and one place to find them in large concentrations is the Rocks Village Bridge off of River Road and Bridge Street. Fish below the bridge and, depending on the run off, either a sink tip or an extra-fast-sinking shooting head will fish well. Some anglers feel that gold hooks increase catch ratios on shad, so you may want to tie flies on both stainless and gold hooks and be your own judge. Below Rocks Village is the Artichoke River, which runs into the Artichoke River Reservoir. It's also a good spot to look for shad and striped bass in the spring.

DEER AND EAGLE ISLANDS

Below the Route 95 overpass are two river islands, Deer and Eagle Islands. The structure around both of these islands is good when the herring and menhaden are in. You'll find bass and bluefish feeding on the bait on the dropping tides in May and in June. There are shallows in between the islands and also on the southwest side of Eagle. Watch for the bald eagles, too. Some big bass are caught up here every year. High tide is a good time to fish up here, particularly on the north side of Deer.

Carr and Ram Islands are the two islands in Newburyport Harbor. The harbor is on the western side, and a back channel follows on the eastern side. The area in between the two islands is a good place to fish on a dropping tide, as bait concentrates on the drop and funnels down in the bottleneck. The water around Ram gets bony in spots, but Town Creek Marsh can be good on the higher water marks. When bass are in along the backside, stealthy anglers use kayaks or will get out of their boats and wade along the banks so as to avoid spooking fish. Both Carr and Ram Islands are just upriver from Cashman Park which is just above the Route 1A bridge. There is a boat ramp as well as plenty of parking for trailers. Kayaks launch from here, too. It's a quick poke to fish the islands.

AMERICAN YACHT CLUB, JOPPA FLATS, AND THE WATER STREET SEAWALL

Most anglers associate Newburyport with Joppa Flats. And with good reason – it's an outstanding fishery. The flats start a bit above the Water Street seawall at the American Yacht Club and continue southeast to Woodbridge Island. Just below the AYC is a cluster of rocks called Gangway Rocks, always worth a few casts, particularly in the spring and fall when you'll see blitzing fish. All along the edges of Joppa are channels, creeks, and ditches, with lots of salt cordgrass and salt hay around the edges. The bottom terrain is a sand/mud mix. Wade fishermen will enter at the seawall around mid-ebb tide, work their way out towards the channel and all around the flats, being back at the seawall by around mid-flood tide. Many shallow draft boats fish this area on the higher water marks, and there are many kayak anglers as well. Water clarity can be murky after a heavy rain (water from upstate washing down) or winds (churned up from the ocean). The proximity to the ocean means fog can be an issue, so be sure to wear a compass even when wading. There is decent parking at the seawall and the short ramp makes for a quick kayak launch.

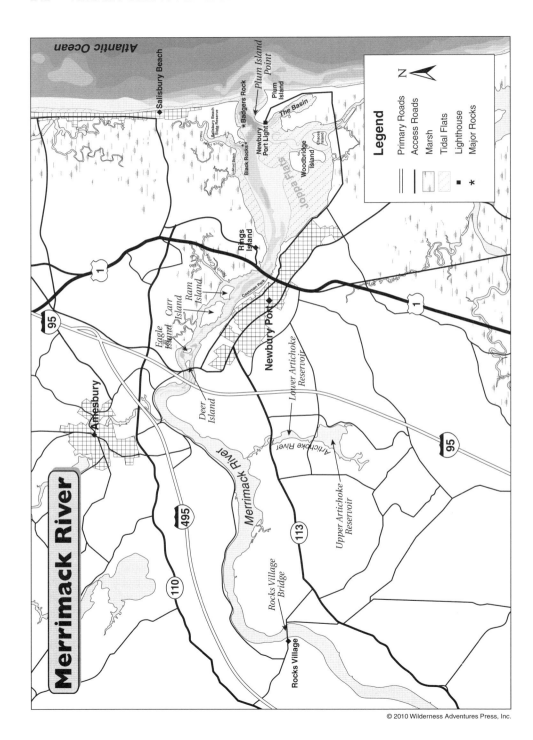

Merrimack River

© 2010 Wilderness Adventures Press, Inc.

WOODBRIDGE ISLAND, CHACES ISLAND, THE BASIN, PLUM ISLAND POINT

At the southeastern end of the flats is Woodbridge Island. Woodbridge Island is well known for outstanding duck hunting. It has a shallow reach on the north side of the island and is full of mussel beds and soft mud. There are shallow creeks and channels on the eastern and southern sides. The water moves constantly on all but dead low tide, and Woodbridge Island fishes well at all times of day. You'll find bass feeding on shrimp and silversides at night, bigger fish around first or last light, and small fish blitzes during the day. The channel that runs between Woodbridge and Chaces Island to the east is the same channel that extends under the bridge going to Plum Island. That channel actually extends south and will run on the western side of the island and ultimately connect with the Parker River and Plum Island Sound. What that means is that on the higher water marks, there are bass and bluefish that trade back and forth between the Merrimack and the southern tip of Plum Island. Kayak fishermen have the best approach for covering the water, just be sure to time your tides so you get more fishing than paddling in. At the northern end of Chaces Island is an interesting structure: water, flats, mussel beds, channels, and three points of land with Woodbridge, Chaces, and Plum Island all connecting. Mid- to higher water marks fish well. The Basin runs on the inside of west end and is the body of water that separates the land that has streets named for people from Newburyport Harbor Entrance Light side which has streets named by numbers. The Basin can be very good in the early and late season for both bass and bluefish, and the bottom can be soft and muddy. It's a good kayak and nightspot, and access points are on both sides. Intermediate lines generally are enough, on the higher tides you may want an extra-fast-sinking shooting head. At the end of the Plum Island Turnpike is a big parking lot. Plum Island Point is the sandy beach that runs from the party boats on the west side to the end of the sand on the east. Spring and fall are great times for fishing the beach and the mouth. Most fly rodders will focus on the three hours on either side of low tide. At the mouth of the Merrimack is a sand flat on the south end of the spit that offers additional deep-water access. Wade anglers should be careful, the current is strong and the waves can be significant if you have tide combined with fishing boats. Extra-fast-sinking shooting heads are typically used due to the current speed.

BADGERS ROCK AND THE JETTIES

Down in the mouth isn't always a bad thing, and with a rock formation and two jetties, the mouth of the Merrimack is a good spot. Badgers Rock on the Salisbury side is a rock ledge that begins a stretch of good water. A point bar separates two crescent-shaped coves along the beach, with river water flowing on both sides of the rocks down to the Salisbury Jetty. Fish move along the entire shore line, and are along all the sides of the ledges when the current is running. The long jetty runs first on a 45-degree angle before extending straight into the Atlantic, thereby necking down the mouth of the river. On the Plum Island side is a second jetty, this one much shorter and running parallel to the Salisbury Jetty. Fishing can be good on and around the jetties, particularly in the bowls that form along the beach.

SALISBURY BEACH

For the most part, Salisbury Beach plays second fiddle to her more famous neighbor, Plum Island. When the fish are on the beaches at Plum Island, at Badgers Rock, or throughout the mouth of the Merrimack, they're probably on the Salisbury side, too. Still, only a fraction of anglers will visit Salisbury Beach per year.

The Salisbury Beach State Reservation is a 521-acre state park, with nearly 4 miles of beachfront access. There is a 484-site campground, two boat ramps on the Merrimack, and day usage as well. What more can you ask for?

Two creeks are on the inside of the Merrimack River that run along the south end of the state park. Black Rock Creek is on the west side and is a saltwater estuary. Once the bait arrives in April, the creek will fish well all season long. In the spring, you'll find shad and striped bass and later in the summer a mixture of bass and blues. There are two branches that form a 'y', thereby making Black Rock Creek a good kayak estuary. It fishes better on the higher water marks, and in particular the dropping tide. Target the confluence and work your way toward the mouth. There you'll find good current and a bar on the east side. The mouth fishes well at low tide, too.

Shad Creek is the next creek on the western side of Black Rock Creek. It is a much smaller estuary, and will hold fish. It splits into two arms: one runs northwest and one runs northeast. As with Black Rock Creek, the confluence of the two arms is a particularly good spot on the dropping tide. As the tide ebbs, continue to move toward the mouth and you're likely to catch fish all along the way.

Heading north along the beach you'll find mostly beach break. There are a few interesting parts of the beach. The first is just above the jetty where a rock pile protrudes and runs along an ocean hole that connects to a bull-nosed bar. The diversity and the current flow here makes for interesting fishing and lots of good structure. A few hundred yards north of that stretch is a parallel offshore bar that holds fish for a good portion of the year. You'll find them at the northern and southern ends of the bar, and the eastern side of the bar. As the tide turns and floods, they'll filter in along the beach.

The Massachusetts/New Hampshire border is about at the Route 286/Route 1A Intersection, an important point if you're planning on keeping striped bass for the table, as the state regulations differ.

Massachusetts Saltwater Public Boat Ramps

BARNSTABLE

Barnstable Harbor (Blish Point). Concrete. Ramps - 1. Lanes - 2. Parking - Yes.

CHILMARK

Great Rock Bight. Ramps - 0. Lanes - 0. Shore Fishing.

DANVERS

Porter River (Popes Landing). Concrete. Ramps - 1. Lanes - 2. Parking - Yes.

DARTMOUTH

Apponagansett Bay. Concrete. Ramps - 1. Lanes - 2. Parking - Yes.

DENNIS

Bass River (Uncle Freemans Landing). Concrete. Ramps - 1. Lanes - 2. Parking - Yes.
Horsefoot Cove. Concrete. Ramps - 1. Lanes - 1. Parking - Yes.
Sesuit Harbor. Concrete. Ramps - 1. Lanes - 2. Parking - Yes.

EDGARTOWN

Cape Poge Bay. Cartop. Ramps - 0. Lanes - 1. Parking - Limited.
Katama Bay. Concrete Pad. Ramps - 1. Lanes - 1. Parking - Yes.

FAIRHAVEN

Acushnet River Basin (Pease Park). Concrete. Ramps - 1. Lanes - 2. Parking - Yes.
Nasketucket Bay (Sconticut Neck). Concrete. Ramps - 1. Lanes - 2. Parking - Yes.

FALL RIVER

Taunton River Basin. Concrete. Ramps - 1. Lanes - 2. Parking - Yes.

FALMOUTH

Falmouth Harbour. Concrete. Ramps - 1. Lanes - 1. Parking - Yes.
Great Bay. Concrete. Ramps - 1. Lanes - 1. Parking - Yes.

Green Pond. Concrete. Ramps - 1. Lanes - 2. Parking - Yes.

Megansett Harbor. Concrete. Ramps - 1. Lanes - 1. Parking - Yes.

Seapit River (Seapit Landing). Concrete Pad. Ramps - 1. Lanes - 1. Parking - Yes.

GLOUCESTER

Annisquam River (Corliss Landing). Concrete Pad. Ramps - 1. Lanes - 1. Parking - Yes.

Annisquam River (Dunfudgen Landing). Concrete. Ramps - 1. Lanes - 2. Parking - Yes.

Jones River (Long Wharf). Concrete Pad. Ramps - 1. Lanes - 1. Parking - Yes.

Lanes Cove. Concrete Pad. Ramps - 1. Lanes - 1. Parking - Yes.

HARWICH

Saquatucket Harbor. Concrete Pad. Ramps - 1. Lanes - 2. Parking - Yes.

IPSWICH

Ipswich River. Concrete. Ramps - 1. Lanes - 2. Parking - Yes.

LYNN

Lynn Harbor. Concrete. Ramps - 1. Lanes - 2. Parking - Yes.

MARBLEHEAD

Marblehead Harbor (Riverhead Beach). Concrete. Ramps - 1. Lanes - 2. Parking - Yes.

MARSHFIELD

Green Harbor. Concrete. Ramps - 1. Lanes - 3. Parking - Yes.

MASHPEE

Popponesset Beach. Ramps - 0. Lanes - 0. Shore fishing area.

MATTAPOISETT

Mattapoisett Harbor (Short Wharf). Concrete. Ramps - 1. Lanes - 2. Parking - Yes.

NANTUCKET

Hither Creek. Concrete Pad. Ramps - 1. Lanes - 1. Parking - Yes.

Madaket Harbor (Jackson Point). Concrete. Ramps - 1. Lanes - 1. Parking - Yes.

New Bedford

Clarks Cove. Concrete. Ramps - 1. Lanes - 2. Parking - Yes.
New Bedford Harbor. Concrete. Ramps - 1. Lanes - 2. Parking - Yes.

Newbury

Parker River. Canoe. Ramps - 0. Lanes - 1. Canoe access.

Newburyport

Merrimack River (Cashman Park). Concrete. Ramps - 2. Lanes - 3. Parking - Yes.

Oak Bluffs

Sengekontacket Pond. Concrete Pad. Ramps - 1. Lanes - 1. Parking - Yes.
Sengekontacket Pond (Pecoy Point). Cartop. Ramps - 0. Lanes - 1. Access for small boats, canoes, and kayaks.

Orleans

Rock Harbor. Concrete. Ramps - 1. Lanes - 2. Parking - Yes.

Plymouth

Plymouth Harbor. Concrete. Ramps - 1. Lanes - 2. Parking - Yes.

Quincy

Fore River. Ramps - 0. Lanes - 0. Shore fishing area.
Fore River (Houghs Neck). Concrete. Ramps - 1. Lanes - 1. Parking - Yes.

Salem

Danvers River. Concrete. Ramps - 1. Lanes - 2. Parking - Yes.
Salem Harbor (Winter Island). Concrete. Ramps - 1. Lanes - 3. Parking - Yes.

Salisbury

Black Rock Creek. Concrete. Ramps - 1. Lanes - 2. Parking - Yes.

Sandwich

Scorton Creek. Ramps - 0. Lanes - 0. Shore fishing area.

Scituate

Scituate Harbor. Concrete. Ramps - 1. Lanes - 2. Parking - Yes.

SWANSEA

Cole River. Concrete. Ramps - 1. Lanes - 2. Parking - Yes.

TISBURY

Lagoon Pond. Concrete. Ramps - 1. Lanes - 2. Parking - Yes.

TRURO

Pamet River. Concrete. Ramps - 1. Lanes - 2. Parking - Yes.

WAREHAM

Wankinco River. Canoe. Ramps - 0. Lanes - 1. Parking - Limited.
Wareham River (Tempest Knob). Concrete. Ramps - 1. Lanes - 2. Sport fishing pier.
Weweantic River. Concrete. Ramps - 1. Lanes - 1. Parking - Yes.

WELLFLEET

Wellfleet Harbor. Concrete. Ramps - 1. Lanes - 2. Parking - Yes.

WEST TISBURY

Tisbury Great Pond. Gravel. Ramps - 1. Lanes - 1. Parking - Yes.

WESTPORT

Westport River. Concrete. Ramps - 1. Lanes - 2. Parking - Yes.

WEYMOUTH

Back River. Concrete. Ramps - 1. Lanes - 2. Parking - Yes.
Whitman Pond. Concrete Pad. Ramps - 1. Lanes - 1. Parking - Yes.

WINTHROP

Winthrop Harbor. Concrete. Ramps - 1. Lanes - 2. Parking - Yes.

YARMOUTH

Bass River. Concrete. Ramps - 1. Lanes - 2. Parking - Yes.
Lewis Bay (Englewood Beach). Concrete Pad. Ramps - 1. Lanes - 1. Parking - Yes.
Parkers River. Ramps - 0. Lanes - 0. Sport fishing pier.

Hub City Information: Massachusetts

Westport

Population - 15,400 Area Code - 508 County - Bristol

Hotels and Motels

Hampton Inn Fall River, Westport, 53 Old Bedford Road, Westport / 675-8500 / www.hamptoninn.com

Paquachuck Inn, 2056 Main Road, Westport / 636-4398 / www.paquachuck.com

Best Western, 737 State Road, N. Dartmouth / 717-0424 / www.bwdartmouth.com

Restaurants

The Back Eddy, 1 Bridge Road, Westport / 636-6500 / www.thebackeddy.com

The Bayside Restaurant, 1253 Horseneck Road, Westport / 636-5882 / www.thewestportbayside.com

Bittersweet Farm Restaurant & Tavern, 438 Main Road, Westport / 636-0085 / www.lafrancehospitality.com

Marguerite's, 778 Main Road, Westport / 636-3040

Fly Shops/Bait and Tackle Shops

Westport Marine Specialties, 1111 Main Road, Westport / 636-8100 / www.westportbaitandtackle.com

Hospitals

Saint Luke's Hospital, 101 Page Street, New Bedford / 997-1515 / www.southcoast.org/stlukes/

St Annes Hospital, 795 Middle Street, Fall River / 674-5600 / www.saintanneshospital.org

Airports

Boston-Logan Airport (BOS), 1 Harborside Drive, East Boston / 800-23-LOGAN / www.massport.com
T.F. Green Airport (PVD), 2000 Post Road, Warwick / 888-268-7222

Trains

Providence Amtrak Station (PVD), 100 Gaspee Street, Providence / 800-872-7245

Other Activities

Westport Winery, 417 Hixbridge Road, Westport / 636-3423 / www.westportrivers.com
New Bedford Whaling Museum, 18 Johnny Cake Hill, New Bedford / 997-0046 / www.whalingmuseum.org

CAPE COD
Population - 226,198 Area Code-508 or 774 County - Barnstable

Hotels and Motels

Chatham Wayside Inn, 512 Main Street PO Box 685, Chatham / 800-CHATHAM or 508-945-5550 / www.chatham-wayside-inn.com
Provincetown Inn, 1 Commercial Street, Provincetown / 508-487-9500 / www.provincetowninn.com
Hyannis Days Inn Hotel, 867 Iyannough Road, Hyannis / 508-771-6100 / www.daysinn.com

Restaurants

Chatham Squire Restaurant, 487 Main Street, Chatham / 508-945-0945 / www.thesquire.com
Mattakeese Wharf Waterfront Restaurant, 271 Millway, Barnstable / 508-362-4511 / www.mattakeese.com
The Paddock Restaurant, 20 Scudder Avenue, Hyannis / 508-775-7677 / www.paddockcapecod.com

Fly Shops/Bait and Tackle Shops

Fishing the Cape, Harwich Commons, 120 Route 137, E. Harwich / 508-432-1200 / www.fishingthecape.com
Goose Hummock Shop, Route 6A, Orleans / 508-255-0455 / www.goose.com
Eastman's Sport & Tackle, 783 Main Street, Falmouth / 508-548-6900 / www.eastmanstackle.com

Marine Supplies

Nauset Marine, Orleans 508-255-0777 / Hyannis 508-563-1110 / www.nausetmarine.com

Hospitals

Cape Cod Hospital, 27 Park Street, Hyannis / 508-771-1800 / www.capecodhealth.org

Airports

Hyannis Airport (HYA), Barnstable Road, Hyannis / 508-778-7770
Provincetown Airport (PVC), Race Point Road, Provincetown / 508-487-2100
Boston-Logan Airport (BOS), 1 Harborside Drive, East Boston / 800-23-LOGAN / www.massport.com

Ferries

Hy-Line Cruises / 800-492-8082 / www.hy-linecruises.com
The Steamship Authority / 508-693-9130 or 508-495-3278 / www.steamshipauthority.com

MARTHA'S VINEYARD

Population - 15,582 Area Code - 508 or 774 County - Dukes

Hotels and Motels

Menemsha Inn and Cottages, PO Box 38, 12 Menemsha Road, Menemsha / 508 645 2521 / www.menemshainn.com
Harborview Hotel and Resort, 131 North Water Street, Edgartown / 508-627-7000 / www.harbor-view.com
Tivoli Inn, 125 Circuit Avenue, Oak Bluffs / 508-693-7928 / www.tivoliinn.com

Restaurants

Home Port Restaurant, 512 North Road, Chilmark / 508-645-2679 / www.homeportmv.com
Giordano's Restaurant & Clam, 107 S Circuit Ave, Vineyard Haven / 508-693-0184 / www.giosmv.com
Offshore Ale Company, 30 Kennebec Street, Oak Bluffs / 508-693-2626 / www.offshoreale.com

Fly Shops/Bait and Tackle Shops

Larry's Tackle Shop, 258 Upper Main Street, Edgartown / 508-627-5088 / www.larrystackle.com

Coop's Bait & Tackle, 147 W. Tisbury Road, Edgartown / 508-627-3909 / www.coopsbaitandtackle.com

Dick's Bait & Tackle, New York Avenue, Oak Bluffs / 508-693-7669

Marine Supplies

Martha's Vineyard Shipyard, 164 Beach Road, Vineyard Haven / 508-693-0400 / www.mvshipyard.com

Hospitals

Martha's Vineyard Hospital, One Hospital Road, Oak Bluffs / 508-693-0410 / www.mvhospital.com

Airports

Marthas Vineyard Airport (MVY), 71 Airport Road, Vineyard Haven / 508-693-7022 / www.mvyairport.com

Boston-Logan Airport (BOS), 1 Harborside Drive, East Boston / 800-23-LOGAN / www.massport.com

Airlines

Cape Air / 800-352-0714 / www.capeair.com / Service from Boston, Hyannis, Nantucket, New Bedford, Providence (seasonally), Provincetown, and White Plains. They have interline agreements for joint ticketing and interline baggage handling for connecting flights with most major airlines. They also have joint fares for discounted travel Continental and JetBlue.

USAirways Express / 800-428-4322 / www.usairways.com / Seasonal service from New York's LaGuardia, Washington D.C.'s Reagan National, Philadelphia and Hyannis.

USAC Aviation / 908-512-9039 / www.usac.com / Private charter flights from several cities to Martha's Vineyard.

Ferries

Hy-Line Cruises / 800-492-8082 / www.hy-linecruises.com

The Steamship Authority / 508-693-9130 or 508-495-3278 / www.steamshipauthority.com

Falmouth Edgartown Ferry / 508-548-9400 / www.falmouthferry.com

Martha's Vineyard Express Ferry / 866-683-3779 / www.mvexpressferry.com

Auto Rentals

AA Island Auto Rentals / Martha's Vineyard Airport/ 508-696-5300 or 800-627-6333 / www.mvautorental.com

Adventure Car Rentals / Martha's Vineyard-Oak Bluffs or Vineyard Haven / 508-693-1959 / www.islandadventuresmv.com

Budget Rent-A-Car / Martha's Vineyard Airport / 508-693-7323 or 800-527-0700 / www.budgetmv.com

Hertz Rent-A-Car / Martha's Vineyard Airport / 508-693-2402 or 800-654-3131 / www.hertz.com

For more information

Martha's Vineyard Chamber of Commerce / 508-693-0085 / www.mvy.com

NANTUCKET
Population – 9,520 Area Code - 508 County - Nantucket

Hotels and Motels

Veranda House, 3 Step Lane, Nantucket / 228-0695 / www.theverandahouse.com
The Wauwinet, 120 Wauwinet Road, Nantucket / 228-0145 / www.wauwinet.com
The Cottages at the Boat Basin, 1 Old South Wharf, Nantucket / 325-1499 / www.thecottagesnantucket.com
Cliffside Beach Club, 46 Jefferson Avenue, Nantucket / 228-0618 / www.cliffsidebeach.com

Restaurants

Centre Street Bistro, 29 Centre Street, Nantucket / 228-8470 / www.nantucketbistro.com
Topper's at The Wauwinet, 120 Wauwinet Road, Nantucket / 228-8768 / www.wauwinet.com
Galley Beach, 54 Jefferson Avenue, Nantucket / 228-9641
Boarding House, 12 Federal Street, Nantucket / 228-9622 / www.boardinghousenantucket.com

Fly Shops/Bait and Tackle Shops

Bill Fisher Tackle, 3 Polpis Road, Nantucket / 228-2261 / www.billfishertackle.com
Cross Rip Outfitters, 24 Easy Street, Nantucket / 228-4900 / www.crossrip.com
Nantucket Tackle Center, 41 Sparks Avenue, Nantucket / 228-4081 / www.nantuckettackle.com

Marine Supplies

Nantucket Moorings, 85 Bartlett Road, Nantucket / 228-4472 / www.nantucketmoorings.com
Grey Lady Marine, 13 Arrowhead Drive, Nantucket / 228-6525
Brant Point Marine, 32 Washington Street, Nantucket / 228-6244 / www.brantpointmarine.com

Hospitals

Nantucket Cottage Hospital, 57 Prospect Street, Nantucket / 825-8100 / www.nantuckethospital.org

Airports

Nantucket Memorial Airport, 14 Airport Road, Nantucket / 325-5300 / www.nantucketairport.com

Boston-Logan Airport (BOS), 1 Harborside Drive, East Boston / 800-23-LOGAN / www.massport.com

Airlines

Cape Air / 800-352-0714 / www.capeair.com / Service from Boston, Hyannis, Nantucket, New Bedford, Providence (seasonally), Provincetown, and White Plains. They have interline agreements for joint ticketing and interline baggage handling for connecting flights with most major airlines. They also have joint fares for discounted travel Continental and JetBlue.

USAirways Express / 800-428-4322 / www.usairways.com / Seasonal service from New York's LaGuardia, Washington D.C.'s Reagan National, Philadelphia and Hyannis.

USAC Aviation / 908-512-9039 / www.usac.com / Private charter flights from several cities to Martha's Vineyard.

Ferries

Hy-Line Cruises / 800-492-8082 / www.hy-linecruises.com

The Steamship Authority / 508-693-9130 or 508-495-3278 / www.steamshipauthority.com

Auto Rentals

Hertz Rent-A-Car / Nantucket Airport / 800-654-3131 / www.hertz.com

Nantucket Island Rent-A-Car / Nantucket Airport / 508-228-9989 or 800-508-9972 / www.nantucketislandrentacar.com

For more information

Nantucket Chamber of Commerce / 508-228-1700 / www.nantucketchamber.org.

BOSTON

Population - 3,406,829 Area Code - 617,857 County - Suffolk

Hotels and Motels

Boston Marriott Copley Place, 110 Huntington Avenue, Boston / 617-236-5800 / www.fairmont.com/copleyplaza

Boston Harbor Hotel, 70 Rowes Wharf, Boston / 617-439-7000 / www.bhh.com

Copley Square Hotel, 47 Huntington Avenue, Boston / 866-891-2174 / www.copleysquarehotel.com

Restaurants

Red Bones, 55 Chester Street, Somerville / 617-628-2200 / www.redbones.com

Union Oyster House, 41 Union Street, Boston / 617-227-2750 / www.unionoysterhouse.com

Barking Crab, 88 Sleeper Street, Boston / 617-426-2722 / www.barkingcrab.com

Fly Shops/Bait and Tackle Shops

Firefly Outfitters, One Federal Street, Boston / 617-423-FISH / www.fireflyoutfitters.com

Bob Smith Sporting Goods, 1050 Commonwealth Avenue, Boston / 617-232-1399

Bass Pro Shops, One Bass Pro Drive, Foxborough / 508-216-2000 / www.basspro.com

Orvis Boston, 8 North Market Bldg. - East End, Faneuil Hall Marketplace, Boston / 617-742-0288 / www.orvis.com/boston

Marine Supplies

Mallard Marine, 28 Damrell Street, South Boston / 617-269-6699

Hospitals

Brigham and Women's Hospital, 75 Francis Street, Boston / 617-732-5500 / www.brighamandwomens.org

Boston Medical Center, 1 Boston Medical Center Pl#1, Boston / 617-638-8000 / www.bmc.org

Airports

Boston-Logan Airport (BOS), 1 Harborside Drive, East Boston / 800-23-LOGAN / www.massport.com

Trains

    Massachusetts Bay Transportation Authority, Boston, MA / 617-222-3200 /
    www.mbta.com

Other Activites

    www.cityofboston.gov/visitors

NEWBURYPORT

Population - 17,189 Area Code - 978 County - Essex

Hotels and Motels

    Essex Street Inn, 7 Essex Street, Newburyport / 465-3148 /
    www.essexstreetinn.com
    Green Leaf Inn, 141 State Street, Newburyport / 465-5816 /
    www.greenleafinnnewburyport.com
    Compass Rose Inn, 5 ½ Center Street, Newburyport / 465-1568 /
    www.compassrosenewburyport.com

Restaurants

    River Merrimac Bar & Grille, 50 Water Street #304, Newburyport / 463-4040 /
    www.rivermerrimacbarandgrille.com
    Tournament Wharf Restaurant, 1 Tournament Wharf, Newburyport /
    462-7785 / www.michaelsharborside.com
    Not Your Average Joe's, 1 Market Square, Newburyport / 462-3808 /
    www.nyajoes.com

Fly Shops/Bait and Tackle Shops

    Surfland Bait & Tackle, 28 Plum Island Turnpike, Newbury / 462-4202 /
    www.surflandbt.com
    First Light Anglers, 21 Main Street, Rowley / 948-7004 /
    www.firstlightanglers.com

Marine Supplies

    Dockside Marine, 356 Merrimac Street, Newburyport / 462-8030 /
    www.docksidemarineboatparts.com

Hospitals

    Anna Jaques Hospital, 25 Highland Avenue, Newburyport / 463-1000 /
    www.ajh.org

Airports

Boston-Logan Airport (BOS), 1 Harborside Drive, East Boston / 800-23-LOGAN / www.massport.com

Trains

Massachusetts Bay Transportation Authority, Boston / 617-222-3200 / www.mbta.com

Other Activites

Plum Island Lighthouse, Newburyport Harbor Light / www.lighthouse.cc/plumisland
Newburyport Cruises, 502-4366 / www.newburyportcruises.com

Rock jetties create good structure, and if they're lining the entrance to a harbor or river system, the currents create a sharp drop off. Slower current runs along the rocks which is oftentimes where the bait concentrates, thereby making a great ambush spot, particularly for bonito or albies.

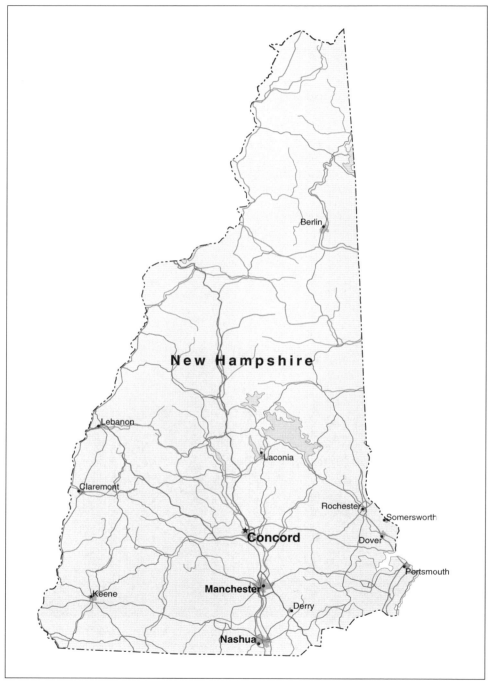

New Hampshire Coast

New Hampshire Waters Overview

With only 18 miles of shoreline, many anglers pass by the Granite State in favor of the Massachusetts North Shore or the Maine coastline. Still, there are some terrific beaches and river systems that get little to no pressure. The best times of year are in the spring/early summer for the estuaries and the rivers, and out front on the beaches in the spring and the fall. The beauty of the New Hampshire fishery is that you can hit prime time in the estuaries and rivers and still have time to hit the other states as you wish.

Still, seacoast New Hampshire has every bit of a distinguished history of fishing and tourism. From the Farragut House in Rye Beach to the Boar's Head Hotel, you'll find plenty of lodging and places to fish despite the short coastline.

REGULATIONS

Fishing regulations (especially saltwater fishing regulations) are constantly subject to change, so we cannot possibly keep up with the current regulations in this guide. Therefore, we can only provide you with a link the website that will have the most current rules.

For New Hampshire, the website is: www.wildlife.state.nh.us/Fishing/fishing.htm.

On that page, locate the current Saltwater Fishing Digest.

NEW HAMPSHIRE SPECIES AVAILABILITY

SPECIES	APR	MAY	JUN	JUL	AUG	SEP	OCT
Striped Bass		+	++	+	+	++	++
Bluefish		+	+	++	++	++	+
School Bluefin Tuna	+	+	+	++	++	++	++

+ = Available, ++ = Prime Time

Seabrook Beach to Portsmouth

Just north of the Massachusetts border are a lot of spots worth checking out. When the fish are moving in the spring and fall, these beaches can fish very well. They are also good night spots during the summer. They can get crowded during the summer time, but dawn and dusk are good times to find a summer bluefish blitz. Floating and intermediate lines get the call.

SEABROOK BEACH/HAMPTON BEACH STATE PARK

Just north of Massachusetts' Salisbury Beach and between the New Hampshire towns of Hampton and Seabrook is the Hampton Beach State Park. There is plenty of parking in the lot (for a fee) or you can park on the Seabrook side along Route 1A and walk. There are three places that anglers typically fish.

SEABROOK BEACH

The grid of houses along Seabrook Beach means that you can expect good crowds of beach goers in the summer. Still, working the beachfront with either a floating or intermediate line is a great option. Spring and fall are the best times. Just after the silversides arrive, you'll find the bass holding for longer periods out in front. You'll also find them when the peanut bunker arrive in the fall. Seabrook Beach is more of a corridor for passing fish.

HAMPTON HARBOR INLET

Beckmans Point is at the top of Seabrook Beach, which is where you'll find Hampton Harbor Inlet. Hampton Harbor is an inlet from the Atlantic Ocean that is formed by the confluence of the Hampton and Blackwater Rivers. The Blackwater River represents the southern portion of the harbor and is principally within the town of Seabrook. The northern portion of the harbor is typically associated with the Hampton River. The channel is some 700 yards long and the beauty here is that you're close to the ocean yet have a place to get into a lee in the event of a storm. The barrier beach and landmass slows down wind and current. River Street runs to the west and provides wade fishermen and kayak anglers access to an excellent early to mid-season estuary. Boat traffic increases throughout the season and many anglers will head outside during the summer and fall, particularly when the fall run is in full swing. Mile Bridge runs over the inlet and to the west is a river estuary system. The Hampton River Marina located on the northwest portion of the harbor is the only privately operated, full-service marina in the harbor area for service. Hampton Harbor Inlet is a good spot which holds bass for a longer part of the early season.

HAMPTON HARBOR INLET JETTY

The jetty is a long breakwall on the inside of the channel with ample amounts of room. You'll find bass at night and blues at both first/last light and during the day. Water depths are good, and either a floating or extra-fast-sinking line works best. The pockets where the jetty runs into the beach can occasionally hold fish.

THE BLACKWATER RIVER

The Blackwater River runs southwest from the inlet. Cross Beach Road connects with the river that is an excellent early season schoolie spot. As with many smaller rivers, the best time to fish the Blackwater is at mid- to high water marks; there isn't much water around low tide. The Route 286 bridge in the lower section provides an easy access point. Begin fishing higher up on the coming tide and continue to work your way up the river as the tide continues to flood. The Blackwater River is also a good spot for kayak fishing. A floating and extra-fast-sinking line works best.

HAMPTON BEACH STATE PARK

The Hampton Beach area was a thriving fishing area in the 1700s and 1800s, and still is a great spot today. Hampton Beach State Park begins north of the Hampton Harbor Inlet. The beach gets heavily fished, partly because of the available camping during the fishing season. Pre-season first-come/first-served camping is allowed from April 24 until May 21. Reservations are accepted from May 22 through October 12. Late season is first-come/first-served camping and runs from October 13 through October 25.

Good news for fishermen – some good fishing just got better. According to the New Hampshire Division of Parks and Recreation: "After several months of anticipation the State of New Hampshire budget was adopted and $14.5 million dollars was appropriated to the Hampton Beach State Park redevelopment project ... Timelines and work schedules are being developed, and right now the first shovels should be in the ground in early spring 2010." Currently there is a $15 fee for standard vehicles to enter the park, a $4 launch fee for car-top boats and a $10 fee for car and trailer boats.

Boats can launch inside the inlet or anglers can work the shoreline from the jetty that is at the mouth of the inlet and north. On a dropping tide, fish stack up along the current seams. At night you'll find them moving at mid-tide on both sides of the parallel bars and into the current. There is no shortage of parking along the beach, and in the fall many anglers will drive along looking for birds and breaking fish. Summer

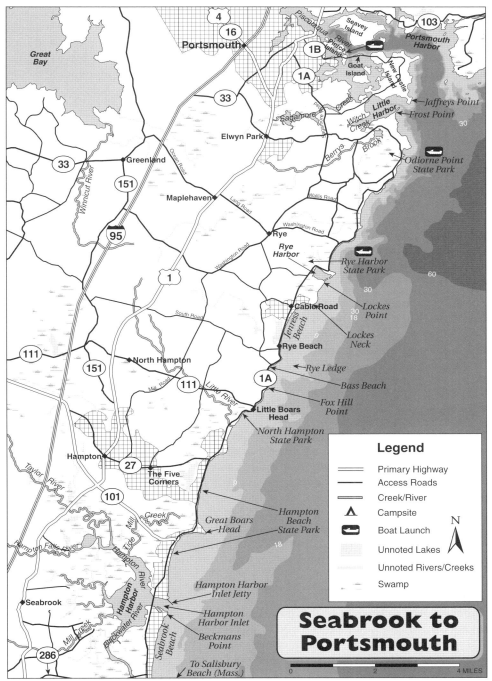

Seabrook to Portsmouth

Legend

Primary Highway	
Access Roads	
Creek/River	
Campsite	
Boat Launch	
Unnoted Lakes	
Unnoted Rivers/Creeks	
Swamp	

N

0   2   4 MILES

is a good time for bluefish, and catching them during the day can be difficult. Head to the beach at first and last light to solve that problem. At the top of the beach on the north end is Great Boars Head, a triangular peninsula that has boulders and rock piles. Fishing has always been strong off of Boars Head, and the structure separates Hampton from the Rye-area beaches. As a result, both hold good amounts of bait in the spring and particularly in the fall.

FOX HILL POINT AND BASS BEACH

Just off of 1A/Ocean Boulevard are two areas that work together to form a cove. They also have a good amount of structure and can be very good for fishing. Fox Hill Point is where the typical beach break meets a cobble/rock point. Bass Beach is near an area that surfers call the "wall". Here at the wall, the beach break meets a long bar that extends to a gravel/rocky shoal known as Rye Ledge. You'll find bass moving in and out of the structure, and an intermediate line is a good call. The cove is a good spot in the fall during the migration, and is relatively clear all season long. In the fall, work the points around the new and full moons and the cove on the quarter moons.

NORTH HAMPTON STATE BEACH/NORTH HAMPTON STATE PARK

Some of the largest bass caught from shore in New Hampshire are caught off of North Hampton State Beach. The heavy surf and offshore bars move a lot of current, and there are good concentrations of sand eels and silversides. In the fall, the bait can be chock a block, with long schools of fish and diving birds. Early morning, dusk and evening fishing is best, particularly since the crowds are typically thinned out. Try a floating or intermediate line.

RYE BEACH

Running from Rye Ledge to Lockes Neck is Rye Beach. The upper shore is also known as Jenress Beach. With the rocky outcroppings north of North Hampton State Beach, you'll find bass and blues. During low tide you can walk out to the rocks; just watch as the tide comes back in. Unless you see fish on the surface, a sink tip or extra-fast-sinking shooting head will put your fly in the strike zone. The structure and current is good here, and the natural curve of the beach makes for a good fall spot, complete with diving birds and blitzing fish. Jenness State Beach with its long beach break can be good when the fish are in. You'll see them in the wash and on the points, moving particularly towards the rocks and structure around Lockes Neck.

RYE HARBOR STATE PARK

Although only 43 acres in size, Rye Harbor has a fascinating history and its story, in microcosm, might well be compared to much larger bodies of water. For more than 200 years, Rye Harbor has been a focal point of the community, first with its tide mills and later because of its hardy fishermen who have harvested from the sea lobsters, shrimp, cod, haddock, pollock, and tuna. Rye Harbor State Park is a seasonal day-use park which opens each year in early May and closes by mid-October. A state marina is located adjacent to the park. There are two breakwalls that close off the mouth of the harbor and protect it from storms. The south breakwall is located off of Harbor Road. Along the ocean front is a rocky/cobble shoreline. On the north side is Ragged Neck Point. Located off of Route 1A, you'll find a bull-nosed peninsula with a similar rocky/cobble shoreline. Sink-tip lines are good choices. Here you'll find an active harbor, complete with fishing, sailing, and lobster boats.

Odiorne Point State Park

Located along the coast on Route 1 is Odiorne Point State Park. Odiorne State Park encompasses 331.5 acres along the Atlantic Coast. The land that makes up Odiorne Point State Park was purchased by the federal government during World War II and built up as a coastal defense base. Today, the old bunkers are camouflaged in the hills and greenery of the park; a few are open for tours on holidays. The park charges admission from May 22 to October 12, and is open from 8:00am to 6:00pm. There is a high water boat launch which carries a $10 charge along with a $4 per person entrance fee. The fishing can be worth it.

On the south end of the park, protected tidal pools of the Sunken Forest adjoin an exposed rocky shore (it is unusual to see hardwoods in a saltwater environment, but this forest is thought to be several thousand years old and remained after the tides claimed much of the surrounding land). Just north, the shore evolves into a pebble beach which features a freshwater marsh. Along the way to Frost Point where a jetty extends into Little Harbor, lies a small sand dune environment. At the end of Little Harbor, Seavey Creek feeds the neighboring salt marsh. Two small river systems, Witch Creek and Berrys Brook, are near the boat ramp and can be fished from shore, boat, or kayak. Jaffreys Point is across from Frost Point.

There is a series of islands north of Odiorne Point State Park that offer good fishing and boating opportunities at the mouth of the Piscataqua River and Portsmouth Harbor. Pierce Island is located across the water from the Seavey Island and the Portsmouth Naval Shipyard.

Goat Island Bridge

The Goat Island Bridge connects Newcastle to Goat Island. A dirt parking lot is maintained by the Fish and Game Department specifically for fishermen. You'll see bait fishermen on the bridge, but the shoreline is good for wade fishermen. The most productive times are at night and on either side of dawn or dusk. A floating or intermediate line works well.

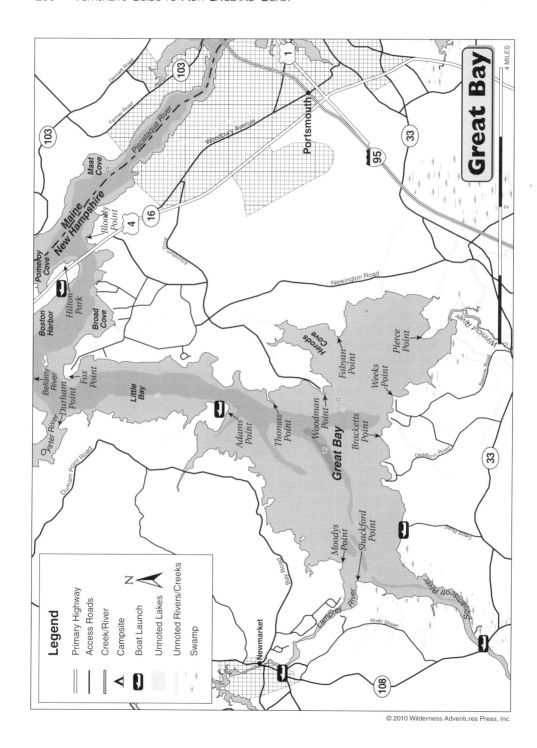

Great Bay

4 MILES

Legend

Primary Highway
Access Roads
Creek/River
Campsite
Boat Launch
Unnoted Lakes
Unnoted Rivers/Creeks
Swamp

N

© 2010 Wilderness Adventures Press, Inc.

Great Bay Estuary

Great Bay has been the state's No. 1 draw for striped bass and duck hunting for over a century. The estuary is formed by the Piscataqua River that runs inland toward Dover. To the south of the river is Little Bay and south of that is Great Bay. The entire area is about 5,000 acres and adds over 50 miles of coastline to the New Hampshire total. Seasons get started later and end earlier in New Hampshire due to the colder waters. As a result, you'll start to see bass and bluefish moving into the river systems in late May and June. Fishing can be good in early through mid-July, and then slows down until the fall. More of the fall-run fishing takes place toward the mouth of the Piscataqua.

Piscataqua River

One of the fastest flowing navigable rivers in the world, the Piscataqua River joins the Cocheco River, Salmon Falls River, and Little Bay en route to the Atlantic Ocean. The river is a migratory route for baitfish like river herring and shad. The river separates New Hampshire from Maine. Boating on the river can be treacherous due to the fast currents, particularly on a dropping tide. Exercise caution.

Bloody Point

Just off the dead end Bloody Point Road is a parking area and a pathway that leads to a rocky point. On a dropping tide, you'll find a tidal rip forming and good current flows. Here, the bass will sit in the quiet back eddies and pick off silversides, shrimp, herring, you name it, as they drift by. Use all of your trout techniques and rig a leader with several droppers. Late spring through the summer is a good time to fish here, and night fishing can be excellent.

Hilton Park

Dover Point's Hilton Park is where the Piscataqua River intersects and joins Great Bay. With all the depth and current changes, you'll almost always find big numbers of baitfish in the area. Conventional and bait anglers typically work the pier on the river side of the park, and fly rodders will work around the rocks that are close to the boat ramp. Extra-fast-sinking shooting heads get the nod due to the current speeds.

The Rivers of Great Bay

The tidal rivers of New Hampshire are where the seawater meets the warmer freshwater. These rivers are also the final destination of large migratory runs of river herring before they spawn and return to sea. Herring and alewives begin to arrive on the full and new moons in April, and by mid- to late May the striped bass have found them.

Lamprey River

The Lamprey River connects with Great Bay on the northwestern corner, just above the Squamscott River. The river runs through the town of Newmarket, and also has freshwater origins. Most anglers know of the Lamprey River due to the New Hampshire Fish and Game's Atlantic salmon stocking program, but there is good fishing below the Lamprey River Reservoir. The river enters into Great Bay, and at the mouth are two points that get a lot of attention. On the northern end is Moodys Point and at the southern end is Shackford Point. The channel runs through the middle, and there are shallows along shore. The more interesting coastline runs north of Moodys Point where there is a series of small coves. Also try the mill buildings on the Lamprey River. The Newmarket Town Landing has a limited number of parking spaces, but if you're there when the herring are piled up below the dam you'll find some outstanding fishing for big bass. Whenever the herring can't access the fish ladders, it is a good time to find the bass swirling on the bait.

Oyster River

The Oyster River runs into the northwest corner of Little Bay in Durham. The top of the river is by Route 108, and the better fishing is down river toward the mouth. Durham Point is at the mouth and there are mud flats that hold fish at half tide. At high tide you'll find bass cruising the shoreline looking for silversides, herring, crabs, and shrimp.

Winnicut River

Located at the southeast corner of Great Bay is the small Winnicut River. At the mouth is Pierce Point and a golf course. The cove to the east of the point fishes well on higher water, and the bass move into the mouth as the current starts to drop. North of Pierce Point is a shallower stretch which is a good early season spot for fresh fish, and the terrain here holds good concentrations of bait in the early season. Some fish will move higher up into the Winnicut River which gets narrow very quickly. Sink tips are good choices.

Squamscott River

Between the towns of Stratham and Newfields is the where the Squamscott River enters the southwestern corner of Great Bay. This river is an important part of spring fishing as the Squamscott River has freshwater origins and attracts tremendous schools of alewives. These baitfish typically arrive later than they do in southern New England, and mid-April through May is the time they begin to trickle in. You'll find fields and woods running down to the estuary that offer reasonably good protection from the spring winds. The river channel runs on the northwest side, that makes for better wade fishing on the southeast side of the river. Flows are about 9 feet, and kayak fishing can be good. Following a heavy rain, the river's clarity can be murky. Fishing the last three hours of the drop and the first three of the flood are good for wade anglers, and the fish will move higher into the river on the higher water marks. There is a good boat ramp in the river.

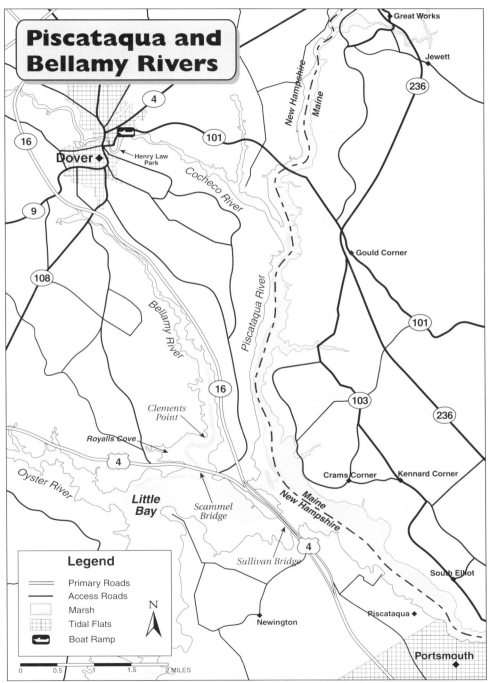

Piscataqua and Bellamy Rivers

Great Works

Jewett

236

4

101

Dover ◆

16

← Henry Law Park

Cocheco River

Gould Corner

9

New Hampshire

Maine

101

108

Bellamy River

Piscataqua River

16

Clements Point

Royalls Cove

103

236

4

Crams Corner

Kennard Corner

Oyster River

Little Bay

Scammel Bridge

Maine
New Hampshire

South Elliot

4

Sullivan Bridge

Legend
Primary Roads
Access Roads
Marsh
Tidal Flats
Boat Ramp

N

Newington

Riscataqua ◆

Portsmouth ◆

0   0.5   1   1.5   2 MILES

© 2010 Wilderness Adventures Press, Inc.

Bellamy River

Above the Scammel Bridge is the Bellamy River. Royalls Cove is to the northwest and has two feeder rivers that enter the cove, and the cove is good for kayak fishing, particularly on the high/dropping tide. Heading up river is Clements Point, a good area on a dropping tide when herring and alewives are dropping out. The deeper water is in the middle of the channel, and the terrain is soft. Scammell Bridge can also be a good night-fishing spot, particularly in the summer when the boat traffic has dried up for the day. Anglers will need to fish this section from either a boat or a kayak, and drift patterns along the fast water and also along the bridge abutments. There are parking lots at both ends of the bridge and wade anglers can get in the water along the shorelines.

Henry Law Park

Anglers can access the Cocheco River from the Henry Law Park in Dover. When the herring are in, the fishing pressure here is usually pretty significant. Near the Central Avenue Bridge is the Cocheco Falls and a fish ladder that allows the herring and returning Atlantic salmon passage higher up into the river. Silversides follow the herring and the area fishes very well through the end of the herring spawn that is in June. You'll also find bass along the mouth of the Cocheco River in the fall when the glass minnows drop out.

Isle of Shoals

With a name that comes from the incredible number of fish "shoaling" (or schooling) throughout the chain of nine islands, the Isle of Shoals is an excellent alternative to the inshore waters. It is located 10 miles from Portsmouth Harbor and 6 miles from Rye. The big tides change the terrain, and these nine islands, at high tide, turn into 18 if you factor in the rocks and ledges that show as the tide ebbs. There isn't much land here, only a total of 205 acres. In the 1800s there were over 1,000 fishermen who lived on the islands.

Isle of Shoals is divided by the Maine/New Hampshire state line (see map). The governing state is listed alongside each island, below.

DUCK ISLAND (MAINE REGULATIONS)

This island was a World War II bombing target that now is a protected wildlife refuge. Its name is fitting, as there are large amounts of waterfowl on and around the island.

Duck is the northernmost island and is a good spot. Rocks and ledges surround the island, so be sure to study a chart carefully before heading out to Duck. Shag Rock and Mingo Rock are two such ledges on the southern side of Duck Island, and that is the best area for fishing. The current sweeps all around these broken structures and the depths vary considerably. Watch your lower unit, as ground swells and currents can be significant. When the bass are in, you'll love casting a big fly into the rocks. On the southwest corner is another cluster of rocks, which is particularly good on the dropping tide.

APPLEDORE ISLAND (MAINE REGULATIONS)

The home to Cornell University's Shoals Marine Laboratory, Appledore offers over 20 undergraduate courses as well as a well-attended adult education center. Appledore is easily recognized, as it is the largest of the islands.

It's shaped like the number 8, with the smaller section to the north and the larger section to the south. The reason it looks like the number 8 is because there are coves on the western and the eastern parts of Appledore Island. The coves can fish well, and the lab is in the middle of the island to the western side. The northeastern end of the island has more breaks in the structure, which holds the fish. The southeastern end

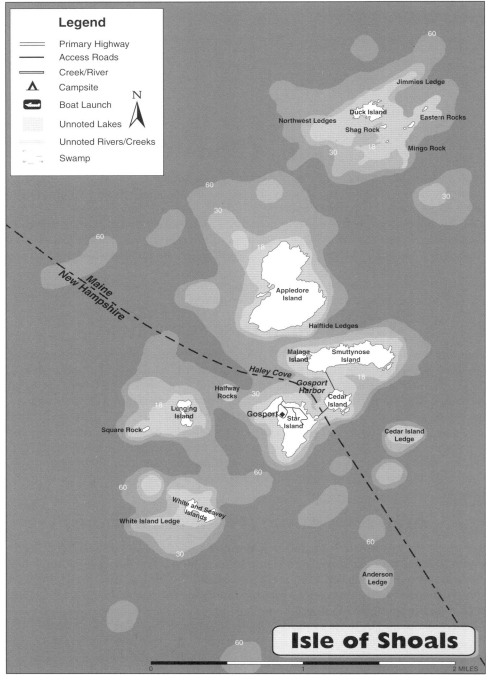

Legend

≡≡≡ Primary Highway
— Access Roads
≡≡ Creek/River
⛺ Campsite
🛥 Boat Launch
Unnoted Lakes
Unnoted Rivers/Creeks
Swamp

N

60

Jimmies Ledge

Duck Island
Northwest Ledges   Eastern Rocks
Shag Rock
Mingo Rock
30   18

30

60

30

18

60

Appledore
Island

Halftide Ledges

Malaga   Smuttynose
Island   Island
Haley Cove
Gosport
Harbor   18

Halfway
Rocks   30   Cedar
Island
18
Lunging
Island   Gosport◆
Star
Square Rock   Island   Cedar Island
Ledge

60

60

White and Seavey
Islands
White Island Ledge

60

30   60

Anderson
Ledge

Maine
New Hampshire

Isle of Shoals

0   1   2 MILES

© 2010 Wilderness Adventures Press, Inc.

is good because a channel is created between Appledore and Smuttynose/Malaga Islands. Watch the ledge that juts out in the middle of Appledore, but make sure you fish all around it. When the tide is moving, it's a good spot for big bass.

SMUTTYNOSE AND MALAGA ISLANDS (MAINE REGULATIONS)

These two islands were founded by Samuel Haley in the late 1800s. Legend has it that Haley did in fact find buried treasure on the island, possibly left by Blackbeard, Captain Kidd, or by Black Sam Belamy, and that he used it to connect the two islands by a breakwall. While those famous visitors may have left more doubloons, the real treasure is striped bass.

Smuttynose is a lateral island, arranged on an east/west tack. The northern side of the island is constantly churning, with the most interesting water being on the northeastern and eastern sides. The terrain is very broken, which offers tremendous amounts of holding spots for stripers. Malaga Island is on the northwestern area, just above a decent-sized cove. Because of the closeness of Appledore Island, this stretch is more protected and can offer a slight respite from the wind. The currents are softer here.

CEDAR ISLAND (MAINE REGULATIONS)

Cedar got its name from a small grove of cedar trees that were on the island. It is connected to Star and to Smuttynose which is how you can remember the island. There is a protected harbor on the northwestern corner that is in between the two breakwalls. I haven't had particularly good fishing off of Cedar, but several anglers favor the southeastern corner.

STAR ISLAND (NEW HAMPSHIRE REGULATIONS)

The Oceanic Hotel, that Victorian gem, has attracted visitors and anglers for over a century. There continues to be an average of 250 visitors per week that arrive at the Star Island Conference Center. The buildings are a blend of clapboard and stone, and the fishing is a short walk away.

Star Island is perhaps the biggest draw. Boat anglers head to the southern portion of the island. Centuries of storms have broken apart the coastline, and there is a very interesting series of rocks and ledges that are detached from the main island. Work your way around here on the higher water marks, and be vigilant of ground swells. On the western side, the island forms a big bowl which can be a very good spot when the fish are arriving in the late spring/early summer.

LUNGING ISLAND (NEW HAMPSHIRE REGULATIONS)

Lunging Island was the original fishing base of the London Trading Company. It's now owned by the Randall family. I remember Lunging Island because it is shaped like the letter 'L.' It's a smaller island, and where I've had the best luck is on the southern end. At the southwestern corner you'll find clusters of ledges and at the southeastern corner you'll find current passing where the island splits. At high tide, the island is split between the northern half (where the Randall family homestead sits) and the southern half. Fish the coves on both sides – bass and blues can stack up when the bait washes over what turns into a high-tide reef. Bigger flies in more natural colors are good choices, particularly when the mackeral, menhaden, or herring are in.

WHITE AND SEAVEY ISLANDS (NEW HAMPSHIRE REGULATIONS)

Built in 1820, the lighthouse makes for easy identification of White Island, and sits at the southernmost tip of the island which is the southernmost island of the group. Some consider White and Seavey Islands to be the same; there is a bridge that connects the two that is visible only at low tide. At high tide, the two are separate. Odds are you'll see a lot of birds while fishing along Seavey Island. That is partly due to the fact that it is the home of one of a tern restoration program. Seeing a large number of birds doesn't necessarily mean that fish are around, but Seavey is a good spot.

Just below the lighthouse is a rocky bowl that looks like an upside down letter 'U.' From half-flood to half-ebb tides, the spot can hold some very large bass. Drop-offs are sharp; work along the cost to the ledges that extend from the southwestern edge of the island. You can work your way in a clockwise or counterclockwise fashion. The northeastern corner can be good as there is more texture due to the jagged edges. Water clarity is excellent, and more natural patterns fished on shock tippet work best. Switch between a floating and an extra-fast-sinking line.

For more information on these fascinating islands, check out www.islesofshoals.com, and to get to Star Island, visit www.starisland.org.

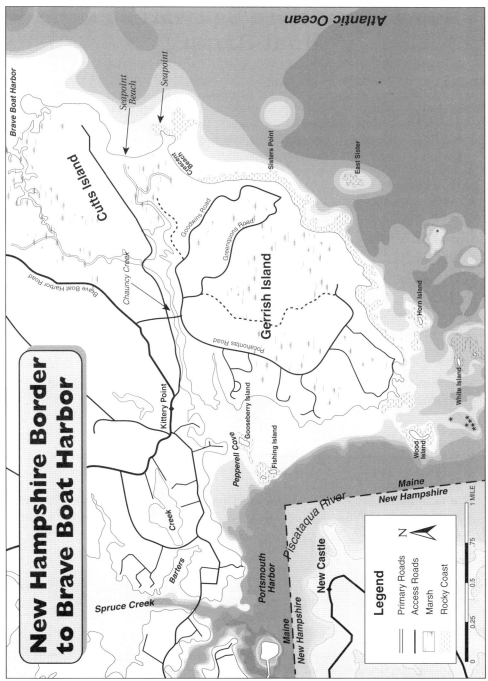

New Hampshire Border to Brave Boat Harbor

Atlantic Ocean

Brave Boat Harbor

Cutts Island

Seapoint Beach

Seapoint

Crescent Beach

Sisters Point

East Sister

Goodwins Road

Greenquons Road

Gerrish Island

Horn Island

Chauncy Creek

Brave Boat Harbor Road

Pocahontas Road

White Island

Kittery Point

Gooseberry Island

Pepperell Cove

Fishing Island

Wood Island

Barters Creek

Spruce Creek

Portsmouth Harbor

Piscataqua River

Maine
New Hampshire

New Castle

Maine
New Hampshire

Legend

N

Primary Roads
Access Roads
Marsh
Rocky Coast

0   0.25   0.5   0.75   1 MILE

New Hampshire Saltwater Public Boat Ramps

DOVER

Piscataqua River. Not accessible at all tides. Hilton State Park. Ample parking. Dover Point. Shore angling. Spaulding Turnpike, Dover.

Little Bay. Not accessible at all tides. Little Bay Marina. Limited parking/fuel pumps. Dover Point, Dover. Fee charged.

Cocheco River. Accessible at all tides. George's Marina. Street parking. Dover. Fee charged.

DURHAM

Great Bay. Not accessible at all tides. Adams Point Boat Launch. Limited parking. Off Durham Point Road, Durham. Shore angling. Fish and Game property.

Oyster River. Accessible at all tides. Jackson's Landing. Ample parking. Old Piscataqua Road, Durham. Shore angling.

Oyster River. Accessible at all tides. Durham Town Landing. Ample parking. Old Landing Road, Durham. Carry-in only. Shore angling.

EXETER

Squamscott River. Accessible at all tides. Exeter Town Landing. Limited parking. Off Water St., Exeter. Shore angling.

GREENLAND

Great Bay. Not accessible at all tides. Sandy Point Discovery Center. Limited parking. Depot Road, Greenland. Carry-in only. Fish and Game property. Shore angling.

Winnicut River. Accessible at high tide. Greenland Town Landing. Very limited parking. Tide Mill Road, Greenland. Four-wheel-drive access only. Remote/carry-in.

HAMPTON

Hampton Harbor. Accessible at all tides. Hampton Harbor State Park. Ample parking. Route 1A, Hampton. Fee charged. Fuel pumps seasonally.

NEWFIELDS

Squamscott River. Accessible at all tides. Newfields Town Landing. Limited parking. Squamscott Road, Newfields. Shore angling.

NEWMARKET

Lamprey River. Accessible at all tides. Newmarket Town Landing. Limited parking. Water Street (off Route 108). Shore angling.

NEWINGTON

Little Bay. Accessible at all tides. Great Bay Marine. Ample parking/fuel pumps. Newington. Private docks. Fee charged.

PIERCE ISLAND

Piscataqua River. Accessible at all tides. Pierce Island. Ample parking. Shore angling. Fee charged.

RYE

Atlantic Ocean. Not accessible at low tide. Odiorne Point State Park. Ample parking. Route 1A, Rye. Shore angling. Fee charged.
Atlantic Ocean. Accessible at all tides. Rye Harbor State Park. Ample parking. Route 1A, Rye. Fee charged. Fuel pumps seasonally.

STRATHAM

Squamscott River. Not accessible at all tides. Stratham Town Landing. Limited parking. River Road, Stratham. Carry-in only. Shore angling
Squamscott River. Accessible at all tides. Chapman's Landing. Limited parking. Route 108, Stratham. Shore angling. Fish and Game property

Hub City Information: New Hampshire

PORTSMOUTH
Population - 20,443 e - 603 County - Rockingham

Hotels and Motels

Ale House Inn, 121 Bow Street, Portsmouth / 431-7760 / www.alehouseinn.com

Hilton Garden Inn, 100 High Street, Portsmouth / 431-1499 / www.hiltongardeninn.com

Anchorage Inn & Suites, 417 Woodbury Avenue, Portsmouth / 800-370-8111 / www.anchorageinns.com

Wentworth by the Sea Marriott Hotel and Spa, 588 Wentworth Road, New Castle / 422-7322 / www.wentworth.com

Restaurants

Jumpin' Jays Fish Café, 150 Congress Street, Portsmouth / 766-3474 / www.jumpinjays.com

Radici, 142-144 Congress Street, Portsmouth / 373-6464 / www.radicirestaurant.com

Four Restaurant, 189 State Street, Portsmouth / 319-1547 / www.fouronstate.com

The Portsmouth Brewery, 56 Market Street, Portsmouth / 431-1115 / www.portsmouthbrewery.com

The Portsmouth Gas Light, 64 Market Street, Portsmouth / 430-9122 / www.portsmouthgaslight.com

The Green Monkey, 86 Pleasant Street, Portsmouth / 427-1010 / www.thegreenmonkey.net

Fly Shops/Bait and Tackle Shops

Eldredge Bros Fly Shop, 1480 US Route 1, Cape Neddick, ME / 207-363-9269 / www.eldredgeflyshop.com

Kittery Trading Post, 301 US Route 1, Kittery, ME / 207-439-2700 / www.kitterytradingpost.com

Marine Supplies

West Marine, 775 Lafayette Road #2, Portsmouth / 436-8300 / www.westmarine.com

Hospitals

Portsmouth Regional Hospital, 333 Borthwick Avenue, Portsmouth / 436-5110 / www.portsmouthhospital.com

Airports

Portsmouth International Airport at Pease (PSM), 36 Airline Avenue, Portsmouth / 433-6536 / www.peasedev.org

Other Activities

Isles of Shoals Daytrip, Isles of Shoals Steamship Company, 315 Market Street, Portsmouth / 431-5500 / www.islesofshoals.com

Portsmouth Harbor Lighthouse, Next to Fort Constitution, Portsmouth / http://lighthouse.cc/portsmouth

USS Albacore, 600 Market Street, Portsmouth / 436-3680 / www.ussalbacore.org

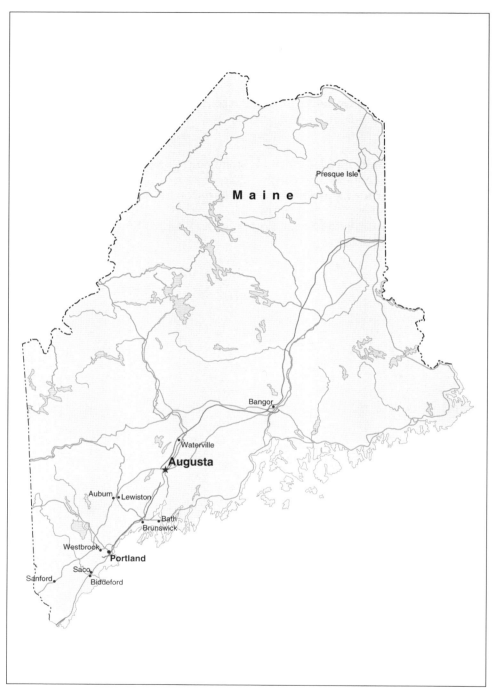

Maine Coast

Maine Waters Overview

Perhaps Maine is best known for the stringers of brook trout, landlocked salmon, and togue taken far inland just after the turn of the century. There are still ample numbers of Maine sportsmen who fish the sweetwater (freshwater) for trout and salmon, but in recent years, many have flocked to the coast for striped bass, bluefish, and tuna. According to L.L. Bean's Mac McKeever, the fishing continues to be strong.

From late April through early November, migratory striped bass inhabit the entire coastal area of Maine, inland to the first upstream dam on major river systems and seaward to the outer Maine islands. These migratory fish are here primarily in pursuit of food, which at that time becomes quite abundant along the coast and in the rivers and streams. One of the most common attractants in the spring is the alewife, followed a few weeks later by sea herring and mackerel.

While Maine has approximately 3,478 miles of tidally-influenced shoreline, the most heavily fished areas are south of Penobscot Bay (from the stateline through Camden). According to McKeever, the water temperature and bait are the two key components to the fishery.

"Many L.L. Bean employees fish every day, typically before or after work," he said. "And the stripers typically arrive in the southern end of the state around May 10. By the third week in May, the fish typically arrive in the Portland area. They chase herring and alewives that have moved in to the rivers to spawn, so the estuary systems with freshwater origins and ponds and herring runs are the most popular. Memorial Day is when you'll see most of the anglers hitting the southern Maine coastline in decent numbers. Because of the colder water temperatures associated with the rocks, ledges, and inshore islands, anglers don't head farther north until June, and the rocks and ledges really are peak in August.

"During the day, the beaches can fish well in May, June, September, and October. The arriving and departing fish are the primary targets. As the water temperatures and beach traffic pick up, night fishing is the focus in July and August. Because the coastline is so far from the Gulf Stream, there are no bonito, false albacore or skipjacks. As a result, the water temperatures cool off gradually instead of abruptly. Bass begin their migration in September and by mid-October, the fishing is just about over. It's thought that there are a number of resident striped bass, and Joseph Zydlewski of the Maine Cooperative Fish and Wildlife Research Unit is conducting several studies to determine how far the bass actually migrate. All in all, Maine has a short but vigorous fishing season."

Maine has a variety of coastline. The beaches and surf are mostly in the south to central regions and are adjacent to the river systems. There are big rivers and small creeks. The top rivers and their tributaries are the Androscoggin, Muddy, Cathance, Abbagadasset, Kennebec, Eastern, Sasanoa, Back, Sheepscot, Cross, Marsh, Damariscotta, Johns, Pemaquid, Meduncook, St. George and Weskeag rivers. Rocks and ledges are what most folks think about, but there are some flats. Due to the 12-foot tides, anglers get brief shots at fish on the flats. Maine fishing has been erratic in the past few years. In 2008, the fish never seemed to arrive. Part of the reason was that during the migration from Massachusetts Bay north, the large schools encountered tremendous schools of bait in the EEZ. With perfect water temperatures, the striped bass never needed to continue their northern migration. Both Maine and Massachusetts' anglers lost, as there were no fish inshore and no striped bass fishing in the EEZ. 2009 was a much better year for bass and blues, and there were many school tuna as well.

REGULATIONS

Fishing regulations (especially saltwater fishing regulations) are constantly subject to change, and as such we cannot possibly keep up with the current regulations in this guide. Therefore, we only provide you with a link the website that will have the most current rules.

For Maine, the website is: www.maine.gov/dmr/recreational/rechomepage. html.

MAINE SPECIES AVAILIBILITY

SPECIES	APR	MAY	JUN	JUL	AUG	SEP	OCT
Striped Bass		+	++	+	+	++	++
Bluefish		+	+	++	++	++	+
School Bluefin Tuna	+	+	+	++	++	++	++

+ = Available, ++ = Prime Time

Stripers Forever

Stripers Forever is a 100-percent-volunteer internet-based organization with one purpose: to enhance public fishing for striped bass by making the striped bass a gamefish and ending commercial striped bass fishing. SF is largely a web-based advocacy group that has partnerships with the American Sportfishing Association, the Federation of Flyfishers, and the International Gamefish Association.

Brad Burns founded the group in 2003 after noticing a decline in mature fish following a 40-percent commercial quota increase. "I was around when striped bass populations were strong and I was around during the collapse. Many would consider fish stocks plentiful, but fisheries managers don't respond to declines until a species has collapsed. I foresee a decline and want to be on the leading edge to prevent the past from reoccuring." Burns was known for his Coastal Conservation Association efforts in the 1990s and his initial push for gamefish status back then.

Former Field and Stream Editor Duncan Barnes has lent his support to the group. Barnes feels that by "getting the message out to recreational anglers and by continuing to communicate the gamefish message, the commercial management practices will be reviewed and hopefully changed to become current with the times." Ed Mitchell is the group's secretary and George Watson is the group's treasurer.

Noted striped bass expert Kenney Abrames wrote about conservation initiatives on his website in 2001. "Take the bounty off the striped bass' head and all commercial fishing ends," said Abrames.

Jerry van de Sande, a Stripers Forever member from New Jersey, drove six hours to attend one of the planning events which was a fundraising dinner and auction. "It's not a local problem," van de Sande says, "it's a regional issue. Stripers Forever needs the support from all states. The fish that are protected in New Jersey are migratory, and they are unprotected in Rhode Island and in Massachusetts. A consistent policy is the answer."

For more information or to join: www.stripersforever.org.

Southern Maine: York to Portland

CHAUNCEY CREEK

Chauncey Creek begins on the east side of Kittery Point's Pepperall Cove and nearly rejoins the ocean at Crescent Beach. Striped bass move throughout the river system, but most anglers concentrate around the mouth of Chauncey Creek. All around Gooseberry Island is a large flat that holds fish on the rising tides. The fish will move into the river system and you'll find them dropping out as the tide ebbs. Most of the time a floating or sink-tip line work best, but for the deeper water and channels bring a sinking line.

CRESCENT BEACH/ SEA POINT BEACH

Early season school fish move in to the rocky/sandy beaches and coves around Crescent Beach and Sea Point Beach. The area all around the sand is good striper fishing, but if you're looking for a big bass, head to the sandy and rocky ledges that separate the two beaches. The currents are strong and with a southeast wind you can get a good surge. If you're looking for good striper water, you'll like this area. Use intermediate lines off the beach, floating or sink-tip lines around the rocks.

Off of Sea Point Road is a rocky point bar that deserves attention. Depths and currents increase here and it's a really good spot for bass. Temperatures are good and oftentimes during the crossover times of late June and in the fall, you'll find bluefish along the beach and bass in the rocks. Parking is limited, so get there early. You can also head north along the shore and fish the coves and ledges, or move south down to Crescent Beach.

YORK HARBOR SEWELL'S BRIDGE

Situated on the York River is an outcropping of rocks that protrudes about 100 yards into the ocean. The surf can be big and the rocks are slick, with drop-offs on either side up to a dozen feet deep. Fish tend to move into these reaches on the flood tide, usually at about half tide, and anglers will use either floating or extra-fast-sinking lines. There are a lot of barnacles on the rocks, so check your tippets and go with heavier pound test or flurocarbon. School fish will arrive in late May, and big bass move onto the bar in June.

Long Beach and Cape Neddick Light are York and Cape Neddick's hotspots. Here you'll find a combination of lots of different terrain, all in a condensed area. Long Beach is at the southern end of this stretch. At the southern end of the beach off of Bayview Avenue is Prebble Point, which is a mix of a bull-nosed bar. On the northern end of Prebble Point where it connects with Long Beach is a deep bowl – a good spot that holds fish. Heading to the north is mostly beach break, a good early season bass spot and a great summer bluefish spot. As you move closer towards Cape Neddick and the light (Nubble Light), you'll trade the beach for rocks. This area holds bass later in June and July and is best fished with either a floating or an extra-fast-sinking line. Nubble Light is off of Sohier Park Road and is housed in, you got it – Sohier Park. Parking along Long Beach is by meter and there are plenty of spaces at Sohier Park.

OGUNQUIT BEACH AND LITTLE BEACH

Off Route 1 is Ogunquit Beach and Little Beach. What makes this area a good fishing spot is that you have a long sweeping beach (Ogunquit), a small river system at the southern end, joined by Little Beach. Ogunquit Beach is good during the early season and in July and August when the bluefish are in. There is also a big parking area where Ogunquit Beach ends and Moody Beach starts.

The river in between the two beaches fishes very well in the early season through June for striped bass. Dropping tides fish best, and you'll want a sinking line for the deeper river water or a floating line if there is a blitz. Floating and intermediate lines are good for the beachfronts. Off of Ocean Street is the Footbridge Boat Launch that has a ramp suitable for smaller craft and kayaks. Anglers can fish from shore all along the ramps, but a kayak or small boat is ideal for the calm water. High dropping tide is the better time to fish. Note that the ramp is not suitable for launching or hauling at low tide.

Wells Beach and the Webhannet River can be a really good spot. It's a popular beach for fishermen and for swimmers, and there is a small town lot and a neighboring lot that charges a fee. Because of the ample available parking, Wells Beach can get crowded.

Early season bass will move along the beachfront and into the Webhannet River. There are two jetties at the mouth of the river: one on the southwest side where it joins Wells Beach, and one jetty on the east side where it joins Drakes Island Beach. Webhannet in Abenaki means "at the clear stream" a proper hint for anglers rigging up; use sparse patterns and fine tippets. You'll find the fish moving into the Webhannet River Marsh, which is located at the northeastern corner. Fish the marsh and higher up in the river system on half to flood tides, and make sure to work the banks.

MOUSAM RIVER, PARSONS BEACH AND WALKER'S POINT (BUSH COMPOUND)

Parsons Beach is at the mouth of the Mousam River. There are a few different ways to fish the river and the beach. One way is to follow Parsons Beach Road to the end and

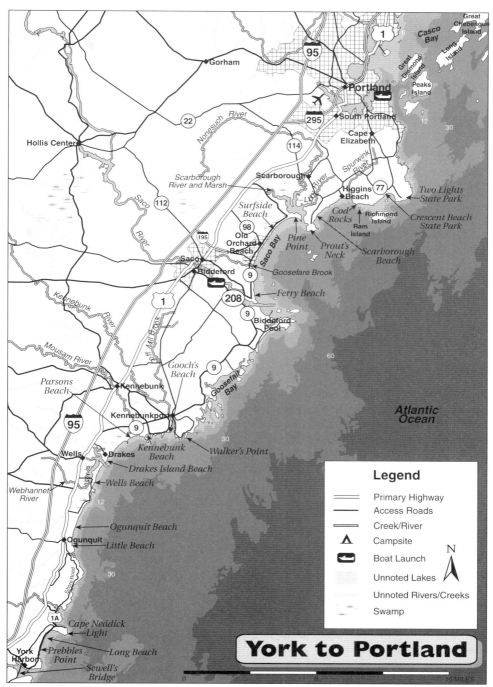

Legend

═══	Primary Highway
───	Access Roads
═══	Creek/River
⚠	Campsite
🛥	Boat Launch
	Unnoted Lakes
	Unnoted Rivers/Creeks
	Swamp

N

York to Portland

0   8   16 MILES

to fish the beachfront all the way down to where the river joins the ocean. Floating and intermediate lines are best along the beachfront. It gets a little tricky at the mouth. The sand flat to the south and to the west of the river mouth holds staging fish around the lower water marks, and as the tide floods, they'll move up into the river system. You also may be fishing along the drop-off where the combination of depth and current call for an extra-fast-sinking shooting head. You'll find early season schoolie bass and mid-season bluefish as well as good schools of fish during the southern migration.

A second way to fish the area is from the Mousam River Boat Ramp off of Route 9. The ramp is a mid- to high tide ramp and perfect for small boats or kayaks. Fishing the dropping tide downstream is good and you can then return to the ramp on the flood tide. You'll see shore anglers fishing upriver as well as downriver from the ramp, too. There is limited parking in both areas. Walker's Point is a peninsula that is the home of the Bush family's compound. The rocks and structure all hold fish and know that you'll encounter visits from the Secret Service when either of the former presidents are in town. Both George Bushes are fanatic fishermen, with the striped bass being one of their favorite species to catch.

Kennebunk Beach is a long sand beach break that is sandwiched in between Libbys and Lords Points. Parking is limited, and when the fishing is good, the lot fills up fast. Kennebunk Beach is a good early and mid-season spot for bass and bluefish. First and last light are good times for bluefish and nighttime fishing for bass can be productive. Intermediate lines are standards along the beach, with floating lines or sinking shooting heads in the points.

KENNEBUNK RIVER AND GOOCH'S BEACH

To the east of Kennebunk Beach is the Kennebunk River. The river has two branches. The main stem runs north/south while the minor branch flows east/west behind a beach. The beach on the westbank of the mouth is called Gooch's Beach. Parking here is also limited and there are two jetties at the mouth of the river that are popular fishing spots. Early through mid-season are the better times to fish for bass and blues, and the fall run can be pretty hot just beyond the beach break. Oaks Neck is the knob of land that is on the southwest corner of the beach and is a good spot for wade and boat fishermen. If you're a boat angler, head down Ocean Avenue to get to the east side of the river. Chick's Marina and Kennebunkport Marina, also at Ocean Avenue, have boat ramps (fee). It's a good way for boat or kayak anglers to fish higher up in the river system, and then work down to the jetties and along the beachfront.

OLD ORCHARD BEACH AND THE SACO RIVER

The Saco River joins the ocean just to the south of Old Orchard Beach. As you move to the north, you'll find that there are four parts to Old Orchard Beach: Ferry Beach, Old Orchard, Surfside Beach, and Pine Point.

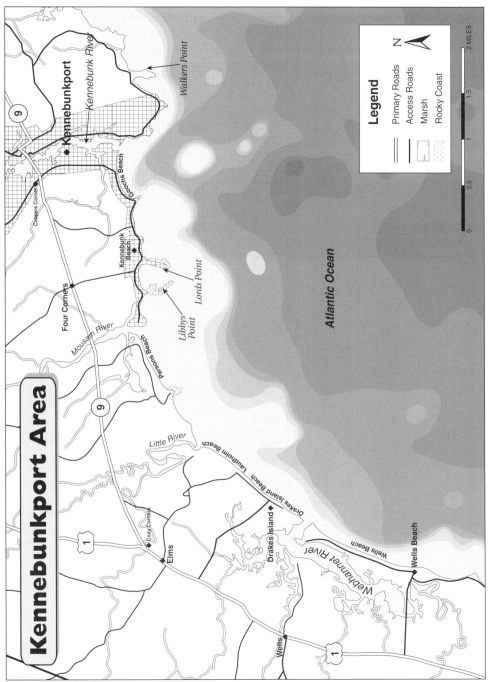

Kennebunkport Area

Legend
Primary Roads
Access Roads
Marsh
Rocky Coast

N

2 MILES
0   0.5   1   1.5

Kennebunkport

Kennebunk River

Walkers Point

9

Coopers Corners

Goochs Beach

Kennebunk Beach

Lords Point

Libbys Point

Four Corners

Mousam River

Parsons Beach

9

Little River

Laudholm Beach

Drakes Island Beach

Cozy Corners

Elms

1

Drakes Island

Webhannel River

Wells Beach

Wells

1

Atlantic Ocean

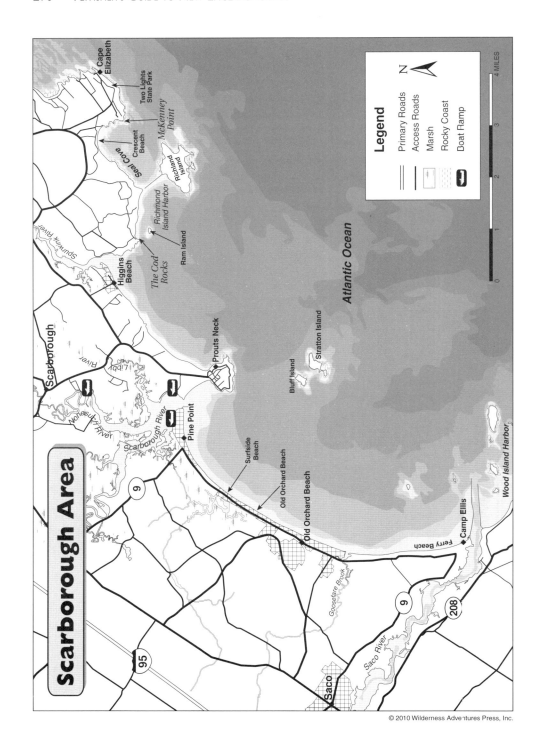

Scarborough Area

Legend
Primary Roads
Access Roads
Marsh
Rocky Coast
Boat Ramp

N

4 MILES

Atlantic Ocean

Cape Elizabeth
Two Lights State Park
McKenney Point
Crescent Beach
Seal Cove
Richland Island
Richmond Island Harbor
Ram Island
The Cod Rocks
Higgins Beach
Spurwink River
Scarborough
Libby River
Nonesuch River
Scarborough River
Prouts Neck
Pine Point
Surfside Beach
Old Orchard Beach
Old Orchard Beach
Bluff Island
Stratton Island
Wood Island Harbor
Camp Ellis
Ferry Beach
GooseFate Brook
Saco River
Saco

95
9
9
208

© 2010 Wilderness Adventures Press, Inc.

The easiest way to think of the Old Orchard Beach area is four beaches with a river system on either end. The amount of space and the two rivers creates a all-season fishy-as-hell area. Floating or intermediate lines are good, and fish the last few hours of the dropping tide and the first three hours of the flood tide are best.

The Saco attracts bass of all sizes in the spring through June. After the water warms, you'll find bluefish blitzing in July and August. There is more bass fishing at night, and in the fall you'll find lots of both species, oftentimes mixed together. You'll want to concentrate your efforts around the beaches and flats around the river mouth on the dropping tide, and then move along the beaches on the flood tide. A small tidal river enters the ocean just south of Porter Road and is a good spring and fall spot on the dropping tides. The baitfish dropping out of the river attract a lot of fish.

The most active ramp is the Meeting House Eddy Boat Launch which is on the west side of the river on Route 9/208. Anglers can find some good shore fishing on a high dropping tide as well. As you're heading down Route 208, check out Biddeford Pool, another good shore spot. If you fish the east end of Biddeford Pool, bring an extra-fast-sinking line as you'll be working rocks and ledges with sharp drop-offs. If you fish the north end bring a floating or intermediate line as there are flats, points, and coves.

SCARBOROUGH RIVER AND SCARBOROUGH MARSH

There are tributaries and branches that form the marsh: the Scarborough River, the Nonesuch River, and the Libby River. The Scarborough runs to the northwest, the Nonesuch to the north then west, and the Libby due east and then north. There are other rivers and creeks such as the New River, Oriocoag River, and Mill Creek. They all collect and form the Scarborough River which connects with the ocean between Pine Point to the west and Prout's Neck to the east. Freshwater drains into the Scarborough and that means herring and alewives in the spring. The jetty at the mouth of the Scarborough River is a good spot, usually on the dropping tide. It can also be good on the early part of the flood tide. The current is quick, and an extra-fast-sinking line is better.

But what really makes this area sing is the 3,000-acre marsh that is somewhat of a baitfish factory. There are silversides, mummichaug, mackerel, menhaden, crabs, and shrimp, all in an area protected from the elements. The boat ramp at the end of Pine Point Road attracts a lot of traffic. The river and marsh make for great kayaking as well.

Prout's Neck is also an excellent place to fish, but due to many private homes, access is limited. The neck, therefore, tends to be a better boat fishery. Checkly Point is at the southwest corner and East Point is at the southeast corner. While fish will hold all along the southern face, the area north of East Point has several ledges with deeper water, perfect cover for striped bass. The rocks also run into the beginning of Scarborough Beach. Then, as the beach moves northeast, you'll find an inshore island that creates perfect striper habitat. L.L. Bean's Mac McKeever favors extra-fast-sinking shooting heads to offset the current and to get deep, and likes the high dropping tide and the first few hours of the coming tide. American artist Winslow Homer was from Prout's Neck.

Scarborough Beach and The Graveyard

Scarborough Beach is a good spot, particularly later in the season after the vacationers depart. When the winds shift to north-northwest in the fall, Scarborough Beach is in the lee. The water is cool and clear, and intermediate or floating lines are best for the beachfront. The Graveyard separates Scarborough Beach from Higgins Beach. There is a series of long, wide rocks and ledges off the coast, and the change from a sandy bottom to a rocky bottom attracts a lot of fish. Mid-summer is the best time to fish here, and the Graveyard is a good, big-fish spot. You'll find pollock and mackerel for bait, and big bait means big fish. The water is especially clear, and Enrico Puglisi's Macs, Brock Apfel's Grocery Flies, and Kenney Abrames' Flatwings are the best bet. Mac recommends an intermediate line for fishing in the rocks, and likes the way the line doesn't get deep too quickly. Cast as far into the white water as possible and rig with shock tippet to offset the sharp edges.

Higgins Beach/Spurwink River

Probably the best way to access these two spots is to park at Higgins Beach for a fee and go south to the Graveyard or fish the beach. The mouth of the Spurwink River on the north side can hold fish. There is good current, rips and a big temperature change. The sandy bottom is mixed with boulders and cobble. Bass will move back and forth on the edges. The depth changes are significant and range from 20 feet at the mouth to 3 to 5 feet higher up in the river. The channel running along the beach is also good, and the best time to fish here is on the higher water marks, namely from the third

The cobble and sand combination makes Higgins Beach a good place to fish.

hour of the flood to the third hour of the drop. Extra-fast-sinking lines with reach casts work well along the trench. The line doesn't have to get deep, as it needs to offset the current. The reach cast will dead drift the fly and get it down so when your line goes tight it'll swing up. If you go farther upriver then a sink-tip or an intermediate line will be fine. You'll find mostly bass around here, but some bluefish along the beach or in the lower sections of the river, particularly in July and in August.

COD ROCKS, CRESCENT BEACH STATE PARK, TWO LIGHTS STATE PARK

East of the mouth of the Spurwink River is a rocky point called Cod Rocks. As the water drains out of the Spurwink, you'll also find bass along the point. From Cod Rocks to the east, you'll find a mixture of sandy beach and rocky ledges, perfect for striped bass. Due to the depth and texture changes, you'll find diverse current flows. Combined with the structure, you'll find good to excellent bass fishing.

Located 8 miles south of Portland is the mile-long beach that is part of the Crescent Beach State Park. Camping is available through the State Park Campsite Reservation System and then on a first-come, first-served basis at the park's headquarters. Beach fishing is best in the spring but is also good in the fall. From the beach east to the Two Lights State Park is a series of points and ledges that hold striped bass. McKenney Point is perhaps the midway point between the two state parks, and its classic rock and ledge fishing. The water is clear and the seas can pick up on the west/southwest summer winds. Two Lights is a 41-acre rocky headland with plenty of parking. Anglers typically leave their vehicles here, head to the water, and move east or west as the conditions dictate. The park's name originated from the twin lighthouses located nearby at the end of Two Lights Road. Built in 1828, these were the first twin lighthouses on the coast of Maine. The eastern light is an active, automated light station and the western light is now a private home. The surf can get very big, so watch for strong winds and directional changes. Due to the rocks and ledges, the higher water fishes better and L.L. Bean's Mac McKeever favors the high dropping tide.

RAM AND RICHMOND ISLAND

There are 21 "Ram Islands" in Maine, but this one is to the west of the private Richmond Island. There is a long bar that forms a rip and it runs from the northwest corner of the island toward shore. When bass are in, the dropping tide in this area fishes well. It's also a good idea to fish the higher water marks from the third hour of the flood to the third hour of the drop and pick pocket the rocks.

To the east of Ram is Richmond Island. There is a bar that extends south from the mainland and runs into the northwest corner of the island. Moving water brings bass and blues into the turbulence, and the eastern part of the island has two points (East Point and Watts Point) and a cove (Broad Cove) in the middle. Be sure to work the rocks/ledges just off of Watts Point as well as the channels in between the ledge and Richmond Island.

Portland Area: Casco Bay

Anglers who are looking for a modified urban fishery need look no further. Catch a flight to Portland's International Jetport Airport and you can be fishing in little more than 15 minutes from leaving the airport. Portland is a wonderful city with plenty of restaurants, shopping, baseball, and museums, all within walking distance.

CAPE ELIZABETH AREA

Running north along Cape Elizabeth to Portland are a series of points and coves. The points and coves alternate and are worth poking around on the higher water marks in June and July. Dyer Cove, Staples Point and Cove, Hunts Point, and Broad Cove among others hold fish. Most of the time anglers will pick-pocket their way through the structure. The next consistently solid fishing spot is Portland Headlight and adjoining 90-acre Fort Williams Park, just south of the city. The park is open from sunrise to sunset which is fine for fish; ground swells, particularly in the early and late season, can be significant, and the summer fishing is best during the day as well. There is ample parking, so walk through the Old Fort and then work down to the rocks on the north side of the lighthouse. Korkers are a must for good footing. Anglers can also work their way north towards Ship Cove. Mac fishes big flies and likes any tide but particularly the high-dropping tide. Intermediate or sink tip lines are best.

PORTLAND HARBOR AND SURROUNDING SHORELINE

SPRING POINT LEDGE LIGHT

At the end of a jetty that extends into the west side of Portland Harbor channel is the Spring Point Ledge Light. The 900-foot granite jetty is in good repair and is easy to walk on. Limited parking keeps crowds down, and the breakwall is separate from the light. The South Portland Municipal Boat Ramp is adjacent to the light and charges a fee for use. Fishing the breakwall is best at mid- to high water marks. The east-southeast side of the breakwall offers more water depth, and there is good structure to the south (where the breakwall connects with Spring Point. On the west-northwest side of the breakwall, you'll find shallower water with a sandy beach onshore. There is a cobble/rock bottom and, with Cushing Point, it forms a big cove. Sink-tip lines or extra-

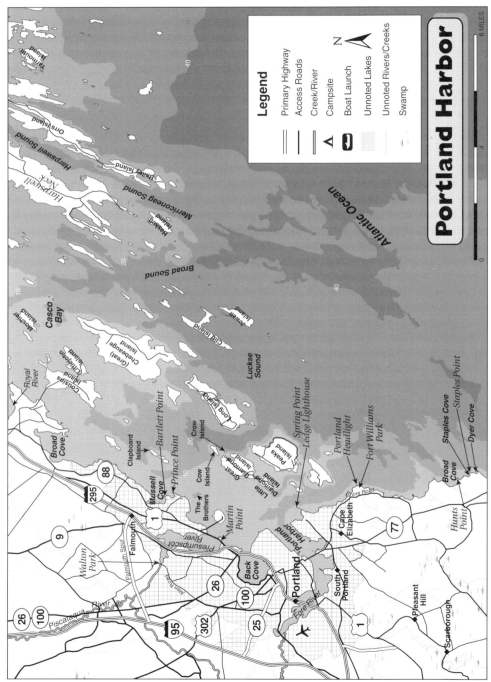

Portland Harbor

Legend

Primary Highway
Access Roads
Creek/River
Campsite
Boat Launch
Unnoted Lakes
Unnoted Rivers/Creeks
Swamp

N

8 MILES

fast-sinking shooting heads are good off the wall, while floating or intermediates are good off the sand.

BACK COVE

To the west of Interstate 295's Tukey Bridge is Portland's Back Cove. The muddy basin makes for difficult wade fishing, but the mud flats provide sight-fishing opportunities from a boat or from a kayak. With a major highway running along the east side, Back Cove has more of an urban feel to it. On quarter moons, the fishing can be good, and the structure surrounding the basin offers some protection from the wind.

The mouth of the cove by the bridge offers the deepest water. Here, the ebb and flow of the current sweep out some of the mud and offer deep water and structure for striped bass. You'll find some early season baits moving in and out of the cove as well as crabs and shrimp. Deeper water runs on a north/south line by the mouth of the cove. On the dropping tides, fish move off the flats and hold in the deeper water as the current sweeps baitfish to them. Finger channels are carved in the basin and reveal edges and water paths on both the flood and ebb tides. Floating and intermediate lines work best, and spring and summer are the better times. Night fishing can be good for bigger bass, too. The tendency in a brackish area such as Back Cove is to use fly patterns that you can see. Back Cove doesn't have a population of starving stripers, so be sure to use selections that match the water color. Even though you might not be able to see the fly, the stripers will. Lower tides can also be very productive for sight casting for fish. Look for 'v' wakes that are telltale signs of cruising fish.

PRESUMPSCOT RIVER

The Presumpscot River that begins at Sebago Lake ends on the north side of Portland. The river is the largest freshwater river to enter Casco Bay, therefore it has been a focal point for two and a half centuries of debate. In the late 1990s, the pulp mills stopped discharging sewage into the Presumpscot, which significantly helped improve water quality. In 2002, the Smelt Hill Dam was removed so the lower 7 miles of the Presumpscot flow freely to Casco Bay. Anadromous fish now can access over 100 miles of tributary water and feeder streams as well. The year 2005 marked a project to enhance fish passage at the Highland Lake Dam so that alewives could return to their spawning grounds. And finally, in 2007, fish passages at existing dams on the mainstem of the river were restored so that herring, alewives, and other fish that swim upriver from Casco Bay could pass.

Is this a big victory? Well, it's not exactly news up here. The topic of rivers and dams has created one of the longest running battles over fishing access on the Presumpscot River that dates back to violent clashes between American Indians and Maine's first industrial settlers more than 250 years ago. It's all good news for returning fish, and that means more anglers on the water. Currently, fishing is from June through October for bass and blues. In the spring, you'll find bait concentrated in the lower sections around Martin Point. The Martin Point bridge gets crowded with

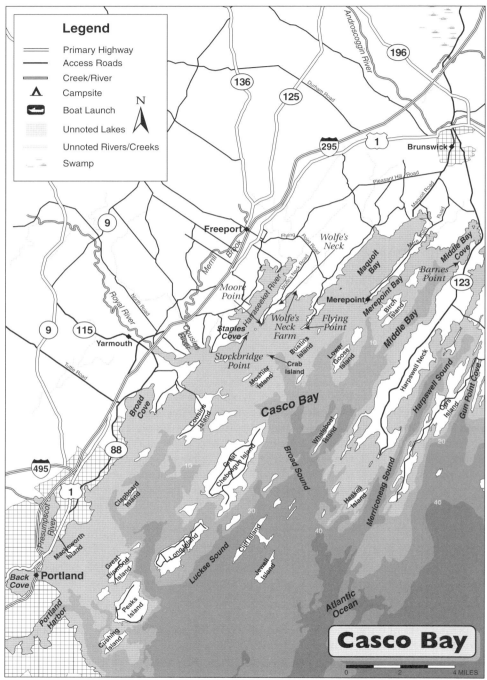

Legend

Primary Highway
Access Roads
Creek/River
Campsite
Boat Launch
Unnoted Lakes
Unnoted Rivers/Creeks
Swamp

N

Casco Bay

© 2010 Wilderness Adventures Press, Inc.

baitfishermen, but head upriver to Walton Park and toss in a kayak and paddle. To get to Walton Park, take the Allen Avenue Extension into Falmouth and park in the lot on the west side, opposite the entrance. There's plenty of signage and the grade from the trail to dockside is an easy walk. To explore the Presumpscot River Falls from another direction, try Portland Trails' new Riverton put-in, located at the intersection of Route 302 and Riverside Street. Park in the lot behind Waste Management. To get to the river, follow the unpaved pathway through the field – some find a wheeled carrier helpful to transport their canoes or kayaks. At the end of the path, you'll need to portage down a flight of sturdy stairs that lead directly into the river. The water can get a bit murky after a rain and in the summer.

The Brothers, Prince Point, Bartlett Point, Mussel Cove

Off of Town Landing Road in Falmouth is a public boat ramp that provides access to three good fishing spots. The ramp is usable only on the higher tides. The Brothers is a pair of inshore islands across from Waite's Landing and the Portland Country Club. The islands run on a northeast/southwest tack, with the smaller, or little brother, being closer to shore. A shoal runs from Waite's Landing to the first island and then a second shoal runs in between the two islands. Both shoals add shallower water and structure on the moving water. At the ends of the islands you'll find deeper water and all the nooks and pockets to hold fish.

Around the corner on the mainland are two points and two coves. Prince Point is first and features an inshore island with a long bar at the top of the cove. The cove is shallow with deeper water at the mouth. Stripers move in during the early season, and you'll find bluefish during the warmer summer months. Neighboring Mussel Cove gets more of the attention. Bartlett Point is at the eastern extreme of Mussel Cove. The rocky terrain out front meshes with the softer bottom of the cove. There is a channel on the northwest corner of the cove off of Old Mill Road. High dropping tide fishes best. A floating or intermediate line fishes best in the cove while a sinking line gets the call out from along Bartlett Point/Prince Point.

Royal River / Cousins River

Yarmouth's Royal River gets a good amount of fishing pressure from shore as well as from the two boat ramps. The Yarmouth Town Landing has a cement boat ramp (a fee is charged for out-of-town residents) and a dock. Parking is plentiful and an outhouse is available. Take Bayview Drive (on the east side of the river) and follow the access signs to the shore. The other is off of Route 88 at the Yarmouth Boat Yard, which charges a fee for use of their private boat ramp. It's a gravel ramp that is unusable at low tide, but there is parking and a float and it's a good option if the Town Landing is full. Competitive anglers may want to hit September's Royal River Striper Tournament that is sponsored by the Yarmouth Boat Yard. Proceeds go to striped-bass conservation and anglers can enter the tournament by going online at www.royalriverstriper.com. Forty-eight acres along the river are protected and open for recreational fishing.

The two rivers (the Royal and the Cousins) join at Casco Bay. Parker and Callen Points are at the mouth of the Royal River, and Browns, Powell, Lambert, and Fogg Points are along the Cousins River. At low water, striped bass stage around these points. Some move into the rivers as the tide rises, but many will move higher up as the tide drops. They'll move about half way up the river systems before turning and heading back to the mouth. The rivers have channels almost in the middle which reveals a consistent flow. Fishing floating or sinking lines are the best bet.

HARRASEEKET RIVER

Freeport's Harraseeket River comes by its name honestly – it is from a Native American dialect and means "river of many fish." You'll see plenty of kayakers on the river; after all, L.L. Bean uses the river for its kayak school. Put the "river of many fish" together with a kayak and you've got one of the best kayak fisheries in the Northeast. While there are numerous bed and breakfasts, inns, and hotels, there is also a campground located on the river at Winslow Park. There is a paved boat ramp but it's not usable at low tide. Winslow Park is a regular park, so there is ample parking, restrooms, wooded picnic areas, campsites, nature trails, and a swimming beach. You will have to pay a fee to access the park and get on the water.

A second way to access the river is through the eastern side at Wolfe's Neck Farm – a historic 626-acre farm that is open to the public. Camping is available next door through the Recompense Shore Campground.

The river is mostly a spring and early summer bass fishery and an early best bet for first arrivals. The bigger fish show in June, and the water warms up in mid-summer making for a better night spot. Bluefish also arrive in the river and there is a lot of structure amidst the muddy, grassy river banks. At the mouth are two points – Stockbridge Point to the west and Moore Point to the east (below Wolfe's Neck State Park). In between the two is a channel that shoots boaters out to Bowman, Pumpkin Knob, and Pound of Tea Islands. All are private so don't pull up on shore. That said, Crab Island is open to the public, so if you want to get out of the boat for a break you can. Fish stage around these islands during the lower water marks, and when there is ample baitfish (like alewives), they'll move into the river on the dropping tide. When the small fish arrive, you'll see lots of activity in the form of blitzing fish and diving birds, and if you don't see that, work the structure.

Carefully navigate your way into Staples Cove around the higher water marks. Mackerel are a common bait in the Harraseeket as are alewives and mendaden, and you'll find them in the coves as well as in the main river. There are a series of points and coves, mostly on the western side of the river near Freeport. Staples, Brewers, Weston, and Bartol Points all have western coves. Fish the points on full moons and the coves on quarter moons.

MERE POINT

After a hotly contested battle between public and private sectors, a dual-lane, concrete ribbed ramp on Mere Point about 6 miles south of downtown Brunswick was built and is ideally situated for easy access to Casco Bay. The new ramp features a large parking lot (55 spaces) and 24-hour all-tide access, however, parking overnight is not authorized. This is a boon to all boat anglers as the southern part of Mere Point is private from shore. The ramp is on the east end of Mere Point and opens on to Mere Point Bay.

From here, head southeast to Birch Island and Middle Bay, southwest to Flying Point or Upper and Lower Goose Islands. The depths vary, and there are channels and ledges throughout. While there are numerous excellent places to fish, and the time of year and bait determine where the fish are, Middle Bay Cove at the northern end is a good place to consistently catch fish. The shore entrance is off of Route 123, and from Barnes Point north you'll find a cove for early through mid-season bass. At low tide the water is only a foot or so deep, so either end of the moving tide is good. Floating or intermediate lines are best, and a kayak enables you to cover some ground. With its proximity so far north off the water, you can get in the lee when the northern winds start to blow.

Bass in the rocks maintain vivid black lines with vibrant purple, pink and blue hues like this Cape Neddick, Maine fish.

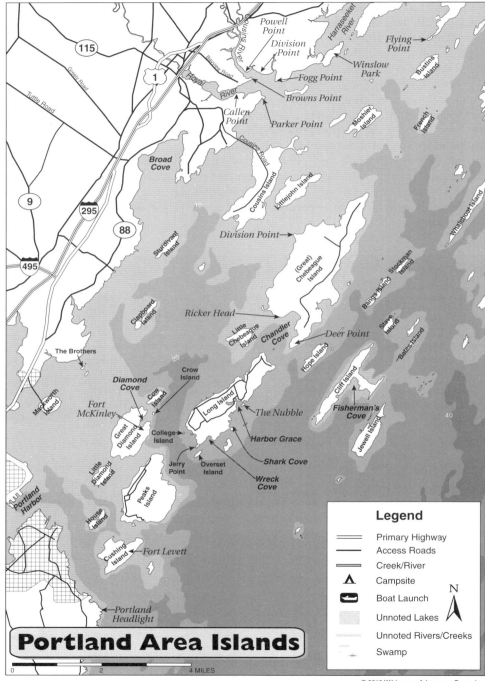

Portland Area Islands

Legend

Primary Highway
Access Roads
Creek/River
Campsite
Boat Launch
Unnoted Lakes
Unnoted Rivers/Creeks
Swamp

N

0   2   4 MILES

PORTLAND HARBOR ISLANDS

Like her big brother Boston, Portland has several inshore islands that are well worth fishing. They are accessible from the Casco Bay Lines Ferry (www.cascobaylines.com/schedules/sailing_schedules.htm), and provide year-round ferry service for passengers, vehicles, and freight between Portland and Peaks Island, Little Diamond Island, Great Diamond Island, Long Island, Chebeague Island, and Cliff Island. The islands were originally called the Calendar Islands because it was thought that there were 365 of them. In truth there are fewer than 200, and the ones listed above have ferry service. As with Boston, explore the remaining islands.

PEAKS ISLAND

With its close proximity to the mainland, Peaks Island has a good-sized summer population of all sorts of characters. It is the most populous Portland-area island. At one time, it was Maine's version of Coney Island, with ferris wheels, theaters, and other entertainment. Peaks Island does have regular car ferry service, but a vehicle is not necessary. There are bike rentals and kayak shops to help anglers access good fishing spots.

Fort Levett (on nearby Cushing Island) is a good area to cast poppers in rocks, and there are numerous sandy and rocky coves that hold striped bass and bluefish. The best time to fish Peaks Island is from high tide dropping down until it gets bony. The fish hold tight to the rocks and focus on the bait as the tide runs out. The terrain is good and the water is more protected with better footing. It's not as abrupt or jagged as some inshore islands are, and the island is reasonably protected from storms (meaning the swells aren't that bad). There are some cobble beaches that are worth fishing on the coming tide, and they tend to fish better in the summer when the bluefish are around, as well as in the fall during the run. Anglers can run out to the island for a day trip or create an overnight fishing package.

Accomodations, etcetera, on Peaks Island:

The Inn on Peaks
Island Avenue
www.innonpeaks.com
207-766-5100

Peaks Island House
Island Avenue
www.thepeaksislandhouse.com
207-766-4400

The Eighth Maine Regiment Memorial
13 Eight Maine Avenue
www.eighthmaine.com
207-766-5085

Maine Island Kayak
  70 Luther Street
  207-766-2373
  www.maineislandkayak.com

Brad's Island Bike Rentals & Repairs
  115 Island Avenue
  207-766-5631

LITTLE DIAMOND ISLAND

As of the 2000 census, Little Diamond Island had a year-round population of five and an elevation of 3 feet. The island is accessible by ferry or by private boat, and if you want to get around on the island bring a bike as there are no cars available. Fishing on the island is good. There is a channel on the southwestern side of the island that is formed by Hog Island Ledge and Little Diamond and serves as a corridor. There is a combination of rocks and sandy beaches; and an intermediate line works best for fishing around here. On the northern point heading toward Great Diamond Island there is a combination of a ledge and shoal that is some of the best striper water you'll see. Rocks, sand, and cobble are all mixed together. Current flows best around the higher water marks and there is a lot of texture. Little Diamond is a better boat fishery.

GREAT DIAMOND ISLAND

Great Diamond Island has a modest year-round population of less than 100. Golf carts and bicycles are the primary modes of transportation because there aren't many roads.

Diamond Cove is a community on Great Diamond Island. Fort McKinley is at the epicenter, and was designed to defend Portland Harbor during the Spanish-American War. The self-contained community offers resort-style living, complete with scenic walking trails and a full-service marina. A small number of restored homes are available as vacation rentals, which may be a great way for anglers to enjoy the island (www.greatdiamondrentals.com).

The mitten-shaped island has Diamond Cove/Fort McKinley in between the index finger and the thumb. A paddle around the area in a kayak is a good way to fish the sandy beaches and the protected rocks without too much fuss. On the northeast side are two separate islands, Cow Island and Crow Island. The channels in between them and Great Diamond are good spots. Indian Cove is also a good spot to pull out an extra-fast-sinking line and work the structure. In the fall on a west-northwest wind, there can be large concentrations of bait piled into Indian Cove. The southwest side of the island has a mixture of sand, rocks, and cobble, and can fish well on a high dropping tide with an intermediate line.

Long Island

Long Island is located 6 miles off the coast of Portland. The off-season population of 200 swells to over 1,000 in the summer, and many of the visitors are fishermen. Many residents, summer and winter, work in the lobster industry. Cars are allowed on the island but are somewhat discouraged, with residents believing that Long is best toured by bicycle. That said, bring your own as there are no bike rentals on the island. Long Island is most well known for its Sandy Beach where the sand "sings" beneath your feet as you walk.

There are more sandy beaches on Long Island which make for good bluefish blitzes in the summer as well as decent night fishing for bass. There is a nice cove off of Fern Avenue called Harbor Grace that holds fish around the higher water marks. Out in front is a rocky peninsula called the Nubble that fishes well from mid- to high tide. The southeast corner is equally good. Shark Cove and Wreck Cove get most of the attention for big bass. The water is clear and fishing a coming tide at first light is a good bet. You'll also find a series of coves and attached islands or heads off of Beach Avenue and Jerry Point Road. Overset Island, Jerry Point, and the College Island ledges off of Harrington Lane are also good for big fish. Hit them around the higher water marks.

Accomodations on Long Island

Chestnut Hill Inn
  Carol Doughty
  209 Beach Avenue
  207-0766-5272
  www.chestnuthillinn.com
  Beautiful rooms and private baths starting at $150 to $260 per night including breakfast.

Chebeague Island

Chebeague Island (also known as Great Chebeague Island) is approximately 7 miles northeast of Portland in Casco Bay. Two ferry services provide transportation to the island: the Chebeague Transportation Company and Casco Bay Lines.

A sandbar connects Chebeague Island with Little Chebeague Island at the southwestern end. There are strong currents between the two islands and when the bait is in you'll find fish on either side. Little Chebeague connects with Chebeague Island at Ricker Head. Between Ricker Head and the Deer Point Peninsula is Chandler Cove. Ferries run through the cove to the island, but this area holds good numbers of fish. On the north end, fish the northwest stretch from Chebeague Point through Division Point. The shoal from Division Point extends far toward neighboring Littlejohn Island. Good current speeds and coves and rocky structures makes for good bass fishing.

CLIFF ISLAND

Cliff Island is the smallest year-round island in Casco Bay. Cars are permitted, but most use alternate methods of transportation (walking, bike riding, etc.).

The southwestern side and the entire south side are good places to fish. Cliff Island is more of a boat spot and it is usually hit in conjunction with other islands. The ledges run very far out into the harbor, and the bass hang around the points on the lower tides and move up and in as the tide floods. Extra-fast-sinking lines are good around here. You'll find some sand along Beach Road where an intermediate line works better. For the most part Cliff Island comes by its name honestly. If you don't like rock fishing or don't want to jeopardize your lower unit, move elsewhere.

CLAPBOARD ISLAND

The private Clapboard Island is just off the coast from Mussel Cove and therefore is a boat-only fishery. It is one of the consistently good places to find summer stripers as there is a tremendous amount of structure. On the southern end of the island, you'll find a series of smaller rocks, ledges, and islands. The currents become diverse due to all of the structure. The southeastern section features a cove with a long, sandy beach, perfect for floating and intermediate lines. The water drops off quickly and you'll find pods of bluefish in the coves during the high dropping tides in the summer. If you're looking for stripers, check out the northern part of the island. Sharper drop-offs and strong currents make for perfect conditions, and you'll find pollock and mackerel during the season as bait. Shift to an extra-fast-sinking line and larger flies.

MACKWORTH ISLAND

At the mouth of the Presumpscot River is Mackworth Island. There is a causeway that connects the island to the mainland in Falmouth. Visitors to the island must pass by a tollhouse; cars can enter the island but parking is limited. There is a footpath around the perimeter of the island with views of Falmouth, Portland, and other islands surrounding the bay, and it runs along the rocky shoreline. The island is the home of the Governor Baxter School for the Deaf, and there you will find an ample parking lot.

Because of the rocky coastline, Mackworth Island fishes best on the higher water marks. Anglers vary between floating and intermediate lines. South of the causeway, you'll find more sand and cobble. The farther south you go, the terrain gets more rocky, and the ledge at the southwest corner is one of the better fishing areas. On a high dropping tide, the baitfish wash over the structure. Casting in and around the reef is a good technique, but also swing your fly through the current. The depth is uniform around most of the island until you reach the northern point. Up here is a shallower shoal that creates a lot of texture and current.

HARPSWELL AREA

Harpswell deserves a bit of an introduction. Due south of the town of Brunswick is a series of islands. Considered a boater's paradise because of the archipeligo of 200-plus islands, multitude of coves, beaches, mud and sand flats, and first-class fishing. These islands are finger-like. The western most island and is known as Harpswell Neck. It has three parts to it: North Harpswell, Harpswell Center, and South Harpswell, with Harpswell Sound to the east. The middle section features Route 24 and Great Island, Orrs Island, and Bailey Island, with Quahog Bay to the east. The third finger has Cundys Harbor with the New Meadows River to the east. All three fingers are integral to the fishing in Casco Bay, with much of the fishing being from a boat. The bass will arrive at the end of May, and June and early July are peak times. Bluefish join the bass during the summer months, and the fall run is tradtionally outstanding. Anglers will pick-pocket the rocks and coves looking for fish and using a combination of floating and extra-fast-sinking lines. For bait, you'll typically find alewives, some herring, menhaden, silversides, mackerel, sand eels, and squid. With all the coves, you'll see worm hatches around the full moon and there is also a good green crab hatch that brings the fish up. If the fish aren't in one cove then pop over to another one. And once you pattern them you'll be on them for the tide. In addition to good fishing, Harpswell has to be one of the prettiest areas along the coastline, with plenty of activities and entertainment for non-fishing spouses/family members.

ROUTE 24, HARPSWELL

The west can have Route 66, Maine has Route 24. Route 24 covers a 10-mile peninsula and three large islands: Sebascodegan (Great Island), Orrs Island and Bailey Island. From the mainland, pick up Route 24 and head south. You'll pass Great Sebascodegan Island, then Orrs Island and finally Bailey Island all the way to the end at Jaquish Gut. Great Sebascodegan Island is almost 5 miles long and 5 miles wide. Orrs Island is almost 5 miles long and less than a mile wide. And last but not least, Bailey Island is almost 3 miles long and less than a mile wide.

There are three boat ramps on the islands. By taking Route 24 south, then Route 123 south you'll find the South Harpswell Boat Ramp. Oddly enough, there is a ramp but car and boat trailer parking are not permitted. Dolphin Marine Service has a paved boat ramp, dock, and parking for a daily fee. Turkey Bridge Boat Ramp is on Prince Point Road just before you leave the mainland and cross over Gurnet Strait to Great Island. This cement boat ramp can't be used around the lower water marks. There is another ramp, the Great Island Boat Yard on Great Island, which is farther south on Route 24. This is a small area so get here early. A daily fee is charged. Another private boat ramp is located at the S.J. Prince & Son Store on Orrs Island. The ramp at this site is gravel and can be difficult to use on extreme low tides. There is a daily fee for using the ramp.

There is some shore access in this area, but much of it is private. Many anglers start with the end of the road which is called Land's End and is where Route 24 terminates on Bailey Island. Park in the large lot next to the gift shop

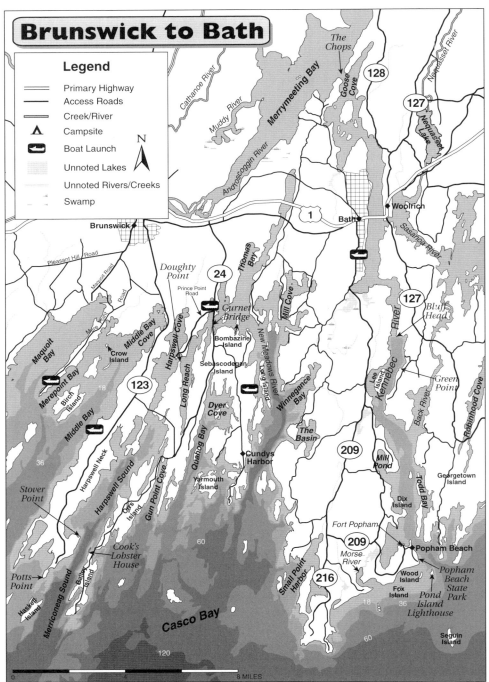

Brunswick to Bath

Legend

Primary Highway

Access Roads

Creek/River

△ Campsite

⬥ Boat Launch

Unnoted Lakes

Unnoted Rivers/Creeks

Swamp

N

COOK'S LOBSTER HOUSE

Off of Garrison Cove Road is the Cook's Lobster House. Founded in 1955, it offers terrific food to be sure. But, the large parking lot adjacent to the water to the west of the Bailey Island Bridge is terrific. Depending on the wind and the bait, you can fish the west side of the point or move over to the east side and access the tidal currents as they sweep through the bridge. Floating or intermediate lines are good. During the summer months you'll usually find bluefish blitzing in the cove. And when you're done fishing, swing by Cook's. You won't regret it.

STOVERS POINT PRESERVE

Stovers Point Preserve is off of Stovers Cove Road. A gravel road leads anglers to the beach. Stovers Point is at the southeastern part of the island and creates one giant cove. Bridge View Lane runs out to the end and features a small saltpond with several creeks that fish well on a high dropping tide. There is a sandy section on the northwest corner. Stovers Cove is to the west of Stovers Point. You'll want to use either floating or sinking lines around here depending on the current.

POTTS POINT PRESERVE

Harpswell Neck Road runs into Potts Point Road that runs down to a long sand bar that connects the preserve to Harpswell Neck. You can't drive to the Potts Point, so you'll need to hoof it or walk along the shoreline. There is a public boat launch at the end of Harpswell Neck Road, too. The water is mostly deep and rocky, but there are some connecting sand/cobble beaches. Using a floating or extra-fast-sinking line is best. At the end is a long sand bar and in the northwest corner is a cove that fishes well on the dropping tide. Bass get closer on the higher water marks along the rocks and ledges. And there can be a lot of lot of seaweed. Fog can roll in very quickly, and boaters should watch for the temperature changes. If you're walking along the houses, make sure you're doing so below the low tide mark.

BAILEY ISLAND'S MCINTOSH LOT PRESERVE

The McIntosh Lot Preserve is a 1-acre parcel of land on the southeastern corner of Bailey Island. It's open from sunrise to sunset, and is a rocky coastline that fishes better on either side of high tide. Because of the current flows, the rocks are arranged on a northeast/southwest line, which makes for good fishing on the dropping tide. Korkers are a must, and you'll need to walk through a residential area to access the preserve. Parking is along the street or at the Episcopal church when services are not being held.

NEW MEADOWS RIVER

The New Meadows River is a 23-mile watershed that covers the towns of Brunswick, Harpswell, West Bath, and Phippsburg. Though known as a river, the New Meadows has little freshwater origins that run into its saltwater sections. Technically it's a big bay, but who cares? The fishing is great and the strong Maine tides move enough water to make it seem like a river. The New Meadows Marina, at the head of the river, offers dock space and boating services.

Striped bass arrive around June and by early to mid-July the bluefish augment the fish stocks. The main channel is anywhere from 50 to 150 feet deep at low tide. The higher up you go the better the water for fly rodders as it gets to shallower depths. Many times you'll see fish working bait at the surface, and if not, work the edges along Cundys Harbor, the backside of Long Island, and into Winnegance Bay. Several other sheltered areas exist along the river, most notably the upper reaches of the New Meadows River, the area between Bombazine Island and the Gurnet Bridge, Mill Cove in West Bath, Winnegance Bay, Cundys Harbor, and The Basin in Phippsburg. Each of these holds fish.

As is typical of inshore islands and ledges, depths vary quite significantly. Floating and extra-fast-sinking shooting heads work best. Shock tippets are good additions and be sure to check your hook points. When dragged across your fingernail the hook point should dig into your nail.

MERRYMEETING BAY

Merrymeeting Bay is the 9,000-acre confluence of six rivers.

This watershed is enormous because the Kennebec, Androscoggin, Cathance, Eastern, Abbagadasett, and the Muddy all drain into the bay. Combined with their distance that runs to their freshwater origins, these six rivers account for a total of 9,524 square miles of water. That's a staggering number for sure, but that number's importance carries much more significance for fishermen. Smelt, shad, alewives, striped bass, and Atlantic salmon are commonly found in Merrymeeting Bay because of a number of variables. First is the combination of fresh and saltwater, perfect breeding grounds for anadromous fish. Second, the bay is a virtual baitfish factory. You'll find fresh and saltwater species from dace, chubs, shiners, fathead minnow, fallfish, suckers, mummichog, stickleback, sculpin along with alewives, herring, and silversides. Be sure to bring lots of smaller fly patterns and in particular blended bucktails to imitate the smaller baitfish. The Kennebec is interesting because it not only runs into Merrymeeting Bay but it also runs out of it.

Stripers arrive around the end of May. As with other areas that have a fresh/saltwater combination, you'll find schoolies arriving with shad. Both fish can become baitfish when the bigger fish arrive in June. One of the early season hotspots is a place called the Sands. The Sands is basically a large shoal that offers structure for the new arrivals. Mature fish are in and around the bay from June through October.

KENNEBEC RIVER

The Kennebec River is under special regulations from mid-October to July 1. With the exception of the mouth of the river, the Kennebec is predominantly a boat river. There are several ramps, and the most common one is at the end of Fiddlers Reach Road. From there, you'll have quick and easy access to a tremendous amount of water. They're all tide ramps.

You could spend a lifetime fishing just the Kennebec. Some guides and anglers do. There is a tremendous amount of water, and there are a tremendous amount of spots to fish, so get a chart and head on out. During the 1990s the menhaden runs in the Kennebec were strong and long, and there were lots of big fish spread throughout the river. The early millennial years were not so kind to the Kennebec. A lot of bait did not return and the fish just didn't seem to be around. In recent years, the fishing has improved and there are good fish stocks throughout the season.

What might help is a methodology. As you work your way upriver from the ocean, you'll find a series of bays and inshore islands. There is an interesting pattern to note, for many of the uptide reaches are better on the flood tides and the corresponding lower tide reaches are better on the ebb tide. That means baitfish and therefore stripers gather in certain spots on the flood tide, then drift apart and regather in a new spot on the ebb tide. There is a peninsula that extends on a southeast tack into the Kennebec, directly across from Parker Head. Mill Pond separates the two land masses. Baitfish move along the channels and shorelines and into Mill Pond on a flood tide. The fishing is good on the seams and drop-offs, along the shoals, and near the shoreline. When the tide turns, the whole party moves southeast into Cox Head and Wyman Bay (just west of Dix Island). There is a river estuary system in Wyman Bay and Dix Island closes off part of the bay on the northeast corner.

With all the inshore islands, coves, points, and peninsulas this theme is repeated. Lee Island and Drummore Bay (just west of Lee Island) uptide and Weasel Point and its cove (downtide) is one example. Bluff Head and Fisher Eddy uptide, and Green Point down below is another one.

For specifics, the Edwards Dam is the top of the tide mark for the river. One place to fish is just below the Edwards Power Plant facility on Water Street. It'll feel more freshwater than saltwater, but a sink-tip line when the herring and alewives are in makes for a good day. There is a boat ramp next to Fort Western where shallow draft boats and kayaks can be launched, and shore fishing around here is good.

Popham Beach State Park is a 529-acre state park which features a 3-mile long white sand beach located on the south side of the mouth of the Kennebec River and the north side of the Morse River. It juts out from land on a northeast position that seems to gather baitfish first, and then striped bass and bluefish. The park has all the usual amenities such as bathhouses and showers.

Because of its eastern position at the mouth/open ocean, the area is buffered from the dominant west-southwest winds which creates a softer surf. The bottom is sandy and unless there are storms or heavy rains upriver, the water stays very clear. It's unsual to find so much sand along coastal Maine, but there is a lot and that makes for numerous flats. There are a number of guides who are able to offer quality sight fishing.

When school is out for the summer, Fort Popham gets very crowded. With a late start to the fishing season, anglers really only have a few weeks of good fishing which are the first three weeks of June. Larger fish arrive in mid- to late June, and the fishing remains strong through the end of September through early October. Parking at Popham Beach State Park costs $4. A sand bar extends out to Fox Island, and fishing along it can be good. Watch for the tidal fluctuations. Intermediate lines are adequate around the lower marks, and as the tide rises the current picks up, making extra-fast-sinking lines a better choice.

The adjoining Morse River runs into the west end of Popham Beach. At the opposite end of the river is a tidal marsh. In the early season there are good numbers of small fish moving into the tidal river, and you'll hear them popping at night. The standard estuary approach applies: Start at the mouth at low water, work your way higher into the system and back down again. You'll find fish holding in some of the mosquito ditches and offshoots, oftentimes feeding on shrimp and crabs.

FORT POPHAM

There are several areas to fish around Fort Popham. The first is along the ledges and the rocks that extend out and along Fort Popham. As the tide floods and ebbs you'll be able to cast to fish moving into the current along the rocks. Most of the time, you'll want to use an extra-fast-sinking line because the current is strong. The rock faces are not jagged like they are downstate, and their smoothness makes for difficult walking, even with Korkers. There are numerous areas to fish, so move cautiously until you find one that is holding fish. Stripping baskets are essential and the currents slow down around either the top or the bottom of the tides.

Or stay at the Popham Beach Bed & Breakfast and walk out the door and fish. As the tide rises, the fish move up and along the beachfront and wind up along the pilings. There are some deep ocean holes that hold the bait on a dropping tide. Overall, a floating and an intermediate line are the best choices. At low tide, you'll see a sand spit that extends relatively far out. You'll find bass and blues below the bar on the dropping tide.

The sand bar that connects to Wood Island is a good spot. If you've got a boat or a kayak you'll be able to cast to fish cruising on the higher water marks, but low tide is best for the wade fishermen. Depending on the wind, one side of the bar – either the east or the west – seems to fish better than the other. More natural patterns with less flash get the nod. As with any body of land that extends out to sea, fish the connection points. Floating or sink-tip lines are good. Currents are strong as the tide rises, so be careful when fishing here, especially at night.

REID STATE PARK

Located on the eastern tip of Georgetown Island in Sheepscot Bay is the 766-acre Reid State Park. The combination of a sandy beach, low-lying marsh, and saltwater pond make for a good fishery. Reid State Park is Maine's first state-owned saltwater beach and was donated to the state in 1946. The lighthouses in the distance are on Seguin Island, the Cuckolds, and Hendricks Head.

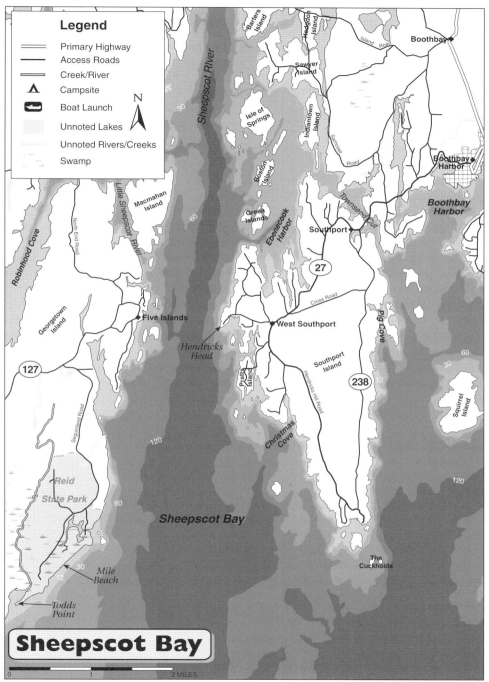

Legend

—— Primary Highway
—— Access Roads
—— Creek/River
▲ Campsite
⛴ Boat Launch
Unnoted Lakes
Unnoted Rivers/Creeks
Swamp

N

Sheepscot River

Barters Island
Hodgdon Island
Island Road
Boothbay
Sawyer Island
Isle of Springs
Indiantown Island
Boston Island
Samoset Road
Boothbay Harbor
Macmahan Island
Little Sheepscot River
North End Road
Green Islands
Ebenecook Harbor
Townsend Cut
Southport
Boothbay Harbor
Robinhood Cove
Georgetown Island
Five Islands
Hendricks Head
Cross Road
27
West Southport
Pig Cove
127
Pratts Island
Southport Island
238
Squirrel Island
Seguinland Road
Hendricks Hill Road
Christmas Cove
Reid State Park
Sheepscot Bay
The Cuckholds
Mile Beach
Todds Point

30
60
120

Sheepscot Bay

0   1   2 MILES

There is nearly a mile and a half of beachfront and nearby are bathhouses, snack bars, and picnic areas. It's broken down into two separate sections, Mile Beach and Half Mile Beach. At the northern end of Mile Beach is a large parking lot off of Griffith Head Road. From there, anglers can fish a variety of spots. The lagoon is a river estuary system and is a combination of sand and mud. It's a good, early season spot as the water warms quickly, and is also a good kayak spot. Out in front on the east side is the lower section of Sheepscot Bay. Here you'll find more rocks and ledges. The water is deeper, and extra-fast-sinking lines are the choice. The northern corner where the ledges meet the beach is a good spot to find fish. As you walk down along the beach you'll mostly find a classic beach break with an offshore parallel bar. Intermediate lines work best.

At the southern end of the beach is a second parking area that is off of Seguinland Road. The two lots connect to Half Mile Beach. At the top of the beach is a series of rocks and ledges and at the southern end is an estuary and river system. Fish arrive in the Sheepscot in late May through early June and will be spread out from the river system, along the beach, and in the rocks depending on the baitfish that are present. Sand eels, silversides, mackerel, and menhaden are the common baitfish. If you're working the rocks and ledges, a sink-tip or an extra-fast-sinking line is best. If you move along the beach you may want to change lines. You can use a floating line in both the rocks and along the beach and adjust to the depth by adding weight to your leader or fly. A few split shot will work fine. Todds Point is at the end of the beach and is at the mouth of a river estuary system. Down here, you'll find a series of flats that are adjacent to a main channel. The best way to access the river is by kayak and from the top of the western parking lot. Pull your boat into the river and fish it on the dropping tide all the way to the point. When the tide turns, float back up. Currents at the mouth get strong, so stay on the inside of Todd's Point.

Maine Saltwater Public Boat Ramps

ADDISON

Eastern Harbor. All-Tide Ramp. Hard Surface, 20'W x 150'L. Parking - Yes.
Pleasant River. All-Tide Ramp. Hard Surface, 20'W x 138'L. Parking - Limited.

AUGUSTA

Kennebec River. All-Tide Ramp. Hard Surface, 20'W x 60'L. Parking - Yes.

BAR HARBOR

Frenchman Bay. All-Tide Ramp. Hard Surface, 20'W x 175'L.Parking - Yes.

BATH

Kennebec River @ South End. All - Tide Ramp. Hard Surface, 40'W x 106'L. Parking - Yes.
Kennebec River @ North End. All - Tide Ramp. Hard Surface, 20'W x 90'L. Parking - Yes.

BEALS

Alley Bay. All-Tide Ramp. Hard Surface, 20'L.

BELFAST

Belfast Bay. All-tide Ramp. Hard Surface, 20'W x 130'L. Fee. Parking - Yes.

BIDDEFORD

Saco River. All-tide Ramp. Hard Surface, 40'W x 133'L. Parking - Yes.

BLUE HILL

Blue Hill Bay. All-tide Ramp. Hard Surface, 20'W x 106'L. Parking - Limited.
Blue Hill Harbor. Part - Tide Ramp. Hard Surface, 10'W x 60'L. Parking - Yes.

BOOTHBAY

Back River. All-tide Ramp. Hard Surface, 20'W x 100'L. Parking - Yes.
Linekin Bay. Part-Tide Ramp. Hard Surface, 20'W x 135'L. Parking - Limited.

BOWDOINHAM

Cathance River. All-tide Ramp. Hard Surface, 16'W x 100'L. Parking - Limited.

BRISTOL

Pemaquid River. All-tide Ramp. Hard Surface, 20'W x 44'L. Parking - Yes.
Round Pond Harbor. All-tide Ramp. Hard Surface.

BRUNSWICK

Androscoggin River @ Water Street. All-tide Ramp. Hard Surface. 20'W x 100'L. Parking - Yes.
Merepoint Bay. All-tide Ramp. Hard Surface. 40'W. Parking - Yes.
New Meadows River. All-tide Ramp. Hard Surface. 20'W x 120'L. Parking - Yes.
Buttermilk Cove. Part-Tide Ramp. Hard Surface. 20'W x 81'L. Parking - Limited.
Middle Bay. Part-Tide Ramp. Hard Surface. 10'W x 90'L.

Calais

St. Croix River. Part-Tide Ramp. Hard Surface. 20'W x 198'L. Parking - Limited.

Chelsea

Kennebec River. All-tide Ramp. Hard Surface. 16'W x 30'L. Parking - Limited.

COLUMBIA FALLS

Pleasant River. Part-Tide Ramp. Hard Surface. Parking - Limited.

DAMARISCOTTA

Damariscotta River. All-tide Ramp. Hard Surface. 20'W x 150'L. Parking - Yes.

EDMUNDS TOWNSHIP

Cobscook Bay. All-tide Ramp. Hard Surface. 20'W x 150'L. Parking - Limited.
Whiting Bay. All-tide Ramp. Carry-in. Parking - Limited.

ELIOT

Piscataqua River. All-tide Ramp. Hard Surface. 20'W x 103'L. Fee. Parking - Yes.

ELLSWORTH

Union River. All-tide Ramp. Hard Surface. 20'W x 155'L. Parking - Yes.

FRANKFORT

Penobscot River. All-tide Ramp. Hard Surface. 20'W x 160'L.

GARDINER

Kennebec River. All-tide Ramp. Hard Surface. 20'W x 140'L.Parking - Yes.

HALLOWELL

Kennebec River. All-tide Ramp. Hard Surface. 20'W x 80'L. Parking - Limited.

HAMPDEN

Penobscot River. All-tide Ramp. Hard Surface. 50'W x 200'L. Parking - Yes.

HARRINGTON

Ripley Cove. All-tide Ramp. Hard Surface.

ISLESBORO

Gilkey's Harbor. Part-Tide Ramp. Hard Surface.

JONESPORT

Chandler Bay. All-tide Ramp. Hard Surface. 20'W x 150'L. Parking - Limited.

KITTERY

Piscataqua River. All-tide Ramp. Hard Surface. 20'W x 65'L.

LAMOINE

Frenchman Bay (State). All-tide Ramp. Gravel Surface. 20'W x 125'L. Fee. Parking - Yes.
Frenchman Bay (Local). All-tide Ramp. Hard Surface. 20'W x 240'L. Parking - Yes.

LINCOLNVILLE

West Penobscot Bay. Part - Tide Ramp. Hard Surface.

LUBEC

Johnson Bay. All-tide Ramp. Hard Surface. 40'W x 210'L. Parking - Yes.

MACHIAS

Machias River. All-tide Ramp. Hard Surface. 20'W x 120'L. Parking - Yes.

MACHIASPORT

Bucks Harbor. All-tide Ramp. Gravel Surface. Parking - Yes.

MILBRIDGE

Narraguagus River. All-tide Ramp. Hard Surface. 20'W x 128'L. Parking - Yes.

MOUNT DESERT

Bartlett Narrows. All-tide Ramp. Hard Surface. 20'W.

ORRINGTON

Penobscot River. Part - Tide Ramp. Hard Surface. 20'W x 102'L. Parking - Yes.

PEMBROKE

Pennamaquan River. All-tide Ramp. Hard Surface. 20'W x 410'L. Parking - Yes.

PENOBSCOT

Northern Bay. Part-Tide Ramp. Hard Surface. 10'W x 75'L.

PERRY

Gleason Cove. All-tide Ramp. Hard Surface. 20'W x 238'L. Parking - Yes.
Passamaquoddy Bay. All-tide Ramp. Hard Surface. 20'W x 192'L. Parking - Limited.

PHIPPSBURG

Kennebec River. All-tide Ramp. Hard Surface. 20'W x 150'L. Parking - Yes.

PORTLAND

Casco Bay. Part-Tide Ramp. Hard Surface. 20'W x 180'L. Fee. Parking - Yes.

PORTLAND PEAKS ISLAND

Casco Bay. Part-Tide Ramp. Hard Surface. 20'W x 75'L.

RICHMOND

Kennebec River. All-tide Ramp. Hard Surface. 20'W x 60'L. Parking - Yes.

ROBBINSTON

St. Croix River. All-tide Ramp. Hard Surface. 20'W x 232'L. Parking - Limited.

Rockland

Rockland Harbor. All-tide Ramp. Hard Surface. 48'W x 140'L. Fee. Parking - Yes.

Rockport

Rockport Harbor. All-tide Ramp. Hard Surface. 20'W x 125'L. Fee. Parking - Yes.

Saco

Saco River. All-tide Ramp. Hard Surface. 20'W. Parking - Yes.

Scarborough

Scarborough River @ Pine Point. All-tide Ramp. Hard Surface.
Nonesuch River. Part-Tide Ramp. Hard Surface. 20'W x 69'L. Parking - Yes.
Scarborough River @ Ferry Beach. Part-tide Ramp. Hard Surface. 20'W x 100'L.

Searsport

Searsport Harbor. All-tide Ramp. Hard Surface. 24'W x 110'L. Parking - Yes.

South Berwick

Piscataqua River. Part-tide Ramp. Hard Surface.

South Portland

Fore River. All-tide Ramp. Hard Surface. 54'W x 156'L. Fee. Parking - yes.

South Thomaston

Weskeag River. Part-tide Ramp. Hard Surface.

Southwest Harbor

Southwest Harbor. All-tide Ramp. Hard Surface. 20'W x 185'L. Parking - Yes.

St George

Port Clyde Harbor. All-tide Ramp. Hard Surface. 20'W x 150'L.
Tenants Harbor. All-tide Ramp. Hard Surface. 16'W x 150'L.

Stockton Springs

Stockton Harbor. All-tide Ramp. Hard Surface. 20'W x 160'L. Parking - Yes.

STONINGTON

Deer Isle Thoroughfare. All-tide Ramp. Hard Surface. Parking - Limited.

SURRY

Patten Bay. Part-Tide Ramp. Hard Surface. 16'W x 150'L. Parking - Yes.

SWANS ISLAND

Mackerel Cove. All-tide Ramp. Hard Surface. 12'W x 100'L.
Burnt Coat Harbor. Part-Tide Ramp. Hard Surface. 20'W.

THOMASTON

St. George River. All-tide Ramp. Hard Surface. 20'W x 138'L. Parking - Yes.

TREMONT

Bass Harbor. All-tide Ramp. Hard Surface. 20'W x 152'L. Parking - Yes.
Seal Cove. All-tide Ramp. Hard Surface. 10'W x 229'L. Parking - Limited.

VERONA

Penobscot River. All-tide Ramp. Hard Surface. 20'W x 100'L. Parking - Yes.

VINALHAVEN

Carvers Harbor. All-tide Ramp. Hard Surface. 10'W x 75'L.

WALDOBORO

Medomak River. All-tide Ramp. Hard Surface.
Medomak River. Part-Tide Ramp. Hard Surface. 20'W x 265'L.

WELLS

Webhannet River. Part - Tide Ramp. Hard Surface. 16'W.

WESTPORT ISLAND

Back River. Part-Tide Ramp. Hard Surface. 20'W x 120'L. Parking - Yes.

WOOLWICH

Pleasant Cove. Part-Tide Ramp. Carry-in/Hard Surface. 10'W x 46'L. Parking - Yes.

Hub City Information: Maine

CAPE NEDDICK

Population - 2,992 Area Code - 207 County - York

Hotels and Motels

Country View Motel, 1521 US Rte One / 363-7160 /
www.countryviewmotel.com

Sands by the Sea York Beach, 15 Ocean Avenue, York Beach / 877-747-8713 /
www.sandsbythesea.com

Admiral's Inn Resort, 95 Main Street, Ogunquit / 646-7093 /
www.theadmiralsinn.com

Beachmere Inn, 62 Beachmere Place, Ogunquit / 646-2231 /
www.beachmereinn.com

The Dunes on the Waterfront, 518 Main Street, Ogunquit / 888-295-3863 /
www.dunesonthewaterfront.com

Restaurants

Clay Hill Farm Restaurant, 220 Clay Hill Road, York / 361-2272 /
www.clayhillfarm.com

Cape Neddick Inn Restaurant, 1273 US Route 1 / 351-1145 /
www.capeneddickinnrestaurant.com

Cape Neddick Lobster Pound, 60 Shore Road Ext / 363-5471 /
www.capeneddick.com

Fly Shops/Bait and Tackle Shops

Eldredge Bros Fly Shop, 1480 US Route 1 / 207-363-9269 /
www.eldredgeflyshop.com

Marine Supplies

West Marine, 775 Lafayette Road #2, Portsmouth, N.H. / 436-8300 /
www.westmarine.com

Hospitals

York Hospital, 15 Hospital Drive, York / 363-4321 / www.yorkhospital.com
Portsmouth Regional Hospital, 333 Borthwick Avenue, Portsmouth, N.H. / 436-5110 / www.portsmouthhospital.com

Airports

Portsmouth International Airport at Pease (PSM), 36 Airline Avenue, Portsmouth, N.H. / 433-6536 / www.peasedev.org

PORTLAND
Population - 64,000 Area Code - 207 County - Cumberland

Hotels and Motels

Hilton Garden Inn Portland Downtown Waterfront, 65 Commercial Street / 780-0780 / www.hiltongardeninn.com
Portland Harbor Hotel, 468 Fore Street / 888-798-9090 / www.portlandharborhotel.com
Holiday Inn Portland By the Bay, 88 Spring Street / 775-2311 / www.holidayinn.com
The Inn at St. John, 939 Congress Street / 773-6481 / www.innatstjohn.com

Restaurants

Back Bay Grill, 65 Portland Avenue / 772-8833 / www.backbaygrill.com
Bintliff's American Café, 98 Portland Street / 774-0005 / www.bintliffscafe.com
Bugaboo of Portland, 264 Gorham Road, South Portland / 773-5400 / www.bugaboocreek.com

Fly Shops/Bait and Tackle Shops

The Tackle Shop, 61 India Street / 773-3474 / www.thetackleshop.net
Cabela's, 100 Cabela's Blvd., Scarborough / 883-7400 / www.cabelas.com

Marine Supplies

Hamilton Marine Portland, 100 Fore Street / 774-1772 / www.hamiltonmarine.com

Hospital

Mercy Hospital, 144 State Street / 879-3000 / www.mercyhospital.com
Maine Medical Center, 22 Bramhall Street / 662-0111 / www.mmc.org

Airports

Portland International Jetport (PWM), Jetport Access Road / 775-5809 /
www.portlandjetport.org

Trains

Amtrak Downeaster, Portland Transportation Center (POR), 100 Thompson's
Point Road / 800-872-7245 / www.amtrakdowneaster.com

OTHER ACTIVITIES

Victoria Mansion,109 Danforth Street / 772-4841 /
www.victorianmansion.org
Wadsworth Longfellow House, 489 Congress Street / 774-1822 /
www.mainehistory.org
Maine Lighthouse Tours, www.visitmaine.com/attractions/sightseeing_
tours/lighthouse

FREEPORT

Population – 1,876 Area Code-207 County - Cumberland County

Hotels and Motels

Harraseeket Inn, 162 Main Street / 865-9377 / www.harraseeketinn.com
Hilton Garden Inn Freeport Downtown, 5 Park Street / 865-1433 /
www.hiltongardeninn.com
Brewster House Bed & Breakfast, 180 Main Street / 865-4121 /
www.brewsterhouse.com
Applewood Inn, 8 Holbrook Street / 865-9705 / www.applewoodusa.com

Restaurants

Azure Café, 123 Main Street / 865-1237 / www.azurecafe.com
Lobster Cooker, 39 Main Street / 865-4349
Broad Arrow Tavern at Harraseeket Inn, 162 Main Street / 342-6423 /
www.harraseeketinn.com
Jameson Tavern, 115 Main Street / 865-4196 / www.jamesontavern.com

Fly Shops/Bait and Tackle Shops

L.L. Bean, 95 Main Street / 877-755-2326 / www.llbean.com

Marine Supplies

Landing Boat Supply, 106 Lafayette Street, Yarmouth / 846-3777 /
www.landingboatsupply.com

Hospitals

Mid-Coast Hospital, 123 Medical Center Drive, Brunswick / 729-0181 /
www.midcoasthealth.com
Mercy Hospital, 144 State Street, Portland / 879-3000 /
www.mercyhospital.com
Maine Medical Center, 22 Bramhall Street, Portland / 662-0111 /
www.mmc.org

Airports

Portland International Jetport (PWM), Jetport Access Road, Portland /
775-5809 / www.portlandjetport.org

Trains

Amtrak Downeaster, Portland Transportation Center (POR), 100 Thompson's
Point Road, Portland / 800-872-7245 / www.amtrakdowneaster.com
Brunswick Amtrak Station (BRK), 162 Pleasant Street, Brunswick /
800-872-7245

CAMDEN/ROCKPORT
Population - 7,560 Area Code - 207 County - Knox

Hotels and Motels

Lord Camden Inn, 24 Main Street, Camden / 236-4325 /
www.lordcamdeninn.com
Hartstone Inn, 41 Elm Street, Camden / 800-788-4823 /
www.hartstoneinn.com
Camden Maine Stay Inn, 22 High Street, Camden / 236-9636 /
www.camdenmainestay.com
Ledges By The Bay, 930 Commercial Street, Rockport / 594-8944 /
www.ledgesbythebay.com
Island View Inn, 908 Commercial Street, Rockport / 596-0040 /
www.islandviewinnmaine.com

Restaurants

Hartstone Inn Restaurant, 41 Elm Street, Camden / 800-788-4823 /
www.hartstoneinn.com
The Waterfront Restaurant, 40 Bayview Street, Camden / 236-3747 /
www.waterfrontcamden.com
Paolina's Way, 10 Bayview Landing, Camden / 230-0555 /
www.paolinasway.com
Cappy's Chowder House, 1 Main Street, Camden / 236-2254 /
www.cappyschowder.com

Fly Shops/Bait and Tackle Shops

Maine Sport Outfitters, Route 1, Rockport, Maine/888.236-7120/
www.mainesport.com

Hospitals

Penobscot Bay Medical Center, 6 Glen Cove Drive, Rockport / 596-8000
Waldo County General Hospital, 118 Northport Avenue, Belfast / 338-2500 /
www.wchi.com

Airports

Knox County Regional Airport, 19 Terminal Lane, Owls Head / 593-9323 /
www.knoxcounty.midcoast.com
Bangor International Airport (BGR), 287 Godfrey Boulevard, Bangor /
992-4600 / www.flybangor.com
Portland International Jetport (PWM), Jetport Access Road, Portland /
775-5809 / www.portlandjetport.org

Trains

Amtrak Downeaster, Portland Transportation Center (POR), 100 Thompsons
Point Road, Portland / 800-872-7245 / www.amtrakdowneaster.com
Camden/Rockport Amtrak Station (CDN), 234 Park Street, Rockport /
800-872-7245 / www.amtrak.com

Other Activities

Maine Lighthouse Museum, One Park Drive, Rockland / 594-3301
Penobscot Marine Museum, 5 Church Street, Searsport / 548-2529 /
www.penobscotmarinemuseum.org

Top Ten Flies for the Fall Run

After a quiet summer, the Northeast Coast comes alive in the fall with outstanding saltwater fishing. Striped bass and bluefish run along the entire coastline from Maine to New Jersey before reaching their winter haunts. Inshore from the Gulf Stream, you'll find bonito, false albacore, and Spanish mackerel. While those five species get most of the attention, there are other fish, too. As a result, fly rodders choose their quarry, 'cause they're all here. And then the schools will gradually thin out and they'll be gone – just in time for duck season.

You'll find lots of different bait forms in the fall, and they range from peanut bunker to sand eels to silversides to bay anchovies to butterfish, to mackerel to herring to mullet, and more. Gotta have flies, sometimes lots of 'em, and while there are tons of them that are excellent, here's a go-to selection that will put fish on your line.

LEFTY'S DECEIVER

Designed by Lefty Kreh

Deceivers are standard streamer templates that can be modified to match your bait. Tie them big and long with schlappen tails and lots of bucktails for menhaden or herring or tie them small and sparse with short saddles and small amounts of bucktail for sand eels and bay anchovies. You can dress them up with various colors such as brown, yellow, and lavender for peanut bunker, or tie them with bright colors as attractor patterns.

SEPTEMBER NIGHT FLY

Designed by Kenney Abrames

The September Night Fly is a go-to mullet pattern. With thin-stemmed hackles tied perpendicular to the hook, flatwings have unparalleled movement in the water. The September Night Fly incorporates both bucktail and marabou, and the bucktail gives the fly its rounded silhouette while the marabou adds movement. The sparse construction closely resembles the mullet's rounded profile without adding bulky materials to add weight. In the fall, you'll find mullet schooled up along the shoreline from the Rhode Island coastline through Maryland. Hint: it's outstanding in the daytime, too.

CONOMO SPECIAL

Designed by Rich Murphy

I first used Murphy's Conomo Special over a decade ago on the Massachusetts' North Shore. The Conomo Special is a loose construction of yak hair, some flash, and a wing. Murphy adds a blue wing for blue-backed herring, a brown wing for menhaden, and varies the length to match the bait. Sometimes he adds a few wraps of lead wire under the E-Z body head for weight which adds action to the fly. While Murphy named the fly for Conomo Point on the North Shore, he favors the fly when fishing the Outer Beaches during the fall run.

RAY'S FLY

Designed by Ray Bondorew

Ray's Fly is a simple bucktail that is without question the single best silverside pattern. It's easy to tie and the colors perfectly resemble a silverside in the water. Silverside length varies proportionately from juvenile to adults (1 inch versus 6 inches or more). Match their size by tying flies with longer or shorter bucktail. Ray's Fly can be fished as a point fly, but I like to use it as part of a dropper rig. Sometimes I'll fish three or four of various lengths to see which one gets the action, and then adjust to the winner. The Ray's Fly works on all species of fish in the fall.

STEEP HILL SPECIAL

Designed by Rich Murphy

The Steep Hill Special is a blended-color, sand eel bendback. Steep Hill is in Ipswich, Massachusetts, at the mouth of Plum Island Sound, known for its cluttered bottom. The bendback construction sweeps the fly over kelp and rocks with few hang-ups. The sparseness of the fly makes it easy to cast and it undulates in the current. While Murphy ties the fly with yak hair, and if you can't find yak hair, substitute bucktail or use synthetics. Like many flies, play around with the color to match the bait. I like to fish the Steep Hill Special with a floating line, adding some split shot when necessary to drift the fly naturally with the current.

Surf Candy

Designed by Bob Popovics

New Jersey's Bob Popovics is best known for his epoxy flies that he created for durability in the 1970s. His flies were designed to withstand the savage jaws of bluefish, and also work well to imitate smaller bait that albies and bonito like. The Surf Candy has been a staple in fly boxes for a long time because of its versatility. A Surf Candy is tied with a synthetic wing, typically Super Hair or Ultra Hair, and with the plethora of available colors, you can make attractor patterns or imitators. Surf Candies cast easily even on lightweight lines. Striped bass eat 'em, too.

Half-and-Half

A combination of flies designed by Bob Clouser, Lefty Kreh, and Kenney Abrames

What happens when you combine two of the most popular saltwater fly patterns? You get a Half-and-Half, a blend of a Lefty's Deceiver and a Clouser Minnow. While the Clouser-with-a-Deceiver wing is the most popular, there are other ways to combine a streamer fly with lead eyes. Try tying a Deceiver with lead dumbbell eyes (also known as a Deep Deceiver) or a Flatwing Clouser, which is a Deep Minnow with an Abrames-style flatwing tail. Anyway you slice it, it's a fly that gets deeper in the water column, has plenty of action, and can be tied in a variety of sizes and colors to imitate any bait you'll encounter.

Mushmouth

Designed by Dave Skok

The Mushmouth series is a recent creation, created around 2004. Skok designed the fly with the help of Capt. Chris Aubut when schools of skipjack, also known as mushmouths, were along the Rhode Island and southwestern Massachusetts coastline. The fly is tied with Wing-n-Flash in a variety of color combinations. Skok has expanded the length of his series to accommodate larger baitfish patterns and calls them Megamushies. He had success with them on false albacore in two of the Martha's Vineyard Derbies.

Gurgler

Designed by Jack Gartside

Gartside's Gurgler is a foam fly that sits in the water's surface. It chugs water when retrieved, is lightweight and easy to cast, and withstands the abuse caused by many landed fish. With a bucktail tail, a palmered-hackle body and a foam wing, you can tie the Gurgler in no time at all. Tie them in bright colors like yellow or lime green as attractors or in natural colors as imitators. I particularly like to fish Gurglers on flat, calm days, for it's exciting to watch fish track and gently take the fly.

CREASE FLIES

Designed by Joe Blados

Long Island, New York's Joe Blados developed the Crease Fly to catch fish that are high in the water column. A Crease Fly is basically a cut-to-shape foam body, colored with markers. By wrapping the foam, you create a cup at the head of the fly which displaces water when retrieved on the surface. Some have bucktail tails, others have hackles, and you can tie them on long- or short-shanked hooks to vary their size. Make 'em bright for attractors or natural for imitators – however you want. Crease Flies cast easily and they catch all fall species.

Fly Shops and Guides

RHODE ISLAND FLY AND TACKLE SHOPS
(alphabetical by town)

Ocean State Tackle-Bristol

1284 Hope Street
Bristol
401-396-5554
www.oceanstatetackle.com

Ocean State Tackle-Coventry

735 Centre for New England
   Boulevard
Coventry
401-226-6626
www.oceanstatetackle.com

River and Riptide Anglers

2435 Nooseneck Hill Road Unit 4A
Coventry
401-392-1919
www.riverandriptide.com

The Saltwater Edge

1077 Aquidneck Ave
Middletown
401-842-0062
www.saltwateredge.com

Quaker Lane Bait and Tackle

4019 Quaker Lane
North Kingston
401-294-9642
www.quakerlanetackle.com

Ocean State Tackle-Providence

430 Branch Avenue
Providence
401-714-0088
www.oceanstatetackle.com

Wildwood Outfitters, LTD

271 Main Street
Wakefield
401-789-1244
www.wildwoodoutfittersri.com

Watch Hill Flyfishing Co.

2 Mastuxet Terrace
Westerly
401-596-1914

Rhode Island Guides

Block Island Fishworks

Block Island
401-466-5392

Patterson Guide Service

Bristol
401-396-9464
www.pattersonguideservice.com

Captain Greg Snow

Snowfly Charters
Conventry
401-439-0953
www.snowflycharters.com

Captain Jim White

White Ghost Guide Services Ltd.
Coventry
401-828-9465
www.whiteghostcharters.com

Captain Ray Stachelek

Cast A Fly Charters
East Greenwich
401-323-5439
www.castaflycharters.com

Captain Rene Letourneau

Pawtucket
401-359-3625
www.primaryflies.biz

Captain Steve Burnett

Watch Hill
860-572-9896
www.fishwatchhill.com

Capt. Ben DeMario

Westerly
401-474-5095
StriperBass40@aol.com

MASSACHUSETTS FLY AND TACKLE SHOPS

Bob Smith Sporting Goods

1050 Commonwealth Avenue
Boston
617-232-1399

Firefly Outfitters

One Federal Street
Boston
617-423-FISH
www.fireflyoutfitters.com

Orvis Boston

8 North Market Bldg. - East End
Faneuil Hall Marketplace
Boston
617-742-0288
www.orvis.com/boston

Red Top Sporting Goods, Inc.

265 Main Street
Buzzards Bay
508-759-3371
www.redtoptackle.com

Roach's Sporting Goods

1957 Massachusetts Avenue
Cambridge
617-876-5816
www.roachssportinggoods.com

Concord Outfitters

84 Commonwealth Avenue
Concord
978-318-0330
www.concordoutfitters.com

Atlantic Angler

433 Washington St
Duxbury
781-934-0242

Fishing the Cape

Harwich Commons
120 Route 137
East Harwich
508-432-1200
www.fishingthecape.com

Larry's Tackle Shop

258 Upper Main Street
Edgartown
508-627-5088
www.larrystackle.com

Coop's Bait & Tackle

147 West Tisbury Road
Edgartown
508-627-3909
www.coopsbaitandtackle.com

Captains Porky's Bait And Tackle

13 Dock Street
Edgartown
508-627-7117
www.captporky.com

The Fin and Feather

103 Main Street
Essex
978-768-3245
www.thefinandfeathershop.com

Eastman's Sport & Tackle

783 Main Street
Falmouth
508-548-6900
www.eastmanstackle.com

Bass Pro Shops

One Bass Pro Drive
Foxborough
508-216-2000
www.basspro.com

Sports Port

149 West Main Street
Hyannis
508-775-3096
www.sportsport.us

Rod Builders Workshop

100 Main Street
Kingston
781-582-1015
www.rodbuildersworkshop.com

Cote's Fly Shop

115 Manville Street
Leicester
508-892-3765
www.cotesflyshop.biz

Merrimac Sport

130 East Main Street
Merrimac
978-346-8835
www.merrimacsport.com

Top Rod Fly & Surf Shop

1082 Orleans Road
North Chatham
800-316-5484
www.capefishingcharters.com

Bill Fisher Tackle

3 Polpis Road
Nantucket
508-228-2261
www.billfishertackle.com

Cross Rip Outfitters

24 Easy Street
Nantucket
508-228-4900
www.crossrip.com

Nantucket Tackle Center

41 Sparks Avenue
Nantucket
508-228-4081
www.nantuckettackle.com

Natick Outdoor Store

38 North Avenue
Natick
508-653-9400
www.natickoutdoor.com

Surfland Bait & Tackle

28 Plum Island Turnpike
Newbury
978-462-4202
www.surflandbt.com

Dave's Pioneer Sporting Center

137 Damon Rd., Suite E
Northampton
413-584-9944

Dick's Bait & Tackle

New York Avenue
Oak Bluffs
508-693-7669

Flagg's Fly & Tackle

189 Daniel Shays Hwy.
Orange
978-544-0034

Goose Hummock Shop

Route 6a
Orleans
508-255-0455
www.goose.com

Nauset Angler

4 Cole Place
East Orleans
508-255-4242

Evening Sun Fly Shop

55 Groton Street
Pepperell
978-433-4910
www.eveningsunflyshop.com

Hunter's Rendezvous/Royal Marine

Rte. 119 (South Road)
Pepperell
978-433-9458
www.huntersrendezvous.com

Nelson's Bait & Tackle

43 Race Point Road
Provincetown
508-487-0034
www.nelsonsbaitandtackle.com

First Light Anglers

21 Main Street
Rowley
978-948-7004
www.firstlightanglers.com

Riverview Bait & Tackle

1273 Route 28
South Yarmouth
508-394-1036

Bear's Den

98 Summer Street
Taunton
508-977-0700
www.bearsden.com

Fin & Feather Sports

10 Milford Street
Upton
508-529-3901
www.finandfeathersports.com

Jake's Fly Shop

11 Jorie Lane
Walpole
508-668-8882

Webster Lake Sporting Goods

144 Gore Road
Webster
508-943-6309

B.G. Sporting Inc.

1460 Russell Road
Westfield
413-568-7569

Westport Marine Specialties

1111 Main Road
Westport
508-636-8100
www.westportbaitandtackle.com

Monahans Marine, Inc.

396 Washington St. (Rt. 53)
Weymouth
781-335-2746
www.monahansmarine.com

The Mountain Goat

130 Water Street
Williamstown
413-458-8445
www.themountaingoat.com

The Lower Forty Fly Shop

134 Madison Street
Worcester
508-752-4004
www.thelowerforty.com

Orvis Company Store, Dedham

960 Providence Highway
Dedham
781-329-7214
www.orvis.com

Massachusetts Boat Rentals

Martha's Vineyard Boat Rentals

Island Water Sports

100 Lagoon Pond Road
Vineyard Haven
508-693-7767
www.boatmv.us

Nantucket Boat Rentals

Brant Point Marine-boat rentals

32 Washington Street
Nantucket
508-228-6244
www.brantpointmarine.com

Massachusetts Guides

Captain Mike Bartlett

B-Fast Charters
Boston Harbor & South Shore
781-293-6402
www.bfastcharters.com

Captain Rich Armstrong
Captain John Mendelson

Boston Fishstix Guides
Boston Harbor
617-233-6090
www.bostonfishstix.com

Captain Mike Conley

Breakwater Charters
Boston Harbor
617-686-7192
www.breakwatercharter.com

Captain Rusty Barry

Boston Harbor & South Shore
781-834-6932

Captain Webb Thompson

Nervous Water Charters
Boston Harbor
617-899-9065
www.nervouswaterboston.com

Captain Wayne Frieden

Reel Dream Charters
Boston Harbor
617-909-7122
www.reeldreamcharters.com

Captain Tom Koerber

Roccus Charters
Boston Harbor & Harbor Islands
617-965-4833
www.roccuscharters.com

Captain Terry Nugent

Riptide Charters
Buzzards Bay
www.riptidecharters.com

Captain Jim Herbert

Cape and Islands Charters
Cape Cod
508-259-6013
www.capeandislandscharters.com

Steve Kean

Cape Cod Flats Fishing
Cape Cod
508-561-7102
www.capecodflatsfishing.com

Captain Curt Jessup

Cape Cod Outfitters
Cape Cod
508-400-5627
www.capecodoutfitters.com

Captain Jeff Smith

Fin Addiction Charters
Cape Cod
508-349-1404
www.finaddiction.com

Captain Mike Mathews

Offshore Angler Charters
Cape Cod
617-997-5209
www.offshoreanglercharters.com

Captain Bob Paccia

Shoreline Guide Service
Cape Cod
508-697-6253
www.reel-time.com

Captain Steve Moore

Slam Dance Charters
Cape Cod
508-631-7506
www.slamdancecharters.com

Captain Will Raye

Sure Thing Charters
Cape Cod
508-432-7856
www.capecodflats.com

Captain Todd Murphy

Well Hooked Charters
Cape Cod
401-808-9642
www.wellhooked.net

Randy Jones

Yankee Angler
Cape Cod
508-258-0701
www.yankeeangler.com

Captain Tom George

Fish Pier Charters
Chatham
508-280-3559
www.fishpiercharters.com

Captain Jaime Boyle

Boylermaker Charters
Edgartown
508-922-1749
www.boylermaker.com

Captain Shawn Bristow

Squaretail Outfitters
Martha's Vineyard & Nantucket
603-498-9518
www.squaretailoutfitters.com

Captain Phil Cronin

Capawock Charters
Martha's Vineyard
617-448-2030
www.capawock.com

Captain Bob Decosta

Albacore Charters
Nantucket
508-228-5074
www.albacorecharters.com

The Waine Brothers

All Hooked Up Charters
Nantucket
508-228-0964
508-221-1115
www.nantucketfishin.com

Captain Tom Mleczko

Captain Tom's Charters
Nantucket
508-228-4225
www.capttom.com

Cross Rip Outfitters

Nantucket
508-228-4900
www.crossrip.com

Captain Bill Toelstedt

Nantucket Outfitters
Nantucket
917-584-5270
www.ackoutfitters.com

Captain Hal Herrick

Sankaty Head Charters
Nantucket
508-325-1575
www.nantucketfishing.com

Captain Peter Sheppard

Rusty Flyfishing Charters
Nantucket
508-982-5398
www.rustyfly.com

Captains Karsten & Matt Reinemo

Topspin Charters
Nantucket
508-228-7724
www.fishingnantucket.com

Captain Kahil Bogden

Downriver Charters
North Shore
978-407-7901
www.downrivercharters.com

Captain Nat Moody

First Light Angler
North Shore
978-948-7004
www.firstlightanglers.com

Captain John Pirie

On-Line Fishing Charters
North Shore
978-468-1314
www.olfc.com

Captain Randy Sigler

Sigler Guide Service
North Shore
888-fly-line
www.striper.com

Captain Jim Ellis

Haystaddle Hill Guide Service
West Barnstable
508-362-9108
www.saltwaterflies.com/haystaddle

Captain Chris Aubut

On Line Charters
Westport River
305-797-5442
www.flyfishwpt.com

New Hampshire Fly and Tackle Shops

Stone River Outfitters

132 Bedford Center Road
Bedford
603-472-3191
www.stoneriveroutfitters.com

North Country Angler

2888 White Mountain Highway
North Conway
603-356-6000
www.northcountryangler.com

WS Hunter

113 Storrs Street
Concord
603-228-0880
www.wshunter.com

Evening Sun Fly Shop

55 Groton Street
Pepperell
978-433-4910
www.eveningsunflyshop.com

New Hampshire Guides

Captain Brett Vaughn

Cast Away Adventures
Amherst
603-345-7131

Captain Dave Beattie

Fly Tide Charters
Epping
603-679-2018

Captain Ken Welsh

K.W. Charters
Bow
603-228-0614

Captain Russ Charleston

Relentless Pursuit Charters
Exeter
603-778-2916

Captain Bill Wagner

Captain Bill's Charters
Deerfield
603-463-9028
www.captainbillscharter.com

Captain Cory Gauron

Northwind Charters
Hampton
603-944-3878
www.northwindcharters.com

Captain Dick Bursaw

Salt By Fly
Derby
603-432-7737
www.saltbyfly.com

Captain Keith LeClair

Runaway Sport Fishing Charters
Hampton
603-765-3639

Captain Jack Grady

Good Times Charters
Hampton Beach
978-663-3829
www.goodtimesfishingcharters.com

Smith & Gilmore

Hampton Beach
603-926-3503
www.smithandgilmore.com

Captain Mike Wheeler

Captain Ned Higson
Adventure Fishing Charters
Hampton Beach
603-247-0924
www.adventurefishingcharters.com

Captain Rick LaPierre

Yellow Bird Fishing Charters &
 Cruises
Hampton Beach
603-929-1995
www.yellowbirdcharters.com

Captain Jim Brown

The Bass Harasser
Manchester
603-627-9041
www.bassharasser.com

Captain Patrick Colby

Roof Rafta Fishing Charters
Merrimack
603-608-8334
www.roofraftacharters.com

Captain Jim Flanders

Sunrise Adventure Charters
Merrimack
603-424-4946
www.sunriseadventurecharters.com

Captain Dave Burkland

Merrimack
603-494-3470

Captain Debbie Jordan

Captain Bill Lussier
Northeast Charter Boat Co.
Portsmouth
603-235-5526
www.northeastcharterboat.com

Captain Doug Anderson

Sushi Hunter Sportfishing Charters
Portsmouth
603-231-7904
www.sushihunter.com

Captain Peter Whelan

Shoals Flyfishing
Portsmouth
603-205-5318
www.shoalsflyfishing.com

Captain Joel Koch

Reel Ecstasy
Rochester
603-332-0242
www.nhsaltwaterfishing.com

Captain Ray Maimone

Harvester Fishing Charters
Rye Harbor
603-926-0264
www.harvesterfishingcharters.com

Maine Fly and Tackle Shops

Eldridge Brothers

1480 US Route One
Cape Neddick
207-363-9269
www.eldredgeflyshop.com

Flyfishing Only

230 Main Street
Fairfield
207-453-6242
www.maineflyfishing.com

LL Bean

95 Main Street
Freeport
877-755-2326
www.llbean.com

Kittery Trading Post

301 US Route One
Kittery
888-439-9036
www.kitterytradingpost.com

Kennebec River Outfitters

469 Lakewood Road
Madison
207-474-2500
www.kennebecriveroutfitters.com

Maine Sport Outfitters

Route 1
Rockport
207-236-7120
www.mainesport.com

Mountain Valley Flies

Route 201
Solon
207-643-2472
www.mtnvalleyflies.com

MAINE GUIDES

Captain Johan Brouwer

Great Gadzooks Tidewater Fishing
Bath
207-442-0729
www.greatgadzooks.com

Captain Doug Jowett

Brunswick
207-725-4573
www.mainestripedbassfishing.com

Captain Eric Wallace

Coastal Fly Angler
Freeport
207-671-4330
www.coastalflyangler.com

Captain John L. Nowinski

North Creek Guide Service
Freeport
207-831-2922
www.northcreekguideservice.com

Captain Nate Gordon

Tidewater Fishing Charters, LLC
Kennebunkport
207-229-0201
www.tidewaterfishing.com

Captain Ethan DeBery

Fish'n'Trips Charters
Phippsburg
207-841-7977
www.fishntripsmaine.com

Gillies & Fallon Guide Service

Phippsburg
207-389-2300
www.mainestripers.com

Captain John Ford

Portland Guide Service
Portland
207-471-5858
www.mainesaltwaterfishing.com

Fishing With Matt and Josh

Slip D2, 1 Spring Point Drive
South Portland
207-450-3549
www.mainecharterfishing.com

Captain George Harris

Super Fly Charters
Warren
207-354-0623
www.superfly-charters.com

Captain Dave Guerard

Rip Tide Charters
York
207-363-2536
www.mainestriperfishing.com

Index

NOTES

NOTES

NOTES

Notes

NOTES

NOTES

Notes